PATTERN

253. Detail of the door in the Cloister of the Pazzi Chapel, Florence. Designed by
Brunelleschi, *c.* 1430

PATTERN

A STUDY OF ORNAMENT
IN WESTERN EUROPE
FROM 1180 TO 1900

By JOAN EVANS

B.Litt. (Oxon.), D.Lit. (Lond.)

VOL. II

A DA CAPO PAPERBACK

Library of Congress Cataloging in Publication Data

Evans, Joan, 1893-
    Pattern.

    (A Da Capo paperback)
    Reprint of the 1931 ed. published at the
Clarendon Press, Oxford.
    Includes bibliographical references and index.
    1. Decoration and ornament — Europe.   I. Title.
NK1442.E8 1976   745.4′49′4   76-10682
ISBN 0-306-80040-3 (v. 1)
ISBN 0-306-80041-1 (v. 2)

ISBN 0-306-80041-1

First Paperback Printing 1976

This Da Capo Paperback edition of
*Pattern: A Study of Ornament in Western Europe
From 1180 to 1900, Volume II,*
is an unabridged republication of the first edition
published in Oxford, at the Clarendon Press, in 1931

Published by Da Capo Press, Inc.
A Subsidiary of Plenum Publishing Corporation
227 West 17th Street
New York, N.Y. 10011

TO
THE MEMORY OF
MY FATHER
JOHN EVANS
1823–1908

PREFACE

AS soon as I began to write this book it became evident that a bibliography of the subject complete enough to be of real use would be of a size to demand a volume to itself,[1] and that it would not be possible to attempt to give a complete set of references for each monument or building cited. I have therefore contented myself with giving references in the footnotes to books that I have consulted on special points.[2] I should like to express a general indebtedness which cannot there be noted to certain books of reference, notably to Michel's *Histoire de l'Art,* to Venturi's *Storia dell'arte italiana,* to Guilmard's *Les Maîtres ornemanistes*, and to the series of books on Renaissance and later decoration in England by Miss M. Jourdain.

My work has been lightened by much kindness from many friends and many courteous strangers.

My thanks are due to all those who have taught me; to all those who have opened to me their own collections and the collections in their charge; to those who drew my attention to relevant books; and to those who have answered my importunate questions on points of detail. I should like to express my gratitude to the staffs of the libraries of the Musée de sculpture comparée at the Trocadéro, of the Reading Room of the British Museum, of the Library and the Department of Engraved Ornament in the Victoria and Albert Museum, and of the Bodleian Library, for their ungrudging service.

Sir Henry Maxwell Lyte, Mr. Samuel Gardner, Mr. J. R. H. Weaver of Trinity College, and Mr. Stokes of Exeter, have generously given me photographs of their own taking and have freely allowed me to publish them; Lady Victoria Manners, Professor de Zulueta, and Dr. G. C. Williamson have given me photographs in their possession with permission to reproduce them; and Mrs. Olive Edis Galsworthy has taken photographs for me at Holkham under conditions of considerable difficulty.

Permission to reproduce objects in the collections in their charge has been granted me by the authorities of the British Museum, and the Victoria and Albert Museum; of the Ashmolean Museum and Bodleian Library at Oxford; of the Whitworth Institute at Manchester; of the Louvre, the Musée de Cluny, the Musée des Arts décoratifs, the Musée de sculpture comparée (Trocadéro), and the Bibliothèque Nationale at Paris; of the Musée des Antiquités de la Seine Inférieure at Rouen and the Musée de l'ancien Evêché at Angers, of the Musées Royaux du Cinquantenaire and the Bibliothèque Royale of Brussels; of the Rijksmuseum of

---

[1] The subject catalogue of the Library of the Victoria and Albert Museum will be found invaluable by London readers.

[2] Where the place of publication is not given it may be assumed that English books have been published in London and French in Paris.

Amsterdam; of the Stadtliche Porzellän Sammlung of Dresden; of the Uffizi Galleries and the Laurentian Library of Florence, and of the Museo Nazionale of Ravenna.

The Provost of Oriel, the Warden of New College, the Warden of All Souls, the authorities of Winchester College and Stonyhurst, and the Corporation of Brighton have allowed me to reproduce objects in their possession. Among private owners I have to thank the Duke of Devonshire, the Duke of Rutland, Lord Leicester, Sir Henry Bedingfeld, the Dean of Westminster, Dr. Forrer, Miss C. A. E. Moberly, and Mr. E. R. Roberts Chanter. Mr. Dyson Perrins has been so good as to allow me to have a page from one of his manuscripts specially photographed for reproduction in this book, and to reproduce another from his Gorleston Psalter. Messrs. Morris & Co. have kindly allowed me to reproduce their *Fruit* paper.

For help on points of detail I owe sincere thanks to Miss Hope Emily Allen, Mr. C. F. Bell, Professor R. W. Chambers, Mr. R. G. Collingwood, the late Monsieur Camille Enlart, Dr. R. T. Gunther, Dr. C. R. S. Harris, Dr. G. F. Hill, Miss M. Jourdain, Monsieur Jacques Meurgey, Professor Daniel Mornet, Mr. C. C. Oman, Professor Rudler, Mr. G. McN. Rushforth, Dr. and Mrs. Charles Singer, the late Professor Paul Studer, Mr. A. Van de Put, Mr. A. J. B. Wace, Mr. W. W. Watts, and Mr. J. R. H. Weaver. To Monsieur J. J. Marquet de Vasselot, Conservateur au Musée du Louvre et du Musée de Cluny, I owe an especial debt of gratitude: he has given me every facility for study in his two museums, he has made me free of his important manuscript bibliography of French decorative art,[1] he has answered innumerable questions, and throughout the writing of the book has helped me by constant encouragement and occasional friendly and constructive criticism. Professor Tancred Borenius has not only acted as supervisor for those chapters of the book that were offered as a thesis for the Doctorate in Literature of the University of London, but has also been so kind as to read the whole book both in manuscript and in proof; I am greatly indebted to him for encouragement and information most generously given.

Finally, my thanks are due to my Mother and to my friends Mrs. Murdo Mackenzie and Miss Agnes Conway, who have done me the great service of reading and criticizing the book in manuscript; to Mrs. E. M. White of Somerville College, who has undertaken the labour of the Index; and to the officers of the Clarendon Press, who have seen the book through all the stages of printing and publication.

LONDON, *March* 1930.   J. E.

---

[1] The section dealing with goldwork and enamel has been published by the Société française de bibliographie, 1925, *Bibliographie de l'orfèvrerie et de l'émaillerie françaises.*

CONTENTS
VOLUME II

LIST OF ILLUSTRATIONS

VOLUME II

VI
THE NEW AGE

I

THE Renaissance was an age of paradox. The heir of the Middle Ages, in spirit it was their antithesis; the spiritual child of Rome, it rejected the Roman ideas of corporation and state and empire, and made the perfection of the individual the aim of human effort. The age which set force and energy over justice and loyalty, it was the time when weightless trifles were first glorified for the modern world;[1] the age which rediscovered and worshipped Plato, it was the time when Idea, no longer supported by Religion, ceded her throne to Fact. An age which lives for posterity in its visible works of art, it identified literature with life, and could say with Petrarch, 'scribendi enim mihi vivendique unus finis erat'.

The orientation of men's lives was changed. The unbeautified present might still repel, but instead of looking forward in the hope of a world to come, they turned back to seek the surer vision of a glory that had already been upon the earth. Petrarch, the first true humanist, declares, 'the very sight of men of the present time wounds me sorely, whereas the memories, the deeds, the illustrious names of the ancients, give me joy, splendid and so inestimable that, if the world could know, it would be amazed that I should have so much pleasure in talking with the dead and so little with the living'.[2] It is this change of orientation that marks the division between the Middle Ages and the Renaissance. A great part of classical literature had formed part of the medieval inheritance, but it was differently used; the earlier scholars had no thought of returning to antiquity, but still went forward towards a Heavenly city, strengthened and increased in moral stature by their classic knowledge. 'We are as dwarfs', they said with Bernard of Chartres, 'that stand upon the shoulders of giants, and, thanks to them, we can see farther than they'.

The scholars of the Renaissance renounced this forward vision. For them the imitation of antiquity was a sufficient end in itself. The poet's function was no longer the revelation of a higher verity, but the veiling of truth in beautiful fictions.[3] Art no longer aimed at a comprehensive vision, but at the exclusion of all that was merely 'plebeian'; 'electio et sui fastidium' were the highest virtues of

---

[1] In 1474 the Ambassador of Ercole d'Este wrote to his master from Florence to report the loss of two of Lorenzo de' Medici's falcons, and adds, 'L'ozio moltiplica per modo in Italia che, se non altro sorge, piu gli sarà scrivere di battaglie di uccelli e cani che di eserciti o fatti d'arme'. *Lettere di Lorenzo de' Medici*, ed. Antonio Cappelli, Modena, 1863, p. 251.

[2] *Epistolae familiares*, ed. Fracassetti, Florence, 1859, vi. 4.

[3] 'Veritatem rerum pulchris velaminibus adornare.' Petrarch, *Opera*, Basle, 1554, p. 1205.

the poet;[1] his highest originality, the ingenious adaptation of passages from the classic writers.[2] Scaliger was content that every artist should be at bottom an echo, and only asked of him grace, decorum, elegance and splendour, all informed by the chief excellence of measure. The classical authors were more than human; and statues of the elder and younger Pliny could in 1498 be set in solitary state on the façade of the new cathedral at Como.[3] Classical literature was as sacred as the Scriptures; so Filarete could set the fables of Aesop (which he was proud to have read in the original) and even Leda and the Swan on the great doors of St. Peter's.[4] So Squarcione preached the doctrine of a rigorous imitation of antiquity; and even Leonardo, though against mere imitation of any sort, found that the imitation of antiquity was more worthy of praise than the imitation of moderns.[5]

Though men of fortune and learning might choose to be scholars, though scholars might be everywhere received and honoured, and though their point of view might have a great public influence, they yet remained a class apart, and Renaissance art cannot be understood in the light of their doctrines alone. Petrarch himself exercised little if any influence upon the artists of the trecento. Moreover, international though humanism itself might be, the vanishing of the medieval dream of unity had helped to intensify the national life of each country, and the force of this life made the Renaissance in every country a conflict, and finally a reconciliation, between classical and national elements. Only in Italy was this conflict hardly perceptible, since only in Italy had the Middle Ages, dominated by French thought, passed as a troubled dream over a sleeping but living classicism.[6] The Renaissance there began in the decline of Gothicism: that alien discipline had only to be removed for a native classicism to awake.[7] In literature the vernacular lapsed into disuse for 'noble' and learned work; in architecture Brunelleschi in 1403 made his pilgrimage to Rome to study the buildings of the Empire, and some twenty years later achieved the classicism of the Pazzi Chapel;[8]

---

[1] Scaliger, *Poetices libri septem*, v, 3; published posthumously in 1561, but written some twenty years earlier; quoted Spingarn, *Literary Criticism of the Renaissance*, p. 128.

[2] Vida, *Ars Poetica;* written before 1520; first known edition, 1527.

[3] When the bones of Livy were taken to the Palazzo della Ragione at Padua, Alfonso V of Aragon sent an embassy to ask for a relic.

[4] See B. Sauer, 'Die Randreliefe an Filarete's Bronzethür von St. Peter' in *Repertorium für Kunstwissenschaft*, xx, 1897, p. 1.   [5] *Traité de la peinture*, ed. Péladan, p. 83.

[6] For instance the end of the Paschal candlestick in the Cappella Palatina of Palermo is upheld by three epheboi wearing the exomis; while Frederick II's gate at Capua (1233–40) had bas-reliefs of trophies and statues of the Emperor, his ministers, and the City, all in classic style. Giovanni Balducci of Pisa, in his shrine of St. Peter Martyr in S. Eustorgio, Milan, made in 1339, uses a classic entablature although his capitals, his canopy and his whole scheme are Gothic.

[7] Italy had never lost the classic predilection for the horizontal line, and consequently for architraves and friezes. Alberti's work in the Temple of the Malatesta at Rimini shows an extraordinary breaking up of Gothic forms to give a horizontal line at any cost.

[8] Another pioneer, if a lesser one, is Jacopo della Quercia. On the tomb of Ilaria del Caretto in San Martino at Lucca, *c.* 1406, he uses classic winged *putti* bearing heavy swags of flowers and fruit; and on the great doorway of San Petronio at Bologna, 1425–37, he combines with completely classical reliefs mouldings that hesitate between classic and late Gothic style.

254. Detail of the balustrade in the Sacristy of San Lorenzo, Florence. Designed by Donatello, c. 1435

255. Ceiling of the Sala dei Gigli, Palazzo Vecchio, Florence. Designed by the brothers del Tasso, *c.* 1475

in sculptured decoration Donatello, about 1434, first brought back into the vocabulary of ornament the acanthus, the shells, the amphorae, the dolphins, the garlands and the festoons that he had studied on the sarcophagi of ancient Rome.[1]

The humanists gradually shook themselves free from their scholastic training; the architects and sculptors gradually lost their lightly-worn medieval mannerisms. But the scholars kept their hardly-won logic, and the architects held fast to some at least of the Gothic tradition; in the Old Sacristy of San Lorenzo, Brunelleschi encircles his classic archways with a bevelled archivolt inherited from the mouldings of the Italian Gothic round arch; on the bronze doors of St. Peter's Filarete completes his characteristically heavy Roman rinceaux not only with the scenes from Aesop and the Metamorphoses but also with little medieval grotesques.

Even in Italy the direct influence of humanism can easily be exaggerated;[2] the scholar and the craftsman were specialized workers, each labouring in his own sphere, each developing his own tradition, and each seeing the world in the light of his own craft. The work of the one was the recovery, the comprehension and the imitation of classical literature; the work of the other the discovery, the comprehension and the imitation of classical sculpture and architecture. The link between them was the enlightened patron, himself neither humanist nor craftsman, who gained a layman's appreciation of classicism from the one and sought to have it satisfied by the craft of the other. Throughout the Renaissance the archaeologists were in every city of Italy the precursors of the artists, and everywhere determined the sources of their inspiration. It is thanks to the collector's instinct, which leads him to start with the mature, and even with the decadent, and to end with the pure and primitive, that Renaissance architecture progresses, not only with a closer approximation to antiquity, but also to antiquity of an earlier date: its first inspiration is drawn from the age of Caracalla and that of its full maturity from the age of Augustus.

Even in the dim and untimely beginnings of the New Age, it was Frederick II who was the patron of Nicolò Pisano,[3] and Charles of Anjou who invited Giovanni Pisano to Naples;[4] and with the true dawn, it was the Medici who fathered the Florentine Renaissance rather than any humanist or artist. It was the Papacy that

[1] e.g. on the pedestal of the Marzocco, the Florentine lily appears within a Roman wreath on a panel rimmed with an egg-and-tongue moulding; though the heavy entablature is crowned with a Gothic frieze.

[2] The great increase in theoretical writings on art comes a little later than the creation of Renaissance art. On such writings see J. von Schlosser, 'Materialen zur Quellenkunde der Kunstgeschichte', Heft IV, 'Die Kunsttheorie der ersten Hälfte des Cinquecento', in *Kais. Akademie der Wissenschaften in Wien, philosophisch-historische Klasse, Sitzungsberichte*, Band 184, 2. Abhandlung, 1917.

[3] Nicolò gained inspiration from the study of sarcophagi with the hunts of Meleager and Hippolytus, now in the Campo Santo of Pisa. He represented God the Father on the model of Dionysus supported by a satyr, and the Nativity according to the scheme of the birth of Romulus and Remus: and used classic egg-and-dart moulding among trefoiled arches and Gothic mouldings.

[4] Giovanni Pisano's pulpit in Pisa Cathedral (1302–11), while Gothic in form and structure, shows traces of classical influence in its sculpture and is crowned by a graceful acanthus frieze.

presided over the destinies of the middle period, that made possible the creation of a grand style as imperial and catholic as Rome; and in every country outside Italy that Renaissance art invaded in its maturity, it was the Monarchy that introduced it, that fostered it, and that ended by making it national. The work of the patrons began as early as that of the humanists: by 1335 Oliviero Forza, a rich citizen of Treviso, had a collection of antique medals, coins, bronzes, marbles and gems;[1] ten years later Petrarch read Cicero's letters for the first time. Indeed the collectors came to be a third branch of specialists in antiquity, so marked that the collector's interest in literary humanism definitely took a second place beside his interest in visible antiquity. Paul II, for instance,[2] the protector of the ancient sculptures of Rome, the collector of coins and gems, the first to impose ancient buildings as models for his architects and classical triumphs as models for his festivals, was not interested in literature.[3] Yet even the collectors who were not humanists brought to humanism that sense of the past as real and living and of one fabric with the present which contact with the visible remains of antiquity almost always inspires; it is Ciriaco of Ancona, the fifteenth-century collector of antique coins and marbles, and not Filelfo or Politian, who replies to those who ask him what he does: 'I am raising the dead'. It is thanks to the collector-patrons, who received, criticized and accepted the work of humanist and artist alike, that the current of Renaissance art flowed towards a closer and more homogeneous imitation of antiquity. Their collections were not merely the diversions of dilettanti, but material for the craftsman, as much as their manuscripts were material for the humanist. Lorenzo de' Medici set apart the Casino Mediceo in his gardens near San Marco as an academy for the study of his antiquities; and it is because of the number of such collections in Florence,[4] and of the enlightened dilettanti who made them, that it was in Florence that Renaissance style, in decoration as in architecture, had its birth. Brunelleschi's fluted pilasters and columns of the Innocenti, begun in 1420, mark the beginning; and by 1430 his Sacristy of San Lorenzo showed the relief and the proportion of classicism as well as the decorative use of classic pilasters, cornice frieze and architrave. Ghiberti's shrine for the relics of Saints Proto, Giacinto, and Nemesio, made in 1428,[5] is adorned with two angels holding a wreath, an adaptation of a classical Victory scheme curiously Roman in conception and even in detail. The artists of Florence spent the thirty years between 1420 and 1450 in rediscovering the proportions and characteristics of column and entablature, first of the Corinthian, then of the Ionic and Tuscan-Doric, and finally of the Compo-

---

[1] It is noteworthy that the French Royal Inventories of 1343 and 1360 include only one cameo, that of 1363 four, and that of 1380 seventy-seven. Laborde, *Glossaire des Émaux*, ii, p. 186.

[2] 1464–71. See Müntz, *Les Arts aux Cours des Papes*, ii, p. 4 *et seqq.* He owned 47 antique bronzes, 227 cameos, over 225 intaglios, and 1,097 ancient medals. *Ibid.*, ii, p. 141.

[3] His panegyrist guardedly remarks that he lent his manuscripts freely and for any length of time, but was very cautious in borrowing those belonging to other people.

[4] See Müntz, *op. cit.*, ii, p. 166.

[5] Now in the Museo Nazionale, Florence.

257. Detail of the sarcophagus from the tomb of Giovanni and Pietro de' Medici in the Old Sacristy of S. Lorenzo, Florence. By Verocchio, 1472

256. Capital of a pilaster in the Church of S. Maria della Consolazione, Todi, c. 1510

258. Details of the tomb of Carlo Marsuppini, S. Croce, Florence. By Desiderio da Settignano, before 1455

259. Sarcophagus of Giovanni Francesco Orsini, Cathedral of Spoleto. By Ambrogio da Milano, 1499

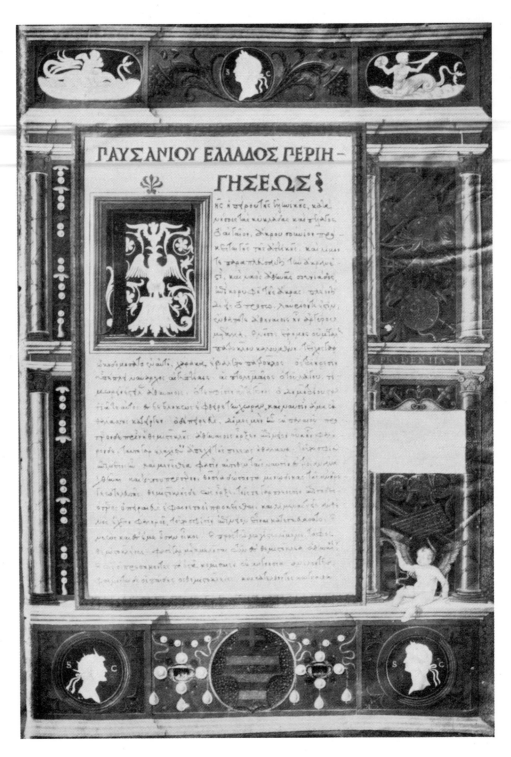

260. Illumination in architectural design. Florentine, *c.* 1480

site Order; and then were free to develop the purely decorative side which for them had a peculiar appeal. By 1445 Michelozzo was using almost over-elaborate mouldings in the Noviciate door at Santa Croce, and in the Chapel of the Annunziata was enriching his work with such fancies as shell-mouldings and paterae filled with rayed heads.

In the beginnings of Florentine ornament all the ages that had made and handed on the classic tradition played a part.[1] Brunelleschi's decorations of the Pazzi Chapel show the coffered vaulting, the patera frieze, and the Corinthian columns of the classic style; a frieze with wavy fluting adapted from a late Roman sarcophagus;[2] the fourfold marble panelling and capitals with the incised carving of Byzantium; the Christian Symbols of the Middle Ages and the winged cherub-heads of the early Italian Renaissance. The search after variety, the enjoyment of a rediscovered pattern, are shown in the varied mouldings of the doors (fig. 253, Frontispiece), where scale patterns, guilloches, linked volutes, scrolls, garlands and anthemia are set like bands of enamel between bosses of metallic design. Similarly he divided the soffit of the arches of San Lorenzo into sections rimmed by double mouldings, and in each section changed the pattern of both mouldings to give a maximum of variety.[3] Donatello made the supports of the pedestal of his Marzocco all different. Sometimes classical themes were so treated in a different technique as to become something new and strange. Donatello's balustrades of the Sacristy of San Lorenzo (fig. 254), with their marble fret of rinceaux growing from a vase, the whole bordered by a shell moulding, are at once classic, Byzantine and new. Baldassare Peruzzi's rather later Palazzo Massimi at Rome has Roman Doric columns with an Attic base, a Greek profile and projection for the echinus, windows of Republican type, and a flat coffered ceiling in the style of the second century. Brunelleschi's more mature work at the Badia di Fiesole[4] has decoration drawn from yet another source; the deep reveals of the doors and window of the cloister are adorned with delicate ornament drawn from Roman *stucchi*, such as those of the 'Tombe Latine', translated into the low relief which Donatello had taught the Florentine sculptors in stone.[5]

The Byzantine element was the first to disappear from Renaissance ornament as from Renaissance humanism; the doorway in the Cloister of Santa Croce, built in 1435, is completely Roman in its architectural form, its pillars and its mouldings,

[1] Brunelleschi drew much of his classic detail from Florentine sources, of which the most important were the little basilica of the Santi Apostoli and the Baptistery. It is thence that he got his pilasters, his capitals, his entablatures, his guilloche, broken roll and bead mouldings, and his fancy of two parallel lines of small ornaments to decorate the soffit of an architrave.

[2] Cf. Alberti's later use of such a frieze on the Church of San Pancrazio, Florence.

[3] Cf. the soffit of the Chapel of St. Benedict in the Cathedral of Monreale, by Francesco Laurana, which is coffered, with each coffer filled with a rosette of a different design, and the quasi-rustication of the Palazzo di Podestà at Bologna, in which each stone is carved with a rosette and almost every rosette is different.

[4] Though not finished until 1462, it was designed earlier.

[5] Similar ornament in Sta. Maria del Popolo at Rome, that dates from 1477, shows a definite thickening of forms in order to adapt the style more fully to the technique of stone.

and in the arabesques on the inner frame. The base of the Idolino,[1] carved—perhaps by Vittorio Ghiberti—some twenty years later, has not merely Roman elements of decoration, Vitruvian scroll and tongue mouldings, swags, vines, lionheaded monsters, and so on, but also the Roman proportion, the dry Roman modelling, the Roman naturalism that is never rustic but always urbane.

Already it was the spirit rather than the letter of classicism from which inspiration was drawn. Donatello's decorations of the presbytery of the Chiesa del Santo at Padua, executed about 1444, show a scheme that is curiously Roman in spirit but yet has no Roman prototype: with Corinthian pilasters set between panels of marble, carved with two-handled vases surmounted by square frames enclosing octagonal panels of precious marbles set in carved rims, the whole crowned by a series of lunettes.[2] By 1490 Andrea da Monte Sansovino's vestibule to the Sacristy of San Spirito had gone beyond the letter into the spirit of classicism; his capitals have no Roman model, and are yet a true development of the Roman tradition; his coffered ceiling has no prototype and yet is worthy of Imperial antiquity. A similar freedom is evident in the vocabulary of decoration. Donatello in his Singing Gallery for the Cathedral of Florence[3] used a series of friezes, the upper of a single acanthus leaf alternating with a two-handled vase, the next based on classical antefixes with rayed heads, the next of concave shells, the next a conventional egg-and-tongue moulding, and the lowest a frieze of swags hanging from winged heads. Donatello and Bertoldo completed the frieze of their Crucifixion in San Lorenzo not with paterae, but with the cruets of water and wine; the designer of the ceilings of the great halls of the Palazzo Vecchio, dating from about 1475 (fig. 255), substituted the Florentine lily for the classic honeysuckle, and set heraldic shields between his Roman swags. The window frames of the Palace of Urbino display a charming frieze of little sirens with leafy tails, who hold up roundels, of which some are charged with the Ducal arms; and on the church of S. Francesco at Ferrara, scale and guilloche mouldings take the place of the usual egg-and-tongue. Similarly there was a new freedom in the design of capitals; volutes and acanthus foliage remained, but were diversified with new devices (fig. 256), as on those of the cloister and refectory of the Convent of Badia Fiesolana near Florence, and on those of the Palazzo dei Diamanti of Ferrara and the palace built for Ludovico il Moro in the same city.

Yet it was not the architects but the sculptors who first recovered the true Roman strength and delicacy. Such work as Desiderio da Settignano's tomb of the humanist Marsuppini, who died in 1455[4] (fig. 258), shows not merely

---

[1] Now in the Museo Archeologico, Florence.

[2] A similar freedom is evident in the small cloister of the Certosa at Pavia, which shows a double row of classic heads carved in full face: one in the frieze, the other in the spaces between the arches; and another example of an unclassical classicism is the lunettes with affronted classic monsters over the windows of the Palazzo del Consiglio at Verona.   [3] Now in the Opera del Duomo.

[4] The tomb was erected between that date and 1464. It is interesting that so early a critic as Vasari finds

261. Window of the Façade, Certosa of Pavia. Designed *c.* 1473

262. Stucco decoration applied to the columns of the Palazzo Vecchio, Florence, in 1565.

classic planning, not merely classic detail in urns and volutes, ribbons and scrolls, acanthus and anthemion, harpies of death and wings of immortality, but that metallic strength of curve, that ideal vitality of growth, that pride of technical execution, that superb conviction of design, which had been lost for some twelve hundred years. Such work is the artistic counterpart of Marsilio Ficino's definition of physical beauty: it 'does not lie in the material shadow, but in light and in grace of form, not in the murky mass, but in a certain shining proportion, not in dark and static weight, but in number and proportion.'[1]

Such classic forms passed over into decorative architecture to form the style of the second stage of the Florentine Renaissance; but however rich the model, the journeyman who copied them had not the sculptor's touch, and for a time there was even in design a tendency to heaviness of form and over-multiplication of members. The tendency is evident in the ceilings of the Palazzo Vecchio; and even in Verocchio's sarcophagus for Giovanni and Pietro de' Medici (fig. 257) the forms are rather heavy and compressed, the curves of growth a little meaningless; compared with the sarcophagus by Desiderio da Settignano (fig. 258), it is definitely a work of decadence. It is true that work in marble and in lower relief kept more of the true classic tradition; Benedetto da Maiano's pulpit in Santa Croce is gracefully designed in some of its panels; but its brackets are clumsy, some of its relief is spoilt by drilling, and outside the rectangular panels its design is neither graceful nor full of meaning. The refinement and ease that Hellenic studies were bringing into literary classicism, especially at Florence, could not find a reflection in decorative classicism, for in the decorative arts Italy had no Greek models to study and to follow; and the characteristic of Florentine decoration after 1450 is not restraint, but abundance: a characteristic intensified by the growing predominance of civil over religious architecture. Moreover, the continued use of ancient forms to express modern thought to some extent led men to forget the significance of form; and conventional use led to illogical construction. Like the early schoolmen, they had to adapt an inherited tradition to new needs with a minimum of change, ere they could through its mastery create a new tradition for posterity. Their abundance and freedom of life had to sweeten the curves that the Middle Ages had left nervous and angular, had to inspire the easy flow and dancing measure of Renaissance decoration and to give it its spontaneous charm; yet they failed to give it the unwearying intellectual beauty that some earlier work achieves.

As the century progressed the tide of humanism began to leave Florence and to pass to Milan, Venice, Naples, and Rome. In all but the last of these centres, classical decoration developed in greater independence of architecture than it had done in Florence, and consequently with less purity of line and greater richness of ornament. Roman art of another date is its inspiration: such ornament as that of

the foliage 'un poco spinosi e secchi'. It served as a model for the tomb of Alessandro Tartagni, in S. Domenico, Bologna, carved by Francesco di Simone Ferrucci in 1477.   [1] *Epistolae*, i. 631.

Ambrogio da Milano's monument to Giovanni Francesco Orsini (fig. 259) is not, like Desiderio da Settignano's, Augustan, but Trajanic. The classical acroterion, such as crowns this sarcophagus, did not pass into the vernacular of ornament; but scrolling leafage and such perching birds as appear on the main frieze were welcomed by sculptors[1] and by wood-carvers,[2] by metal-workers and by architects alike. Each craft set its own stamp on the style; the Milanese iron-workers turned it into a grotesque, with sirens and dragons alternating with the birds; the potters of Faenza and Castel Durante adapted it to a circular field. The journeyman carvers made it a little more grotesque, and then the Florentine sculptors, by the middle of the sixteenth century, once more classicized the style.

The very enumeration of outstanding examples of Renaissance classical ornament shows how far they are sculptural. This was inevitable; not only were the surviving examples of ancient decorative art works of sculpture, but the most common artistic discipline, whether gained in the marble-worker's shed or the goldsmith's *bottega*, was a training in modelling in relief. Cellini expresses the view of his age: 'Sculpture is the mother of all the arts that employ design, for he who can be a great sculptor will very easily be a great architect, will have a grasp of perspective and will be a greater painter than any who have not a grasp of sculpture.'[3] This influence and this training had a great and lasting effect upon ornament. The decorative tradition of work appearing on a single plane was lost; even decoration painted or embroidered on a flat surface had to mimic relief. The old conventional perspective of decorative work gave place to a new representational perspective. For a time—and indeed for a long time—the ancient freedom of pattern was attacked, and ornament was dragged an unwilling captive behind the chariot of the fine arts. Usually it was the craftsman who attempted a plastic or pictorial technique;[4] sometimes it was the sculptor or painter who attempted decoration.

Colour, one of the chief glories of ornament, was deliberately relinquished in certain schemes; the men of the Renaissance, who saw antique sculpture denuded by time of its former colour, accepted a marble fairness as a standard of beauty. Not only were the lights and shadows of relief imitated on flat surfaces, but they were imitated in grisaille.[5] Even enamel gave up its jewel colours and was content

[1] As by Luciano da Laurana on the Palace of Urbino, 1468–82.

[2] As by the Brothers del Tasso in the panels of the Tribunal of the Collegio del Cambio at Perugia, carved in 1497.

[3] Letter to Benedetto Varchi, L. J. Jay, *Receuil de lettres*, p. 105.

[4] The most elaborate Italian Majolica plates are representations and distortions of pictures, and like them are intended for hanging on the wall.

[5] The fashion arose in sculpture-loving France even earlier than it did in Italy: a French missal written not much later than 1317 (Bodleian MS. Douce 313) has many grisaille illuminations, some touched with purple; and the Breviary of Queen Jeanne d'Évreux (now at Chantilly) written about 1350 has delicate grisaille pictures. An advanced grisaille technique is evident in such later manuscripts as a *De Civitate Dei* of *c*. 1370–80 in the British Museum (Add. MSS. 15244–5). In 1416 the Duc de Berry had 'Unes petites heures de Nostre Dame ... enluminées de blanc et de noir' and in 1454 the Duc de Bourgogne paid 'Johannes le Tavernier,

263. Bronze bowl, with the arms of the Venetian family of Contarini. Venetian, *c.* 1510

264. Arabesques from the Loggie of the Vatican. By Giulio Romano and the pupils of Raphael

with night-blue and black grounds on which the swags and scrolls of sculpture were imitated in shaded grey. Only from Venice, the city of Italy most influenced by the East and least by humanism, did a wave of colour gradually flow back over the provinces.

As lasting in its effect as the influence of sculpture was the cognate influence of classical architecture, not only in its obvious influence on architecture, but also on purely decorative design. The Orders ranked with sculpture as the visible remains of antiquity; to measure and draw the architectural relics of Rome was part of the training of artist and sculptor as well as of architect. So they were familiar not only to those who understood their structural necessities, but also to many who considered them as pieces of ornamental sculpture detached from any structural background.

In Italy, too, the habit of richness, which inevitably entailed the painting of plain surfaces with an imagined wealth of architectural detail when poverty prevented its more solid creation, had gradually accustomed artists to a wholly non-constructive use of architectural forms. They were used decoratively without regard to purpose and often in contradiction to it. The Italian genius was not dynamic, but static, and found its finest expression in such buildings as the Strozzi Palace. Hence its decoration was 'applied' and little influenced by constructive needs;[1] and therefore it was possible for architectural motives, detached from structure, to enter ornament. Cellini is perpetually recording some such inspiration for his work; and *la belle Ferronière* has a charming little Ionic frieze to edge the neck of her dress. Manuscripts (fig. 260) and printed books have their pages framed in classic columns, with the stylobate below and architrave above enriched with classic medallions. Occasionally such detail appears on a Gothic structure: the crockets on some of the flying buttresses of Milan Cathedral are formed like the volutes of an Ionic capital.

Complete architectural compositions of a fanciful kind came into decorative use: at San Satiro in Milan they mimic a sanctuary for which there is no space, but by 1485 they appeared on the Scuola di San Marco at Venice as decoration pure and simple.[2] In the Church of Santa Maria del Organo at Verona the choir stalls have

pour avoir fait de blanc et de noir deux cent trente histoires'. The fashion may, however, have been derived from the liturgical hangings for Lent, which, like the famous Parement de Narbonne, were decorated with drawings in black and grey on a white ground. Similarly in great houses a whole set of 'Vaisselle de Karesme' was kept for use in Lent, of silver decorated only in niello. (See Labarte, *Inventaire du mobilier de Charles V*, p. 212 (1380)). The hatched ornament of many grisaille windows (e.g. those of about 1290 at Stanton Harcourt, Oxon) may reflect such influences. The fashion in illumination was encouraged by the use of a particular white paint, used to render faces and even architecture almost in relief. (See e.g. Bodleian MS. Douce 131). The fashion continued until the last quarter of the century (e.g. the moral and religious treatises illuminated at Ghent in 1475 for Margaret of York, Duchess of Burgundy; Bodleian MS. Douce 365). At the same time much grey and black was worn, for instance by Philippe le Bon and René of Anjou.

[1] Cf. Alberti, *De re Aedificatoria* (trans. Leoni, 1755, p. 113): 'So that then Beauty is somewhat lovely which is proper and innate, and diffused over the whole Body, and ornament somewhat added or fastened on, rather than proper or innate.'

[2] Such work was occasionally imitated in France, e.g. in the panelling of the Church of Cormeilles-en-Parisis.

their backs adorned with an elaborate marquetry picture of the interior of a church in perspective.[1]

Architecture, indeed, had a peculiar charm for the men of the Renaissance, for there is in architecture and in architectural ornament a quality of massiveness and of endurance, and this quality met a need that weighed heavy upon an age that had no certain hope of the future. Even the greatness of Rome had fallen; and men cried, with Alain Chartier:

'Où est Ninive la grant cité qui duroit trois journées de chemin? Qu'est devenue Babiloine, qui fut édifiée de matière artificieuse pour plus durer aux hommes, et maintenant est habitée de serpens? Que dira l'en de Troye la riche et la renommée? Et de Ylion le chastel sans per, dont les portes furent d'ivoire et les colonnes d'argent: et maintenant à peine en reste le pié des fondemens, que les haulx buissons forcloent de la vue des hommes?'[2]

Every perfected thing that visibly endured unchanged gave the lie to the haunting thought that

Everything that grows
Holds in perfection but a little moment.[3]

Art found a new ideal to express: the ideal of permanence. Men might seek it in a Virgilian world, timeless and ever mature; they might seek to build it anew in writings for which they dared hope for the immortality they doubted for their souls; or they might find it, for life at least, in the unchanging beauty of marble, of metal, and of precious stones. So architecture, sculpture, and jewels came to be worthier models for the craftsman than the flowers of the field that are withered in a day.

Marsilio Ficino,[4] a man full of the especial sensibility of this day, could thus define the feeling of his generation: 'Pure colour, lights, voices, the shining of gold, the whiteness of silver, knowledge and the soul, these things do we call beautiful.' All of these beauties that are tangible are to be found in jewels, which came to be regarded as types of beauty and of magnificence. Not only did men own and wear jewels of incredible splendour of colour and workmanship, but representations of them crept into many of the sister arts. They adorn the margins of the choir books of the Cathedrals of Florence and of Siena, the manuscripts of the Medici,[5] the Bible of Mathias Corvinus, the Glockendon Missal in Nuremberg,

[1] Such work was much used for furniture, notably at Brescia and Cologne.
[2] *Quadriloge invectif*, 1422, ed. Duchesne, p. 403.
[3] The great men of the Renaissance for the most part died young; Leonardo, Alberti, and Cousin are among the few notable exceptions.
[4] Quoted P. Monnier, *Le Quattrocento*, i. 59.
[5] e.g. in the Laurentian Library at Florence, Plut. xvi. 17; xviii. 17; liv. 4; lxv. 12, 28, 31, 33; lxvi. 7, 9, 10; and lxviii. 33. Müntz notices (*Précurseurs de la Renaissance*, p. 157) that some of these manuscripts date from before the addition of the fleurs-de-lis to the Medici arms, and are therefore earlier than 1465. The influence spread to the northern countries even before that of classical architecture, and the fine illuminated Flemish Books of Hours of the second half of the fifteenth century have commonly some borders with enamelled flowers with jewelled centres, jewelled crosses, pendants, rosaries, and pilgrim's badges. e.g. Bodleian MS.

265. Dish of Italian maiolica: Faenza or Castel Durante, dated 1520

266. Majolica plate with arabesque decoration. Urbino, c. 1570. Louvre

267. Back of a cuirass. Milanese, *c.* 1525

and the Grimani Breviary at Venice.[1] A Book of Hours in the Siena Library [2] has a frontispiece that is really a sheet of delicately wrought gold gemmed with painted pearls and rubies and set with miniatures. Not only were the canopied figures of allegory from Renaissance shrines and tombs reduced to the measure of an enamelled pendant, but jewels themselves, and the goldsmith's training which most artists received, influenced the design even of architecture, and created a style that, seventy years after Brunelleschi's beginnings, was to blossom into the plateresque architecture of Spain. Not only were houses built with their masonry cut like four-sided jewels,[3] but churches were erected so chiselled and wrought in filigree-like sculpture as to suggest some silversmith's shrine. Such is the Madonna dei Miracoli of Brescia, begun in 1495, with great candelabra [4] pilasters, panels of conventional foliage, an elaborately decorated architrave and variously fluted columns,[5] that all seem magnified out of an original in precious metal; such too is the lower part of the façade of the Certosa of Pavia,[6] begun in 1473 and finished in 1496, with candelabra mullions [7] so rich as to recall the rather earlier work of silversmiths such as Libero Fontana, and friezes with hanging busts and medallions that have their prototypes in chalcedony cameos and Roman gold medallions (fig. 261). Here, too, as in the cabinets of the collectors, ancient and modern are curiously mingled: [8] some of the medallions are copied from medals of Antoninus Pius, Nero, Octavian, Vespasian, Titus, and Hadrian; some from the Renaissance medals of Bolu and Cristoforo di Geremia. Bucrania alternate with death's heads and seraphim, and classic and Christian mythology are set on an equal footing. The windows of Como Cathedral, built in 1510, are each framed by a series of twenty-one medallions with heads, many of them derived from Roman coin types.

Douce 256, Douce 311 (c. 1488); Burlington Fine Arts Club Exhibition, No. 165 (Sir George Holford); *ibid.*, No. 164 (Pierpont Morgan Collection), Roman Breviary of Queen Eleanor of Portugal; Bodleian MS. Gough Liturg. 7, private prayers written for the use of George Talbot, Earl of Shrewsbury.

[1] Other typical examples are Bodleian MS. Douce 29, Hours of Leonora Gonzaga, Duchess of Urbino, with imitations of engraved cornelian gems set in silver. Artists who particularly affected this style were Liberale di Giacomo da Verona, who worked at Siena after 1466; the Florentine, Giovanni da Giuliano Boccardi, the Dominican, Fra Eustachio, Antonio di Girolamo, Attavanti, and others: see H. Clifford Smith, *Jewellery*, p. 175.

[2] That of Litti di Filippo Corbizi, 1494.

[3] For example the Palazzo de' Diamanti at Ferrara, a house in the Via Nicolo at Verona, the Palazzo Bevilacqua at Bologna, and the 'hostel de Salerne' described in the *Vergier d'honneur* of André de la Vigne. The Granovitaïa Palata in the Kremlin of Moscow, built by two Italians in 1491, has its stones cut diamond-fashion.

[4] Lighted candelabra appear on the margin of the frontispiece of the Duke of Urbino's copy of Jerome on the Psalma (Vatican, Urbino MSS. No. 54) and delicate and elaborate candelabra pilasters adorn the *Sforziad* of Gambagnola. (Bibl. Nat. fonds. ital. No. 372.)

[5] On fancifully fluted columns see A. Sartorio, 'Le colonne vitinee e le colonne tortili,' in *Rassegna d'Arte*, xii, 1912, p. 175.

[6] A similar type is to be found at the Certosa in the monument of Gian Galeazzo Visconti, begun in 1493 and finished in 1497.

[7] Cf. the elaborate candelabra pillars that frame the side door of Como Cathedral, 1507.

[8] Collectors, such as Mazzuchelli, filled up the gaps in their series with modern versions of the missing medals. See Courajod, *L'imitation et la contrefaçon des objets d'art antiques aux XVᵉ et XVIᵉ Siècles*, p. 8.

Coins, indeed—next to potsherds the commonest discovery on Roman sites—had come to typify the individual *virtù* of antiquity; and hence influenced a far wider sphere of decoration than that of medallic art.[1] They were a shorthand symbol for antiquity; and so Jacopo Bellini, in his drawing of the Flagellation, now in the Louvre, ornaments the palace of Pilate with medallions copied, even to their inscriptions, from coins of Elis with the seated figure of the Olympian Zeus; and a late fifteenth-century manuscript of the *Romuleon*[2] is adorned with many medallions copying the coins of Rome.

Naturally it was in the Lombard provinces, which were the centres of goldwork in the late fifteenth century, that the plateresque[3] style was most developed;[4] but even in Rome the door of the Palazzo di Venezia[5] had earlier showed the marked influence of jewel design; its architrave is studded with facetted gems carved in stone, and the little window above is connected with it by scrolls that look as if they were wrought in beaten metal. A subtler form of the same influence is to be found in the elaborate surface decoration of architectural members: a decoration in some instances literally applied, as in the *stucchi* added to the columns of the cortile of the Palazzo Vecchio in 1565[6] (fig. 262). It is hardly surprising that the best ornament of the mature Italian Renaissance is to be found in metal-work itself, and especially in the elaborate armourers' work of Brescia and Milan.

The strongest direct classical influence on pure decoration lay in the revivals of 'grottesche'.[7]

'These grotesques', says Cellini,[8] 'have acquired this name from modern people through their being found by students in certain caverns in the ground at Rome, which caverns were in ancient times chambers, baths, studios, saloons, and other similar places. These students found them in these cavernous places, which because since ancient times the ground has risen in those spots, whilst they have remained below, and because the term applied to those low places in Rome is "grottoes"; from this circumstance they acquired the name of "grotesques" (*grottesche*).'

In their earliest form they are characteristic of Rome; the Florentines Brunelleschi and Michelozzo never use them, and it is at Rome and after Roman models that Pinturicchio first paints them. It is from the painted grotesques, to keep the

---

[1] Vasari tells us the Lorenzo Ghiberti 'dilettosi anco di contraffare iconj delle Medaglie antiche': *Vite*, ed. Milanesi, ii. 223.

[2] Paris, Bibl. de l'arsenal, 667.

[3] This adjective, generally reserved for the Renaissance architecture of Spain designed in silversmith's style, may well be used for the north Italian work from which the Spanish style is derived.

[4] e.g. also in the Chapel of the Colleoni at Bergamo and in the terra cotta decoration of the Palazzo Stanga at Cremona.

[5] By Francesco del Borgo di Santo Sepolcro, 1455.

[6] By Marco da Faenza. The custom of covering architectural forms with decorative stucchi may owe something to Spain, where it appears as early as 1483, perhaps by analogy with the faience and stucco revetments of Musulman architecture.

[7] This style I have consistently termed arabesque, in accordance with eighteenth-century usage; reserving 'grotesque' for the deliberately monstrous, and 'moresque' for patterns ultimately of Arab inspiration.

[8] *Life*, Bk. i, chap. vi, 1542; ed. Cust i. 113–14.

ancient word, found in the ruins of the Palace of Titus on the Esquiline that Raphael's and Giovanni da Udine's decorations of the Loggie of the Vatican (fig. 264)[1] are derived; but if they imitate antiquity, they do it with a difference. The principle of median symmetry in the main lines, varied by a free treatment of the detail, the heterogeneity of the ornament,[2] the convention that divides the panel horizontally into three, and the greater number of the forms employed, are all classical, but the style of the whole is informed with a new spirit. Cameos of modern life, including one that shows the pupils of Raphael working at the very *stucchi* the medallion adorns, take their place beside scenes of classic allegory and mythology. We are farther from Attic, and even from Pompeian grace; the ponderation is heavier, the curves less sweet, the line less pure; in many a detail there is a certain *mièvrerie*. The difference is that which distinguishes a lyric of the Renaissance from an Horatian ode. The best description of Renaissance arabesque is Henry Peacham's:[3]

'The form of it is a generall, and (as I may say) an unnatural or unorderly composition for delight sake, of men, beasts, birds, fishes, flowres etc., without (as we say) Rime or reason, for the greater variety you shew in your inuention, the more you please, but remembering to observe a methode or continuation of one and the same thing throughout your whole worke without change or altering. You may, if you list, draw naked boyes riding and playing with their paper-mils[4] or bubble-shels upon Goates, Eagles, Dolphins etc., the bones of a Ram's head hung with strings of beads and Ribands, Satyres, Tritons, Apes, cornu-copias, Dogs yoakt, and drawing Cowcumbers, Cherries, or any kind of wild traile or vinet after your owne invention, with a thousand more such idel toyes, so that herein you cannot be too fantastical.'

The Renaissance desire to find human prototypes for its architectural forms—a desire that obsesses such writers as Serlio—is reflected in compositions that have the line or proportion of a human face or figure. For tombs and the 'Heures des Morts' of Books of Hours arabesques of skulls and crossbones were commonly used. Occasionally they were translated into other than Roman style, as in the Egyptian arabesque of obelisks, hieroglyphs, sphinxes, beast-headed statues, cartouches and reliefs that adorns the page of a missal written for Pompeo Colonna, Archbishop of Monreale and Viceroy of Naples, who died in 1532.[5]

Andrea di Cosimo, called Feltrini, who founded the Florentine school of arabesque painting between 1456 and 1476, and Giuliano da San Gallo, who worked in the last quarter of the century, designed fine and comparatively severe arabesques (fig. 270),[6] but by the end of the century, Nicoletto Rosex da Modena was

[1] Early engraved by the 'Master of the die' and again before 1540 by Agostino Musi; they continued to be reproduced all through the Renaissance; a set engraved by F. de la Guertière was published in Paris, c. 1670.
[2] This includes classic bas-reliefs, arabesques of every sort and kind—some light in style, some heavier and more sculptural in type—trophies of all kinds, from fishes to musical instruments; there is endless liveliness and variety, and a total absence of any constructive idea.   [3] *Graphice*, 1612, p. 49.
[4] Cf. the frieze of *putti* playing with paper windmills on the Hotel Pincé, Angers.
[5] Rome, Biblioteca Sciarra, MS. 1.
[6] San Gallo's are now in the Library of Siena; see E. Müntz, *Précurseurs de la Renaissance*, p. 197. Similar

publishing arabesques with long-necked winged female sphinxes and other elaborations of the classic style (fig. 273). Soon after this Agostino de' Musi, called Veneziano, published arabesque designs of an especially monstrous sort, with lion's legs that end in fish, devil- and dragon-headed eagles, man-headed cocks, winged sphinxes with scrolls for paws and tails, and other nightmare inventions oddly fused into the classic gravity of the conventional scheme.[1] The style soon came to be transferred from wall painting[2] to other forms of decoration; about the middle of the tenth century Rost was weaving tapestries in the arabesque style at Florence, and between 1565 and his death in 1571 Orazio Fontana developed arabesque decoration on the pottery of Urbino (fig. 266).[3]

2

The Renaissance was an age of individualism; the medieval instinct that subjugated individual pride to corporate loyalty was dead. In the earlier Middle Ages the arts flourished in the service of collective needs; in the Renaissance the 'fine' arts were developed of which the primary function was the self-expression of the individual. But besides this individualism of the artist—an individualism reflected in our personal knowledge of the artists of the Renaissance—the arts had to glorify the individualism of their patrons. Money must always be at the roots of individualism; without it, the individual must seek strength in association. In the course of the sixteenth century the money supply of Europe was quadrupled, and Italy became the richest country in Europe. Its 'tyrants' were rich enough to hold their lands not by feudal right, but by sheer weight of power. Not loyalty or duty, but freedom was their justification. A new conception of citizenship was formed; Alberti could say that 'he who cultivates his personal gifts thus performs service enough to the State'. The old idea of social function was dead; 'we are born into this condition', writes Pico della Mirandola,[4] 'that we may be whatsoever we wish to be.' The upstart Doge Agnello of Pisa used to show himself at the window of his palace 'as relics are shown';[5] man shared no longer in the Divine Passion, but in the Divine Transfiguration into glory. The triumph[6] is the characteristic ceremony of the epoch, as the sacrament is of the Middle Ages. The quality that

arabesques appear on the doors from the Palace of Federigo, Duke of Urbino, at Gubbio, now in the Victoria and Albert Museum (103, 1888).

[1] Other grotesque designs of this type were published by Giovanni Antonio da Brescia, who worked in the first quarter of the century, and the tradition was perpetuated in Italy by Antonio Tempesta, 1555–1630.

[2] Such arabesques of 'candelabra' form in an architectural setting are painted on Alberti's Cappella di Sant' Andrea at Mantua and in the choir of San Satiro at Milan.

[3] Hannover, *Pottery and Porcelain*, ed. Rackham, i. 156. The style was copied all over Italy and perpetuated far into the seventeenth century.

[4] *Opera*, Venice, 1557, p. 56.

[5] Burckhardt, *Civilization of the Renaissance in Italy*, p. 11.

[6] On triumphs in art see Werner Weisbach, *Trionfi*, Berlin, 1919; and Prince d'Essling and E. Müntz, *Pétrarque*, chap. iv (p. 101), et seqq.

268. Panel over the door of Andrea Doria's palace at Genoa. By Montorsoli, soon after 1529

269. Panels from the New Sacristy, Cathedral of Florence. By the Armadi, 1460

FIG. 270. Design for an arabesque by Giuliano da San Gallo, c. 1485. Library of Siena.

it held up for admiration was that which concerned the individual alone, independently of his relation with others: Machiavelli's *virtù*—a combination of force and intellect divorced from any moral consideration. It cast a reflection of antique glory on the conquerors of the New Age. The entry of Alfonso of Aragon into Naples in 1443 was staged as a triumph; he rode in a Roman chariot, and behind came triumphal cars with representations of the four Virtues and of his device of the Sege perilous; in 1500 Cesare Borgia enjoyed the honours of the Triumph at Rome. Such classic triumphs were represented on north Italian *cassoni* from about 1445 onwards,[1] and occasionally formed the subject of reliefs. A relief with the triumph of Sigismondo Malatesta was set up in his Tempio at Rimini; and Andrea Doria set a carving of his shield borne in a Triumph over the door of his Palace at Genoa (fig. 268). The accessories of the Triumph soon passed into current decorative use. The victor's wreaths of oak and laurel figure on the Arco del Cavallo at Ferrara, designed by Alberti about 1445, and adorn the inlaid panels of the new sacristy of the Cathedral of Florence, set up in 1460 (fig. 269). Triumphal trophies of ancient armour appear set in scrolls between the winged horses of Renown on the pedestal of Colleone's statue; they adorn the reliefs of the tomb of Doge Pietro Mocenigo, erected between 1478 and 1487[2] and the pilasters of that of Gian Galeazzo Visconti, begun in 1493 and finished in 1497.[3] Nor was their use confined to such monuments; the principal story of the Palazzo Contarini delle Figure at Venice, built in the first quarter of the sixteenth century, has similar trophies suspended from the tops of trees, from which all the branches have been lopped, leaving only a few stray leaves; and a frieze of close-packed trophies adorns a rather later chimney-piece from the Palazzo Borgherini at Florence.[4] Trophies of arms appeared on Castel Durante pottery all through the sixteenth century (fig. 271). Such engravings as those of Enea Vico and Zoan Andrea helped to diffuse the style.[5] Even the church had to have its trophies; Benedetto da Rovezzano arranged its censers and candles, its snuffers and aspergils, its psalters and lecterns, to look as trophy-like as the weapons of a conquered host.[6]

3

Renaissance Italy was revealed to France only by her invasion of Italy in 1494,[7] and then as a strange and alien civilization. France had at that time a knowledge

[1] P. Schubring, *Cassoni, Truhen und Truhenbilder der Italienischen Frührenaissance*, Leipzig, 1915, figs. 111, 115, 116, 125, &c. [2] In the Church of SS. Giovanni e Paolo, Venice.

[3] In the Certosa of Pavia. [4] Now in the Museo Nazionale, Florence.

[5] Trophy pilasters decorate the translation of Livy published at Venice in 1511. Other important engravings of trophies of ancient armour are those published by Polidoro da Caravaggio in 1550, by René Boyvin in 1575, and by Jakob Floris of Antwerp in 1567.

[6] The fashion was perpetuated by French trophy designers. Examples of it may be found in many French provincial churches with *boiseries* of the time of Louis XV: e.g. at Saint Thibault, near Saulieu. Similar trophies in stone appear on the façades of some churches in Lorraine, such as Saint Sebastien, Nancy.

[7] The French were in Italy from September 1494 until October 1495.

271. Plate of Castel Durante faience, *c.* 1530

272. Tomb of the children of Charles VIII of France. By Jean Juste and Guillaume Regnault, 1506. Tours Cathedral

FIG. 273. Arabesque panel by Nicoletto Rosex da Modena, *c.* 1495

of classic literature at least as great as that current in Florence about 1420; but she had long since absorbed her heritage as a Roman province, and had created a civilization of feudalism that forbade any resurrection, whether artistic or political, of Empire. When at last she saw Renaissance Italy, it appeared as a new creation, and not as a resuscitation of the past. It is the absolute deadness of ancient Rome that strikes the Frenchmen of the Renaissance; Montaigne expresses the view of all the other French travellers when he finds there nothing but 'le ciel sous lequel elle avait été assise et le plan de son gîte. . . . Ce n'était rien que son sépulcre.' Du Bellay had vision enough to see that

> le daemon Romain
> S'efforce encor d'une fatale main
> Ressusciter ces poudreuses ruines;

but there was no suggestion that it was only in these ruins that artistic salvation was to be found. In the first stage of the French Renaissance, indeed, it was the influence of modern and not of ancient Italy that came to enrich the Gothic tradition;[1] it was Petrarch, not Horace, who affected the style of French verse. Francesco Laurana was at the court of Anjou from 1460 to 1467, and again after 1470; he designed an Italianate tomb for Charles d'Anjou's father, and built the Italian Chapel of St. Lazarus at Marseilles.[2] Italian artists came to found the 'School of Amboise'[3] soon after 1495; but though they were brought over 'pour ouvrer de leur mestier à l'usage et mode d'Italie' there was no real classicism. The tomb of the children of Charles VIII in the Cathedral of Tours, made by Jean Juste and Guillaume Regnault in 1506 (fig. 272), attempts to capture the Florentine style, but is in no sense antique; even the little satyr of the frieze is a medieval satyr, fitly balanced by a medieval mermaid.[4] The scrolling foliage is more nearly Renaissance; but it grows from the mouth of French dolphins, who most unclassically rise from a sculptured stream. Even in the middle cornice, where we should expect dentils, we find leafage set in opposing directions, a moulding with no antique prototype; while a knotted cable serves as cornice to the whole. Moreover in such a detached piece of sculpture the Renaissance influence was more strongly felt than in a strictly architectural composition; the Gothic structure might totter, but it had not yet fallen; France had not lost her medieval balance. She still had a nation and a religion to fight for; the Italian *virtù* was a quality alien to her soil;[5] the fear of

[1] Similarly when Ducerceau was in Rome he made careful drawings of the projects for St. Peter's, of the Palazzo della Cancelleria, the Palazzo dell' Aquila, &c. (H. de Geymüller, *Les Ducerceau*, p. 15).

[2] 1479–81; see Palustre, *La Renaissance en France*, iii. 114.

[3] Besides sculptors, Charles VIII brought from Italy to Amboise the famous designer of parks and gardens, Passelo da Mercogliano.

[4] The satyr and mermaid arabesques, putti, and wreathed medallions of arms reappear on the otherwise Gothic tomb of Raoul de Lannoy and his wife at Folleville, Somme, ordered from Antonio della Porta and his nephew c. 1510.

[5] Cf. Rabelais' idea of Honour as the only rule of the Abbaye de Thélème: 'Fay ce que vouldras, parce que gens liberes, bien nayz, bien instruictz, conversans en compaignies honnestes, ont par nature ung insting et aiguillon qui tousjours les poulse à faictz vertueux, et retire de vice, lequel ils nommoient honneur.'

274. Frieze from the house called that of Agnes Sorel at Orléans, *c.* 1525

276. Engaged capital from the Escalier d'honneur.
Château de Chambord, *c.* 1535

275. Capital from the exterior. Château de Chambord, *c.* 1535

death still carried a moral lesson, and was not merely an incitement to eat, drink, and be merry. She had no need to turn back to a greater past to find nobility and beauty. She might seek a brand wherewith to light her fire from a neighbour, but she did not linger by a stranger's hearth. Gaillon, the first French Renaissance building of any importance, had only three Italians among its hundred craftsmen,[1] and Ducerceau could describe it: 'fort bien baty, de bonne manière et d'un riche artifice, toutefois moderne' (that is, late Gothic) 'sans trace de l'antiquité, sinon en quelques particularités.'[2]

Chambord[3] may show perfect Renaissance detail; but even Chambord, seen dark at sunset against a radiant sky, has the pinnacled and soaring outline of a castle in a fifteenth-century miniature. Du Bellay was not the only Frenchman to feel:

Plus que le marbre dur me plaît l'ardoise fine
Et plus que l'air romain, la douceur angevine.

France had to acquire humanists, patrons, and craftsmen of Renaissance spirit before she could produce a true Renaissance style. The literature and history of Rome were part of her medieval heritage; the encouragement of their study was the chief task of printed books. She had only to go back again to the sources and to attempt once more to imitate Rome's literary style to attain the humanist ideal. By 1539 Latin verse by Italian writers was being published in French editions[4] and it was soon imitated by the humanists of France. The study of Greek was an academic fact, and was even reflected in decoration; on the Hôtel Lancreau are Greek inscriptions from Pindar, Callimachus, and Menander.[5] A knowledge of Roman architecture likewise became easier to attain; Vitruvius, of which the first printed edition came out at Rome in 1496, was published in Lyons in 1523,[6] Leone Battista Alberti's *de re aedificatoria*, issued at Florence in 1485, appeared in Paris in 1512; the *Roma Instaurata* of Blondus of Forlì had been printed as early as 1474 and his *Roma Triumphans* in 1482. It was not long before every element of Renaissance decoration was to be found in France. At first, it is true, detail alone was affected, and affected by the silversmith decoration of northern Italy, just past its height in the very provinces that the French had invaded.[7]

---

[1] Two of these had long been settled in France.

[2] Quoted Blomfield, *History of French Renaissance Architecture*, i. 42.

[3] Begun in 1519, interrupted by the Italian wars 1524–6, and finished soon after 1545.

[4] de Nolhac, *Ronsard et l'humanisme*, p. 15.

[5] Palustre, *op. cit.* iii. 204. Cf. the pavement of tiles in the Chateau de Polisy, Aube, with the inscription 'Η ΤΥΚΗ 'ΑΚΟΛΟΥΘΟΣ 'ΕΣΤΙ ΤΗΣ 'ΑΡΕΤΗΣ, and the Greek motto sometimes used by Henri II. The use was not confined to France. A shield and casque made for the Emperor Charles V by Lucio Piccinino of Milan about 1551, chased with figures of Fame and Victory, are inscribed ΠΡΟΣ. ΤΑ. ΑΣΤΡΑ. ΔΙΑ. ΤΑΎΤΑ (*Catalogue of the Tudor Exhibition, New Gallery*, 1890, p. 164) and the façade of the University of Salamanca, begun in 1520, has medallions of Ferdinand and Isabella with the inscription: 'ΟΙ ΒΑΣΙΛΕΙΣ ΤΗ ΕΓΚΥΚΛΟΠΑΙΔΕΙΑ ΑΥΤΗ ΤΟῖΣ ΒΑΣΙΛΕΥΣΙ.

[6] It was also published in an Italian translation at Como in 1521.

[7] It is definitely from Como, Pavia, Brescia, and Verona, and not from Florence or central Italy, that the first Renaissance influences to affect French architecture are derived: and it is definitely the forms that are

The portal of Guingamp might be framed in candelabra pilasters, the choir-screen at Fécamp might have dolphin-headed acanthus scrolls;[1] the woodwork at Brou[2] might have Renaissance olive wreaths, strapwork, jewel-cutting, and medallions of classic heads; heavy rustication might appear in the *grotte des Pins* at Fontainebleau;[3] the characteristic north-Italian diamond-cut stones might rim the arches of the bridge at Fère-en-Tardenois;[4] but the basis of art was unchanged. Even Hector Sohier's work of 1518–45 at Saint Pierre de Caen, perhaps the finest example of the French plateresque style, shows all the rich ornament of Lombardy expressed with an added complication of line through the survival of the pinnacles, gargoyles, parapets, and buttresses of the Gothic tradition. Yet little by little each of the Italianate elements was naturalized and perfected, and so little by little the French were weaned from their national medieval style. The influence of engraving helped to propagate the arabesque (or 'grotesque') plaster decoration which Bramante had made a feature of the north-Italian decorative tradition. Such arabesques were probably first introduced by Italian workmen, but they were early copied by French craftsmen, who drew inspiration from such woodcuts as those that frame the pages of the Venice *Ovid* of 1494 and the *Terence* of 1499.[5] The most ordinary Italian printed book had a page or two framed in them; and the French versions of such ornaments, such as those used in Simon Vostre's Paris Hours of 1508, doubtless helped to disseminate the style.[6] Their decorative use, especially in woodwork, commonly shows a strange mixture of ready-made classicism and French provincialism. Such a mixture is evident even in the woodwork of Gaillon.[7] The choir screen in the chapel there had one side carved in the traditional late Gothic style, the other adorned with sculptured arabesques copied or modified from engraved Italian patterns, including some by Zoan Andrea of Mantua. Occasionally, too, the actual use of arabesques was modified by a Gothic tradition; on the wooden screen of Saint Bertrand de Comminges they are cut out to form a fretted cresting to the whole, while they are carved in fretted stone to form parapets for Hector Sohier's Chateau de Lasson and Church of Saint Pierre at Caen. Carved in relief in stone they are usually more Italianate, but even thus they first take their place in an architectural scheme that is entirely Gothic. One of the earliest French instances of their use is on the otherwise completely Gothic

just beginning to fall into disuse in Italy that France adopts. The persistence of the plateresque style in France can be shown by a comparison of the extraordinarily rich ornament of the Church of St. Pierre at Caen, dating from 1518–45, and the organ loft of the Church of SS. Gervais and Protais at Gisors, carved in 1578.

[1] Part of these sculptures were ordered in Italy by Antoine Bohier and imported ready made.

[2] Probably by the Bressan artist, Pierre Terrasson, *c.* 1530.

[3] Built between 1530 and 1537.   [4] *c.* 1537.

[5] They occasionally appear in the early sixteenth-century illuminations, e.g. Bodleian Douce 72 and Douce 112.

[6] See J. Lieure, *La gravure en France au XVIᵉ siècle dans le livre et l'ornement.*

[7] See J. J. Marquet de Vasselot, 'Les Boiseries de Gaillon', in *Bulletin Monumental*, Nos. 3–4, 1927, p. 30 et seqq. The woodwork from Gaillon (now in the Musée de Cluny) may be compared with the wooden doors carved for the north porch of Gisors by Pierre Adam in 1523.

277. Capitals from the Cour Ovale, Palais de Fontainebleau, *c.* 1540

278. Capitals from the North Aisle, Church of Saint Maclou, Pontoise, *c.* 1540

279. Panel and misericord from the Chapel of Gaillon, *c.* 1510

280. Pilaster from the Choir
Screen of Chartres Cathedral,
1529

281. Detail of the Jubé of the Cathedral of Limoges,
1533–4. Made for Jean de Langeac, Bishop of
Avranches and Limoges, Ambassador of Francis I at
Rome

282. Detail of the former Choir Screen, Cathedral of Rodez.
Ascribed to Nicholas Bachelier, 1531

Entombment of Solesmes, dating from 1496;[1] again, they fill the flamboyant arcadings of the portal of Troyes Cathedral, and appear on the Gothic façade of Rouen
Cathedral in 1527. On the choir-screen at Chartres, two years later, they frame
late Gothic doorways; but here they attain a higher level of accomplishment, and
in their Satyrs, Pans, cornucopiae, birds, and candelabra betray the influence of the
designs of Agostino Musi and Nicoletto da Modena (fig. 280). Similar influences
are evident in the elaborate arabesques of the door of Angoulême Cathedral, and
again in the pilasters, curved to frame the arch, of certain decorations from the
Château de Charcus now at Nogent-les-Vierges. Even in the best work the influence of engraved patterns betrays itself; on the screen at Rodez (fig. 282), dated
1531, used to frame admirable fretted panels derived from the usual 'candelabra'
pattern but completely sculptural in style and treatment, there is an odd half-
pilaster, with half a titulus, half a knot of ribbon, half of all its elements, which at
once betrays the use of ready-made designs instead of ornament specially planned
for the place it was to occupy. Soon after 1540 Primaticcio naturalized the style
of Giulio Romano in France, and some of the arabesques of his decoration of the
Galerie d'Ulysse at Fontainebleau[2] were copied and engraved by Ducerceau.[3]
Their curved architraves broken by a pediment, their compositions framed by
terminal figures, their trellised backgrounds, and even their details of birds and
fish, monkeys and monsters, lanterns and trophies, show an arabesque style so
mature that later decorators such as Bérain could do little more than perpetuate it.

Arabesques were applied to many arts besides that of sculpture: they are one of
the commonest *genres* of sixteenth- and early seventeenth-century tapestry, and
they were used in the decoration of many stained glass windows. Even the goldsmiths made use of them; Daniel Mignot, at the end of the century, applied arabesque decoration to his enamelled jewels, and the inventory of the possessions of
Florimond Robertet made after his death in 1532[4] describes:

'Une grande cuvette faite en fontaine, ou sont de ces gentilles crotesques nouvellement
inventées qui jettent miles fleurons a petits jambages tortus, portant les uns des paysages sur
de simples lignes, mesmes des elephants des bœufs et des lyons, des chevaux, des chiens et
des singes, des paons, des herons et des chahuans, des vases, des lampes et des grenades de
feu d'artifice, des aspics, des lezards et des limaçons, des abeilles, des papillons et des hanne-
tons, des fées, des masques, des cornes d'abondance et autres fanfares.'

Nor were the arabesques the only Italianate schemes of decoration used in
France. Jean de Berry had begun to collect ancient and modern medals as early

[1] Other early instances of their use are the pilasters of the tomb of Francis II of Brittany, at Nantes,
carved by Italian and French artists between 1502–7, and of the tomb of Guillaume Guegen in the same
cathedral, erected soon after his death in 1508: Palustre, *op. cit*. iii. 12. Rather later examples appear over
the chimney-piece of the Château d'Omerville, *c.* 1522. *Ibid*. ii. 62.

[2] Destroyed 1738. The arabesques were designed by Primaticcio and painted by Antoine Fantose.

[3] Watercolours in the Musée des Gobelins show tapestries in the style that may have been used to complete
the scheme. Ducerceau also designed arabesques based on those of Nicoletto da Modena and Enea Vico,
and published them at Orléans in 1550 and 1562.

[4] E. Bonnaffé, *Les Collectionneurs de l'ancienne France*, p. 22.

as 1416,[1] and heads of Emperors, derived from coin-types and named, were used to adorn the courtyard of Gaillon[2] and the choir-screen of Chartres.[3] Set in flamboyant tracery they appear on the Hôtel de Ville of Vendôme and on a house at Amiens; one fills the gable of the turret door of the Hôtel Lallemant at Bourges; and a series of them in intarsia decorates the back of the choir-screen of Saint Bertrand de Comminges, finished in 1536. The other type of head-medallion, ultimately derived from those at San Satiro in Milan, appears on a screen on the Church of Saint Martin at Laon, and others of the sort, once more transformed as the Apostles holding the instruments of the Passion, are carved in high relief on a frieze in the Church of Ennery, Seine et Oise.

The triumph seems hardly to have figured in French pageantry before Henri II's entry into Rouen in 1550, but it had much earlier figured in the decoration of tombs. The tomb of Louis XII shows his entry into Genoa in the guise of a Roman triumph, complete with trophies and tituli; the unfinished tomb of Gaston de Foix, ordered by Francis I in 1515, has bas-reliefs of triumphs as its chief decoration;[4] while the completely classical tomb of Guillaume de Langey at Le Mans, of about 1546, has trophies of helmets, cuirasses, lances, javelins, axes, swords, standards, and battering-rams. In 1565 Cramoy and Martin le Fort were paid for the trophies of the upper story of the courtyard of the Louvre; 'corselets, toraces, tarques, parvois, expées, dagues, arcques, carquoys et autres sortes d'armes antiques.'[5] But ancient armour soon became too remote and visionary a symbol: a Henry IV chimney-piece at Cheverny is adorned with trophies of sixteenth-century arms and guns.[6]

4

The next stage in the progress of the French Renaissance depended upon the influence of the 'amateur' who did most to encourage its development. Francis I, who ascended the throne in 1515, was the first Frenchman to approach the ideal of the Renaissance patron. With little learning, but a strong 'sens du décor', he is fitly shown on the fresco of his gallery at Fontainebleau, crowned with laurel and armed with book and sword, opening the door of the temple of the Muses to a

[1] His inventory of that year includes a jewel with medallions of Tiberius and Faustina, bought in Paris in 1401, others with medallions of Octavian and Julius Caesar, and another with a medallion of Constantine, bought from a Florentine merchant in Paris in 1402. (Guiffrey, *Les inventaires de Jean Duc de Berry*, i. 70.)

[2] Carved by Paganino. All that now remain of them are in the courtyard of the École des Beaux Arts at Paris.

[3] Labelled Titus Cesar (twice), Vespasianus Cesar, Neron le cruel Cesar, Julius Cesar, Domigianus Cesar.

[4] Palustre, *op. cit.*, iii. 148. Similar trophies also appear on the panels of Francis I's Gallery of Fontainebleau, on the frieze of the Gros Horloge of Rouen, and on Henri II's doors in the Louvre, now between the Grande Salle and its alcove.

[5] Laborde, *Comptes des Bâtimens du Roi*, 1877, ii. 112.

[6] Italianate trophies of chalices, cruets, aspergils and the like also came into use; they appear on one of the pilasters of the screen at Rodez, carved in 1531.

283. Fragment of a frieze from the tomb of Jean de Vienne, *c.* 1535. Château de Pagny.

284. Front of a chest. French, Valley of the Loire, *c.* 1535.

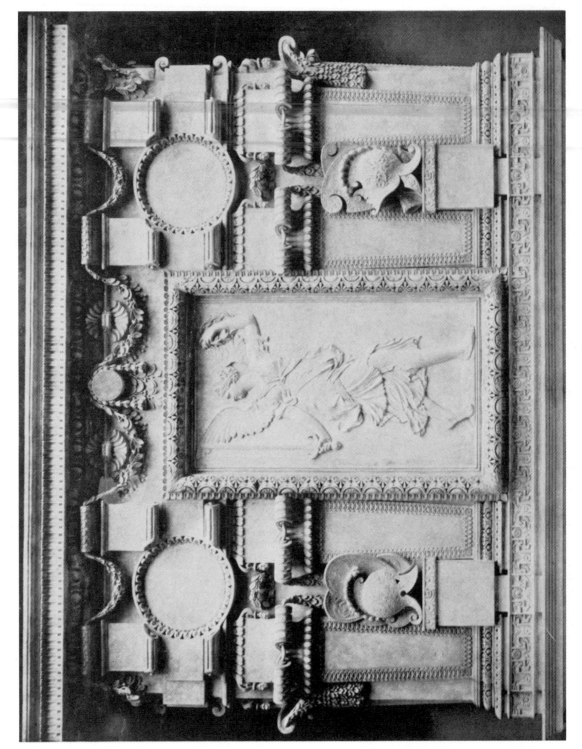

285. Upper part of a chimney-piece in the Castle of Écouen. Probably by Jean Goujon, *c.* 1540.

crowd of his subjects, who enter it as blind men with bandaged eyes.[1] Not only
did he offer his protection to such alien artists as Primaticcio, but under his patronage there grew up a generation of artists both truly French and truly of the
Renaissance.

Philibert de l'Orme was the first Frenchman to go to Rome to study architecture,[2]
and to study not the Renaissance, but antiquity. For three years, from 1533 to
1536, he measured 'les édifices et antiquités avec grand labeur, frais et despens,
selon ma petite portée, tant pour les échelles et cordages que pour faire fouiller les
fondements, afin de les connaître et pour retirer toutes choses rares et exquises en
l'art d'architecture.' He studied the Pantheon; the theatre of Marcellus; the
classical columns built into St. Peter's, the Lateran and Santa Prassede; the cornices
of the Arch of Constantine; the Baths of Diocletian; the Temple of Faustina; the
Forum of Nerva and the Coliseum; he explored the vineyard of Cardinal Gaddi
and the remains of the villa of Hadrian, and found broken architraves and capitals
'fort antiques et plus qu'admirables à l'œil humain,' which he hurriedly drew
before they were broken up and burnt for lime.[3] Then, when he was back in
France again, he scoffed at those who used classical forms as 'filets à prendre les
hommes ou ce qui est dans leurs bourses,'[4] and instead of recommending a slavish
adherence to the Vitruvian orders, suggested new forms which, he says, you may
call what you please. His training and his point of view illustrate the two aspects
of French Renaissance classicism. On the one hand there was a light and graceful
Gallicism: on the other a classicism that, however gracious, was in its essence severe.

The first was the earlier manifestation. By 1540, Gothic detail might be elimi-
nated from secular work, but classicism came in, not as a rigid discipline but as an
elegant arabesque.[5] Men loved decoration for its own sake; it is characteristic that
even the rustication of the château de Tanlay is carved with a running pattern.
France developed her own style of plateresque decoration; in such work as the
apse of the Trinité at Falaise, the transept of the church of Fenioux, the turrets and
oriels of many châteaux of the same date, we find the same delicacy of relief and
richness of decoration that appear at Bergamo and Pavia, transposed into the key
of another race and another civilization. France took much that was Italian, some
that was Roman; but 'ce n'est plus thin ny marjolaine;' the honey she distils is all

---

[1] Cf. Castiglione, *Il Cortegiano*, written in 1514 (Lyons, 1562 ed., p. 94) 'Ma oltra alla bontà, il vero e principal
ornamento d'ell animo in ciascuno penso io, che siano le lettere; benche i Francesi solamente conoscano la
nobiltà d'ell'armi e tutto il resto nulla estimino, di modo, che non solamente non apprezzano le lettere, ma
le abhorriscono, e tutti letterati tengon per vilissimi huomini . . .' He goes on to predict that the Count of
Angoulême, when King (as he later became under the title of Francis I) will make the supreme ornament
of letters flourish there also.

[2] It is not a Frenchman, but the Italian Giuliano da San Gallo, who first studied the Roman remains of
Provence: H. Clousot, *Philibert de l'Orme*, p. 11.

[3] H. Clousot, *Philibert de l'Orme*, p. 31.   [4] *Livre premier de l'architecture*, chap. viii. 16.

[5] It is characteristic that the copy of Clement Marot's version of Ovid's Metamorphoses presented to the
King by the poet before his death in 1544, is illustrated with completely French miniatures with nothing
classical about them. Juno appears in modern dress, and even Apollo wears jerkin and hose.

her own. Moreover the style that was developed under the stress of individual needs, individual taste, and individual caprice grew into a style that was characteristically national alike in its restraint and in its freedom.

It is freedom which is first made manifest. The ornaments of architecture were modified at will. The French sculptor had too many centuries of freedom behind him to treat even the classic capital with over much respect. Sometimes, as at the Hôtel Lallemant at Bourges, the capital has a winged death's head between the volutes, and the volutes themselves are the tails of dolphins. At Chambord[1] some of the classical foliage on the capitals is treated according to the medieval tradition, and all the eight hundred capitals are differently designed (figs. 275–6). Some have pegasi and baby centaurs, others Gallic cocks and grotesque monsters; there is one with a little devil and many with projecting heads. The volutes may be lizards, horses, masks, dolphins, griffins or birds; some are formed of elegant and slender cornucopiae. No words can give an idea of their delicacy and variety.[2] France hated 'un scavoir pédantesque' above all things; and such decoration is exactly as classical as Ronsard's verse. It has the same varied rhythm, now rapid and now weighty; the same change of emphasis and scale; the same classical conceits, and the same freshness that comes from the observation of nature. Just as French verse achieved a lyric delicacy of its own, so French decoration achieved a style of peculiar charm, which has no true prototype in Italy. Its scrolling forms may be classical, but the dancing measure, the fastidious ponderation, the vitality of the figures and the subtlety of modelling in such work as decoration of a tomb at Château-de-Pagny (fig. 283), are characteristically French.[3] The little figures that dance among its scrolls are the chorus of Ronsard's verse:

> Faunes, Satyres, Pans, Napées, Oréades,
> Aigipans qui portaient des cornes sur le front,
> Et qui, ballant, sautaient comme les chèvres font,
> Et les Nymphes, suivant les fantastiques fées
> Autour de moi dansaient à cottes agrafées.

The style was translated into woodwork, which sometimes has the dry perfection that is characteristically French (fig. 284), and sometimes reverts to the tradition of the later Gothic style. On a heavier scale it played a part in architectural decoration, as in the 'frise de festons composée de plusieurs fructages aux petis enfans et oiseaux y entremeslés' carved for the south wing of the Louvre in 1562–3;[4] but it never flourished outside France. France thus had a new birth as

---

[1] The visitor may find Blois more interesting than Chambord, but must remember that nearly all the sculptural decoration there dates from 1845–8 and not from the sixteenth century.

[2] The Chambord capitals show an advance even on such contemporary Italian work as the capitals from the Castle of Mondolfo now in the Victoria and Albert Museum.

[3] The style is derived, but with a difference, from such light Italian scrolling ornament with *putti* as that of 1527 reproduced by Reynard I, p. 5; other designs were published by Vico, *c.* 1530. Those of Battista Pittoni of Vicenza, published *c.* 1560 (Victoria and Albert Museum, E. O35, E, 1389, 97) are inspired by French models.   [4] M. Vachon, *Le Louvre et les Tuileries*, p. 75.

287. Detail of the soffit, Salle des Caryatides, Louvre, 1558

286. Detail of the door of the Church of Gisors, c. 1550

288. The 'French Order' of the Tuileries. Designed by Philibert de l'Orme in 1564. Burnt
in 1871. Since demolished

delightful as the Florentine Renaissance a hundred years before; a Renaissance content with allusion in its erudition, occupied with grace rather than with correctness, and saved by the national genius from the tyranny of the Fine Arts.

But at the same time architectural knowledge increased, and a humanist style of severe classicism was created. Serlio's *Livre d'Architecture* was published in French in 1545, and paved the way for the first French version of Vitruvius two years later;[1] at the same time such good plates of Roman orders as those of Agostino Veneziano and of Enea Vico were available; and a greater sense of *ensemble* was encouraged by engraved views of Roman ruins and remains.[2] At first even classic Orders had been unclassically used; at the castle of Bournazel in the Rouergue, for instance, the metopes are filled with little patterns from engraved designs—half-bulls, sacrificial fillets, trophies, cartouches, mermaids, centaurs, and tragic masks, all used with no regard to uniformity of ponderation and scale. French classicism had to discover its own code and to formulate its own canons. Bellay was commanding his fellow countrymen 'La donq, Françoys, marchez couraigeusement vers cete superbe cité romaine, et des serves dépouilles d'elle . . . ornez vos temples et autelz.' By 1555 the ideas of the Pleiade had been formulated by Pelletier, and Ronsard had declared the imitation of the moderns to be so odious that he would accept no masters but Pindar and Horace. In decoration Ducerceau naturalized the classic style of Enea Vico in France,[3] and thus set the note for all lighter French classicism down to the Empire.[4] At the same time Bullant and Lescot were setting the pitch for French classical architecture. Bullant was a man of learning and an archaeologist, and betrays it in his style; while Lescot's designs for the Louvre of 1546 show a finished and urbane Roman style unsurpassed under Louis XIII.[5] The contemporary church of Belloy, built in the style of Bullant, has wreathed bucrania alternating with rosettes and paterae on its frieze, and heavy classical consoles instead of triglyphs; an equally severe classicism appears on the Church of Conches, Eure, and on the portal of that of Luzarches. Similarly austere ornament decorates even such less architectural constructions as the

[1] By Martin, with an introduction by Jean Goujon. An abstract of Vitruvius had been printed by S. de Colines in 1539.

[2] Such as Jacobus Mazochius *Epigrammata Antiquae urbis* of 1521. Ducerceau's *Vues d'Optique* of 1551 are imitated, if not copied, from those of Crecchi of Lucca. Others appear in Jean Cousin's *Livre de Perspective* of 1560. From 1553 to 1577 the greater number of engravings of Roman antiquities published were by Frenchmen, notably by Antoine Lefrère. The most important attempts at restoration are those published in Ducerceau's *Livres des edifices antiques romains* of 1584.

[3] It is Vico's vases of 1530, 1531, and 1532 that Ducerceau copies with immense success, and Vico's arabesques and trophies that Ducerceau reproduces as his own in 1566.

[4] Ward, *French Renaissance Architecture*, i. 133, remarks, 'So completely did France come into her definitive manner in architecture at this time (c. 1540) that certain of its buildings, as, for instance, the house known as du Cerceau's at Orleans, might, with slight modifications, have been the product of almost any period from 1540 to 1870, while every reign, from Henry III to the last Napoleon, has produced work which, but for minutiae, might have been built when Henry II was King'.

[5] The style has marked analogies with such Italian work as the Madonna di San Biagio at Montepulciano.

Fontaine des Innocents of 1550 and the tomb of Guy III d'Espinay of 1553.[1] Gradually, however, this constructional style came to be more freely treated; the porch of the Church of Montjavoult of about 1565[2] is heavily and rigidly classical, but the portal of the Church of Othis,[3] finished eight years later, shows a marked freedom of treatment. An upper frieze—a Vitruvian scroll—crowns a rose window of plateresque design rimmed with a delicate moulding; the metopes of the lower frieze, filled with a design of crossed olive branches, vary in width, while the triglyph remains constant. On the Hôtel d'Assézat at Toulouse, built in 1555, there are roundels with trophies instead of paterae upon the frieze, and the consoles are adorned with lovely pea-pod anthemia that are purely of the Renaissance.

1572, the year of the St. Bartholomew, marks a stage in the French Renaissance. Many of France's most national artists, such as Étienne de Laune, had to fly to a Protestant country. As a consequence French art suffered a certain loss of coherence on French soil and developed on more northern lines outside France itself.

The designs published by René Boyvin in 1575 show a fantastical treatment of classical motives and masks; even Ducerceau's later designs[4] show arabesques with an increasing tinge of northern *diablerie*, pilasters and consoles so broken up as to have lost their architectural strength of form, columns with medallions and other ornaments on the shafts, and such details as paired and tripled dentils to mark the decline of a classical tradition.[5] It is characteristic that the one element of classical decoration that attains a new importance is the least architectonic of all: the Caryatid. Caryatids were first introduced into France by Cellini, who used them to frame his nymph at Fontainebleau, to correct a little the arch above, 'in the bad French style'; they appear again on the reliefs of the Altar of the Chapelle d'Écouen by Jean Goujon and Jean Bullant and figure magnificently on Goujon's façade of the Louvre;[6] but they were little used in French architecture or decoration until the last quarter of the century. Ducerceau then published his 'Série des Termes', and Hugues Sambin made them a characteristic of the richer French furniture of the last two decades of the century (figs. 289–90). Extremely fine ones frame the windows of the Hôtel du Vieux Raisin at Toulouse; but even here a certain lack of architectonic feeling is evident in two sets with monstrous legs entwined round each other.[7]

[1] The French architect Pierre de la Roche imported the style into Sweden; it appears in his work at Wadstena, dating from between 1556 and 1563.   [2] Perhaps by Jean Grappin; Palustre, *op. cit.*, i. 70.

[3] In the Ile de France; *ibid.*, i. 146; a similar style is evident in the Church of Le Grand Andely of about the same date.   [4] e.g. Victoria and Albert Museum, EO, 1208–1923.

[5] A similar decline is evident in the detail of the Château de Sully, Saône et Loire, in the parts built between 1567 and 1596.

[6] He, however, there cuts off their arms to intensify their architectural function. On the French use of caryatids see H. Lemonnier, *L'Art Moderne*, 1500–1800, p. 50; on the Italian use, *c.* 1550–60, see C. Gurlitt, *Geschichte des Barockstiles in Italien*, pp. 103 and 123.

[7] Similar caryatids may be found in some of Ducerceau's designs for furniture, and also occur on a door of the Église Saint-Pierre at Avignon and on a dormer of La Labenche at Brive.

289. Table of carved walnut. French, *c.* 1570

290. Cupboard of carved walnut. French, *c.* 1570

Dorica

11

291. Design for a Doric order. By Vredeman de Vries, 1563

Humanist, patron, and artist were alike suffering from the political anarchy of France; 'Ronsardiser' became a term of reproach,[1] and the sense of splendour and victory, that must accompany the progress of a classic style, was lost. Political troubles, moreover, precluded any revival of a more national style, though a new interest was felt in the national past,[2] and was even reflected in such work as Virgil Solis' and Jost Amman's *Effigies Regum Francorum Omnium*, published at Nuremberg in 1576. But until the King returned to Paris in 1594, and even until the Edict of Nantes was passed four years later, there was a weakening of the continuity of the French tradition.[3]

5

The idea of a re-birth rather than a re-creation of classicism is especially true in that classic style was not achieved before the seventeenth century, except in the countries on which Rome had set her imprint, and in which Roman monuments remained visible. In other lands classicism, necessarily derived chiefly from engravings, had to be grafted on to an alien stem; and when at length it flowered the result was too often a strange and sterile hybrid.

Even in the southern country of Spain the classicism of the Renaissance had to contend against the double influence of Moorish tradition and an imported Flemish style.[4] Yet one by one all the marks of classic influence appeared in due order: diamond-cut points on the façade of the Infantado Palace at Guadalajara in 1483,[5] all the plateresque detail of the Certosa of Pavia on Enrique de Egas' Hospital of Santa Cruz at Toledo, begun in 1504 and left unfinished some ten years later,[6] and all the arabesques of the engravers on the staircase of the Archbishop's Palace at Alcalá, begun in 1535. By the middle of the century Alonso Berrugete used arabesques in the manner of Musi on his choir stalls in San Benito at Valladolid; head-medallions are almost the only decoration of the arcades of the Irish College at Salamanca; and caryatids adorn the columns of the Zaporta house at Saragossa. The great artists of Spain had a sense of the geometric basis of classic design; Juan de Arphe not only warns his compatriots against the use of pretty ornament copied from French and Flemish pattern books,[7] but also emphasizes the element of strict proportion in all his work.[8] But though her

[1] No new edition of Ronsard's works was published between 1629 and modern days.
[2] In 1579 Claude Fauchet begins to publish his *Antiquités gauloises et françoises*.
[3] Philibert de l'Orme died in 1570, Ronsard in 1585, Jean Cousin in 1589, Germain Pilon in 1590, Montaigne in 1592.
[4] For a good account and illustrations of Spanish early Renaissance work, see A. Byne and M. Stapley, *Spanish Architecture of the sixteenth century*, New York and London, 1917.
[5] Later instances are the Palacio de los Hozes at Segovia and the Palacio de Javalquinto at Baeza in the province of Jaén.
[6] See also the Royal Hospital of Santiago, 1511, the Casas Consistoriales of Seville, 1527.
[7] *Descripción de la traza yornato de la Custodia de Plata de la Sancta Iglesia de Seville*, 1587.
[8] Notably in the *De varia comensuración para la escultura y Architectura* of 1585.

architects did achieve a Peruzzi-like classical style in architecture with very little ornament—notably in the Palace of Grenada, built for Charles V between 1526 and 1550—Spain's contribution to Renaissance decoration was an oriental richness which was ever at war with the principles of classicism. The conventional elements of Italianate decoration were multiplied inconceivably on her choir stalls and altars; but there were curiously few original developments either in style or in ornament.[1]

The Netherlandish provinces shared to some extent in the early French Renaissance:[2] Guy de Baugrant's chimney-piece at Bruges (1529)[3] is in the Italianate style with *putti* upholding classical profile medallions within wreaths; the window given in the same year to the Church of Saint Jacques at Liége[4] has a background in regular plateresque style; while very rich classical ornament restrained by a strong architectural feeling appears on the alabaster retable of 1533 in the Church of St. Martin at Hal.[5] At the same time Lucas van Leyden was producing characteristically Teutonized arabesques after the style of Niccolo Rosex of Modena (fig. 292), and Alaert Claes adequate, if rather heavy, foliage patterns (fig. 293). After 1540 or a little later, artists such as Pieter Koeck van Aelst, who had studied in Italy, brought back a truer ideal of classicism. Such ornament, however, is derivative; and even the good rich decoration of the Maison de l'Ancien Greffe of Bruges, built in 1537, and the more characteristic carvings on the door-frame of the Hôtel de Ville at Audenarde bear no later fruit. The work of Hans Vredeman de Vries, the most influential of the Low Country ornamentists,[6] shows less an ignorance of the classic canon than a national distaste for line and proportion at the expense of decoration[7] (fig. 291). Cornelis Matsys, again, was familiar with the Roman tradition of arabesque ornament, but he not only added *bizarreries* of his own, but also falsified the architectonic tradition by designing his arabesques not as panels, but as continuous bands. This tendency reappears after the pause in artistic production in the Netherlands due to the wars with Spain between 1566 and 1584, intensified into a horror of an unbroken line: the classic forms of Heinrich Muntinck's pattern book of 1604 and of Rotger Kaseman's designs of 1615[8] and 1616 are all broken up by diamond-cut panels and moulded and

[1] The contribution of Portugal is still less important. Renaissance style there appears in the cloister of St. Jerome at Belem, 1500–20.

[2] They had, however, from the beginning markedly less architectural sense. The triptych (dated 1523) by Lancelot Blondeel in the Church of Saint Jacques at Bruges has a background of curiously unintelligent classical architecture; the pilasters are broken by medallions in the most unlikely places, and the whole is crowned with pinnacles, some plateresque and some late Gothic in style.

[3] See Paul Clemen, *Belgische Kunstdenkmäler*, Munich, 1923, vol. ii, chap. i.

[4] *Ibid.*, ii. 46.   [5] *Ibid.*, ii. 93.

[6] His designs, cartouches (1555), grotesques (1563), caryatids, and columns (1563) and his version of Vitruvius (1577) influenced not only the Netherlands but also England and Denmark.

[7] It is significant that the Town Hall at the Hague (1564) is almost the first Dutch building in the Renaissance style.

[8] *Architectura lehr-seivlen Bochg.* The part of the Town Hall of Ghent built between 1595 and 1628 shows

FIG. 292. Arabesque panel by Lucas van Leyden, 1528.

FIG. 293. Panel designed by Alaert Claes, *c.* 1545.

decorated bands. The Dutch use of oblique lines of light and shadow, that makes such lines the basis of Dutch pictorial composition, is everywhere reflected in Netherlandish decoration in the precise angular adjustments of complicated mouldings, giving a similar effect on another scale.

Neither Germany nor the Low Countries could produce a true classicism; their humanists leant towards pedantry, their patrons were merchants or petty princes who confounded ostentation with magnificence, their craftsmen were trained in a provincial medievalism from which they could not escape. Curiously little fine architecture in true Renaissance style was produced; and so classical decoration lost its purpose, and suffered a corresponding degeneration when its use was determined by the minor arts alone.

In the German provinces, moreover, the Renaissance hardly got beyond a compromise between classicism in detail and Gothicism in mass. Only three buildings of any importance can claim to be considered of true Renaissance style: the Residenz at Landshut, the Belvedere in the Schlossgarten of Prague, and the Fürstenhof at Wismar. All these were built in the twenty years between 1535 and 1555, and for all of them Italianate architects were employed.

German decoration, however, was generally affected through the medium of engravings, and a plateresque style that comes ultimately from Lombardy[1] is to be found alike in the south and in Saxony and Silesia. Candelabra pilasters are combined with Gothic ornament on the monument of St. Sebald in the Sebalduskirche of Nuremberg, carved by Peter Vischer and his sons between 1508 and 1519; medallions, pilasters, dolphins, and sirens, all appear in the chapel erected in 1512 by the great merchant family of Fugger in the church of St. Anne at Augsburg; and even columns and architrave were used by Peter Flötner to mask his door to the Hirschvogel House at Nuremberg in 1534. But the principles of classic architecture were not realized; the triumphs of the German engravers are in designs which are not classical, though they are of the Renaissance. Hans Sebald Beham and Peter Flötner came nearest to classicism in the patterns they published round about 1540; but even in these there is not only a false emphasis on the accidents of classical decoration at the expense of its essentials, but also an introduction of incongruous elements. Beham's illustrations of the Vitruvian Orders, engraved in 1543, are curiously unclassical; his style is freer even than that of the carvers of Chambord, and, unlike their modifications, what is added is not harmonious.

a severer classic style, with three superimposed orders crowned by ordinary Flemish gables; but this style quickly degenerates into such work as the church tower of Saint Amand-les-Eaux, near Valenciennes, built in 1633, which has stumpy versions of the Five Orders superimposed upon its façade, and every detail overloaded with ornament.

[1] Admirable candelabra pilasters frame the gilt bronze 'Croy epitaph' of 1519 in Cologne Cathedral treasury. A pilaster and a fanciful capital appears in 1523 in the background of a portrait of Erasmus by Holbein, now at Longford.

294. The Façade of the Otto Heinrichsbau, Castle of Heidelberg. Begun 1556

295. Screen of Middle Temple Hall, *c.* 1570

148

FIG. 296. Design for a chimney-piece by Wendel Dietterlin, 1598.

Splendour and greatness are markedly absent: goldsmith's patterns predominate over anything architectural; and in idea as in fact the pattern-making centres of the German States were the goldsmiths' towns of Nuremberg and Augsburg. Such designers as Höpfer and Holbein could produce delicate and even beautiful designs for gold and silver, but classical construction was not apprehended. Even in such work as the Otto Heinrichs Bau at Heidelberg, begun in 1556 (fig. 294), a wealth of Italianate ornament of the pattern-book type is merely applied to a Gothic shell, and the same insignificant richness is visible in all the series of German Renaissance buildings down to the end of the sixteenth century.[1]

A northern classicism, indeed, was impossible until the north had learned a new civilization from the south. Until then it could approach neither the magnificence of Italy nor the grace of France; northern individuality, with no unity of experience or culture behind it, could not hope to found a school. So even sixteenth-century England could add nothing but her own provincialism to Renaissance decoration of a classic kind. Our country had humanists and patrons, but native craftsmen with the classic sense were lacking. Pietro Torrigiano might set up a Renaissance tomb to Henry VII in 1516 in his Gothic chapel; by 1521 Wolsey might employ Giovanni da Maiano on his medieval palace at Hampton Court, and the medallion heads of the Emperors that Italy set as her seal upon the countries she influenced might appear on the turrets of his courtyard;[2] his closet might have 'a border of antyke' such as is described in his accounts, with dolphins and candelabra patterns in Italianate style; his arms might be supported by *putti* and framed in pilasters with a frieze of swags between the leopard's faces of his blazon; but it was all an importation, and when Henry VIII added his own arms in 1530 the slab was of pure late Gothic style. The various stages of the French Renaissance found spasmodic expression in England: the chantry of the Countess of Salisbury at Christchurch, erected about 1529, and Bishop West's contemporary chapel at Ely are of late Gothic form with Italian friezes and pilasters, like the façade of Rouen. Fairly good arabesque panels and pilasters of the French type decorate the Greenway Chapel at Tiverton;[3] the chapel screen of King's College, Cambridge (1532–6) shows an English version of the plateresque style, and in the background of its Nativity window appears a good architectural ensemble. Henry VIII's startlingly rich late-Gothic ceiling in the great Hall at Hampton Court (1536) has Renaissance

---

[1] e.g. the Rathaus of Cologne, built between 1569–71, from designs of Wilhelm Vernickel, and the Gasthaus zum Ritter at Heidelberg, dated 1592.

[2] Heads of the same sort appear again on Bishop Fox's screen at St. Cross, Winchester, rather before 1528, and over the dining-room door at Haddon Hall, *c.* 1545. The medallions with Caesars' heads on the façade of Old Gorhambury (1563–71) are definitely Italian, perhaps imported ready made. Head medallions survive in minor decoration as late as 1585, when they appear on the loving-cups presented by John White to the Corporation of Plymouth. Jewitt and Hope, *Corporation Plate*, 1895, i. 152. Some later examples may be derived from R. Reynolds, *A Chronicle of all the Noble Emperours of the Romaines*.

[3] Coverdale's Bible, printed abroad in 1535, has its title-page framed in good candelabra arabesques which may have helped to disseminate the type.

297. Ceiling in Thorpe Hall, 1656

298. Detail of the ceiling of the Sala di Giove, Palazzo Pitti, Florence. By Pietro da Cortona, 1650

pendants under the hammerbeam of the roof, and classical brackets to its Gothic corbels.[1] Caryatids[2] (with feet awkwardly appearing below the term), triglyphs, and rosette metopes adorn the screen of Middle Temple Hall,[3] carved about 1570 (fig. 295). One house—Kirby Hall, Northamptonshire, dating from 1570–5—even shows the superimposed orders, 'giant' pilasters, and Vitruvian scroll frieze of the severer French style;[4] but none of these found a development in England in any way comparable with that they enjoyed in France. The Tudor appropriation of many of the monastic houses as homes for the new rich (and as additional houses for great lords of older family) was in itself a certain check on the development of the Renaissance style in sixteenth-century English building. It was, indeed, only in such detached and isolated objects as plate that a pure classicism was achieved.[5]

The classic orders played an important part in Elizabethan architecture, but played it simply as ornaments applied with no conception of their structural use. The middle of the century, indeed, that marks the beginning of architectural classicism in France, is in England the date at which Dutch influence definitely replaced that of the Latin countries. Dutchmen were employed at Nonesuch after 1547; Dutch influence is already apparent in such buildings as Burghley House, Northampton, of about 1556; such chimney-pieces as that in the Solar of Stokesay Castle, dating from 1571, show a purely Low Country version of Venetian classicism; while the influence of Vredeman de Vries is clearly evident in John Thorpe's design of Wollaton Hall (1580–8), in the west porch of Charlton House, Kent (1607), and in such woodwork as the Hall screen of Chastleton House, Oxon.[6] Peacham, writing in 1612, finds that in choosing an 'Antique' design, 'except it be a Dutch peece, you shall have it either lame, ill cut, false shadowed, or subject to some such grosse error'.[7] Even Shute's digest of Serlio had to wait a decade after its author's return from Italy in 1553 before it found a publisher.[8]

The selective taste and the sense of permanence that are essential to the creation of a classic style were both absent in England. Sir Thomas Browne was willing to find that 'there was never anything ugly or misshapen but the Chaos, wherein, notwithstanding, to speak strictly, there was no deformity because no form'. The variations of Elizabethan pattern were like the variations of Elizabethan attire: 'It is a world to see the costliness and the curiositie; the excess and the varietie; and finally the fickleness and the follie, that is in all degrees.'[9] Until Thomas Lord

[1] Carved by Richard Rydge of London.

[2] They also appear on the Foljambe tomb of 1592 in Chesterfield Church, and become commonplaces of English title-pages about 1610.

[3] Cf. the similar style of the dining-room mantelpiece at Madingley Hall, Cambridge.

[4] In the comparatively few instances in which such architectural forms appear in woodwork (e.g. on the doorway of the great Chamber of Maxstoke Castle, Warwickshire, c. 1587) they are produced with rather mean flat carving all over the members, giving a curiously northern and provincial effect.

[5] e.g. in the Barber Surgeons' cup of 1523 and the Goldsmiths' goblet with a crystal bowl of 1545.

[6] His *Panoplia* influence the ornament of the great staircase of the Charterhouse.

[7] *Graphice*, p. 50.   [8] *The First and Chief Grounds of Architecture*, 1563.

[9] William Harrison, *Description of England*, ed. Furnivall, pt. I, Bk. 2, p. 168.

Arundel[1] had established the English tradition of collecting, until Inigo Jones had studied classical architecture in Rome and could work for a patron of Latin tastes, true classicism remained foreign to England. Even so, political events hindered the development of English classicism, and her medieval tradition was not really broken until the Restoration of 1660.[2]

6

Meanwhile Italian classicism was itself entering upon another phase.[3] The imitation of antique motives had become a commonplace; for such motives, together with the style, the relief, and even the spirit of Roman models had become part of the artistic heritage of Italy; and her artists were free to use this heritage in new creation. Knowledge of classical myth and story was equally widespread; and after a time of apprenticeship to the illustration of such stories[4] the artists were free to use them with a new significance. The figures of the *imagini* books were transmuted by the hands of great artists, and turned from their use in isolated medallions to figure in great allegorical schemes. In 1560 Veronese painted the gallery ceiling of the villa of the Barbaros at Maser near Treviso, with eight planets figured as Olympian deities circling round an allegorical figure of Earth, and divinities personifying the elements in each corner: Juno for Air, Cybele for Earth, Vulcan for Fire, and Neptune for Water; with figures of the four seasons in lunettes below. Variations of the scheme adorned many of the great palaces of the early seventeenth century. About 1610 Francesco Albini painted a ceiling in the Palazzo Verospi (Torlonia) at Rome with the sun chariot of Apollo crossing the Zodiac, among figures of the Seasons, Day, Night, and the seven days of the week; and Guido Reni's more famous fresco of Aurora and Phoebus is but one of many similar contemporary paintings,[5] alike in subject however much they may vary in artistic merit. In 1642 Francesco Rondinelli planned a scheme of decoration for the royal apartments of the Palazzo Pitti at Florence, that was carried out by Pietro da Cortona, one of the ablest decorative painters of his day. Each room was dedicated to a Planet,[6] with all its decoration in connexion with that planet's divine personification. In the room consecrated to Venus the ceiling is painted with Pallas snatching Youth from the arms of Venus, with the eight lunettes beneath painted with classic examples of continence: Scipio, Massinissa, Seleucus, Alexander, Antiochus, Crispus, Octavia, and Cyrus.

[1] 1585–1646.

[2] See F. Lenygon, *Decoration in England from 1660 to 1770*, and H. Avray Tipping, *English Homes*.

[3] The classic account is still C. Gurlitt, *Geschichte des Barockstiles in Italien*, Stuttgart, 1887.

[4] See vol. I, p. 144.

[5] e.g. Guercino's Aurora in the Casino Ludovisi at Rome, twelve years later than Guido's, completed with lunettes with figures of Day and Night.

[6] The first rudiments of such a scheme appear at Verona in the first half of the fourteenth century. Sagazio Muzzio Gazzata, in exile from Reggio at the court of Can Grande della Scala, tells how his guests were each assigned a suitable room, dedicated to Victory for Soldiers, to Hope for Exiles, to the Muses for Poets, to Mercury for Artists, and Paradise for Preachers. A. Wiel, *Story of Verona*, p. 74.

299. Cassone of carved walnut. Italian, c. 1565

300. Detail of the decoration of the dome, Capella Ugo, San Pietro in Montorio, Rome, c. 1630

When Venice added the triumphs of her victory to her own comprehension of the classic spirit, such impersonal allegories were quickly turned to a modern application. Tintoretto's decorations in the Doge's Palace, painted between 1573 and 1587, show a tendency to such an application in their figures of Ariadne crowned by Venus, Peace protected by Minerva, the Three Graces, and Vulcan's forge, with their implicit allusions to the glories of Venice. By 1575 Veronese completed his allegorical picture of the victory of Lepanto in the Sala del Collegio with a ceiling with the figure of Venice herself painted between Justice and Peace, with subsidiary figures of Faith triumphant, Neptune, and Mars, and in the spandrels the virtues of Moderation, Industry, Vigilance, Abundance, Sweetness, Fidelity, Simplicity, and Fortune. In the same year Tintoretto paired a scene of Jupiter giving Venice the empire of the world, and an allegorical figure of Venice as Queen of the Seas; while three years later Veronese adorned the ceiling of the Sala del Gran Consiglio with a great Triumph of Venice,[1] like an apotheosis, with scenes of Venetian history below.

Outside Venice such victories were wanting, and allegorical and mythological scenes were used with less special significance. The Loves of the Gods provided the theme for the Carraccis' decoration of the Gallery of the Palazzo Farnese at Rome, finished in 1609. Here, splendid and rich though the effect may be, both in detail and in mass, a certain weakness is apparent. The scheme, unlike the Venetian schemes of victory, has not significance enough to lift the whole on to a higher artistic plane; and yet the 'Fine Arts' of representation are here encroaching too far on the sphere of decoration for the result to be purely ornamental. These medallions imitating sculpture, held and framed by painted figures that are yet more plastic in style, lack that architectural quality which would make them decorative, and that intellectual significance which would give them another value. From the Carraccis' work at the Palazzo Farnese two currents divide: one of decoration of such pictorial quality (culminating in Tiepolo's Venetian schemes) as to be in another category from that of ornament; and another in which pictorial elements are made subsidiary to a decorative scheme. The finest type of this second style is the more decorative work—notably the Sala di Giove—of Pietro da Cortona in the Palazzo Pitti (fig. 298). Here the flowing line and rounded modelling of true classicism are restrained by an architectural scheme; painting and sculpture, colour and relief, the hues of marble, fresco, gold and bronze, the forms of nature and of architecture, are combined to form a single whole, as facile, as complex, and as well orchestrated as an Italian Opera.

On the whole, however, the development of such pictorial decoration helped to weaken the hold of the canons of classical architecture. Men began to look upon it *picturesquely*; they had learnt the secrets of its decoration and construction; it offered fewer problems to their intellect though it still delighted their eyes.

[1] A similar subject adorns the ceiling of the saloon of the Palazzo Pesaro, painted by Niccolo Bambini in 1682.

In Rome classical architecture appears in two guises—the one finished and complete as the Triumphal Arches, the other massive, ruined and rough as the remains of the Golden House of Nero, bereft of its revetments of marble and stucco, and yet noble in boldness of plan and richness of relief. As appreciation grew from admiration of the delicacy of classic finish to comprehension of the majesty of classic scale the picturesque beauty of these ruins imposed themselves upon men's imaginations. They turned from the composition of detail to the creation of picturesque *ensembles*. In architecture a comparatively severe and simple style sufficed, with ornaments that were few but handsome and correct;[1] but its whole scale was altered by making the house a part of a greater architectural scheme in which terraces, fountains, and formal gardens became part of the plan. Gradually, as the delicate chisellings of Roman arabesques came to pall, and the need for sheer magnificence was felt more strongly than the need for grace, palace and garden architecture were fused. The statues of the gardens became a part of architecture, the relief of nature a part of decoration. The baroque style was created out of this appreciation of grandeur of scale, emphasis of expression, and picturesqueness of effect.

The classic orders became units not of construction, but of picturesque composition; the pediments, columns, and entablatures of the classic orders came to be used as freely and decoratively as the gables and canopies of Gothic architecture had been in the Middle Ages. The long lintel line was twisted and tortured into a hundred angles and returns, pediments were broken, cornices were made to vanish in false perspective. But baroque, however much it ignored construction, was essentially a style of architecture and not of decoration, and its influence on ornament, though visible, is hard to define. The commonplaces of classical decoration were used here and there to emphasize a plane or to crown a pediment; but their importance lay not in their motives but in their plastic relief. By the middle of the sixteenth century a certain restlessness is apparent even in architecture that conforms to the canons of classic structure. Sanmichele's Palazzo Bevilacqua at Verona shows it in the broken lines of the subsidiary pediments of the alternate windows of the *piano nobile*, and on his famous library at Venice, the same quality, plastic rather than architectural, is evident in the addition of Victories in high relief over the arches. From Venice the usage spread to her rival, Genoa; the Palazzo Pallavicini, built about 1550, shows a wealth of plastic decoration in stucco—figures reclining on pediments, caryatids, terms, and heavy sculptured framing to the windows. The famous Genoese Church of the Annunziata, built by Giacomo della Porta about 1570, translates this plastic feeling into marble and bronze; capitals, soffits, frieze, and vault are all enriched, to create a

[1] See for instance *Racolta di Diversi Ornamenti copiati da fragmenti antichi di Roma, c.* 1600; Cherubino Alberti, engravings of classical urns and vases drawn by Polidoro da Caravaggio, Rome, 1582; Horatius Scoppa's engraved patterns published at Naples in 1642 and 1643, &c.

301. Ceiling of the Chapel of Santa Cecilia, San Carlo ai Catinari, Rome. By Antonio Gherardi, 1690

302. Façade of the Church of the Maddalena, Rome. By Sardi, 1686

303. Chimney-piece in a room of the Palace of Fontainebleau, *c.* 1620

Scena della Festa Teatrale in occasione delle Sponsale del Prencipe Reale di Polonia ed Electoral di Saßonia

304. Design for a theatrical setting by J. G. Bibiena, c. 1710. Engraved by J. A. Pfeffel, 1740

general effect of splendour that can hardly be analysed. At Florence the hold of architectural form was stronger; but in detail[1] there was a freer use of swelling cartouche forms, a rounder modelling, a sense of greater scale imparted even to small things. At Milan architectural line was sooner affected; the Church of S. Alessandro, built by the Barnabite father Lorenzo Binago in 1602, has a waved line used for its gable pediment.

With the turn of the century this plastic quality of decoration reached Rome, there to receive the consecration of the Papacy and the stamp of Bernini, the greatest sculptor of the age. But the hold of architectural style was strong in Rome; and though towards the end of the sixteenth century the cultivated classical style of Peruzzi was more freely treated, any really baroque element was absent. The stucco decoration of the Porch of St. Peter's, dating from about 1625, is exceedingly rich, but it keeps the traditional coffers and ribs of classic decoration, and except for its emphatic cartouche might be much earlier in date; the decoration of the dome of the Chapel of the Passion in S. Pietro in Montorio (fig. 300) shows a richer modelling and a charming use of figures of child angels in the round; but its lines are purely architectural, its style relatively severe. The tendency was rather to an abuse of pedimental line and to an increasing emphasis of modelling than to any greater extravagances.

Gradually, however, the hold of style relaxed; in the Church of SS. Luca e Martina, built about 1640, an otherwise architecturally designed interior is adorned with florid rhetorical sculpture in the spandrels; while in 1647[2] Lorenzo Bernini was permitted to add to the piers and arches of St. Peter's the cartouches and statues that were imitated on the multitude of churches that can claim it as their greater prototype.[3] Bernini's decoration of the Church of S. Andrea al Quirinale shows sculptured cherubs and angels invading the regularity of the coffered dome; and the next and more unhappy stage is reached in the cherubs in relief that gesticulate against a painted background on the vault of S. Maria dell' Orto, built about 1690. The sharp and clear-cut lines of the classical tradition are fused into plumpness and softness; the planes of relief have disappeared; everything swims or flies in space. The three dimensional sense, lost in an architecture of fine façades, was transferred to a decoration bereft of the sense of the flat plane; and such artists as Father Pozzo learnt so to add illusions of paint and stucco to architectural realities that the moment of transition is not perceived.

At the same time the constructional lines, of which the logical and traditional form had at first been respected, were modified; Borromini in 1667 did not hesitate

[1] The doors of the Uffizi, by Buontalenti, c. 1575, are crowned by a rounded pediment, cut in two, with the halves set back to back, and a bust on a console in the middle.

[2] The baroque element in his baldaquin of the High Altar, finished in 1633, is far less pronounced; its classicism is extremely ornate, but the most baroque features are the curved architrave (masked by lambrequins) and the theatrical line of the canopy.

[3] A certain reflection is also to be found in secular decoration, for instance in the graceful figures of cherubs in the round on the spandrels of the Palazzo Pesaro at Venice, built by Longhena in 1679.

to curve the architraves of his Church of San Carlo alle Quattro Fontane, alike on both stories of the façade, on the tower, over the door, and indeed wherever he could; and a similar and even greater freedom is evident in such more ornate work as Sardi's Church of the Maddalena, dating from 1686 (fig. 302).

Rome became a centre from which the Jesuits[1] helped to spread the baroque style to all the southern provinces of Christendom. About 1690 Serpotta arranged a richer and clumsier version of the dome of the Chapel of the Passion in S. Pietro in Montorio to frame the windows of the Oratorio di Santa Cita at Palermo; at the same time the twisted curves and exaggerated relief of Sardi's style appeared in a provincial form in S. Gregorio at Messina. All over Italy such more or less successful provincial imitations sprang into being. Renaissance style was once more adapted for secular use; the saloon of the Palazzo Albrizzi at Venice[2] shows the simple lines of the earlier architectural features altogether transformed by stucco additions made in 1692: reliefs in pictorial style, flying amorini, and trumpeting Victories supporting a scrolling cartouche over the door: the whole obviously too rhetorical for its purpose, and derived from buildings on a larger scale.

Though the style continued in provincial use, in Rome itself it soon found its final expression, not in architecture, but in the stage settings of the Bibiena (fig. 304).

7

The mature classical style of Italy was one of richness and splendour, applicable only on a large scale; great personal wealth and comparatively settled conditions were essentials of its existence. Such conditions were far from prevailing at the beginning of the seventeenth century in France, torn by religious and civil war on her own soil, and at war with Spain beyond her frontiers. When the Wars of Religion were at an end, the League and the War with Spain[3] still precluded the monarchy from undertaking building schemes on a large scale,[4] and prevented the Court from becoming an important artistic centre. However much it was urban and civilized, the Court was forced to lead a nomadic life, and so, in nomadic fashion, its interest in the arts was focussed upon small, highly finished, and portable objects.

[1] A curious collection of drawings in the Bibliothèque Nationale shows how the designs for Jesuit churches projected even in Mexico and Peru were submitted for the approval of the General of the Order in Rome. Michel, *Histoire de l'art*, vi. 108.   [2] Molmenti, *Venice : the Decadence*, ii. 8.

[3] A lesser decorative influence of these wars is the increasing importance of the trophy; J. M. Kager's *Suite des trophées* was published in 1632, and A. Pierretz' studies for trophies *c.* 1640. Light trophies of arms adorn the pilasters on the stairs of Cheverny (1634) and the stairs of Gaston d'Orleans' wing at Blois; they even figure on Lyons brocade. Similar trophies appear in England on the great staircase at Ham House.

[4] In such exceptions as the Hotel de Ville at La Rochelle, begun in 1587 and finished in 1607, richness of detail and a certain lack of harmony in the whole are evident. At La Rochelle reversed and broken pediments and caryatids adorn the dormers; the columns of the lowest story are thick and stumpy, and are replaced by pendants at intervals.

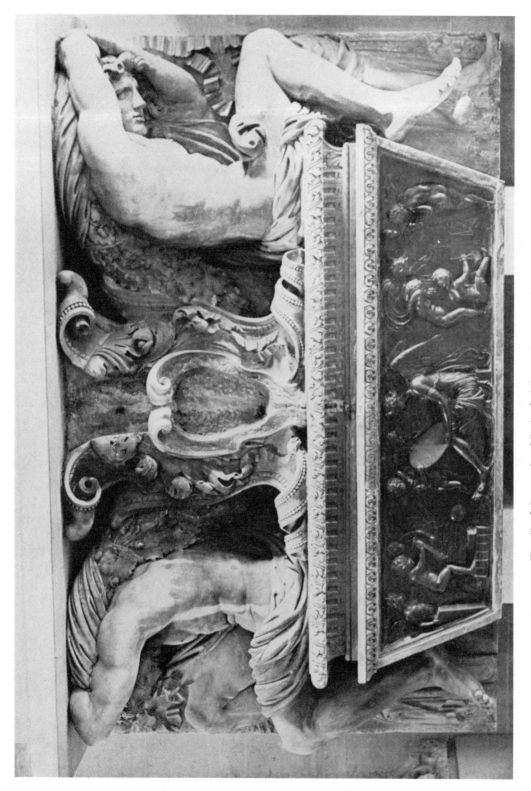

305. Detail of the tomb of J. A. de Thou. By François Anguier, 1617

306. Doorway of the Hôtel de Lavallette (École Massillon), Paris, *c.* 1620

The persecution of the Huguenots had driven many of the ablest workers of France into exile. Many did not return with more tranquil times, but from centres like Strasbourg, Augsburg, and Amsterdam, they and their pupils and imitators produced engraved designs for ornament that influenced pattern in France itself. The patterns they produced were intended for a particular technique—most often for that of the goldsmith—and the style they followed was that of professional craftsmen little influenced by the views of those outside their *métier*.

When the King had once more power to influence art, he had to concern himself with providing material and training, not for an École de Fontainebleau, but for the humble craftsmen of his court. Henry IV and Sully had to create fresh silk manufactures, to import mulberry trees and silk-worms, to induce spinners of gold thread and blowers of glass to come from Italy, tapestry-makers from Bruges, and fine-linen-weavers from Flanders. In 1618 the king still further allied himself with the craftsmen by decreeing that the galleries of his palace of the Louvre were to be at their disposal, in order that they might exercise their crafts and train their apprentices in freedom, 'sans être inquietés par les compagnies des maîtres de Paris ou autres'.[1] They entered into the King's service and were attached to his court as Primaticcio and Il Rosso had been to that of François I; and as the early stages of the art of the French Renaissance had been dominated by Italian artists, so the decoration of the earlier part of the seventeenth century was dominated by French craftsmen.

As a consequence of these conditions, the style of the early seventeenth-century Renaissance was in France far more closely linked with the decorative arts than in Italy, where the 'Fine' arts dominated style. There was everywhere a smaller scale, and schemes of decoration that, whatever their subject, were less pictorial in treatment, and tended to be more ornate. Catherine de Medicis' Salle des Antiques, finished for Henry IV, was so encrusted with marbles that Sauval likens it to a reliquary or a German cabinet; while the decoration of the Galerie de Diane at Fontainebleau, painted by Ambroise Dubois for Henri IV, in spite of the Italianate schemes of panels of mythological subjects set in an arabesque composition, was too restless and cut-up in design for its classicism to make a good effect. Even when a more settled state of affairs was restored, the scale of decoration was only gradually broadened and some Louis XIII work (fig. 303) shows a large scale minimized by its being broken up into many small spaces.[2] The close association between scholars, patrons, and artists necessary to the development of a classical style had not yet been re-established. The strongest link between them at the beginning of the century was not classicism, but national history. When the great gallery of the Louvre was finished in 1600 Sully consulted Antoine de Laval as to

[1] Quoted, M. Vachon, *Le Louvre et les Tuileries*, p. 93.
[2] Similar small panels appear in English work, for instance in the Kederminster Library, Langley Marish, Bucks. (1617) and in the gilt room at Holland House, *c.* 1624. See M. Jourdain, *English Furniture and Decoration of the Early Renaissance*, p. 96.

the best scheme for its decoration. He recommended a strictly historical scheme, with effigies of the sixty-three Kings of France, each in his niche with appropriate ornaments, emblems, devices, letters, verses, panegyrics, and inscriptions, in terms 'esloignez du vulgaire, ressemblans la gravité antique':[1] and Brunel carried out the scheme.

The Jesuits returned to France in 1603, and the education they gave the generation of Louis XIV was based not upon national history but upon classical mythology. Their teaching was perpetuated throughout the century:[2] the first lessons that Bossuet and Fénelon had to give to the Dauphin and the Duc de Bourgogne were 'Fables de la théologie payenne'. Such an education trained men to a particular way of thinking from which they could never wholly escape; it is only half in mockery that Boileau writes:[3]

> Chaque vertu devient une divinité,
> Minerve est la prudence et Vénus la Beauté.
> Ce n'est plus la vapeur qui produit le tonnerre,
> C'est Jupiter armé pour effrayer la terre.
> Un orage terrible aux yeux des matelots,
> C'est Neptune en courroux qui gourmande les flots.'

By 1630 the centre of literary and artistic creation was once more established at Paris; and the bases of a classical civilization were once more laid. But it was no longer enough to regard or to understand antiquity; the time had come to create beauty that was both national in its purpose and antique in its style.

The century had begun with Malherbe's insistence on the canons of order, balance, conciseness of statement, perfection of form, and unity of conception; Descartes[4] in 1644 re-expressed the idea of men's perfectibility: his doctrine of the 'progrès à l'infini' turned men from viewing the Golden Age in some Lucretian past to seek it in troubled visions of the future. But the seventeenth century was

[1] Blomfield, *History of Renaissance Architecture in France*, i. 33; M. Vachon, *Le Louvre et les Tuileries*, p. 91. A set of full-length miniatures of all the French kings, from the Merovingians to Francis I, was painted to illustrate the *Recueil des rois de France* of Jean de Tillet, finished in 1566 (Bibl. Nat. MS. fonds français, 2848), and this may have initiated the scheme. It finds a parallel in the embroidery (probably of much the same date) recorded in the *État du mobilier de la couronne* of 1701: 'de riche broderie d'or, relevée sur un fond de broderie d'argent à grain d'orge, enrichi de figures en petit de broderie d'or, d'argent, et soye, représentant les Roys, Reynes, princes, princesses du sang royal depuis la Reyne Blanche jusqu'à aujourd'huy, habillez selon les modes des temps, consistant en un lit, quatre fauteuils, dix-huit sieges ployants et quatre carreaux' (quoted Havard, *Dictionnaire de l'ameublement*, s.v. Imparfait.) A series of the Kings of England, painted in the time of Charles I for the panelling of Keevil Manor in Wiltshire, is now at Westwood Manor House, Wilts. The exiled Bussy Rabutin developed the scheme in decorating one room in his Burgundian castle with a series of great warriors, from Duguesclin to himself, and another with a series of the mistresses of the Kings of France. The prototypes of such decoration are such Italian paintings as the series of the Seven Kings of Rome and the twelve heroes of the House of Doria painted by Pierino del Vaga in the vestibule of the Palazzo Doria at Genoa about 1530.
[2] It was extended even to the artists: the students of the *Beaux Arts* in the seventeenth and eighteenth centuries had to study Calmet's *Histoire des Juifs*, Herodotus, Thucydides, Zenophon, Tacitus, and Livy, but no French history. (Courajod, *Leçons*, iii. 33.)
[3] *Art poétique*, chap. iii.   [4] See also Krantz, *L'Esthétique de Descartes*, Paris 1882.

307. Ceiling of a room on the first floor, Château de Vaux le Vicomte. By Le Brun, c. 1655

308. Detail of the Galerie d'Apollon, Louvre. Designed by Le Brun, *c.* 1663

able to see even its visions in classic guise: 'On peut voir l'avenir dans les choses passées.'[1] This assimilation of the classic point of view influenced the very basis of decoration. 'Ce qu'on ne voyait plus que dans les ruines de l'ancienne Rome et de la vieille Grèce, devenu moderne, éclate dans nos portiques et dans nos péristyles.'[2]

Classic detail was no longer merely applied to walls and monuments of which the skeleton was Gothic: classic structure became the inspiration of architecture, and so decoration ceased to be an extraneous beauty and once more grew out of construction. Consequently it becomes far harder to analyse; like the descriptive adjectives of classic verse, it is merged into the fabric of the whole. Detail ceased to be interesting except as a part of a whole; a universal sense of mass, of form and of plan made architecture so much the mistress art that decoration was dominated by it even when free from its necessities. France entered on the full Latin inheritance of magnificence; her king was the grandson of a Medici, and under him the country reached the assurance of grandeur that Italy had reached before. King and court did not attempt to master the technical sciences of the arts, nor to descend to minute criticism; but they set the standard. 'Louis XIV n'étoit pas un connoisseur . . ., mais il étoit né pour sentir le grand.'[3]

Descartes's *Discours de la Méthode* in 1637 glorified reason in restating the importance of order and unity in the world of thought. In France unity became as universal an aim as it had been in the thirteenth century. Richelieu's centralization of power showed one side of this aspiration: a desire for the voluntary association of men of taste and learning represented another. The Renaissance cult of the individual tended to develop into the cult of the type, and in every branch of activity like-minded men found in association that strength that is always felt when the ideal and the actual, theory and action, are voluntarily balanced. The men of the time were trained together in schools, in corporations, in *salons* and in cloisters; all those who had received a classical education were linked in thought, and all those who had not could only be admitted as artisans within the real France. Thus in each group of society a golden mean of moderate opinion was accepted by all, and the common basis of race and education made it possible for a definite sum of these moderate opinions to be accepted by society as a whole. Men felt with Pascal that it was such opinion that creates happiness, righteousness, and beauty. An intellectual aristocracy was established in art; the Précieuses proposed to 'dévulgariser la langue', and the artists to free the classic style 'de la rouille qu'elle avait contractée sous terre'.[4]

With the foundation of the Académie Française in 1634 and the Académie Royale in 1648[5] the sum of literary and artistic opinion found expression in

---

[1] Rotrou.   [2] La Bruyère, *Caractères*: 'Des Ouvrages de l'Esprit.' (1687–96).
[3] Watelet, *Dictionnaire des arts de peinture*, 1792, i. 590.   [4] Blondel, 1698.
[5] On this foundation see H. Jouin, *Charles le Brun*, pp. 63 et seqq.

corporate action. Local academies, concerned with every interest of educated men, began to arise in various provincial centres.[1] Artist and patron were banded together for the production of an art classical in its homogeneity and national in its application, and for the justification of such art before the tribunal of reason. It is Minerva, Goddess of Reason and Learning, whose head appears on the medals of the Academy of Architecture.

In the early years of the century, sculpture was the only art that had kept the secret of the grand manner. The seventeenth-century Renaissance in France was heralded by such work as François Anguier's magnificent tomb of J. A. de Thou, carved in 1617 (fig. 305); its architectonic composition, its beauty alike of line and relief, make it an *œuvre de maîtrise* that once more justifies the admission of France into the guild of classic art. Baroque influence is evident in the heavy central cartouche; and such influence again appears in such decorative work as the door of the Hôtel de Lavallette a few years later (fig. 306), in a sense of greater scale, a thickening and enrichment of classical forms, a bossing and complication of cartouches, a massing of swags and trophies, and a masking of mouldings with sculptured enrichments. The Pavillon de l'Horloge of the Louvre, built about 1630, in its triple pediment, its caryatids, and its wealth of sculptured decoration shows a similar style applied not to a simple doorway but to an architectural scheme on a larger scale; while engraved patterns produced by Barbet, Collot, and others, helped to disseminate the style in the provinces.[2]

In architecture and architectural decoration, however, France, whatever inspiration she received from Italy, continued her national tradition of style from the point where political events had broken it off. Bullant's *Règle générale de l'architecture,* republished in 1619, and Philibert de l'Orme's *Architecture,* republished in 1628 and 1648, were the main sources of this tradition; and what Italian influence there was came rather from Vignola[3] and Palladio[4] than from the Jesuit school of architects. Such churches as that of Saint-Paul-Saint-Louis in Paris show the calm architectural lines of the Italian academic style of about 1550; while the Church of the Val de Grâce, begun in 1645 and finished in 1665, though it has baroque reclining figures over the spandrels of the arches, has them changed from the Italian figures in the round to a more restrained type in low relief. The French academic code everywhere imposed its canons and restraints.

Like all codes it was most definite on the negative side: the irregular, the fantastic, the trivial, the ugly, the undisciplined were proscribed from every region of human activity. Mere prettiness and mere imitation of nature had become

---

[1] 1674 Soissons, 1682 Nîmes, 1685 Angers, &c. Colbert in 1675 wished to establish teaching academies for the arts in all the chief provincial cities, but only succeeded at Bordeaux.

[2] Good provincial examples are the Hôtel de Pierre at Toulouse, and the Chateau de Tanlay, Yonne.

[3] His *Regola delli cinque ordini* was published in French in 1629.

[4] His *Quattro libri dell'architettura* was published in French and four other languages in 1570, and in a French edition in 1650.

309. Detail of the Galerie des Glaces, Versailles. By Le Brun and Mansart, 1680–4

310. Decoration in copper gilt applied to marble, *above*, from above a door in the Salon de la Guerre and, *below*, from the Salon de la Paix, Versailles, *c*. 1680

uninteresting to a generation that subordinated feeling to reason and rejoiced in man's domination over nature.[1]

If Italian architectural influences were thus modified, Italian pictorial influences were strong. The government of Louis XIII strove in vain to induce Pietro da Cortona to come to Paris,[2] but Mazarin succeeded in importing a pupil of his, Romanelli, to act as his court painter. He painted the Cardinal's palace and the Queen's apartments at the Louvre with scenes of biblical, mythological, and classical history, in settings enriched by classical stuccoes by French modellers. Such of his decorations as remain—notably the ceiling of the Salle des Antonins in the Louvre—show the schemes and style of Pietro da Cortona, a little colder and more academic for having crossed the Alps. His style was perpetuated by the French school of Lebrun; but national feeling gave it a new significance. Three currents of Renaissance activity united to form a new impulse. Individualism and nationalism culminated in the apotheosis of the monarchy of Louis XIV, and the force of humanism was turned to the constructive interpretation of antiquity in order to create for the modern king a legend and an atmosphere as splendid as those of Greece and Rome.

At first a scheme of type and antitype was chosen; Richelieu had the gallery of his Château de Richelieu painted with twenty pictures of the conquests of Louis XIII compared with the conquests of the Greeks and Romans.[3] But soon it was enough to leave the modern parallel to the spectators' imagination. The gallery of the Louvre and most of Brunel's decoration was burnt in 1660,[4] and when Le Brun began to decorate the new Gallery (fig. 308) two years later he planned not a national, but a cosmic scheme. Veronese had used classical mythology to symbolize the trophies of Lepanto; Le Brun dared to use it to symbolize the whole history of Louis XIV.[5] Louis attained apotheosis[6] as the Sun-God Apollo. A scheme of decoration that had been a commonplace in Italy[7] and had already been used in France[8] was given a new force and significance by the identification

[1] Cf. Pascal: 'Quelle vanité que la peinture qui attire l'admiration par la ressemblance des choses dont on n'admire pas les originaux.'

[2] Michel, *Histoire de l'art*, vi. 203.

[3] The same idea may have inspired the set of hangings of the taking of Rome by the Gauls, woven at Aubusson at this time.

[4] Blomfield, *History of French Architecture*, ii. 84. It appears that the pictures of the kings were saved. Hautecœur, *op. cit.*, p. 10.

[5] The contemporary hero was appearing in novels like *Clélie* and *Le grand Cyrus*, in transparent disguise against a remote historical background. Moreover, the strong dramatic element in the pleasures of the court made personification an element of its life; antiquity and mythology were actually and visibly a part of the life of Versailles.

[6] As early as 1600 Ambroise Dubois had painted Henri IV going heavenwards in a chariot drawn by lions. In his decoration of Vaux le Vicomte Le Brun tentatively identified Fouquet with Hercules, and designed a representation of his apotheosis for the great oval saloon in 1665.

[7] See p. 34.

[8] Perrier had painted Apollo in his chariot with Time, Aurora and the Zephyrs, and night flying towards him, on the ceiling of the long gallery of the Hôtel de la Vrillière.

of the monarch with its divine hero.[1] The ceiling shows Apollo driving his chariot through the midday heavens, within a circle of medallions of which four show stages of the day and night, four the seasons, and twelve the figures of the months.[2] The wall on the side of the Seine shows the *Triomphe des eaux* under the symbol of Neptune and Amphitrite; the opposite wall has the *Triomphe de la terre* figured as Cybele. Round the cornice of the ceiling children play with the signs of the Zodiac; on the side of the *Triomphe des eaux* are figures of river gods, and on the other side the captive giants of the earth. Each leaf of the doors bears the name and attributes of a Muse; even the subjects of the cameo-like medallions on the jambs are Apolline.

A breadth and comprehensiveness of symbolism hitherto unknown in secular decoration began to appear in the royal schemes. The identification with Apollo[3] in 1664 provided inspiration for the first day of the fêtes of the 'Plaisirs de l'Isle enchantée' at Versailles. In the next year the famous grotto of Tethys was added to the garden there, and Perrault had the idea of creating a scheme of Apolline decoration for all Versailles.[4] For the first time in history a great palace was decorated in accordance with the mythology of a single god of a past religion: Versailles is the temple of *le Roi Soleil*. The myth of Apollo can be read in all its details as clearly as the Christian legend can be deciphered in the symbolism of a thirteenth-century cathedral. Félibien tells us[5] that every figure and every ornament in the palace is in relation either with Apollo or with the particular purpose of the rooms they adorn. We find there, as Perrault says,[6] 'les principales actions de

[1] Before the king had become finally identified with Apollo, Le Brun's task was harder; his scheme for the ceiling of the 'Petit Chambre de Conseil' of the Louvre, drawn up in 1654, was so clumsy that it was never executed. 'Premièrement sera représenté au milieu du platfonds un ciel ouvert dans lequel sera assis la Justice accompagnée de la Clémence et de la Sévérité, et toutes les vertus des ministres, comme la Sagesse, l'Intelligence et autres qui composeront comme un cercle autour de cette déesse. Tout au haut du ciel sera représenté un Jupiter sur un aigle accompagné de la Providence, qui toutes deux mettront entre les mains de la Justice un bouclier de diamant tout lumineux et la Justice semblera le recevoir avec joye et aussi le soutenir avec fermeté. Jupiter sera représenté soubz la figure du feu Roy et le bouclier couvert de celle du Roy de présent. Et la Justice soubz la figure de la Reyne.' In the corners there were to be figures of the four ages—Golden, Silver, Brazen, and Iron—accompanied by appropriate Virtues and Vices. Above there were to be four clouds, one bearing Peace and Abundance, going towards the group of the Golden Age; one with Riches and Fortitude, going towards the Silver Age; with Severity, Chastisement, Mars, and Bellona proceeding towards the groups of the Ages of Brass and of Iron. Jouin, *Le Brun*, p. 680.

[2] These, painted by Jaques Gervaise between 1666 and 1670 (Hautecœur, *Le Louvre et les Tuileries de Louis XIV*, p. 116) show how the medieval tradition, when it was rooted in antiquity, survived into the full Renaissance. In March the vine-dressers are shown pruning the vines; in June there is the sheep-shearing; in July, harvest; in August, the second haymaking; in September, the vintage; in October, ploughing and sowing; in November, pig-killing; in December, woodcutting.

[3] The identification first appears in medals. The medal struck to commemorate his birth in 1638 shows the astrological state of the heavens at the time of his birth, and has the figure of the young Apollo in his chariot with the motto 'Ortus solis gallici'. The same allegory appears on the medal for 1643 (Menestrier, *Histoire du Roy Louis le Grand*, Paris, 1691).

[4] de Nolhac, *La Création de Versailles*, 1925, p. 89. The closest parallel with the scheme is Diane de Poitier's Diana-decorations at Anet more than a hundred years before; and already at Vaux le Vicomte Le Brun had experimented in identifying Fouquet first with Hercules and then with Apollo.

[5] *Description de Versailles*, p. 279.   [6] *Parallèle des Anciens et des Modernes*, 1688 ed., p. 120.

Louis le Grand à demi cachées, sous le voile agréable d'une ingénieuse allégorie';
every detail is an ode to his glory, but his name does not appear once in the palace
he created. Félibien thus describes the suite of seven rooms for the king's own
use: [1]

'Et comme le Soleil est la devise du Roy, l'on a pris les sept planètes pour servir de sujet
aux Tableaux des sept pièces de cet appartement; de sorte que dans chacune on y doit repre-
senter les actions des Héros de l'antiquité, qui auront rapport à chacune des Planètes et aux
actions de Sa Majesté. On en voit les figures symboliques dans les ornemens de sculpture
qu'on a faits aux corniches, et dans les plafonds.'

The *Salon de Vénus*, for instance, has on the ceiling Venus bringing the gods and
empires under her power; in the angles are Theseus and Ariadne, Jason and
Medea, Antony and Cleopatra, Titus and Berenice, each couple linked by garlands
held by little cupids. Two round and four square medallions frame mythological
and historical scenes referring to the marriage of Louis XIV, all painted in cameo
fashion.

Even the commonplaces of Renaissance decoration were developed to fit in with
the mythological scheme; the great staircase showed trophies of arms of Hercules
and Minerva to symbolize the power of Force and Wisdom, the capitals of the
Corinthian pilasters of the Galerie des Glaces have Delian palm in place of
acanthus, and a 'tête de soleil' instead of the usual rose.

Most elaborate of all is the symbolism of the exterior of the palace, that set the
mythology of the Roi-Soleil in relation with the realm of nature. Félibien tells us,[2]

'On the side of the flower garden they have had in mind the outlook, which is the flowers
of this same garden, and the fruits of the orangery. . . . This has furnished the idea of setting
on the first projection or balcony figures to preside over the flowers, that is, Flora, their
goddess, Zephyr her lover, who by the sweetness of his breath makes the flowers arise from
the earth with the coming of Spring, Hyacinth, the sun's favourite, and Clytie the sun's
lover, who were both changed into flowers. . . . On the projection or balcony opposite . . .
are four figures of the divinities of fruit, that is, Pomona, who is the goddess of fruit,
Vertumnus, her lover, one of the Hesperides with one of the orange trees laden with golden
fruit, guarded by the dragon, and the nymph Amalthea holding the horn of plenty. . . . On
the side of the grotto they have also had the outlook in mind, that is the grotto, and the
fountains which are seen thence. . . . On the projection or balcony near the grotto the four
figures are the nymph Echo, who was changed into a rock, Narcissus whom she loved, and
Thetis and Galatea who represent the springs that are the chief beauties of grottoes.'

On the side giving on to the gardens were statues of the twelve months, with bas-
reliefs beneath showing children engaged in pastimes suited to each month. 'On
the key-stones of the ground floor they are to represent heads or masks of men
and women from childhood to extreme old age . . . for the year is the perfect
image of human life.' Apollo rules equally over the gardens. The most important

---

[1] *Description de Versailles*, p. 291.   [2] *Ibid.*, pp. 294–5.

FIG. 314. Design for a panel by Daniel Marot, *c.* 1685.

312. Grille of carved gilt wood. Versailles, *c.* 1680

311. Bronze balustrade of the Escalier de la Reine,
Versailles. By Le Brun, *c.* 1685

313. Panelling of the grand salon of the Hôtel de Lauzun, Paris, *c.* 1670

fountains are the 'Bassin d'Apollon' and the 'Bassin de Latone'; the sun-god's emblems appear in many others, and in a retired spot was the grotto representing 'le palais de Téthys où le soleil se retire après avoir fini sa course'.

A real interest in minutiae—which is after all one aspect of a comprehensive view—ensured that the classical style should decorate even the lesser furniture of the palace. Bérain designed a chandelier with a royal crown surmounting a terrestrial globe, charged in sign of dominion with the arms of France, and borne hanging from garlands of laurel by four winged genii. Ballin made four great basins, two with trophies of arms between figures of captives to symbolize the vices, and two with the attributes of Apollo between six female figures to symbolize the Virtues.[1] Verbeckt made two more, one with Time drawn in a chariot by horses, and the other with the crowned figure of a woman holding a horn of plenty, drawn by lions, to represent the Golden Age.[2] Two great silver sconces were 'cizelées dans le milieu de la figure du Roy sous la forme d'Apollon qui conduit ses quatre chevaux environné de deux palmes, par les costez des Travaux d'Hercules, et par le hault de deux Renommées et de la devise du Roy, *Nec pluribus impar*'.[3]

It was an age of splendour, expressed in the forms of metal and fine stone. The relief and decoration of the art of Versailles are based on the technique of metal; for art it was literally a Golden Age.[4] The State Apartments have lost the furnishings which completed their play of reflected light, but the bare list remains in the *Mercure Galant* of November 1679: 'Brancards d'argent portant des girandoles, quaisses d'orangers d'argent, posées sur des bases de mesme métal: vazes d'argent accompagnant les brancards, torchères dorées portant de grands chandeliers d'argent; girandoles d'argent sur des guéridons dorés; foyers d'argent de deux pieds en haut sur trois et demy de diamètre. . . .' Precious marble formed the background and the frame, valued not for its magnificence but for what Madame de Sévigné calls its 'forte et royale beauté'.[5] Colour was revived,[6] and revived in its most natural and most beautiful forms: marble, stone, woods of curious grain and warm tone, agate, gold, and tortoiseshell. Recent experiments in repolishing have shown that it is time alone that has spread a film of grey over the marbles of Versailles: when they were new the columns and revetments of the state apartments

---

[1] Guiffrey, *Inventaire général du mobilier de la couronne*, i. 69 (1673).

[2] Ibid, i. 71.

[3] *Ibid*., p. 43. The motto appears on medals from 1666 onwards. The *Mercure Galant* of November 1679 tells us 'Il n'y a point de morceau d'argenterie qui ne soit historié. Des chandeliers représentent les douze mois de l'année. On a fait des saisons sur d'autres et les travaux d'Hercule en composent une autre douzaine. Il en est de même du reste de l'argenterie. Tout a été fait . . . sur les dessins de M. Le Brun.'

[4] It has been estimated that at this date one-fifth of the total supply of precious metals was used for decorative purposes. See W. Jacob, *An Enquiry into the Production and Consumption of the Precious Metals*, ii. 131.

[5] Letter of April, 1685.

[6] Madame de Maintenon regretted that the Cardinals joined the Court only at Fontainebleau, 'car ils parent fort le Cour, et leur couleur de feu sied parfaitement dans le vert de Marly'.

glowed and sparkled with brilliant colour. We are reminded of the saying of St. Francois de Sales:[1]

'Le Beau étant appelé beau, parce que sa connaissance délecte, il faut que, outre l'union et la distinction, l'intégrité, l'ordre et la convenance de ses partis, il ait beaucoup de splendeur et de clarté, afin qu'il soit connaissable et visible . . . les couleurs [pour être belles, doivent être] éclatantes et resplendissantes; l'obscurité, l'ombre, les ténèbres sont laides et enlaidissent toutes choses, parce qu'en icelles rien n'est connaissable, ni l'ordre, ni la distinction, ni l'union, ni la convenance.'

Even colour had its hierarchy; as Dangeau tells us in 1688, 'le rouge pour le roy, le vert pour Monseigneur (le Dauphin), le bleu et l'aurore pour Monsieur et Madame'. Further, 'on a observé d'employer [les marbres] qui sont les plus rares et les plus précieux dans les lieux les plus proches de la personne du Roy. De sorte qu'à mesure qu'on passe d'une chambre dans une autre, on y voit plus de richesses soit dans les marbres, soit dans la sculpture, soit dans les peintures qui embellissent les plafonds.'

The seventeenth century, moreover, was a time when painters were concentrating their energies upon the study of reflected colour. Similarly the decorators enlisted reflected colour into their schemes, and wood, marble, and metal were polished as mirrors, while the glories of the ceilings were faintly doubled in the shining floors.[2] Thus by daylight or candlelight both form and colour were balanced and harmonized by reflection.

The desire for balance and harmony in form and effect is indeed the vital inspiration of the art of Versailles. The echoes of the 'vingt-quatre violons' seem to have passed into visible form, to create a stately saraband of bronze and stone. Symmetry is one of its dominating principles; but symmetry conceived in terms not of mathematics but of human psychology.

Pascal writes[3] 'notre œil, s'inspirant des exemples que lui fournit le corps humain—lequel est symétrique seulement dans le sens de la largeur—ne considère pas comme indispensable la symétrie dans le sens de la hauteur'. Symmetry in this sense governs the whole of Louis XIV architecture and decoration; it helps to emphasize those horizontal lines which always symbolize stability, endurance, and order. Restraint and repetition are there, not because the artist had little to express but because he could find ample beauty within a simple but delicate expression. We are apt to conceive our recollections of the decoration of Versailles in images of figure-sculpture alone; in point of fact the underlying principles of classic pattern have never been expressed with greater force or universality, but 'quand on excelle dans son art, et qu'on lui donne toute la perfection dont il est capable, l'on en sort en quelque manière, et l'on s'égale à ce qu'il y a de plus relevé'.[4]

---

[1] *Traité de l'amour de Dieu*, chap. i.

[2] It is noteworthy that when they were covered with Savonnerie carpets these often reproduced the architectural lines of the ceilings.

[3] *Pensées*, xxv. 77.   [4] La Bruyère, *Du mérite personnel*.

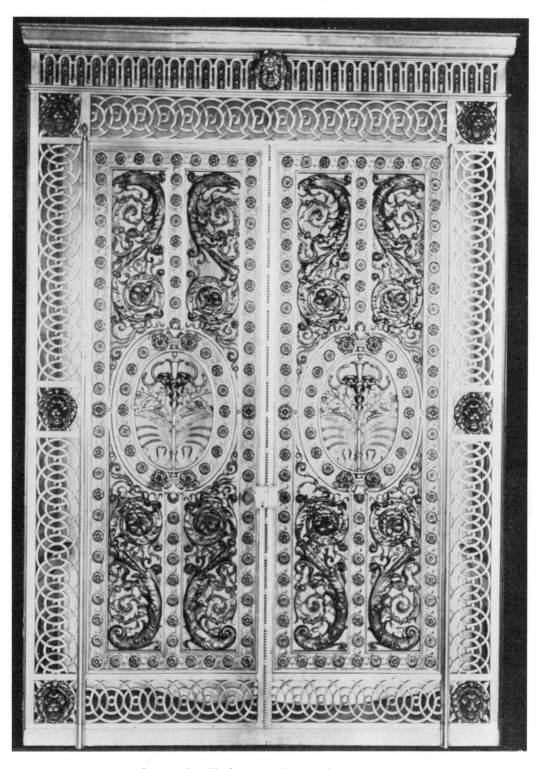

315. Ironwork grille from the Château de Maisons, *c.* 1670

316. Cupboard in gilt metal inlaid in tortoiseshell.
By André Charles Boulle, *c.* 1690

So classic decoration became merged in the Fine Arts whose handmaiden it was content to be.

A classic symmetry had come to be for the men of the seventeenth century the symbol of human civilization. As early as 1642 Savot wrote,[1] 'Plus les symmetries sont gardées en un bastiment, plus il est agréable à l'homme, s'il ne tient plus de la beste que de l'homme, parce que l'effet de la grâce dont il a esté précipué y reluit davantage: au contraire le bastiment dénué de cette industrie humaine n'a rien qui le puisse rendre recommandable par dessus le repaire de la beste.' Consequently the plans and designs of the period are very rarely broken even by carefully balanced inequalities, and gain their most impressive effects from perfect regularity and constant repetition. Variety is achieved by the use of elements—columns, pilasters, brackets—grouped in pairs: that is, by the repetition of a unit itself symmetrical on the smallest scale. Symmetry and balance were achieved in every degree and dimension: one of their frankest expressions was in the use of mirrors, which made even the spectator an actor in the ordered pattern of the room.[2] Even the splendid trifles of the Cabinet du Roi were given a certain dignity by their reflection in mirror-pilasters crowned with the royal sun, in a setting of lapis lazuli and gold.[3] In rooms of a certain shape it is the view from the windows that is repeated to decorate the room; then—as in the Galerie des Glaces—the mirror plates are framed in window mouldings, 'et fait des Tableaux qui par leur ressemblance et par leur brillant charment et éblouissent également les yeux.'[4] The great pools of the gardens play the same part without; and water thus becomes 'l'âme des jardins'.[5]

Though the students of the French school at Rome (founded in 1666) spent their days in measuring her ancient monuments, and though the study of proportion in architecture was simplified for those who had to stay at home by the publication in French of Palladio in 1650, of Vignola in 1653 and of Degodetz' *Monuments antiques de Rome dessinés et mesurés tres exactement* in 1682, the accepted canon was no arbitrary one, but that of humanity. Just as the spectator feels himself, however humbly, in direct relation with the tragic heroes of Corneille and Racine,

[1] *L'Architecture françoise des Bastiments particuliers*, p. 205. Montesquieu, *Essai sur le goût* (*Œuvres*, t. vii, p. 140), says, 'La raison qui fait que la symmetrie plaît â l'âme c'est qu'elle lui épargne de la peine, qu'elle la soulage et qu'elle coupe, pour ainsi dire, l'ouvrage par la moitié.'

[2] Mansard was the first to introduce mirrors over chimney-pieces. They were known first as 'à la Mansarde' and then as 'à la royale'. The manufacture of mirrors was introduced into France by Colbert. Le Brun first experimented with mirror panels in Madame Fouquet's apartment at Vaux le Vicomte in 1661 (J. Cordey, *Vaux le Vicomte*, p. 81). Other 'cabinets de glace' were made for Mlle de la Vallière in 1668, the Duchesse de Bouillon in 1694 and the 'alcôve du Régent' in 1726.

[3] See Mlle de Scudéry's description, 1669. Quoted de Nolhac, *La Création de Versailles*, 1925, p. 121.

[4] Piganiol de la Force, *Description de Versailles*, 4th ed., i. 168.

[5] Charles Perrault says of Versailles: 'S'il est vrai que l'eau soit l'âme des jardins, quels jardins ne paraîtraient morts ou languissants à côte de ceux-ci?' Quoted Bertrand, *Louis XIV*, p. 202. Cf. Sir William Temple, *Gardens of Epicurus*, 1685: 'In every garden four things are to be provided for: flowers, fruit, shade and water.'

so the *poilu* that stands sentinel at Versailles is in his own figure the epitome of the proportions of the great building behind him.[1]

So strong was the power of classicism that even the crafts to which technical difficulties had given a characteristic style had to bear its yoke. Not only in the châteaux of the Court but also in the lesser houses of the provinces the style of ironwork was turned into classical channels. Even lace fell under the same influence (fig. 317) and Bérain's designs were used not only for wall decorations, tapestry, Boule inlay, and goldsmith's work, but also on the pottery of Moustiers.[2]

Le Brun,[3] the high priest of the style, had himself been a pupil of Poussin's at Rome. In his lectures to the academy, begun in 1667, he set before his hearers two objects of admiration: 'l'antique et le Poussin'; the classical plastic ideal and the modern creation of the picturesque.

To seventeenth-century France antiquity meant the ruins of Rome considered as an expression of Roman greatness.[4] Rome could at last exercise all the power of her glamour over France, when the fear of neither Papacy nor Empire intervened between her glories and the French imagination. But her greatness served less as a model than as a stimulus. Fréart de Chambray's *Parallèle de l'architecture antique et de la moderne* (1650) might do much to purify the French classical style, but its gospel was not to make a slavish copy of antiquity, but 'faire renaistre pour ainsi dire de nouveaux antiques'.

Moreover, only certain elements of classical art were admitted into ornament. Under Colbert a cast of Trajan's Column was made for the second time at the expense of France, but the French sense of the appropriate prevented any such monumental art from influencing decorative style.[5] It is significant that Poussin's designs for the decoration of the long gallery of the Louvre (1640–42), incorporat-

[1] Cf. Pascal, *Pensées*. 'There is a certain pattern of charm and beauty which consists in a certain relation between our nature . . . and the thing which pleases us.'

[2] They were perpetuated as late as 1754 on the faïence of Martres, Haute Garonne (examples in the Musée Raymond, Toulouse).

[3] Court painter and President of the Academy, he was responsible for the design of all the most important work at Versailles: artists like Coypel and Coysevox, Girardon and Caffieri, only translated his designs into their own materials. He was Director of the *Manufacture royale des meubles de la couronne*, founded at the Gobelins in 1667; and as Desportes tells us (quoted, Harvard, *Histoire et philosophie des styles*, p. 416) 'he furnished the designs for most of the *bosquets* of Versailles, for the fountains, for most of the statues and vases . . . true works of art, with which the gardens were adorned. He likewise provided the designs for the great gallery, even to the woodwork and the locks.' His obituary notice in the *Mercure Galant* (February, 1690, pp. 257, 267) says, 'Il avoit un génie vaste et propre à tout . . . son goût étoit général aussi bien que son sçavoir. Il tailloit, en une heure de temps, de la besogne à un nombre infiny d'ouvriers. Il donnoit des dessins à tous les sculpteurs du roy. Tous les orfevres en recevoient de luy. Ces candelabres, ces torchères, ces lustres, ces grands bassins ornéz de bas reliefs de *l'Histoire du Roy*, n'étoient que sur ses dessins et les modèles qu'il en faisoit faire . . .'

[4] Pompeii and Herculaneum lay undisturbed beneath the lava of Vesuvius; Greece was a country almost unknown. Jacques Carrey was the first modern artist to study the Parthenon when he drew it for M. de Nointel in 1674, but he characteristically brought it into relation with Rome by labelling it 'Temple de Minerve à Athènes par Adrien'.

[5] Perrault, *Parallèle*, p. 78. 'Depuis qu'on les a apportés moulés en France, il ne s'est pas trouvé un seul peintre ni sculpteur qui ait été les copier, quoique l'on ne les ait fait venir que dans cette intention-là.'

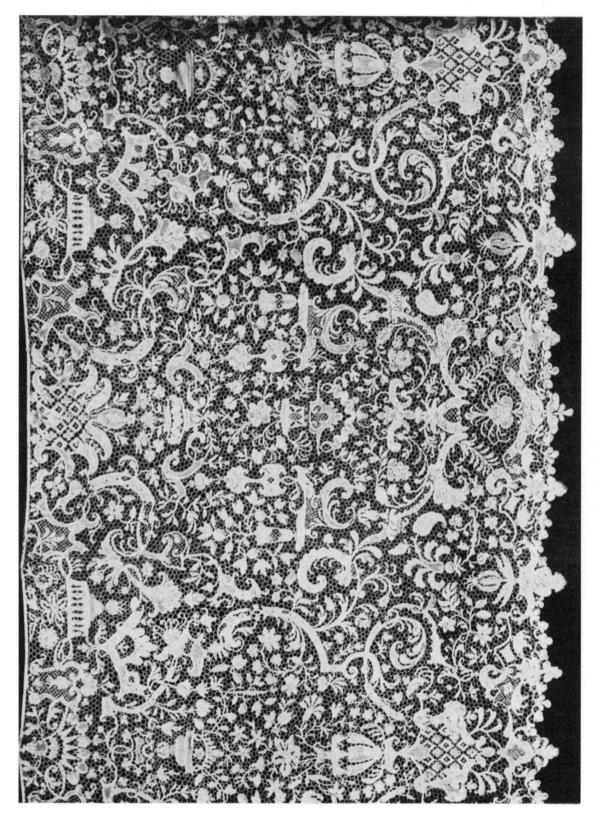

317. Needlepoint lace (Point de France), c. 1680

318. Console of carved gilt wood. Versailles, *c.* 1710

ing casts of antique reliefs, were never carried out.[1] Such 'antiquailles' as were admitted into the decorative scheme of the interior of the palaces and chateaux of the French court were statues in niches, or busts of the emperors on pedestals;[2] even these were most commonly confined to such slight garden buildings as the Pavillon de Marly. I do not recall an instance of an exact copy from the antique in all Versailles; they desired not strictly classical ornament, but decoration in a national style 'assaisonné du sel de nos grâces antiques'.[3] Such decorative art of classical times as survived at Rome was carefully studied, and formed a lexicon of ornament for the artist: but it was treated not as a dead but as a living language, to be enriched and modified and recast at will. The greatness of scheme, the largeness of scale, the limitation of appeal to the educated classes, the attributes and allusions were all classical; but in spite of this, and in spite of mouldings and cofferings, vases and urns, wreaths and ribbons, scrolls and sphinxes, the whole was modern. The trophies of the King's riches on the *Escalier des ambassadeurs*[4] include not only the craters and drinking vessels of Greece and Rome, but also the nautilus cups and *nefs* of Augsburg and Paris. The frieze of the Galerie des Glaces is adorned with Herculean lion-skins and Apolline suns, but under the cornice are crowns of France and collars of the King's Orders,[5] while the capitals have cocks and fleurs-de-lis to decorate the new 'ordre composite français'.[6] The scrolls and urns might be classical, but the flowers they bore were studied directly from nature. Even when art became learned and turned to Dionysiac ivy, Delphic laurel, Dodonaean oak, and Delian palm the subject might be 'dans la manière grecque et dans le goût romain',[7] but the treatment was new and French. Le Pautre impresses

---

[1] At the Château de Richelieu, it is true, the roundels and niches of the front were filled in with busts and statues, some ancient and some modern. In all the chateau 100 full-length statues and 106 busts were used. Blomfield, *History of French Renaissance Architecture*, ii. 83. Colbert writes to the Director of the newly-founded French Academy at Rome: 'faites travailler diligemment aux termes, vases et généralement à tout ce que je vous ai ordonné; mais prenez garde que les sculpteurs copient purement l'antiquité sans rien y ajouter', but such copies from the antique were used for the adornment not of *salons* and galleries but of gardens in the style of Lenôtre.

[2] Such busts were then as common in France as they were to become in England a century later: Gaston d'Orléans in 1630 had eighty busts and heads sent from Rome, and Richelieu in 1633 received from the same source sixty busts and sixty garden statues. The fashion owed much to Mazarin; a contemporary (quoted by Guilmard, *Connaissance des styles*, p. 125) states: 'Les François auroient mesprisé toujours ces idoles, mais ce pompeux cardinal les a rendues chères en leur faisant bailler de l'or pour avoir des pierres taillées'. It is interesting that the busts set on the façade of the Versailles of 1665 were removed later in the reign. Inigo Jones used such busts on the gate-piers and in the interior decoration of Coleshill in 1650, and they appear again imitated in painting in the pavilion at Wrest Park.

[3] Molière, *Val de Grâce*.

[4] Remains of these paintings, which had been thought to have wholly disappeared, were discovered in the course of the repairs undertaken at Versailles in the summer of 1923.

[5] As early as 1654–5 Le Brun adapted the collar of St. Michael to form a moulding, bordered with fleurs-de-lis, for Louis XIV's apartment in the Louvre. Hautecœur, *Le Louvre et les Tuileries de Louis XIV*, p. 51.

[6] Le Brun first used this capital in his design for the decoration of the second story of the Cour Carrée of the Louvre in 1671. Cottart in his designs for the same competition also used the cock and rayed head on his capital, and ornamented his architecture with fleurs-de-lis and his frieze with shields of France linked by garlands. Hautecœur, *Le Louvre et les Tuileries de Louis XIV*, p. 184.   [7] Molière.

the curves of a breaking wave upon his *rinceaux*, and makes his trophies swim upon its flood and his Tritons and Naiads rise from its foam; his lightest arabesques float as easily upon the surface as seaweed in the ocean. French seventeenth-century pattern is never merely static; its curves are the curves of growth, its straight lines the lines of gravity.

Men agreed with Perrault in feeling that Nature remains the same from one age to another, and never degenerates. The moderns could claim the same divine heritage of beauty and variety as had inspired the ancients. Félibien expressed the true contemporary point of view in the advice he gives to painters in his *Entretiens*:[1] 'Les antiques doivent estre aux peintres comme des verres au travers desquels ils puissent voir la Nature: ou bien des miroirs qui leur en découvrent les défauts'.

His phrase gives the real link between 'l'antique et le Poussin' as viewed by the men of the seventeenth century. The emulation of either involved two things: the study of nature, and the conscious and deliberate intellectual recomposition of the elements of beauty which such study revealed. Batteux faithfully reproduced the view of the generation before his own when he found that art is 'une imitation où on voit la nature, non telle qu'elle est en elle-même, mais telle qu'elle peut être, et qu'on peut concevoir par l'esprit'.[2]

The union of 'l'antique et le Poussin' is to be found in the composition of the great parks and gardens of the seventeenth century, that combine in perfect proportion the beauty of formal regularity of plan and the beauty of changing effects of natural growth. They increased the vocabulary of decoration in two ways; it is not only their vases and terminal figures that grace the severer style, but also their trellises and arcadings that form the backgrounds of tapestries, their cascades and fountain-figures that appear in the Louis XIV versions of classical *groteschi* (fig. 312),[3] their yews and orange trees that beautify the silks of Lyons.

An art as congruous as this could become the basis of the generalizations of aesthetics. Even so a generation elapsed between the completion of Versailles and the publication of the first strictly aesthetic treatise in French—the *Traité du Beau* of J. P. de Crousaz, Professor of Mathematics and Philosophy at Lausanne, which was published in 1715. He found, naturally enough, that beauty consists in 'la relation de toutes les parties à un seul but'; and Montesquieu was content to follow him.[4]

The mature classicism of France was essentially monarchical and aristocratic. Its

---

[1] *Op. cit.*, p. 3.   [2] *Les Beaux Arts réduits à un seul principe*, 1746, p. 24.

[3] For the importance of *treillages* in French seventeenth-century gardening, see d'Aviler, *Cours d'Architecture*, i. 195, and Lister, *Voyage à Paris*, p. 169. The most famous were near Paris, at St. Cloud, Sceaux, Chantilly, Meudon, Clagny, &c. They were received into dramatic art as the background of such plays as Molière's *Princesse d'Élide*. Such decoration was also used to supplement the vistas of a small garden; painted treillages were so used at Marly, Saint Cloud, and the Hotels de Freubert, d'Aumont, and de Dangeau.

[4] *Essai sur le goût: Œuvres complètes*, vii. 140.

319. Carved wood bracket in auricular style. Dutch, *c.* 1630

320. Oak chair in the style of Daniel Marat. English, *c.* 1695

321. Mirror frame of gilt wood. Probably designed by William Kent for Frederick Prince of Wales. English, *c.* 1743

322. The State Bedroom, Chatsworth, *c.* 1700

323. Choir Stalls, St. Paul's Cathedral. By Grinling Gibbons, 1697

324. Staircase of the Castle of Bruhl, near Cologne, *c.* 1745. The Trophy, 1766

art was a 'fine' art, depending for its design upon more than a craftsman's skill. Outside this privileged circle artists had to accept classical decoration reduced to the flat in drawings and engravings.[1] Thus though designers like Le Pautre[2] (who was also an architect) laid great weight upon mouldings and relief, the lesser men (and even Le Pautre upon occasion) were apt to treat their classical motives, however plastic, in one plane, as decoration in low relief upon a flat and definite background. This treatment did in its decadence produce a certain effect of aridity, but in work of the best period its restraint satisfies by the suggestion of power unused, and its limitations respect the two-dimensional character of decoration on the flat which the Renaissance too often outraged.

The art of Versailles was based on pride, assurance, and security; Apollo need not always bend his bow, but that bow must never be broken. The true flowering time of any classical age is always short, however long and fruitful its autumn may be. When men cry with La Bruyère 'tout est fait, et parfait!' the end is near. Saint Simon was of opinion that the year 1688 marked the apogee of the reign of Louis XIV, the height of his glory and prosperity. After it there was decline in power, in splendour, and in coherence of thought. In 1689 reverses abroad compelled Louis XIV to melt the treasures of gold and silver plate which formed part of the decorative scheme of such rooms as the Galerie des Glaces. For twenty-five years the monarchy was impoverished, and the centre of attraction gradually passed from Versailles to Paris, from the king to his courtiers. Hope lay with the young, and to them the arts began to turn. Bossuet's books for the Dauphin's education were published in 1681, to be followed by Fénelon's *Éducation des Filles* in 1688 and *Télémaque* in 1699. In 1697 appeared Perrault's fairy stories, and before twelve months had elapsed there were three rival publications.[3] In the autumn of the last year of the century Louis XIV wrote on Mansard's report on the decoration of the rooms of the Ménagerie at Versailles: 'Il me paraît qu'il y a quelque chose à changer, que les sujets sont trop sérieux, et qu'il faut qu'il y ait de la

---

[1] 1607, French edition of Palladio, *Merveilles de la Ville de Rome*; 1608, Maggi, *Fontane diverse*; 1627, Parasacchi, *Racolta delle principali Fontane di Roma*; 1651, Damery, *Vases Antiques*, &c. The importance of such engravings is shown by Felibien in his *L'Idée du Peintre parfait* of 1707 (p. 57).

[2] Le Pautre published at least 2,250 engraved plates, for the most part worked out directly upon the copper, with no preliminary sketch. The most important of his decorative works are:

1657. Frises ou montants à la moderne	1661. Lambris à la Romaine
1659. Portes de chœur	„ Cheminées à la Moderne
„ Chaires de Predicateurs	„ Vases à l'Antique
1660. Clostures de chapelles	1663. Grands cheminées à la Romaine
„ Inventions pour faire des plaques ou des Aubenistiers	„ Chasses et feuillages
	1667. Ornements de panneaux à la Romaine
„ Vases à la moderne	„ Cheminées à l'Italienne
„ Dessins de Lambris à l'Italienne	„ Aubenistiers et plaques à la Romaine
1661. Recherches de plusieurs beaux morceaux d'ornements	1678. Alcoves à la française
	1680. Trophées à l'antique

besides more than 130 suites of decorative engravings for the most varied purposes.

[3] Madame de Murat's *Contes de Fées* (1697), Mlle de la Force's *Les Fées* (1698), and Madame d'Aulnoy's *Les Illustres Fées* (1698).

jeunesse mêlée dans ce que l'on fera. Vous m'apporterez des dessins quand vous viendrez, ou du moins des pensées. Il faut de l'enfance répandue partout. Louis, Fontainebleau, 10 Septembre 1690.' [1]

8

Naturally, since the very existence of baroque style depended on a complete mastery over the elements of classic architecture and decoration, its development outside Italy was less complete than on Italian soil.[2] France, as we have seen, achieved a characteristic mature classic style of her own. In the Low Countries the influence of baroque could fatten and enrich the ornate decoration of the school of Vredeman de Vries, but the plastic and picturesque qualities that mark it in Italy were lacking, and such houses as those of the Grand' Place at Brussels, rich and ornate though they be, have no kinship with the work of the school of Bernini. With the increasing influence of the Society of Jesus in the Low Countries baroque influence became evident;[3] the Jesuit Church at Antwerp, built between 1614 and 1621, shows all its characteristics, only a little flattened by a northern environment. This flatness remained a characteristic of Netherlandish baroque as compared with its Italian prototype; the one appears to be built from drawings in the flat, the other from models in the round. In decorative detail, however—and notably in such sculpture as the confessional of Notre Dame d'Hanswyck at Malines—this disability is less evident. There was little real novelty of style; the old tendency to over-elaboration was turned into new channels, cartouches and console forms took the place of the strapwork of Vredeman de Vries, but however skilful the execution a new style was not created. It is characteristic that a certain monstrous kind of decoration exceptionally found in Italian baroque of the late sixteenth century—for instance in the consoles of the gallery of the Palazzo Marucelli at Florence and in the dreadful door decorated with a grotesque human face in the Casa Zucchero at Rome—was developed in the Netherlands into the peculiarly repulsive *style auriculaire* (figs. 319, 327). Though occasionally found in

[1] Quoted, Lechevallier Chevignard, *Les Styles Français*, p. 337. Stella's *Les Jeux et Plaisirs de l'Enfance*, published in Paris in 1657, are pictorial rather than decorative, but may have had some connexion with Le Brun's decorations of the King's cabinet at Saint Germain, described by Le Laboureur in 1669 (*Promenade de Saint Germain*, p. 16), with cupids playing with lions and leopards, building, hunting, working, and otherwise diverting themselves. Claude Torchebœuf, who published at Paris in 1701 a *Livre nouveau de toutes sortes d'ouvrages d'orfevreries*, included in it panels 'animés au milieu par des enfants se livrant à plusieurs métiers', and the Salon de l'Œil de Bœuf at Versailles, finished in 1701, is decorated with a frieze of children at play. About the same time the Gobelins produced tapestries with child gardeners, of which examples are in the Gardemeuble Nationale, the Galleria degli Arazzi at Florence, and in private collections. See H. Goebel, *Wandteppiche*, II Teil, *Die Romanischen Länder*, Band 2, figs. 81–4. Similar figures appear on the central medallions of Roman dishes, *c.* 1710.

[2] The most baroque church in France, the Chapel of the Visitation of Nevers, was built between 1639 and 1641, when Nevers was under the Gonzaga, and is therefore markedly Italianate.

[3] See M. S. Briggs, *Baroque Architecture*, p. 197.

325. The Sacristy, Cartuja, Granada. By Juis de Arévalo, 1727–64

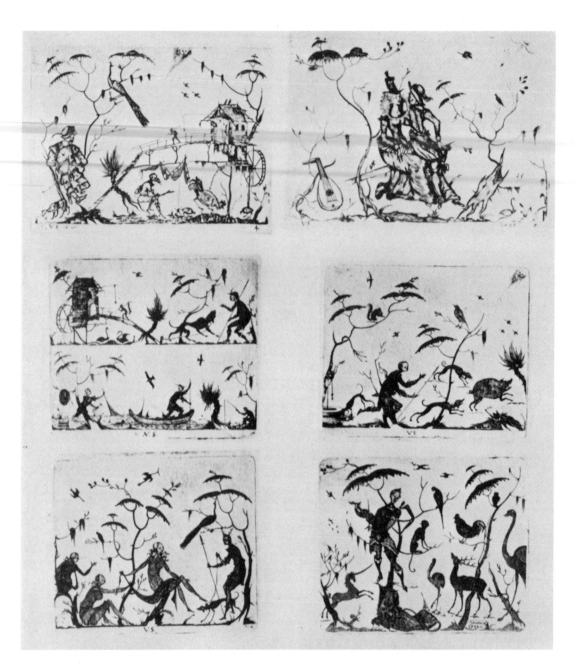

326. Six designs in the Chinese taste. By Valentin Sezenius, 1623–6

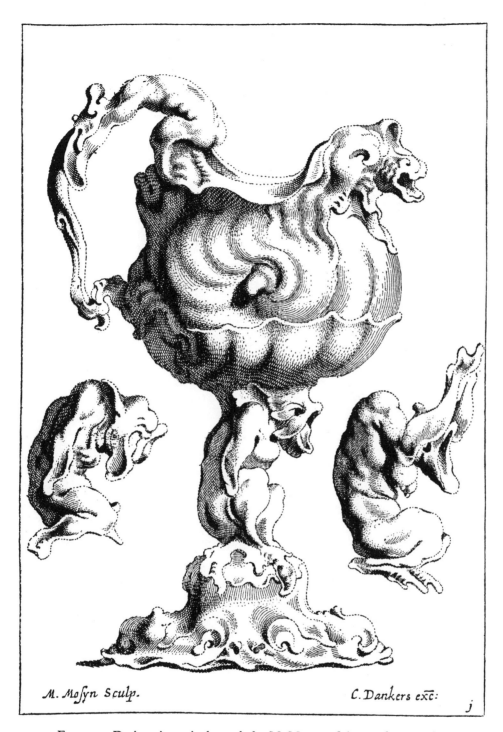

M. Mosyn Sculp.   C. Dankers exc:

j

FIG. 327. Designs in auricular style by M. Mosyn of Amsterdam, c. 1620.

wood, it was essentially a silversmith's style, and seems to have originated in the workshop of C. van Vianen of Utrecht.[1]

With the progress of the seventeenth century Netherlandish baroque was modified by French influences. Daniel Marot, exiled in 1685, became the chief agent in introducing the style of Versailles to the northern nations; but his work, and that of lesser men such as Van Somer and Le Juge of Antwerp, shows how much the style was dependent upon the court for which it was created. Even Le Pautre's engravings, faithfully representing its royal richness, could not convey its spirit to an alien atmosphere: and the true success of his work and of that of his imitators has rather lain in recording its glories for posterity.[2]

In England, it is true, where there were no Jesuit churches, a generation of courtiers that had spent years of exile at the French court was able to produce a classic style, sobered and simplified, in sombre oak rather than in gold and bronze, that perpetuates at once the traditions of Inigo Jones and of Le Brun (figs. 322–3). How far such work was dependent on that of the French engravers may be guessed from a passage in a letter written by Sir Christopher Wren from France in 1665: 'I have purchased a great deal of Taille-douce, that I might give our countrymen examples of ornaments and grotesks, in which the Italians themselves confess the French to excel.'[3]

Hugh May's work of 1665 at Eltham Lodge, Kent, and the queen's bedchamber of 1671 at Ham House show, perhaps, the nearest approach to French magnificence; but the style of Louis XIV reached its full development in England only under William Kent, who definitely based his style on that of the final stages of the classicism of Louis XIV, before a changing taste had modified and lightened its proportions and its scale. Similarly Vanbrugh, the only exponent of baroque art in England, began to build Castle Howard only in 1701, and Blenheim in 1705: and both of these are rather examples of a rich classicism than of true baroque.

In Germany, as in the Low Countries, baroque influence was first felt in the enrichment of the earlier style of Vredeman de Vries. The Friedrichs-Bau at Heidelberg, built between 1601 and 1607 from designs by Johann Schoch, show

[1] See W. W. Watts, 'Recent Acquisitions for Public Collections', in *Burlington Magazine*, vol. xxxii, 1918, p. 209. One of the earliest pieces in the style, belonging to Mr. R. E. Brandt, is dated 1618; another in the Victoria and Albert Museum is dated 1635. Van Vianen came to England early in 1637 and worked for the Chapel of the Garter. Adam van Vianen published designs (engraved by T. van Kessel) in 1650; others in the same style were published by Friedrich Unteutsch, of Nuremburg. A cup in auricular style bears the London hall-mark for 1668–9. See Jackson, *English Plate*, i. 233.

[2] A curious instance of the influence of engraved designs such as he published is afforded by the dining-room in Läckö Castle, Sweden, which has its woodwork painted in imitation of the carved decoration of the Louis XIV style.

[3] J. Swarbrick, *Robert Adam and his Brothers*, p. 7. While in France in the autumn of 1665 Wren visited Paris and Vaux, Maisons, Verneuil, Meudon, and Chantilly. A curious instance of French monarchical decoration adapted to English aristocratic use is provided by tapestries woven by Vanderbank at Soho. Their design is based on that of Le Brun's set of the elements, glorifying Louis XIV, modified to glorify Ralph, Earl of Montagu. A. F. Kendrick, 'Tapestries in the possession of the Duke of Buccleuch', in *Old Furniture*, v, Sept. 1928, p. 22.

329. Delft plate, c. 1700

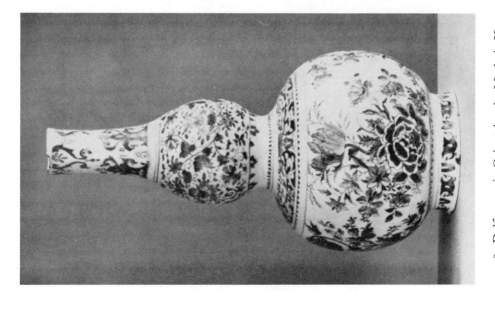

328. Delft vase, in Oriental style, Mark A. K.
in Monogram, c. 1690

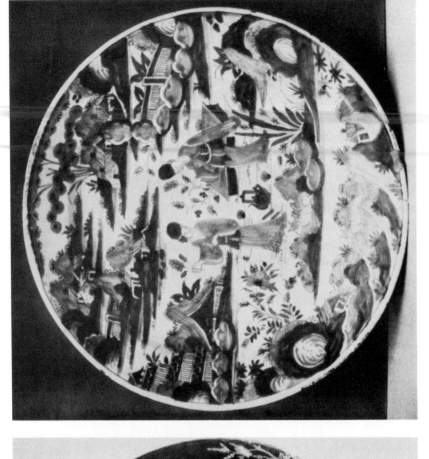

331. Delft plate, *c.* 1710

330. Delft plate in Oriental style, painted in green and yellow on a
black ground in imitation of lacquer, *c.* 1700

de Vries' characteristic breaking-up of classical forms and use of diamond-cut ornament modified by a profusion of baroque cartouches, applied to every blank panel
or pilaster. Gabriel Krammer (1611) and Buxenmacher (1613) produced engraved
pattern-books that helped to disseminate this Netherlandish style. Nor was the
medieval tradition yet at an end; the Jesuit Church of Cologne, built between 1618
and 1629, which has all its detail of this bastard classicism, has its vault, tracery, and
balustrades in flamboyant style; the Gothic spirit survived the outbreak of the
Thirty Years' War that brought the first phase of the German Renaissance to an
end. In the next stage of German classicism the absolutely unstructural use of
architectural motives was flagrantly abused: over the windows of the *piano nobile*
in Elias Holl's Zeughaus at Augsburg, there are two pediments (and those broken);
on the Mausoleum of Graz, built between 1614 and 1622, there are three; while on
the 'Palais' in the Grosse Garten at Dresden, built between 1679–80, volutes like
those of Santa Maria della Salute at Venice are quite meaninglessly applied to
a flat façade.

The Jesuits, however, taught Germany how to translate into stone the play of
angles, the multiplication of mouldings, and the effects of exaggerated perspective
that appear in the theatrical perspectives of Italy; but such freedom is not found
until late in the seventeenth century.[1] Thenceforth it is noticeable how closely the
most successful interiors—such as the chapel at Kloster Melk, begun in 1718, and
the Frauenkirche at Dresden, built between 1726 and 1740—approximate to the
theatrical style of the Bibiena. Elsewhere, as in the stalls of Mainz Cathedral, with
their erratic cornice line, their curves based on an infinity of planes, and their
gesticulating caryatids at varying heights; or as in the main arch to the Zwinger at
Dresden, with two halves of a pediment set back to back, each awaiting a ghostly
completion in the spectator's mind, the extravagance of the baroque is pushed to
its utmost limit: and the style comes to an end in exhaustion.

In Spain, that received and developed its Renaissance styles late, the baroque
style was not developed until the end of the seventeenth century. The severe
classicism of Herrera remained dominant all through the seventeenth century,
rather enriched in such work as the great Jesuit Church of Salamanca, begun in
1617, and in the later Church of the Hospital of Charity at Seville, but still
respecting the classic simplicity of line. Josef de Churriguera, who died in 1725,
was the true baroque architect of Spain, though in his best work, for instance the
façade of the University of Toledo, the baroque elements are confined to decoration and hardly influence architectural line. It was in the third and fourth decades of
the eighteenth century that the exaggerated baroque style appeared in Spain:[2] in

---

[1] The classical academies were equally late in foundation; that of Vienna dates from 1692, Berlin 1696,
Dresden 1697; while most of the lesser provincial academies were founded in the last half of the eighteenth
century.

[2] The style of Sardi only appears episodically, for instance, in the Palace of the Duque de la Victoria at
Logroño.

1720 in the Church of Our Lady of Montserrat at Madrid, and in the Palace of San Telmo at Seville. In some late work it seems as if the feeling for Gothic line revives, and such baroque forms as broken lintels and pediments and twisted architraves are applied to form a whole that—like the front of Murcia Cathedral, begun in 1737—is hardly classical at all; while in such interior work as the Sacristy of the Cartuja of Granada (fig. 326) classical elements are broken and multiplied as in a kaleidoscope to create an effect not Roman but Indian. Yet Jesuit influence was already declining; in 1759 the members of the Society of Jesus were deported from Portugal, in 1767 they were expelled from France and Spain; and with them passed the vitality of the baroque style. Even in Italy by 1770 Milizia was inveighing against baroque extravagance, and demanding a scientific plan and logical ornament: a return to the style of Palladio.

VII

THE FAR EAST

I

THE medieval travellers overland to China had been unable to return with any heavy baggage-train of merchandise;[1] but by the end of the fifteenth century the growth of the sea power of Spain and Portugal had begun to create a great Eastern trade that exercised an influence more profound than that of casual embassies. In 1480 Portugal gained the West Coast of Africa; six years later Diaz rounded the Cape of Good Hope; in 1497 Vasco de Gama inaugurated the Indian trade by his voyage to Calicut, and in 1510 Albuquerque took Goa. Indian influence was soon apparent in Portuguese art and architecture. Some trace appears in the cloister of Batalha, and it is clearly evident in a fountain erected in Cintra under John I. The early sixteenth-century window of the chapter house in the Convent of the Christ of Thomar has drawn inspiration from India in its inconceivable elaboration both of form and surface, that in spite of certain flamboyant elements is strangely un-European in effect; while the tower of Belem owes its balconies and ribbed cupolas to the palace of Udaipur.

Not India, but Cathay, was the final goal; as early as 1511 the Portuguese were in Siam, the clearing house of the trade with China and Japan, while by 1517 Fernando Perez had reached the coast of China itself. A sea-borne trade with the East was quickly established, whether it was carried in Portuguese and Spanish bottoms only from the end of the land route in India or from the half-way house of the sea journey at Siam.

The 1503-5 inventory of Isabella the Catholic includes a considerable quantity of oriental porcelain;[2] Charles V even possessed plates made to order in China with his cipher and badge,[3] as well as the quantity of porcelain recorded in his 1561 inventory; and Philip II owned over three thousand pieces.[4] Spain sent to

[1] For their influence on Italian art see vol. I, p. 63. The early importance of land-borne trade with the East is shown by a bottle of oriental porcelain in a silver gilt mount enamelled with the arms of Lewis the Great of Hungary, 1326–82. *Gazette des Beaux Arts*, 1897, vol. xvii, 3rd series, p. 55. Gaignières includes a drawing in his collection (Bib. Nat. Fr. 20070, fol. 8) of a vase in the collection of M. de Caumartin. It appears to be a ewer of greyish white Chinese porcelain mounted in silver gilt, enamelled with the arms and inscribed with the name of Jeanne I d'Anjou, Queen of Sicily, who was assassinated in 1382. See Bouchot, *Inventaire des dessins exécutés pour Roger de Gaignières*, ii. 423. The Sultan Barsbay sent Charles VII by Jacques Cœur's nephew 'trois escuelles de pourcelaine de Sinan, deux grands plats ouvrés de porcelaine, deux bouquets de porcelaine, un lavoir es mains et un garde à manger de porcelaine.' P. Clement, *Jacques Cœur et Charles VII*, p. 116.

[2] Davillier, *Les Origines de la Porcelaine en Europe*.　　　　　　　　　[3] Now at Dresden.

[4] Havard, *Histoire des faïences de Delft*, i. 23. References to porcelain will also be found in the inventories of Elizabeth of Valois (1569) and Don Carlos (1599), and in those of Margaret of Austria (1523–4) and Margaret of Navarre (1534). See Davillier, *op. cit.*

the East not only merchants but also missionaries; and so achieved a far more intimate contact with China and Japan.[1]

Through the Jesuits the East was opened up to the merchant venturers who trod close at their heels. Trade was to some extent organized, and at the end of the sixteenth century, in the reign of Wan Li, much of the blue and white ware produced in China was frankly intended for the European market.[2] The taste for oriental art followed the succession of maritime supremacy, and in 1579—the year of the foundation of the Dutch Republic—the English had leave to trade in the Ottoman Empire and established a consulate at Constantinople, one terminus of the caravan route.[3] By 1587 Burleigh was presenting Elizabeth with New Year's gifts of porcelain, and in 1592 the capture of the Spanish vessel *Madre de Dios* coming from Goa brought much Chinese merchandise to England.[4] The incorporation of the English East India Company in 1600 was followed in 1606 by a licence being granted to Sir Edward Michelborne and others to trade 'to Cathay, China, Japan, Corea, Cambaya', and in 1609 by a treaty of commerce between England and Russia, another half-way house to the East. By 1612 the English were at the great trading centre of Siam, and communication with China was thus secured. Already John Taylor, publishing an ordinary set of patterns called *The Needle's Excellency*, put himself in the fashion by describing them as:

> Collected with much praise and industrie
> From scorching Spaine and freezing Muscovie,
> From fertile France and pleasant Italie,
> From Polande, Sweden, Denmarke, Germanie,
> And some of these rare patterns have been set
> Beyond the bounds of faithlesse Mahomet,
> From spacious China and those kingdoms East
> As from great Mexico, the Indies West.

By 1615 Lady Arundel was busy matching curtains to her 'bedde of Japan'.[5] But the East India Company was not in direct touch with Canton between 1634 and 1673, and English interest was focussed on the Indian trade, which after the fall of Spain remained chiefly in British hands. Its variety is shown by Charles I's proclamation of 1631,[6] which mentions satins, taffetas, and carpets, as well as porcelain, from China.

Some early seventeenth-century lacquer, such as the ballot box of the Saddlers'

---

[1] See Linschoeten, *Discourse of Voyages*, Dutch edition, 1596, English trans., 1598, for an account of the visit of three Japanese princes to Europe with their Jesuit tutors.

[2] Hobson, *op. cit.*, p. 134.

[3] The Levant Company was founded in 1581.

[4] Birdwood, *Old Records of the India Office*, p. 198. The Goanese trade with China was so considerable that the city had an industry of its own in making decorative plates of the broken fragments of Chinese dishes set in rims of lacquer. Hobson, *op. cit.*, p. 136. The caravans went overland from China to Agra.

[5] M. F. S. Hervey, *Life of Thomas, Earl of Arundel*, p. 90.

[6] Birdwood, *Report on the old Records of the India Office*, 1891, p. 37.

Company, made for the East India Company in 1619, seems to be of Indian origin,[1] and Indian style had a marked influence on certain branches of decoration in England. The patterns of the characteristically English crewel embroideries are derived from printed cotton palampores from Masulipatam, where the East India Company established an agency in 1611.[2] Such cottons provided inspiration for the designs of tapestry also; in 1625 an English company was founded to weave hangings with Indian figures, histories, and landscapes,[3] and Indian hangings or 'chints'[4] continued in common use for decoration. Evelyn tells us that Lady Mordaunt's room at Ashstead was 'hung with pintado full of figures great and small prettily representing sundry trades and occupations of the Indians, with their habits', and in 1663 Pepys brought his wife 'a chint, that is, a painted East Indian callico for to line her new study'.

By 1670 the trade had become so important that artisans were sent from England to India to introduce designs suited to the European taste. A few years later, we are told 'from the greatest gallants to the meanest cook maids, nothing was thought so fit to adorn their Persons as the fabrick from India! Nor for the ornament of Chambers like India Skreens, Cabinets, Beds, or Hangings, nor for Closets like China and lacquered ware.'[5] In 1676 further attempts were being made to imitate oriental work in England; in that year Will Sherwin was given a patent to print on broad cloth in 'the only true way of East India printing and stayning such kind of goods'.[6]

England, however, did not remain unchallenged as mistress of the seas. In 1660 the Dutch fleet first reached Canton; two years later the Dutch East India Company was established, in 1610 commercial importation on a large scale was started from Bantam to Holland, in 1619 Batavia was built, and by 1641 Dutch agents were busy in Siam. Soon Dutch factories were established in Formosa and in Japan, and by the middle of the century they were in occupation of Ceylon, the half-way house between Europe and the Far East.

The commerce of Holland was at its highest point between 1651 and the beginning of the war with France in 1672.[7] In one year forty-five thousand pieces of oriental porcelain entered the port of Amsterdam. Her foreign trade and navigation was greater than that of all Europe besides, and the Dutch were merchants of chinoiseries for the rest of Europe. They introduced to the painters of China designs with their favourite tulips, and ordered from them plates with the radiating

[1] Cf. the 'Indian Brewhouse for tee, which hath beene very good Black Lack worke' for which Lord Stafford 'payed exceeding deare' at Amsterdam in 1643 (M. F. S. Hervey, *Life of Thomas, Earl of Arundel*, p. 443).   [2] Jourdain, *English Secular Embroidery*, p. 85.
[3] W. R. Scott, *Constitution and Finance of English, Scottish, and Irish Joint Stock Companies to 1720*, ii. 119.
[4] The word chintz has nothing to do with China but is derived from the Hindustani *chint* = coloured.
[5] Pollexfen, *A Discourse of Trade, Coyn and Paper Credit*, 1697, p. 99.
[6] Anderson, *History of Commerce*.
[7] Havard, *Dictionnaire de l'Ameublement*, s.v. Chine. Between 1665 and 1675 Jacob de Meurs published at Amsterdam richly illustrated accounts of the numerous Dutch embassies to China.

patterns of Rouen pottery.[1] Holland, moreover, gave letters of denization to the art of the Far East by herself producing manufactures in the Chinese style. As early as the 4th of April 1614 Claes Wytmans obtained from the States General the privileges of making at the Hague 'porcelain'—that is, fine, Delft faience—like that of the Indies, and soon after 1642 Aelbrecht de Keizer was imitating Chinese blue and white porcelain at Delft. Once such manufactures were established it was inevitable that the oriental style should be brought into some relation with other national arts. For the first part of the century, however, decoration was so eclectic and varied that Eastern ornament offered little attraction to designers already occupied with styles that had not lost their novelty.

The first trace of Chinese influence in engraved ornament appears in the minute patterns issued by Mathias Beitler in 1616,[2] which show trees, bridges, and little figures *à la chinoise*, together with the Pans and fauns and cats and other beasts of a Dutchman's fancy. These were followed in 1623 by the work of Valentin Sezenius, a remarkable and little-known set of designs in the Chinese taste (fig. 327). Some of the figures are more or less Chinese; some are in ordinary seventeenth-century dress, and some—Orpheus playing to the beasts and Actaeon surprising the nymphs—are classical. In each instance, however, the background, the style, and the ponderation of the design is recognizably Chinese. At about the same date, doubtless under the inspiration of the Danish East India enterprise of 1616, a room in the Rosenborg Slott at Copenhagen was panelled in green imitation lacquer with mouldings of tortoiseshell; but beautiful though it is, it seems to have been little imitated.

France, though not herself actively engaged in the oriental trade before the middle of the seventeenth century, had early received Chinese merchandise from other nations. Père Daniel states that Francis I had in his cabinet several porcelain vases and 'une infinité de petites gentillesses' from India, China, and Turkey.[3] Oriental porcelain and other merchandise were first brought by Portuguese merchants to the Foire St. Germain in 1610,[4] and were soon imported from Holland into France on a large scale: Lord Stafford writes in 1643, 'now the Eastern comodities are soulde [in Zeland] there is 47000 peeces of purcelane which will be bought there to send to France.'[5] Scarron[6] describes the oriental merchandise of the Foire Saint Germain:

Menez-moi chez les Portugais
Nous y verrons, à peu de frais,
Des marchandises de la Chine.

[1] See *L'Art ancien à l'Exposition de 1878*, p. 483.

[2] Victoria and Albert Museum, Engraved Ornament, EO 6, E2157–61, 1911.

[3] In his *Trésor des merveilles de la maison royale de Fontainebleau*, quoted Havard, *op. cit.*, s.v. Porcelaine. In 1599 Gabriel d'Estrées owned 'un pavillon de taffetas de la Chine où il y a toutes sortes d'oyseaulx et animaux représentez' (H. Belevitch Stankevitch, *Le goût Chinois en France au temps de Louis XIV*, p. xxxiii), and in 1605 Louise de Coligny brought from Holland chinoiseries and lacquered vases for the Dauphin and his sister (Havard, *Dictionnaire de l'Ameublement*, s.v. Chine). [4] Havard, *op. cit.*, s.v. Chine.

[5] M. F. S. Hervey, *Life of Thomas, Earl of Arundel*, p. 443. [6] Quoted, Havard and Vachon, p. 359.

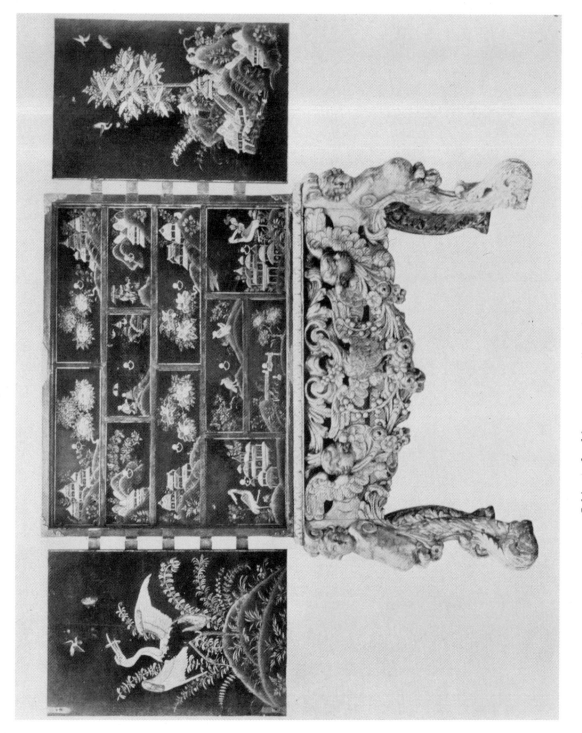

332. Cabinet of red lacquer on a silvered stand. English, c. 1680

333. Silver tankard engraved with Chinoiseries. London, 1650.

334. One of four tapestry panels in Indo-Chinese style made by Vanderbank at Mortlake for Elihu Yale, c. 1700.

335. Soho tapestry in the Chinese taste, *c.* 1740

Nous y verrons de l'ambre gris,
De beaux ouvrages de vernis,
Et de la porcelaine fine
De cette contrée divine
Ou plustot de ce paradis.

The fashion for *chinoiseries* at the French court probably owed something to Mazarin's desire to develop trade with the Orient. He certainly encouraged it by example; in 1649 he owned three Chinese chests, as well as much porcelain and many embroideries. By 1653 he had not only added much more, including beds and other furniture, but had witnessed the establishment of rival 'Chinese' industries in France, for his inventory mentions 'Dix pièces de serge de soye à plusieurs couleurs façon de la Chine faites à Paris.'[1]

The Chinese trade in France was also, like that of Spain, indebted to the missionaries. In 1658 the 'Compagnie pour les voyages de la Chine, du Tonkin, de la Cochinchine et des iles adjacentes' was founded with the double aim expressed in the first article of its statutes: 'la propagation de la foi et l'établissement du commerce dans ces contrées'. This particular company did little, but in 1663 missionaries to Asia, finding it impossible to enter China itself, endeavoured to establish instead a colony in Siam, the centre of the Eastern export trade; as Monseigneur Pallu stated, 'à cause des marchandises du Japon, dont on trafique à Siam, comme dans le Japon même.'[2] Commerce and religion worked hand in hand, and the French trade with the East grew and prospered.[3] With the foundation of Colbert's Chinese trading company in 1660 and of the Compagnie des Indes et du Levant in 1664 the oriental fashion was admitted among the *menus plaisirs* of the King of France. In 1662 Monsieur appeared at a fête at Versailles as the Shah of Persia and Condé as the Sultan of Turkey,[4] and in the Carnival of 1667, Louis himself 'avait un habit moitié à la persienne, moitié à la Chinoise.'[5]

[1] Stankevitch, *op. cit.*, p. 85. Another imitation of oriental textiles in Europe at the same time was the manufacture of carpets. See *Stromatourgie, ou de l'Excellence de la manufacture des tapits dits de Turquie*, 1632, by Pierre Dupont, first decorator of the Savonnerie.

[2] *Memoire*, ii. 309.

[3] In 1685 missionaries sent by Louis XIV were able to reach Pekin.

[4] Molière's *Bourgeois Gentilhomme* (1670) was written as a pretext for a Turkish ballet by Lully.

[5] In 1671-2 Perrault planned a building to join the Louvre to the Tuileries. He proposed to decorate its apartments 'à la manière de toutes les nations célèbres qui sont au monde, à l'italienne, à l'allemande, à la turque, à la persane, à la manière du Mogol, du Roi de Siam, de la Chine, &c.' (Hautecœur, *Le Louvre et les Tuileries de Louis XIV*, p. 190). Not only would such a scheme provide diversity of ornament, but when ambassadors came to France from any country they would find there a microcosm in which their own land was represented. A similar vague exoticism appears in a series of painted panels formerly in a house in Botolph Lane, Eastcheap, painted by R. Robinson in 1696. (Now in Sir John Cass's School, Duke St., Aldgate; see E. W. Tristram, 'A painted room of the seventeenth century,' in *Walpole Society Annual*, iii. 75.) These show more or less oriental scenes with motives borrowed from Chinese, Indian and West Indian sources: palm trees, feathered Indians, monkeys, crocodiles, rhinoceroses and elephants—all given a certain factitious congruity by a classical style and merged into a single romantic scheme. Similar, if less varied, exotic elements are equally evident in contemporary French and Flemish tapestry design. The famous 'tentures des Indes' of the Gobelins, first woven about 1690, copied and re-copied for 150 years, were of the 'Indes

By 1663 the king's apartments were already 'adorned with the two things that please His Majesty most, that is Chinese filigree work in gold and silver, and jasmines. Never has China itself seen so much of this work together, nor Italy so many of these flowers.'[1] Ten years later the royal inventory mentions not only Chinese lacquer screens but also whole sets of Chinese hangings and upholstery,[2] while between 1673 and 1715 no less than nine hundred and twenty-three pieces of oriental porcelain are enumerated.[3]

Only gradually was a real admiration for Chinoiseries cultivated, and even then comprehension and consistency lagged behind; thus in 1666 Louis XIV had silver plaques engraved with the labours of Hercules added to a Chinese lacquer cabinet.[4] The devices of oriental art remained enigmas; in 1668 La Fontaine's sightseers at Versailles,[5] 'entre autres beautés s'arrêtèrent longtemps à considerer le lit, la tapisserie, et les chaises dont on a meublé la chambre et le cabinet du Roy: c'est un tissu de la Chine, plein de figures qui contiennent toute la réligion de ce pays-là. Faute de Brachmane, nos quatre amis n'y comprirent rien.'

The style, however, was already domiciled in France; and when in 1670 the king desired to build the first Trianon, Félibien tells us, 'l'engouement pour la Chine suggéra l'idée de faire un petit palais d'une construction extraordinaire'— an erection of one story modelled on the Porcelain Tower of Nankin, covered with blue and white pottery with stylized decoration—'le tout travaillé à la manière des ouvrages qui viennent de la Chine.'[6] European taste, indeed, had at last been so closely disciplined in the classic style that a reaction in favour of the outlandish was experienced. Some alternative was needed to academic classicism: something that should be different in style, in scale, and in association, but should none the less appeal to tastes trained in the canons of Le Brun's academy and the Court of Versailles. The East offered exactly what was needed: an art associated with a mighty Empire, and therefore not ignoble; an art of pure and glowing colour, and of rare and precious material; an art of exquisite finish and infinite sophistication, yet one neither solemn nor pompous, nor (to the European eye) consistent: an art, moreover, which had never been measured by the five orders, and had never felt the heavy impress of Rome. All this China offered, 'enwrapped in an exquisite sense of the strange'. It is exactly this quality which is seized upon by De la

Occidentales', America and the Antilles. Their designs were adapted by Monnoyer, Houasse, Bonnemer and Yvart from pictures given to Louis XIV by Prince John Maurice of Nassau, representing, according to the inventory of 1681, 'des figures d'hommes et de femmes grandeur naturelle, plusieurs plantes et fruits, oiseaux, animaux, poissons ou paysages du Brésil.'   [1] *Lettres, instructions et mémoires de Colbert*, vi. 470.

[2] Havard, *Dictionnaire de l'Ameublement*, s.v. Chine.   [3] *Ibid.*, s.v. Porcelaine.

[4] Stankevitch, *op. cit.*, p. 132. Cf. the Delft plate by Jacob Wemmersz Hoppesteyn (admitted to the guild of St. Luke in 1661) now in the Berlin Museum, with large medallions of Roman figure subjects in blue and white set among Chinese designs in colours and gilt. Hannover, *Pottery and Porcelain*, ed. Rackham, i. 245.

[5] *Les Amours de Psyche*, ed. Regnier, viii. 31.

[6] Félibien, *Description de Versailles*, p. 332. It was pulled down and replaced by the present Grand Trianon in 1687. Lemonnier, *Art français au temps de Louis XIV*, p. 209. Even the seats in the neighbouring *bosquets* were painted in imitation of porcelain.

336. Curtain of English embroidery in Oriental style, *c.* 1700

337. Panels from a dressing room, Château de Champs, c. 1730

Loubère in his contemporary analysis of Chinese art:[1] 'Ils veulent donc de l'extra-ordinaire dans la peinture, comme nous voulons du merveilleux dans la poésie. Ils imaginent des arbres, des fleurs, des oiseaux et d'autres animaux qui ne furent jamais. Ils donnent quelquefois aux hommes des attitudes impossibles, et le secret est de répandre sur toutes ces choses une facilité qui les fasse paraître naturelles'.

The development of perspective in European painting and the strongly pictorial tendency that made itself felt in tapestry designs had destroyed the decorative flatness of medieval wall decoration; this again was provided in a new guise in the artificial simplicity of Chinese perspective. The curiously complete break made in the seventeenth century with all the decorative traditions of the Middle Ages, even in peasant art, is perhaps partly due to this discovery of an art that met the same needs as the medieval tradition, but that could not incur the reproach of age. Bright colour, engaging narrative, natural observation, and skilful stylization were all to be found in the wares of China; and the illuminations, the enamels, and the embroideries of an earlier day were soon forgotten.

The taste for chinoiseries received its greatest impetus after 1678, when the peace with Holland removed some of the dangers of navigation in Eastern waters. In 1684 the first embassy from Siam was received at the French Court,[2] but it was forgotten in the brilliance of the second embassy which arrived four years later. The ambassadors were laden with presents: sixty trays, about twenty each of cabinets, chests, tables, desks, screens, and bedheads; boxes innumerable; for the king over 1,500 pieces of porcelain, as well as 84 for the Dauphin, 640 for the Dauphine, and 190 for the French ambassador. Such presents naturally represented only a tithe of the Siamese trade; in 1691, for instance, Louis XIV purchased over 9,000 livres worth of porcelain from Lemaire. Siam, too, was far from being the only centre; from Surat in a typical year (1661) 7,600 pieces of Japanese porcelain and a hundred lacquer bureaux were imported, and the other factories all sent their tribute of oriental wares.[3]

Not only was there much traffic by sea, but after 1692 trade between Russia and China was organized and regulated, and knowledge of the country was increased by such books as Lecomte's *Nouveaux Mémoires sur . . . la Chine* published in 1696. Chinoiseries were everywhere; Dancourt's comedy of *La Maison de Campagne*, first acted in 1688, shows a lady going to a friend's house and breaking 'toutes ces porcelaines d'Hollande' since 'il n'en faut avoir que de fines', that is, genuine Chinese. The Duc d'Aumont, wishing to decorate his stable, adorned it with

[1] *Du royaume de Siam*, i. 273; quoted Stankevitch, *op. cit.*, p. 35.
[2] The ambassadors came in an English boat and were introduced to the King of England on the way.
[3] In 1660, a Portuguese embassy to Pekin gained the right to send an annual fleet to Macao; in 1666 there was a French expedition to India; in 1668, a French factory was established at Surat; in 1671, the Compagnie du Sénégal was founded; in 1673, there was an expedition to Ceylon; in 1681, an Embassy from Morocco; in 1677, an English factory was established at Amoy; in 1690, an English factory at Calcutta; in 1691, the New East India Company was founded; in 1698, the new and old Companies were united; in 1670, the Dutch gained right to send an annual fleet to Macao; and in 1693, the Dutch took Pondicherry.

'une corniche fort recherchée tout autour, qu'il garnit partout de pièces de porce-laine.'[1]

In Holland nearly every house of any pretensions had a room specially decorated to contain the owner's collection of porcelain; the designs of Daniel Marot (*c.* 1690) show whole mantelpieces designed simply as étagères for china. In England in 1694, Wren planned chimney-pieces similarly loaded with china.[2] Evelyn tells us that in July 1682 he 'went to visit our good neighbour Mr. Bohun, whose house is a cabinet of all elegancies, especially Indian; in the hall are contrivances of Japan screens, instead of wainscot . . . the landscapes of the screens represent the manner of living and country of the Chinese'.

In the three countries, Holland, England, and France, most familiar with chinoiseries there was a corresponding increase in the imitation of Chinese pro-ductions. Lacquered furniture, at first found only in costly imported specimens, began to be imitated at home (fig. 332). In all three countries professional cabinet-makers exercised the art.[3] In England oriental lacquer was cut to fit occidental forms, and supplemented with English imitations. In the Duchess of Lauderdale's bedroom at Ham House there is a mirror, dating from before 1679, set in Japanese lacquer cut and fitted to fill the usual European frame, with a table of English lacquer to match. We are told as early as 1683 that 'English varnished cabinets might vie with the Oriental',[4] while by 1697 a company of 'The Patentees for Lacquering after the manner of Japan', formed three years earlier, were offering for sale 'cabinets, secretaries, tables, stands, looking-glasses, tea-tables and chim-ney-pieces.'[5] Lacquering even took its place among genteel female accomplish-ments; Edmund Verney in 1689 permitted his daughter to learn it at school.[6]

The year before the amateur's need for instruction had been met by Stalker and Parker's *Treatise of Japanning and Varnishing.*[7]

Their preface shows how lacquer appealed to the seventeenth-century taste for polish and gilding.

'What can be more surprising', they ask, 'than to have our chambers overlaid with varnish more glossy and reflecting than polisht marble? . . . The glory of one Country, Japan alone, has exceeded in beauty and magnificence all the pride of the Vatican at this time, and the

[1] Saint Simon, *Mémoires*, x. 432.

[2] His design is now in the Soane Museum; see Lenygon, *Decoration in England, 1660–1770*, Fig. 87.

[3] Abraham du Pradel's *Livre Commode des Adresses de Paris* of 1691 tells us, that 'Les sieurs Langlois père et fils font des cabinets et paravans façon de la Chine, d'une beauté singulière', while commodes were made with ormulu mounts to harmonize their oriental patternings with classically decorated rooms.

[4] William Whitewood, *The Present State of England*, 1683, quoted in Gillespie, *Influence of Oversea Expansion of England to 1700* (Faculty of Political Science, Columbia), p. 141.

[5] In spite of home production, however, so much Oriental lacquer was imported into England that the Joiners' Company declared in 1700 that 'the said trade is in danger of being ruined'.

[6] 'I find you have a desire to learn to Jappan, as you call it, and I approve of it; and so I shall of any thing that is good and virtuous, therefore learn in God's name all Good Things, and I will willingly be at the charge so farr as I am able—though they come from Japan and from never so farr and Looke of an Indian Hue and colour, for I admire all accomplishments that will render you considerable and Lovely in the sight of God and man . . .' *Verney Memoirs* ii, p. 312.   [7] Published at Oxford.

338. Panel from the Salon des Singes, Château de Chantilly. Probably by
Huet Père, *c.* 1740

339. Porcelain jardinière. Meissen, *c.* 1730

Pantheon heretofore . . . Japan can please you with a more noble prospect, not only whole Towns, but Cities too are there adorned with as rich a covering; so bright and radiant are their Buildings, that when the sun darts forth his lustre upon their golden roofs, they enjoy a double day by the reflection of his beams.'

The plates give designs for little boxes for powder and patches, some Chinese and some Japanese in style, brushes and comb boxes, mirror frames and drawers for cabinets. There are besides two plates of Japanese storks, one of trees, two of great flowering sprays, one of beasts, and two of curiously European figures.

The authors profess that they have in their designs closely followed the towers, figures, and rocks of Japan as figured on imported specimens, but add: 'perhaps we have helped them a little in their proportions where they were lame or defective, and made them more pleasant, yet altogether as Antick. Had we industriously contrived prospective, or shadowed them otherwise than they are; we should have wandered from our Design, which is only to imitate the true genuine *Indian* work.' Mrs. Delany's criticism of such japanning was just: 'it put me in mind', she wrote, 'of the fine ladies of our age—it delighted my eyes, but gave no pleasure to my understanding'.[1]

For the first time in European history clay was held in as high estimation as silver, and the smith accepted his designs from the potter. In England, where this tendency was most strongly felt, silver was engraved with designs in the Chinese taste at least as early as 1670 (fig. 333).[2] Besides useful plate of all sorts, whole *garnitures de cheminée* were made, imitating Chinese porcelain alike in form and pattern.[3] Nor was porcelain the only source of design; de Moelder's pattern book of 1694[4] includes a silver vase with panels of hawthorn and birds and of a Chinese lady, all in the manner of lacquer work.

By 1670 Ary de Milde was copying Ming tea-pots in Delft, and Dwight and Elers followed William of Orange to England to make imitations of the red wares of Japan at Bridewell. About 1690 Adrian Pijnacker was imitating Japanese Imari porcelain, and others were imitating the black-ground wares of China. The potters of Nevers followed suit with blue and white wares combining Persian flowers and Chinese and oriental figures in their patterns; and by 1686 M. Perrot was reproducing the patterns of Oriental porcelain at Orléans.[5] Dutch 'chintzes' had early imitated oriental textiles, and though up to 1686 painted and printed

[1] Lenygon, *Furniture in England, 1660–1770*, p. 275.

[2] Cf. the Goldsmiths' Company's two-handled cup and cover, with Chinese birds and trees and a classical fountain, 1680, and tankard with birds and palms in style of Nankin porcelain, 1683; St. John's College, Cambridge, the Burleigh standing cup with Chinese figures, birds and trees, oddly mixed with the arms and supporters of the college, 1683; the Coachmakers' Company's two-handled porringer, 1688.

[3] e.g. those of 1688–9 and 1696–7 belonging to the Duke of Portland. Jackson, *English Plate*, i. 259.

[4] Published in London with a dedication to Lord Ranelagh. Cf. a silver tea-pot of 1682 illustrated in Jackson, *English Plate*, ii. 945; and two small silver-gilt bowls made in London by David Williams in 1712, exhibited at the London Amateur Art Society's Exhibition in 1928.

[5] For a strange allegory of the introduction of porcelain, painted by Vernansal in 1700 and now in the Museum of Orléans, see H. Jouin, *Charles le Brun*, p. 99.

stuffs were the chief import of the Compagnie des Indes Orientales, after that date the French Protectionist policy limited their importation.[1] They were freely imitated, though Charpentier Cossigny tells us[2] that 'La teinture des toiles des Indes a été imitée en Europe, mais celle-ci n'approche pas du degré de perfection que les Indiens lui donnent pour vivacité et pour la solidité des couleurs.'

Oriental subjects, moreover, began to make their appearance in purely European crafts. The English tapestry-maker Vanderbank wove hangings in oriental style with such success that he found not only private patrons but also royal favour. One such set was made for the withdrawing room at Kensington Palace in 1699. Those made for Elihu Yale (fig. 334) show the influence of Chinese lacquer screens in their composition and of Mogul miniatures in several of their subjects; Yale, who retired from the Governorship of Madras in 1699, may well have provided Vanderbank with Indian paintings as models for parts of the design.[3] The beginning of the year 1700 witnessed many Chinese fêtes at the French Court; there was in January a *divertissement* called 'Le Roi de la Chine' at Marly, with the king in a palanquin escorted by thirty Chinamen, and a month later Monsieur gave the Duchesse de Bourgogne a collation in a room 'ornée à la Chinoise' with his officers dressed 'en pagodes'. Yet the *Amphitrite*, returning in 1703 from its second voyage in Chinese waters, found it difficult to dispose of its cargo of china, lacquer, paper, textiles, and embroidery, and its voyage was the last trading expedition to China for some years. The War of the Spanish Succession, the loss of the Netherlands, Piedmont, and Provence, the death of the Duc de Bourgogne and his son, and the ascendancy of Madame de Maintenon sobered France. For a few years the tide of orientalism slackened, until in 1717 the Triple Alliance between England, France, and Holland re-established conditions of maritime trade favourable to intercourse with the Orient. Law founded the Compagnie d'Occident in 1717 and the Compagnie des Indes et du Mississippi in 1719. In the latter year the existing French companies were fused into the Compagnie universelle des Indes Orientales, of which the operations greatly increased the Chinese trade.[4] By 1722 the Beauvais weavers had finished several sets of tapestries designed by Vernansal with Chinese subjects treated in European perspective, of which a set was sent by Louis XV to Kien Lung, Emperor of China.[5] At the same time the gradual supersession of the symmetrical ideal of classicism by a taste for the

[1] England enacted in 1701 that 'all wrought silks, Bengals and stuff mixed with silk or herba, of the manufacture of China, Persia or the East Indies, and all calicoes painted, dyed or stained there, which are or shall be imported into this kingdom, shall not be worn or otherwise used in Great Britain'. M. Jourdain, *English Secular Embroidery*, p. 92.

[2] *Voyage à Canton*, 1699, p. 490.

[3] The type was reproduced at Brussels rather later. See J. Guérin, *La Chinoiserie en Europe au XVIIIᵉ siècle*, 1911, Plate 8. A panel of English embroidery imitating one of the Soho tapestries in Chinese style was lent by Mr. Detmar Blow to the Amateur Art Society's exhibition held in London in 1928.

[4] The Swedish East India Company received its charter in 1723 and began to import on a considerable scale about 1731.

[5] A fine panel, *Le Prince en Voyage*, is now in the smoking-room of the Army and Navy Club, Pall Mall.

balanced irregularity of the picturesque added a new charm to chinoiseries. Watteau, indeed, the chief creator of the new style, himself included *chinoiseries* in his decorations. Before his death in 1721 he had designed panels with Chinese divinities,[1] Chinese Emperors, 'La Déesse Thvo-chvu dans l'île d'Hainane', and 'L'Idole de la déesse Ke Mao Sao'. All these have their titles correctly given in Chinese characters, showing that they were based on Chinese pictures similarly inscribed.[2] Watteau, however, added his own illusion and his own grace to the style of the Chinese painters, and naturalized Chinoiseries in France as the artists of Versailles had naturalized classicism. The East reappeared in literature, and the 'conte oriental' became a recognized genre between 1710 and 1776.[3] Even the classical Blondel, though he would not admit oriental decoration elsewhere, considered that Chinese and Indian plants and figures were the proper decoration for the room 'où l'on passe pour prendre le caffé' in a country house.[4] The elder Boucher painted several chinoiseries between 1730 and 1740, and in 1742 redesigned the 'tentures Chinoises' of Beauvais, in the new style of picturesque naturalism, against a background of pictorial perspective in the manner of Watteau.

The Chinese style in decoration was continued by Jeaurat and Aubert. Baptiste and Fontenay designed more Chinese tapestries for the Beauvais looms, and Dumont invented the famous set of the *Délassements de la Chine*, while weavers of the Gobelins, Aubusson and Brussels followed suit. The connexion between the missionaries and the East even added devout amateurs to those who practised the style. About 1753 Marie Leczinska was busying herself with painting one of her 'petits cabinets' at Versailles, which was full of fine oriental porcelain and lacquer, with scenes of Jesuits preaching to the Chinese against a Chinese background.[5]

A new genre, however, was soon developed. As early as 1709 Claude Audran had painted at Marly the famous 'berceau où des singes sont à table', and Christophe Huet now designed *singeries*, with monkeys playing the parts of men against a Chinese background.[6] La Fontaine's *Fables* had once more endowed

[1] 'Les Divinités Chinoises, peints au Château de la Muette d'après Watteau', were engraved and published by Jean Aubert. Much less intelligent variations on the same theme were published by Mondon fils in 1736: 'Puzza tenant son fils Horus Divinitez qui président aux grains et fruits chez les chinois'. They combine rocaille framing, cartouches with pseudo-Chinese script, and 'gods' with Egyptian heads.

[2] There can be little doubt that the originals were the Chinese paintings, of which forty-nine volumes were presented to Louis XIV by the Jesuit Father Bouvet in 1697. Some were reproduced in the *Estat présent de la Chine*.

[3] Cf. Grimm, Letter of September 15, 1766: 'L'empire de la Chine est devenu de notre temps un objet particulier d'attention, d'études, de recherches et de raisonnements. Les missionnaires ont d'abord interessé la curiosité publique ... Les Philosophes se sont ensuite emparés de la matière et en ont tiré, suivant leur usage, un parti étonnant pour s'élever avec force contre les abus qu'ils croyaient bons à detruire dans leur pays. Ensuite les bavards ont imités les philosophes, et ont fait valoir leurs lieux communs par des amplifications prises à la Chine.'

[4] *De la distribution des maisons de plaisance*, 1737, i. 87.

[5] P. de Nolhac, *Marie Leczinska*, p. 257. The paintings are now in the Château de Monchy.

[6] The revival of *singeries* may have been due to the importation of Indian palampores with a design of monkeys aiding Vishnu against his demon adversaries (e.g. one in the Museum of Toulouse). Figures of

animals with intelligence, and they were again admitted for a time to their medieval share in the human comedy. Huet painted *singeries* at the Hotel de Rohan and at Chantilly (fig. 338) and Clermont came to England to execute the same kind of decoration at Kirtlington (1745), at the Duke of Marlborough's pavilion on Monkey Island and at Lord Baltimore's Belvidere. Charles Huet, the painter's son, published engraved designs in the style: 'Singeries, ou différentes actions de la vie humaine représentées par des singes', and similar decorations are to be found in the work of J. C. Weigel of Nuremburg.[1] This translation of the orient from romance to satire had as short a life in art as it had in literature,[2] and soon after 1745 the style came to an end in France, as it did in England after Clermont's departure in 1754.

Meanwhile Johann Friedrich Böttger had succeeded in discovering the secret of true porcelain at Dresden in 1711. In its early stages his factory not only imitated Chinese buccaro, but even cast moulds for stoneware from Chinese originals. All his earliest work[3] was purely Chinese in its decoration: some of his black-glazed stoneware even had paintings in lacquer style.[4] Augustus the Strong planned a Japanese palace, and between 1720 and 1725 the Meissen factory was busy copying Japanese Kakiemon porcelain, followed a little later by Imari ware. The French porcelain factories soon stole Böttger's secrets and his styles. The potters of Chantilly, founded in 1725, imitated the patterns of Chinese and Japanese porcelains, but simplified the forms; and like the Meissen potters specialized in the Kakiemon style. Saint Cloud and Vincennes imitated Fukien *blanc de Chine* and *celadon*, and soon were adept in versions of the flower and figure designs of China and Japan. The coarser wares of France followed their lead; Chinese and Japanese motives appeared in Rouen faïence after 1720, and the factory of Guillibaud (1720–39) specialized in Chinese flower, bird, insect, and trellis patterns.[5]

Oriental china, and its European imitations, were now, indeed, so plentiful that an attempt had to be made to provide them with a harmonious background. Lazare Duvaux's office accounts show not only an enormous quantity of vases and

monkeys were to be found among the oriental porcelain figures imported at the time. They were even copied by the European manufacturers. Cf. *Livre Journal de Lazare Duvaux*, ii. 71: December 1750: 'M. de Boulogne: Une pagode d'un singe avec son petit, 300*l*. . . . Mme. la Duchesse de Rohan: un groupe de singes en pagodas remuant lâ tete, 336*l*.'; and ii. 146, December 1752, 'M. le Marq. de Castries: Deux singes groupés de porcelaine de Saxe.' Singerie-chinoiseries of Huet's type appear on the so-called 'Callot' pottery of Moustiers, *c.* 1750–60.

[1] *Neu Inventirtes Laub Bandl und Groteschgen Wirk*. Weigel died in 1746. The style was revived for Toile de Jouy about 1773, but had small success.

[2] Contemporary social and political criticism with oriental background:

1721. Montesquieu, *Lettres Persanes*.
1745. Dubourg, *L'Espion Chinois*.
Toussaint, *Mémoires pour servir a l'histoire de Perse*.

[3] Submitted to Augustus the Strong in 1710 and now in the Porcelain Collection at Dresden.

[4] Cf. Chelsea china of *c.* 1760–5, with chinoiseries in gold on a blue-black ground, imitating lacquer.

[5] The potteries of Sinceny (1737–75), Bordeaux, Nevers, and Marseilles likewise attempted to produce cheap versions of the wares of the East.

340. Wallpaper in the Chinese style from a house at Wotton-
under-Edge. English, *c.* 1745

341. Printed linen. French, *c.* 1760

ornaments of all kind bought by the ladies and gentlemen of the Court[1] but also an important trade in oriental wall hangings and furniture. His day-book records endless 'garnitures' and 'dessus de portes' in 'papier des Indes, représentant des armoires',[2] 'à fleurs figures et oiseaux',[3] 'à fond d'argent à magots',[4] 'à pagodes',[5] and 'à fond blanc nuées bleues',[6] as well as commodes and corner cupboards of 'lacq de Coromandel' and 'vernis la chine'.

In the first half of the century the silk weavers of Lyons wove brocades in imitation of Chinese fabrics, and designed stuffs decorated with Chinese lacquer cabinets and tea caddies.[7] Silk and gauze were painted 'dans le goût des Indes',[8] elaborate embroideries were wrought in the Chinese and Indian taste, and J. B. Huet and his school made many designs for the Manufacture de Jouy (founded by Oberkampf in 1758) for printed cottons and linens in the style of the Chinese wallpapers.[9] Indeed, the whole style of textile printing was under the influence of China; and *toiles de Jouy* of the late eighteenth century, with scenes drawn from novels of sentiment such as the *Nouvelle Héloïse*, owe their episodic treatment, their purely decorative perspective, and their mannered scheme to Chinese art. A few fantastic rocks and an over-slender bridge may be the only visible borrowings, but the spirit that informs them is oriental.

Lacquer was extensively imitated in *vernis Martin*; in February 1744 a decree was passed, permitting 'le sieur Simon-Etienne Martin le cadet, exclusivement à tous autres a l'exception de Guillaume Martin, de fabriquer pendant vingt ans toutes sortes d'ouvrages en relief et dans le goût du japon ou de la Chine,'[10] and Duvaux's day-book includes several items of 'vernis vert poli' and 'vernis fond blanc', 'peint dans le goût des Indes'. Even marquetry was influenced, and about 1770 imitated the angular forms of the lacquers of Japan. The craftsman's need of models was met by numerous pattern-books. About 1740 J. G. Huquier published at Paris his 'Livre de différentes espèces d'oiseaux, plantes et fleurs de la Chine', and 'Livres . . . propres à ceux qui veulent apprendre à dessiner l'ornement chinois'. Soon afterwards Jean Pillement, the most prolific of all designers of

---

[1] Published by Courajod. In June 1756 the Comte de Valentinois bought no fewer than twenty-four 'magots' as well as forty other pieces of oriental porcelain (ii. 286); ii. 9 (Dec. 1748) 'M. de Boulogne: Deux magots doubles de terre des Indes remuant tête et mains, 336l.'; ii. 39 (Dec. 1749) 'M. le Président Hénault: Un magot de terre des Indes couché, de 96l.'; ii. 50 (May 1750) 'Mme. la Marq. de Pompadour: Deux singes du japon remuant la tête, 960l.'; ii. 105 (Dec. 1751) 'Mme. la Ctesse d'Estrades: Deux pagodas du Japon remuant la tête, assises sur les cerfs, 384l.'; ii. 148 (Dec. 1752) 'Mme. la Marq. de Pompadour: Un palanquin du vernis du Japon, avec une pagode de terre couchée dedans, porté par deux magots, ajusté et tenu sur un pied à contours en vernis noir et aventurine'.

[2] Jan. 1755, ii. 231.

[3] Sept. and Oct. 1748, ii. 2.

[4] July 1749, ii. 18.

[5] Aug. 1753, ii. 166.

[6] Aug. 1749, ii. 28, &c.

[7] Specimens in the Musée des Arts Décoratifs, Paris.

[8] See Duvaux, ii. 55.

[9] An English print in this style stamped 'Collins, Woolmer', is dated 1766. MacIver Percival, *The Chintz Book*, p. 77.

[10] *Ibid.*, i. cxxviii. The *Recueil de dessins pour meubles et pour ornemens exécutés en partie, le surplus proposé en 1752* in the Bibliothèque Nationale (Recueil Hd 64) includes several gouache compositions in the manner of Chinese lacquer.

chinoiseries, began to publish his pattern-books at Paris. They included a book of 'Fleurs persannes' and 'Cahiers d'oiseaux Chinois', 'de Parasoles Chinois', 'de balançoires chinoises' (fig. 342), 'de cartels chinois' and 'de figures chinoises'—all conceived in a style combining French elegance with Chinese fantasy. They inspired the design of many Louis XV Lyons silks, with mountains, bridges, pagodas, vases, and even sledges *à la Chinoise*.[1]

The extension of oriental commerce had by this time made the taste for chinoiseries international. Imari ware was being imitated at Ansbach and Vienna from about 1725, and famille verte porcelain from about 1730–50; and with the middle of the century Capo di Monte, Venice, and Buen Retiro began in their turn to continue Böttger's tradition. Between 1730 and 1740 Count Dubsky had a room[2] entirely decorated with 1570 panels of porcelain, with consoles to hold yet more, all decorated in Chinese style; some fifteen years later another was made for Portici, followed in 1763 by another, from the Buen Retiro factory, at Aranjuez.[3] Even Tiepolo painted naturalistic chinoiseries in the Villa Valmarana near Vicenza. Salons were decorated with panelling made from oriental lacquer screens from Schönbrunn to Lisbon and from Drottningholm to Modena; everywhere bedrooms and boudoirs were hung with painted silk or printed paper either Chinese or in the Chinese taste.

In England the demand for chinoiseries made London as important a centre as Paris for the publication of pattern-books in the Chinese taste.[4] Batty Langley's large fretwork schemes of 1740 were accepted for the decoration of some houses;[5] and Elizabeth Montagu, 'the Queen of the Blue Stockings', writes ten years later to describe her dressing room, 'like the Temple of some Indian God. . . . The very curtains are Chinese pictures on gauze, and the chairs the Indian fan sticks with cushions of Japan satin painted.'[6] Chinoiseries reached the theatre in the year 1754, when David Garrick appeared at Drury Lane in the *Chinese Festival*, brought over from France by Noveterre.[7]

The English porcelain factories were just being founded—Bow in 1744, Bristol in 1750, Derby, Longton Hall, and Lowestoft at about the same date—and were soon busy imitating oriental wares. *Blanc de chine* with plum blossom in relief was imitated at Chelsea about 1750, at Bow about 1755, and then at most of the other

---

[1] See Havard and Vachon, *Les Manufactures Nationales*, p. 575.

[2] At Brünn, now in the Austrian Museum, Vienna.

[3] See C. Moran, 'The Royal Porcelain Factory of Buen Retiro', in *Connoisseur*, lxxx, 1928, p. 153. The fourth, and slightly later, Salon de Porcelana at the Royal Palace in Madrid is occidental in the style of its decoration.

[4] The only Chinese pattern-book that I have found published elsewhere than in Paris or London is the *Neue Arth Blumen Die so wohl zum Laquiren, Sticken und Nehen, alss auch auf Porcelan zue Mahlen*, published at Nuremburg. One or two of Huquier's publications (e.g. those designed by Bellay) have German as well as French titles.

[5] The only other patterns published in England before 1750 are some unimportant designs for snuff-boxes by Elias Baeck.

[6] E. J. Climenson, *Elizabeth Montagu, The Queen of the Blue Stockings*, i. 271.

[7] Bolton, *Robert Adam*, ii. 291.

342. Lacquered and gilt bedstead from Badminton. English, *c.* 1760

FIG. 343. Design from Jean Pillement's *Cahier de Balançoires Chinoises*, c. 1750.
Engraved by Jeanne Deny.

factories; the Kakiemon style followed, and Chelsea imitated Imari wares. England was classical enough to be as much interested in form as in pattern, and chinoiseries were in England consequently translated from the background of wall decoration to a more solid existence as chairs and tables.[1] Chippendale includes in his *Director* of 1754 designs for chairs in Chinese style, which he advocates for 'its usefulness because of the scope for variety which it affords'; and his mirrors are classics of chinoiserie.[2] In the same year Edwards and Darly published '*A new book of Chinese Designs, calculated to improve the present taste, consisting of Figures, buildings and furniture, Landskips, Birds, Beasts, Flowers and ornaments, etc.*', which includes bedsteads as well as much wall decoration.[3]

The description given in a *Connoisseur* of the following year (No. 65) of 'A Pretty Fellow's Dressing-room' shows the prevailing style:

'I was accordingly shown into a neat little chamber, hung round with Indian paper and adorned with several images of Pagods and Bramins and vessels of Chelsea China, in which were set various-coloured sprigs of artificial flowers. But the toilet most excited my admiration, where I found everything was intended to be agreeable to the Chinese taste. A looking-glass, enclosed in a whimsical frame of Chinese paling, stood upon a Japan table, over which was spread a coverlid of the finest chintz. I could not but observe a number of boxes of different sizes which were all of them Japan, and lay regularly disposed on the table.'

In 1756 began the war with France which diminished for seven years the influence of the lighter French styles in England, and consequently prolonged the life of the Chinese taste in that country. The style, indeed, took such hold in England that about half of Jean Pillement's designs were published in London: *A new book of Chinese Ornament* in 1755, the *Four Elements* à la Chinoise in 1759 and 1774 and *Receuil de fleurs Chinoises, de Fontaines chinoises, de Tentes chinoises,* and *de baraques chinoises* in 1760 and 1770.[4] While the Chinese porcelain-painter was learning to depict English hounds and hunters, and English cottages beneath an English sky, his European brother was painfully learning the elements of Chinese perspective, in order to depict Chinese tea-gardens, pagodas, and fine ladies for the Squire's delight.[5]

In England, moreover, attempts were made to raise *chinoiseries* to a standard of historic correctness. William Chambers, a member of an English family domiciled at Gothenberg, the home of the Swedish East India Company, as a boy of eighteen went to China on one of their ships and in 1775 returned to England by

[1] They likewise influenced the design of silver: see, for instance, the epergne in the shape of a Chinese pagoda illustrated in Jackson, *English Plate*, ii. 927 (1762).

[2] e.g. the very fine set designed to go between the windows in the long drawing-room at Crichel.

[3] The Master's chair of the Joiners' Company was carved in this year by Edward Newman, and is Chinese in style with some *rocaille* influences.

[4] Some of Pillement's designs were used by Hancock to decorate his black transfer-printed wares.

[5] The Emperor Kien Lung had the principal scenes of his successful campaigns of 1759 drawn by four European missionaries at his court, and in 1765 sent the drawings to France to be engraved. H. Cordier, 'La Chine en France au XVIIIᵉ siècle', in *Journal des Débats*, Nov. 21, 1908.

344. Painted panel with Russian subjects. French, *c.* 1785

way of Rome and Paris.[1] He there made use of his eastern experience and published in 1757 *Designs of Chinese buildings, furniture, dresses, machines and utensils,* which, he tells us, were intended 'to put a stop to the extraordinary fancies that daily appear under the name of Chinese, though most of them are mere inventions, the rest copies of the lame representations found on porcelain and paper hangings'.[2] But picturesqueness rather than correctness was what the public required, and chinoiseries ended by being curiously modified by the prevailing classicism.[3] A late eighteenth-century Chinese room at Wellington shows the whole style formalized into a classical arabesque; while the 'Pagode de Chanteloup' near Amboise, built between 1775 and 1778, has the diminishing shape of a pagoda but is completely classical in architecture and decoration. Choffart's designs of 1772 seem to have been the last in Chinese style published in France, while Mairan's *Lettres sur la Chine* and Raynal's *Histoire philosophique et politique des établissements et du commerce des Européens dans les Indes,* both published in 1770, are the last books on the East of any importance before the next century. The silks of the period show how far the tradition of chinoiseries was breaking down; a design in the Galais Collection[4] shows classical ruins, rocaille motives and chinoiseries all framed in a hideous trellis of cactus; and a Lyons brocade[5] has Pompeian panels interspersed with a few Chinese medallions. Theoretical criticism hastened the decline of the style; Watelet[6] considered that in China they had not 'la moindre idée des beaux arts'; they did not suspect that perspective existed; they only knew a few decorative lines which they repeated to satiety; they had no sense of form, and they had not even begun to study nature.

Diderot condemned it: 'Un amas d'ornemens confus ne peut avoir de raison apparente; une varieté bizarre, et sans rapport ni symmetrie, comme dans l'Arabesque ou dans le goût Chinois, n'annonce aucun dessin.'[7] By 1780 it was only the remoter factories, such as Warsaw, which maintained the tradition of Chinese porcelain decoration.

[1] He seems there to have acquired French tastes, for in 1756 he congratulated the world on the triumph of true taste over the Chinese, which, he said, 'was now left to cake houses and Sunday apprentices'. Lenygon, *Furniture in England, 1660–1770,* p. 22.

[2] Two years later P. Decker published in London his *Chinese Architecture, Civil and Ornamental*—a good repertory, but only intended for reproduction in the flat.

[3] J. Dinglinger most oddly associates Chinese figures with a classical altar on a tazza of sixteenth-century style. Victoria and Albert Museum, EO 15, 13548.

[4] Paris, Musée des Arts décoratifs. It is for Tours silk, *c.* 1775.

[5] Lyons, Musée historique des tissus.

[6] *Dictionnaire des arts de peinture,* 1792, iv. 66.

[7] *Grande encyclopédie,* art. Beau. Moreover the style made no appeal to the sentimentalists. Its condemnation was indirectly pronounced in the *Nouvelle Héloïse*: 'Au reste, j'ai vu à la Chine des jardins . . . faits avec tant d'art que l'art n'y paraissoit point, mais d'une manière si dispendieuse et entretenus à si grands frais, que cette idée m'ôtoit tout le plaisir que j'aurois pu goûter à les voir . . . On y voyoit entassées à profusion des merveilles qu'on ne trouve qu'éparses et séparées.' After this even Chambers's *Dissertation on Oriental Gardening* of 1772 and Le Rouge's *Jardins anglo chinois* of 1776–86 had no success. (Chambers definitely wrote his book in reaction against the return to Nature. See his Preface. Mason in 1779 dismissed it as 'an ingenious want of taste'.)

2

Alison, writing in 1792, found the explanation of the 'Chinese taste' in the fact that 'however fantastic and uncouth the forms in reality were, they were yet universally admired, because they brought to mind those images of Eastern magnificence and splendour, of which we have heard so much, and which we are always willing to believe, because they are distant'.[1] The enchantment of distance had indeed been an important element in the charm of chinoiseries; but by the end of the eighteenth century it had become lessened by familiarity, and other oriental styles were found to have a more delightful strangeness. When Desportes redesigned the 'Tentures des Indes' of the Gobelins in 1737–41 he enriched them with elephants and negroes, plantains and bananas and a wealth of other tropical fruit. A similarly composite scheme appears in some Brussels tapestries by G. Van der Borght of about 1735, now in the Kunstgewerbemuseum of Cologne.[2] The most important rivals to China in decorative art were India and Persia;[3] and their influence was perpetuated by the English textile manufactures. When between 1764 and 1775 the basic inventions of the English cotton trade were made,[4] English commerce with India was at its height[5] and nearly every house in England contained hangings from the East Indian warehouses.[6]

Thus it was natural that the English calico printers should print cottons in the Indian style,[7] since their aim was to supersede the Indian fabrics with their own. The French trade with India had in the meantime developed by being opened to all in 1769 and by the foundation of a new Compagnie des Indes in 1780. The china painters of Chantilly were soon using 'Indian flowers' in their patterns, and

[1] *Essays on Taste*, 1825 ed., p. 194.

[2] Hannover, *Pottery and Porcelain*, ed. Rackham, i. 239. The tendency is evident in such Delft ware as a vase of about 1700 in the Kunstindustrimuseum of Copenhagen, with naturalistic illustrations of Eastern scenes, including elephants.

[3] As early as 1735 Fraisse published a 'Livre de dessins Chinois tirés de Perse, des Indes, de la Chine et du Japon'.

[4] 1764 Spinning Jenny; 1765 Watt's steam-engine; 1768 Arkwright's spinning-machine; 1770 Taylor and Walker's apparatus for printing cotton from cylinders instead of blocks; 1775–6 Crompton's spinning mule. The right of cutting log-wood for dyeing in Honduras was secured in 1763.

[5] The English gained Madras in 1749.

[6] Mrs. Delany, writing in 1746, describes a room at Cornbury, 'hung with the finest Indian paper of flowers and all sorts of birds; the ceilings are all ornamented in the Indian taste. The bed chamber is also hung with Indian paper on a gold ground, and the bed is Indian work of silk and gold on white satin' (Jourdain, *English Secular Embroidery*, p. 94). Even Robert Adam, designing a state bed and candlestands *en suite* for Kedleston, about 1760, decorated them with the stems and leaves of Indian palms, and used naturalistic palm tree pilasters for his tea room at Moor Park in 1763. Similar palm trees appear in a chimney-piece of about the same date, now in one of Madame du Barri's *salons* at Versailles. Their previous use in French art had been for presents for Eastern potentates: e.g. the four silver palm trees by Ballin given to the Sultan in 1742. Mazé-Sencier, *Livre des Collectionneurs*, p. 99.

[7] The manufacture of English muslin dates from 1774. In 1760 Pillement had published in London his *Recueil de différentes fleurs de fantaisie dans le goût chinois, propres aux manufactures d'étoffes de soie et d'indienne*, which was quickly followed by his *Recueil de nouvelles fleurs de goûts pour la manufacture des étoffes de perse*.

the Manufacture de Jouy was quick to imitate the English cotton printers. By 1783 it was producing coloured chintzes in the Indian style.[1]

But meanwhile a growing acceptance of a rather mechanical classicism was driving out from decoration any oriental style that could not be classically adapted.[2]

The East had ceased to be the country of romance, which men began to find afresh in past times and in less civilized parts of the world. There was a definite revival of interest in travel; in 1785 Lavallée Poussin designed a set of tapestries for Beauvais with 'La Conquête des Indes'—Vasco da Gama, John II holding his Council, and the departure from the island of Porto Santo.[3] Five years later a set of 'Les Parties du Monde' was designed by Lebarbier for the same factory.[4] Decorations inspired by a foreign country could be more easily fitted into a classical building than could oriental *ensembles*. The *cabinet Turc* at Fontainebleau, for instance, designed by Mique in 1775, has nothing but a few turbans and crescents to distinguish its ornaments from the usual classical arabesque.[5] For a few years the fashion turned to Russia; and little Russian scenes displaced any more oriental types of decoration alike in tapestry and wall-painting[6] (fig. 344). On his return from Russia in 1769 J. B. Leprince painted various schemes of decoration with Russian scenes and designed a set of 'Jeux Russes' for the Gobelins,[7] while Casanova provided the Beauvais looms with cartoons of 'fêtes russes'. At the Château de Raincy a 'maison russe' was even erected in the Park. Only in England did Oriental influence survive, and there chiefly in textiles.[8] Such influence, indeed, depended much upon the English dominion in India; and

[1] In the following year Jacques Charton published a 'collection de douze cahiers de plantes étrangères en fleurs, fruits, corail et coquillages', described as 'Fleures des Indes—Plantes de la Libie, du Japon, du Pérou, de Cayenne, &c.' About 1785 such motives were used in designing Toile de Jouy 'à motifs Persans, dit à l'Ananas'.

[2] In France even textiles in oriental style went out of fashion. Madame de Genlis, writing of the time immediately after the treaty of commerce with England in 1786, says, 'Les toiles des Indes qu'on appeloit *perses* étoient jadis fort magnifiques, fort à la mode. Une belle robe de perse à fleurs, coûtoit soixante-dix à quatre-vingts louis; cependant, les dessins en étoient affreux, comme ceux des schalls de cachemire. Quand les anglois voulurent s'approprier ce commerce . . . ils firent des rayures et des mouchetures sur de jolies toiles, et ces toiles anglaises ont fait tomber les perses.'

[3] Badin, *La Manufacture de Tapisseries à Beauvais*, p. 65. A set was ordered for the king in 1788.

[4] *Ibid.*, p. 66. About the same time a Toile de Jouy with the same subject was printed. The fashion continued under the empire and the restored monarchy. In 1807 Joseph Dufour produced his wallpaper of 'Paysage indien et Voyage du Capitaine Cooke.' Then in 1819 Bolivar brought South America into fashion, and Zuber produced a wall-paper with scenes of virgin Amazonian forest, and South American village scenes and bull-fights.

[5] The same is true of the Cabinet Turc of the Hotel Beauharnais, and of the Kiosk à la Turque included in Queverdo's *Arabesques* of 1788. The mosque erected in 1784 in the park of Swetzingen near Heidelberg is rather more oriental, but keeps some classical elements. Tapestries of Turkish scenes were woven at the Gobelins between 1781 and 1784; some are now at Compiègne.

[6] In 1775 a Tragedy by La Harpe, *Menzikoff*, was played at Fontainebleau with Russian dresses.

[7] A set is in the Archbishop's Palace at Aix.

[8] Cashmere shawls were first imitated at Norwich in 1784, and at Paisley and Edinburgh a little later. The first French imitations were made at Paris in 1802.

in its best-known expression—the Pavilion at Brighton[1]—Indian architecture on the outside[2] is combined with Chinese decoration within. The music-room (fig. 345) was decorated by the Frenchman Lambelet with Chinese landscapes in yellow on a crimson ground, to imitate lacquer; but the other rooms show a more hybrid style. One with a paper imitating red lacquer is finished with Gothic fireplaces; and in several rooms Chinese ornament is combined with tropical naturalism. Palm tree columns appear alike in the south drawing-room and in the great kitchen; an immense fruited plantain tree covers with its broad and branching leaves the ceiling of the banqueting room, while from its centre a Chinese dragon holds a great chandelier with lesser dragons and lotus blossoms among its lustres.[3] The Brighton Pavilion, however, is an isolated fantasy, and even in England exotic decoration was dead. Not till Napoleon had taught France to dream of Oriental Empire did any eastern style reappear there; then Josephine draped her classic shoulders in 'véritables cachemires', had her robes fashioned of India muslin, and her jewels set in Indian filagree.[4] In 1811 patterns like the 'pine-apples' of cashmere weaving appeared in lace, in brocade, in printed textiles; and Züber was producing wallpapers representing draperies of cashmere shawls hanging from heavy gilt hooks on a background of pale blue brocade.

Meanwhile a romantic generation was once more seeking glamour in the Nearer East:[5] Chateaubriand, Hugo, and Lamartine pictured it in words,[6] Delacroix, Vernet, Marilhat, Decamps, and Fromentin described its many aspects with their brush. The Orient had the unfailing glamour of distance, the dignity of classic antiquity, and the romance of a medieval survival. But since men's interest in the East was romantic and pictorial and in no wise archaeological, there was no study

[1] The exterior was finished in 1787, with additions in 1801 and 1802. It was remodelled by Nash in 1817, and the interior decoration finished 1819–20.

[2] An important factor in the creation of this style was the work of English artists painting in India. Repton acknowledges his indebtedness 'to the beautiful designs published by Daniell, Hodges, and other artists' (*An Enquiry into the Changes of Taste in Landscape Gardening*, 1806, p. 4). Similarly Thomas Hope designed an Indian room as a frame for four of Daniell's paintings of Indian architecture. (*Household Furniture and Interior Decoration executed from Designs by Thomas Hope*, 1807, p. 24). Daniell's *Views of Indian Architecture* were published between 1795 and 1808. Repton's account of how the Indian style came to be chosen is illuminating. 'I considered all the different styles of different countries, from a conviction of the danger of attempting to invent anything entirely new. The Turkish was objectionable, as being a corruption of the Grecian; the Moorish, as a bad model of the Gothic; the Egyptian, as too cumbrous for the character of a villa; the Chinese, as too light and trifling for the outside, however it may be applied to the interior; and the specimens from Ava were still more trifling and extravagant' (*Designs for the Pavillon at Brighton*, 1808, p. vi).

[3] The same room shows the influence of the Empire style in a Chinese guise; it has columns shaped as fasces of lances and darts bound together by serpents, a tented roof, and trophies of Chinese standards and pennons in the Napoleonic manner.

[4] Morvins tells us that for the official first meeting between Napoleon and Marie Louise a boudoir was decorated 'tellement plafonné, tapissé et drapé en magnifiques châles de l'Inde et en telle quantité, que ce cadeau impérial était estimé cent mille francs. C'était l'invention de Napoléon, homme à la fois taillé à l'antique et à l'orientale. L'ameublement était complètement asiatique' (C. Simond, *Paris de 1800 à 1900*, i. 202).   [5] A Persian ambassador was appointed to Paris in 1819.

[6] 1828, Chateaubriand, *Itinéraire de Paris à Jérusalem*; Hugo, *Orientales*; 1835, Lamartine, *Voyage en Orient*. The Société Asiatique was founded in 1822.

345. A corner of the Music Room, Royal Pavilion, Brighton, 1784

of detail. Colour was brightened and strengthened, but the East did not seriously influence decoration until Adrien de Longpérier, armed with his legendary magnifying glass, initiated the serious study of Arab art in 1842. His theories of the relation between Arab and Christian art in the Middle Ages served to affiliate Eastern decoration with the Gothic revival. By 1855 Gothic was moribund and the Renaissance influence was beginning to decline before Arab models.[1] Marchand and Petiteau were making jewels in Moorish designs; the weavers of Beauvais and Kidderminster were imitating Persian, Turkish, and Indian carpets,[2] and Falloise was damascening in Arab style. At the 1851 Exhibition there were shown carpets[3] and hangings[4] woven with designs from the wall decorations of the Alhambra, copied from the publication of Owen Jones, as well as a complete tea set in Persian style.[5] Seven years later Indian textile patterns were being recommended as models to the weavers and calico printers of Lancashire and Yorkshire.[6] At the 1862 Exhibition Deck of Paris was showing *faïence* with patterns imitated from Arab glass and damascened metal, and the Austrian and Bavarian glass manufacturers were exhibiting imitations of the Alhambra Vase in gilded glass. The oriental styles became part of the repertory of the learned eclectic designers.[7] Dr. Dresser explains the procedure.

'I may settle that the pattern is to be Arabian, Chinese, Indian, or Moresque in style, and decide to produce Arabian, Chinese, Indian, or Moresque ornament. Knowing what the Arabians, Chinese, Indians, and Moors have for centuries produced when they have ornamented a fabric, or surface, such as I desire to decorate, I commence to produce forms similar to those employed by the particular people that I elect to follow, and thus I produce an Arabian, a Chinese, or Indian, or Moresque pattern. But my success in the production of such a pattern depends largely upon the extent to which I become, in feeling, for the time a Chinaman, or Arabian, or such as the case requires. But I must not only become, in spirit, a citizen of the country whose ornament I wish to simulate, but I must become, in a sense, a scholar of that country. . . . In order that I enter into the Spirit of the Oriental, I often find it necessary to inform myself of the religion, mode of government, climate, and habits of a people; for it is only by understanding their faith and usages that I can comprehend the spirit of their ornament, and become for a time one of them in feeling.'[8]

In 1863 the traditional feudal isolation of Japan was broken by the French,

[1] e.g. in E. Julienne's pattern-book, *La Pandore*, of that year.
[2] *1851 Exhibition, Reports of Juries*, ii. 1634.
[3] *Ibid.*, ii. 1635. [4] *Ibid.*, ii. 1638.
[5] *Ibid.*, ii. 1121. Owen Jones (*Grammar of Ornament*, 1857, p. 67) sets the Alhambra at the apex of art.
[6] M. Digby Wyatt, *On the Principles of Design applicable to Textile Art*, 1858.
[7] The theoretical criticism of the day condemned oriental art. Ruskin decides (*Two Paths*, lecture 1) that such art, produced by semi-barbarous, cruel, and licentious races, beautiful as its conventional designs may be, does not come up to his requirements as great art. It appeals only to the love of pleasure, and not to the love of truth; it is a one-sided development of the artistic instinct. The same opinion is expressed by L. de Laborde, *De l'Union des Arts et de l'Industrie*, 1856, i. 262. Their influence, however, was not strong enough to condemn the style. Brocard copied Arab glass with good results from about 1880; and Morris owed much to Persia in his brocade designs. Racinet's *Ornement Polychrome* helped to familiarize commercial designers with Persian and Indo-Persian ornament. [8] C. Dresser, *Studies in Design*, p. 3.

English, and American fleets. Three years later Japanese ambassadors were received at the Tuileries. As a consequence there was a fresh revelation to Europe of the art of Japan, and it had as strong an appeal as that of China had had two centuries earlier. It appealed to a naturalistic generation by its truth of observation, and yet refreshed them by its sense of style. They were wearied of flowers massed as closely as a carpet bed; here was composition in which space was as important as form. They were tired of a flat-footed realism; here was truth that was none the less artistic. Men were beginning to feel with Beaudelaire that 'le beau est toujours bizarre'; here was beauty spiced with strangeness. Soon after 1867 a little group of artists and critics founded at Sèvres a dining club called the 'Société Japonaise du Jinglar'[1] which became the centre of Japanese influence in French art. The brothers de Goncourt encouraged the appreciation of Japanese art in France; Japanese poetry appeared in a French guise; a dramatic fantasia, *La Belle Saïnara*, was produced, and in 1879 the style was officially naturalized in a Japanese ballet at the Opera. In decoration Japan offered new models both in technique and in design; Falize studied the processes of its cloisonné enamel, and then produced exquisite jewels in Japanese style, in 1874, in designs taken from Japanese lacquer, and about two years later in a more elegant style inspired by Japanese painting. Reiber designed in the Japanese style for the potteries of Deck and for the enamels and bronzes of Christofle (fig. 347); Bracquemond interpreted the flora of France according to the canons of Japan.[2] Whistler painted the 'Peacock Room' for Mr. Leyland; Tiffany brought over Japanese workmen to New York. The commercial designers copied Japanese prints for china and bronze, enamels and textiles, and those who worked for the connoisseurs found easy access to models from Japan itself.[3] But it was not long before such influences were assimilated; they helped to purify European style but were merged in it. Meanwhile increased trade with the Far East brought to Europe enough *chinoiseries* to satisfy even the humblest possessor of exotic tastes, and European craftsmen turned to the satisfaction of other needs.

[1] See *L'Art moderne à l'Exposition de 1878*, p. 464.   [2] See p. 157.
[3] In Exhibitions: Arts du métal, 1880; Exposition rétrospective de l'art japonais, 1883; Gravure japonaise, 1891; and in books such as L. Gonse, *Art japonais*, 1883, and S. Bing, *Japon artistique*, 1888.

L'ESCARPOLETE

346. Design for a panel. By Watteau, engraved by L. Crépy fils, *c.* 1715

FIG. 347. Furniture and ornaments in Cloisonné enamel and bronze.
Exhibited by Christofle at the Paris Exhibition of 1878.

VIII

LES AMATEURS

IN the early eighteenth century men were conscious of disillusion; neither the
political nor the intellectual splendours of the *grand siècle* had proved so endur-
ing or so sufficing as their creators had deemed them to be. Velasquez, Poussin,
Borromini, Rembrandt, and Molière had been dead for more than a generation;
Bernini, Le Pautre, Corneille, Racine, Madame de Sévigné, La Bruyère, Le Nôtre,
and Bossuet had died between 1680 and 1704; their successors were of a different
stamp, men of another and a lesser world.

Louis XIV outlived the art and the society he had created;[1] by the turn of the
century the reaction against the standards he had helped to impose had already
begun: a reaction of which the succeeding generation could recognize the origin.
The Chevalier de Boufflers wrote to the Duchess de Biron:[2] 'If Madame de
Maintenon were to come to life again, and if her old coachman and her old horses,
likewise resuscitated, were to take her to Versailles, she would no longer find
Louis XIV there, or anything like him. . . . Yet, after a little time she would see
that it is this same Louis XIV who is the cause of all the change.' His classicism
was too selective and too exclusive to endure long; he might build, pull down, and
rebuild Versailles again and again, but a limit alike of creation and of appreciation
was eventually achieved beyond which he had neither force nor money to go.
As Louis XIV passed beyond his prime of maturity and of conquest, the splendours of courts were dimmed, and men turned from power to delight. In every
department of intellectual and artistic activity there was a demand for a quicker
measure and a smaller scale. Locke and Hobbes inspired a new generation of
politicians; the vast state rooms were cut up into *petits appartements,* and *le delizie del
fiume Brenta* succeeded the fêtes of Versailles.

As early as 1692 Gravina[3] was demanding *novità* and *maraviglia* as essentials of
art. *Genres* and unities had to rank with the unity and elasticity of life; 'Tous les
genres étaient bons, hors le genre ennuyeux.' Couperin could make music out of
everything that he came across, from his wife's chatter and the musicians' quarrel
with the Ménestrandise to the shower that spoilt the Court's picnic at Saint Germain
en Laye; Watteau and Lancret could find themes as diverse for their decorative

[1] Saint Simon says that at his death 'le peuple, ruiné, accablé, désesperé, rendit grâces à Dieu, avec un éclat
scandaleux, d'une délivrance dont ses plus ardens desirs ne doutaient pas'.
[2] Letter of 20 March 1791 quoted by the Duc de Noailles, *Histoire de la maison royale de Saint Louis.*
[3] *Ragionamento sopra l'Endimione*; quoted, J. G. Robertson, *Studies in the Genesis of Romantic Theory in the
Eighteenth Century*, p. 28.

348. Panels. By Lancret, *c.* 1720

349. Panel of carved wood. French, c. 1710

350. Panel with gesso decoration. French, c. 1720

paintings.[1] Every degree of pleasure could be admitted into art; Montesquieu writes,[2] 'ce sont ces différens plaisirs de notre âme qui forment les objets du goût, comme le beau, le bon, l'agréable, le naïf, le délicat, le tendre, le gracieux, le je ne sais quoi, le noble, le grand, le sublime, le majestueux, etc.'.

Such a point of view made a link of a new kind between the artist and his public; the artist[3] was received into society, and society itself took to art. The touch of the amateur appears in literature, decoration,[4] and the Fine Arts.[5] Even Madame de Pompadour tried to acquire the art of drawing, and had Cochin to touch up her prentice essays in engraving. Those who did not create invested themselves with the privileges of the 'donneurs d'idées' and dictated to those who did. Not only style but criticism developed along new lines.[6] The artist's view of art became of importance. Hogarth wrote his *Analysis of Beauty* 'with a view of fixing the fluctuating ideas', and says in his Preface: 'It is no wonder this subject should have so long been thought insoluble since the nature of many parts of it cannot possibly come within the reach of mere men of letters.' Almost every member of polite society considered himself an authority on art, and Père André, writing his *Essai sur le Beau* in 1741, begins it: 'Tout le monde en parle, tout le monde en raisonne. Il n'y a point de cercles à la cour, il n'y a point de sociétés dans les villes, il n'y a point d'échos dans les campagnes, il n'y a point de voûtes dans nos temples, qui n'en retentissent.'

Science was being established on a new basis of observation, and such observation was giving a new value to direct expression in the arts. The generation that fathered the *Encyclopédie* felt little need of symbolism except as a convenient shorthand; and correspondingly in the visual arts mythology and allegory retired into the background, leaving only a few attributes behind for the use of the new generation. None the less there was no real break in tradition. The grand style of Versailles had obscured the other national tradition of direct observation but had not destroyed it; and styles that drew their inspiration from such observation yet

[1] On the painting of the period see P. Marcel, *La Peinture française de la mort de le Brun à la mort de Watteau, 1690–1721*, 1906.
[2] Second article, s.v. Goût in the *Grande Encyclopédie*.
[3] The *Dictionnaire de l'académie* of 1694 defines *Artiste* as 'Industrieux, qui travaille selon l'art. Il est aussi substantif et signifie celui qui travaille dans un art. Il se dit particulièrement de ceux qui font les opérations chimiques.' But the edition of 1762 recognizes the modern sense of the word; the artist had in the interval received his patent of nobility.
[4] Even the amateur mathematicians of the day took a hand in it, and Père Dominique Donat published in 1722 a *Méthode pour faire une infinité de dessins différens avec des carreaux mie partis de deux couleurs par une ligne diagonale*, with 22 plates.
[5] The Regent himself may serve as the type: Hisson wrote of him: 'Il a beaucoup d'esprit . . . il sait beaucoup de choses, il a bonne mémoire, et ce qu'il sait, il le dit sans pédanterie aucune. Il ne se sert pas d'expressions nobles et ses sentiments ne sont pas élevés. Il préfère la société des gens du commun, de peintres, de musiciens, à celle des gens de qualité. En ce moment, il peint un tableau dont le sujet est emprunté à la Fable, car tout ce qu'il fait est forcément historique.'
[6] It is significant that no one published a book on aesthetics in France between Dubos in 1719 and Père André in 1741. T. M. Mustoxidi, *Histoire de l'Esthétique française*, 1920, p. 34.

remained as undercurrents to the main stream of classicism. Some of the work of Bérain epitomizes these lesser styles.[1] To the classical eccentricities of Ducerceau's arabesques he added the whimsicality of his native Lorraine; his subjects might be exotic and theatrical—he set Red Indians, Chinese, Arabs, and Moors in the niches of his arabesques and staged pastorals, operas, Lulli ballets and bacchic scenes of comedy[2] in the arcades of his tapestries—but he treated them in the spirit of his fellow citizen, Jaques Callot. His figures have a Chinese strangeness, a peasant comicality or a diabolic twist; but their extravagance, their contrast, and their variety are drawn from direct observation.

The beginning of the eighteenth century witnessed a change in both the chief elements of the classical art of the preceding age; the repertory of antiquity had become so fully naturalized that it had almost ceased to be antique, and the pictorial landscape compositions had become so familiar as to seem natural. The gardens of Versailles, finished in 1688, had grown into natural beauty during the next twenty years. The most important influence of the new charm of their perspective lay in the creation of the arabesque style of Gillot, Audran and Watteau, which opened fresh horizons of decoration.[3] The movement which their style initiated can best be appreciated by comparing a panel by Bérain with one of the same kind by Gillot (fig. 351). The subjects are parallel: there is similar use of medallions, of terms, of trellis and of vine, even the perspective of the panels is in a sense alike; but Gillot's design is wholly reinformed by an admixture of a new element of picturesque naturalism.[4] His figures, his architecture, his leafage, are not things drawn but things seen; there is not merely light falling upon them, but there is air round them. With Watteau (fig. 346) there is more: the lines of composition run not only along the planes facing the spectator but also along the lines of airy space that recede into the background.[5] He studied his trees in the gardens of the Luxembourg and his perspectives in the avenues of Montmorency. He applied to his Elysian vistas the principle that Hogarth enunciated in his *Analysis of Beauty*: 'Observe that a gradual lessening is a kind of varying that gives beauty. The pyramid diminishing from its basis to its point, and the scroll or voluta, gradually lessening to its centre, are beautiful forms. So also objects that only seem to do so, though in fact they do not, have equal beauty; thus perspective views . . . are

[1] The earliest dated 'Bérinade' was published in 1663. He had several imitators, notably Jean le Moyne, who published his arabesques in 1710.

[2] Mariette notes that he excelled in stage design.

[3] Watteau, a Fleming from Hainault, came to Paris in 1702, at the age of eighteen, to work on the New Opera house. He tried and failed to get a Prix de Rome in 1709, but so rapidly did the vogue for his style grow that three years later he was elected to the Academy without opposition as *peintre des fêtes galantes*.

[4] His *Livre de portières* and *Nouveau livre de principes d'ornemens* were engraved by Huquier.

[5] Watteau's tradition was carried on not only in France by Lancret and his followers, but also in Venice, where Amiconi (1676–1758) composed designs of the four seasons, the four elements, and the four quarters of the globe in his manner. But the peculiar grace of his style was too personal to survive him long, though its influence made itself felt for thirty years after his death; the panels in his style by Oudry are curiously flatter and duller than their prototypes.

Fig. 351. Design for tapestry by Gillot, *c.* 1715.

Gillot inv. et sculp.

FIG. 351. Design for tapestry by Gillot, *c.* 1715.

always pleasing to the eye.' Watteau felt the universal need of his time to unite poetry and gaiety, romance and humanity, observation and illusion, and combined in his art all the guises of beauty that Père André could distinguish—'un beau de génie, un beau de goût, et un beau de pur caprice'.

Decoration rested on a basis at once wider and more personal. The opening of the *Salon* in 1737 set the seal on the gradual decline of the artistic power of the monarchy, and marked the transference of art patronage from the king to the educated society of Paris. The Court was succeeded by 'la bonne compagnie', and 'l'homme du monde' usurped the position of the courtier. The official glorification of royalty was at an end, and the tastes of ordinary men made themselves felt. The cipher of the individual played as important a part in the decoration of the Régence as did the cipher of the king under the Grand Monarque. The financier-collectors brought antiquity down to the level of the private cabinet, and noble ladies, without being *femmes savantes*, ruled over the arts and sciences. Women, indeed, set the keynote of Parisian society and of its setting.[1]

The best Régence decoration has 'the illogical but impeccable concatenation' that La Bruyère ascribes to feminine writing. Woman had come into her kingdom, and remade the visible world as she would have it be. It is women's heads that appear as the central ornaments of the panels of Régence decoration, and that adorn the keystones of Régence architecture. Even the Sphinx is represented with the head of a lady of the Court. It is feminine taste that gives to the Régence style an impression of graceful yet rapid movement, as if its scrolls and leaves had in some moment of swift motion seen Medusa. It is feminine preoccupations that are the subjects of Watteau's decorative panels; their very titles—La Folie, Le Théâtre,[2] Le Galant, Colombine et Arlequin, L'Escarpolette (fig. 346), La Coquette, L'Amusement, La Chasseuse, Le Repos gracieux—are the quintessence of the

> Tems fortuné, marqué par la licence,
> Où la Folie, agitant son grelot,
> D'un pied léger parcourt toute la France:
> Où nul mortel ne daigne être dévot,
> Où l'on fait tout . . . excepté pénitence.[3]

Even the commonplaces of Renaissance decoration owed women service, and reappeared as symbols of the arts and diversions cultivated in the boudoirs they adorned. A very light and graceful design of Gillot's for a ceiling shows trophies of the arts treated in a gay arabesque style. The Salon Ovale of the Hotel de

---

[1] Caylus tells us, 'Tous ceux que l'on rencontre sont gaillards, animés, empressés; rien ne languit en eux. Quelle est la cause de cette aimable vivacité? Je n'en trouve point d'autre que celle-ci; c'est que les femmes donnent absolument le ton à tout ce qui se passe dans cette grande ville.' *Mémoire et Reflexions, 1717–40,* p. 25.

[2] Theatrical scenes also appear on the Beauvais tapestries designed by Oudry with subjects from Molière between 1726 and 1736, and on the 'Fragments d'Opéra' series woven at the Gobelins between 1733 and 1741. A design for a rocaille chimney-piece Chippendale published in 1761 has Harlequin and other figures of comedy included in its decoration.   [3] Voltaire, *La Pucelle,* Chant xiii; *Œuvres,* xx. 346.

353. Panel with a trophy of music, from the Salon of Marie
Adelaide, Versailles. Probably by Verbeckt, c. 1750

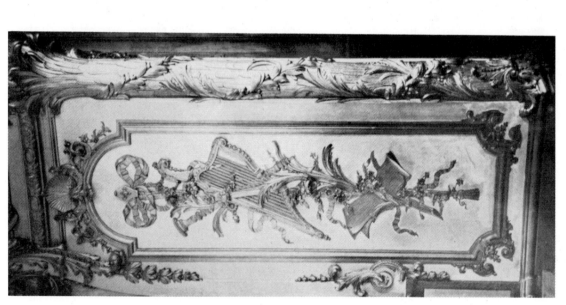

352. Panel with a trophy of music, from the
organ of the Chapel, Versailles. Designed by
R. de Cotte. 1710

354. Panel with a scene from the fable of the Wolf and the Lamb. Cabinet Vert, Hôtel de
Rohan-Soubise (Archives Nationales), Paris, 1738.

Soubise, finished in 1740, has a charming light decoration, completed by groups of the Muses, Tragedy and Comedy, Geography and Astronomy, Painting and Poetry, History and Fame, all women of the world ready to preside over a feminine *salon* which should comment the works of Fontenelle and Voltaire.[1] The variety of women's pastimes was equalled by the variety of trophies that adorned their walls.[2] Metra describes Madame de Genlis' room, 'On the right an easel, on the left a violoncello; here flutes and bows hung in a sheaf; there drawings and maps in touching disorder; in one corner dresses, in another globes and telescopes'. Trophies of a most elegant and graceful classicism were designed that include all these symbols of feminine pursuits, and these were reproduced on panelling, in Aubusson tapestry and in Lyons brocade. Trophies of music adorn the panels of the cabinet of the musical Madame Adelaïde at Versailles (fig. 353), and the library of Louis XV is likewise decorated with trophies—one of music, lyric, pastoral, and dance, and another of declamation, comedy, burlesque, satire, and epic.[3] Even in minor decorations amusements provided the theme, and 'plats à musique' with scores and instruments and others decorated with packs of cards came into fashion.

The ladies of the court shared in the chase, the real and official pleasure of the Monarchy; and this too was celebrated in the great series of the *Chasses de Louis XIV* designed by Oudry in 1733 and woven at the Gobelins. But except for the decoration of hunting-chaises and the like, such subjects and such trophies were not treated with any realism, and ordinarily their bows and arrows, quivers and baldrics can hardly be distinguished from the attributes of Cupid.[4]

Women's liking for pet animals brought these too into the scheme of decoration. The Cartesian view of them as automata had driven them from the *genres nobles*, but La Fontaine re-created them as living creatures, and the beginning of the study of animal behaviour by de Réamur (1734–42) led to Julien de la Mettrie's theory[5] that there is no difference in kind but only in degree of organization between man and animals. La Fontaine's Fables soon appeared in every kind of decoration:

[1] The *Salon* of 1761 included designs for the manufactory of Beauvais of *Les Génies de Poésie, Histoire, Physique et Astronomie*, by J. J. Bachelier. Havard and Vachon, *op. cit.*, p. 215.

[2] J. F. Blondel in 1737, describing the antechamber of an ideal county house, says 'Les dessus des portes y sont ornés aussi de tableaux, et c'est dans leurs sujets que l'on doit exprimer les inclinations ou les emplois du maître.' *De la distribution des maisons de Plaisance*, i. 69.

[3] The seventeenth-century trophy tradition in Grinling Gibbons's technique was perpetuated in England up to about 1725, as in Leoni's saloon at Lyme Hall. About 1730 the saloon at Downton Hall, Salop, was decorated with plaster trophies in the French manner (Jourdain, *English Decorative Plasterwork of the Renaissance*, fig. 146). The eighteenth-century French tradition commonly appeared in rather a clumsy form, in English work of the middle of the century, as on the staircase of Powderham Castle (1755) and at Hagley Hall, Worcestershire (c. 1765). Both these instances appear to be derived from French engraved pattern-books.

[4] It was only in England that fox-hunting squires demanded masks and brushes, stirrups, bits, and hunting horns to decorate their chimney-pieces. *Some Designs of Mr. Inigo Jones and William Kent*, 1744, shows such a chimney-piece designed by Kent for the Prince of Wales.

[5] *L'homme Machine*, 1748.

woodwork (fig. 354), painting, china,[1] tapestry (between 1736 and 1750), embroidery, and even marble.[2]

Feminine influence, moreover, modified the scale and style of classicism. A new standard of fitness was applied to architecture, and Blondel had to adapt classicism to the needs of a generation that thought a columned front suited to a palace but not to a private residence. Even more fundamental was the change in decoration; from being raised to the level of architecture and sculpture it was deliberately brought down to the level of upholstery and goldsmith's work. A certain smallness and frivolity invaded every sphere of decorative art,[3] and some designers were willing to use the pelmets and lambrequins and tassels of the upholsterer even in architectural decoration.[4]

Le Blond's edition of d'Aviler's *Cours d'architecture*, published in 1710, shows how the colouring affected in decoration was equally chosen with a view to gaiety and lightness. The rich colours of the seventeenth century no longer formed an ideal background: 'White is at the moment the colour most commonly used for painting panelling. The lines and ornaments are picked out in gold to show them up from the background. . . . They thus affect to give great lightness and variety to the whole panelling.'[5] Such classicism as survived was greatly modified; Vanloo's and Boucher's Apollo and Aurora, all in 'camaïeu bleu et rose' in the Salle du Conseil at Fontainebleau, are very different beings from the divinities of Lebrun. Strict classicism, indeed, had no admirers left even among the *femmes savantes*. Madame Geoffrin's circle was divided for and against the antique, but its supporters were only 'pour l'antique, jusqu'à un certain point', and 'contre l'archéologie en art, tout à fait'.[6] Classical art had to submit to *parfilage* at

[1] e.g. on Chelsea china, *c.* 1750–3.

[2] The fashion quickly spread to England, and the Countess of Hertford, writing to Lady Luxborough in June 1749, says of a proposed alteration to Northampton House in the Strand: 'The chimney piece in the dressing room is to be of statuary marble and *giallo*; and just in the front of it the fable of the stork inviting the Fox to dinner, very neatly executed.' Lenygon, *Decoration in England, 1660–1779*, p. 91. Curiously the scenes from the fables on the woodwork of the Hotel Soubise were based on English engravings published by Francis Barlow in 1668. (See F. Kimball and E. Donnell, 'Les Boiseries du Cabinet Vert de l'Hotel de Soubise' in *Gazette des Beaux-Arts*, 5th series, vol. xvii, 1928, p. 185.) The same engravings served as models for plaster medallions at Kirtlington Park about 1750 (Jourdain, *English Decorative Plasterwork of the Renaissance*, figs. 142 and 143) and were used by Chippendale and Johnson as the basis of some of their designs.

[3] See, e.g., the *Nouveaux desseins* of Masson. The influence of such engraved ornament is evident in such work as the interior of Schloss Schleissheim, *c.* 1715.

[4] e.g. Paul Decker, who published his architectural plates before 1713. The earliest dateable lambrequin decoration on Rouen pottery occurs on a barber's bowl in the Rouen Museum dated 1699; similar patterns occur about the same time on the Delft ware of Lambertus van Genhorn (Hannover, *Pottery and Porcelain*, ed. Rackham, i. 244). Similar decoration was used by Charles François and Paul Hannong on Strasbourg pottery, *c.* 1730–45.

[5] The decorations in 'blanc et or' and in 'blanc des carmes' were in fact executed in a warm pearl or stone grey, to which the absence of true white in their surroundings gave the effect of a paler tint. In 1782 Wailly painted the Théâtre Français (Odéon) in true white, and 'les femmes se plaignent que l'éclat du blanc qui règne généralement dans la salle affadit les traits et les éclipse tout à fait'. Bachaumont, *Mémoires secrets*, t. xx, p. 210.

[6] Rocheblave, *Goût en France*, p. 188.

355. Decoration of the Salle des Bourbons, Hôtel de Rohan-Soubise (Archives Nationales), Paris, *c.* 1740

356. Console in carved and gilt wood. French, *c.* 1730. Versailles

357. Console in carved and gilt wood. French, *c.* 1740. Versailles

women's hands: a little heap of glittering tinsel was all that was left of its splendid fabric.

> Our age was cultivated thus at length
> But what we gained in skill we lost in strength;
> Our builders were with want of genius curst,
> The second temple was not like the first.

2

Symmetry had seemed an essential part of beauty in the seventeenth century, but with the decline of magnificence and the rise of individualism its rule was felt to be too severe. A new appreciation of dancing rhythm, picturesque variety, and structural lightness had to find expression in an art less static than that of the great age of Versailles. Hogarth's *Analysis of Beauty* expresses the current view:[1]

'If the uniformity of figures, parts or lines were truly the chief cause of beauty, the more exactly uniform their appearances were kept, the more pleasure the eye would receive, but this is ... far from being the case. ... The eye is rejoiced to see the object turned and shifting, so as to vary these uniform appearances. ... Simplicity, without variety, is wholly insipid, and at best does only not displease; but when variety is joined to it, then it pleases, because it enhances the pleasure of variety, by giving the eye the power of enjoying it with ease.'

Anti-classical though such an appreciation of variety might be, it found expression in a form that itself owed something to antiquity. It was not, however, from the serious and devoted study of the details of classical remains that it drew its inspiration, but from the romantic vision of classical ruins as a whole.

Such ruins had had a definite influence upon the style of Italian garden architecture. Where a mass of crumbling brick and stone did not exist to add the romance of antiquity to the scene, some more formal grotto had been created, combining art and nature in its symmetry of plan and its roughness of material. For water gardens such *grotte* were commonly adorned with shells;[2] Alberti in 1452 had recorded 'I was extremely pleased with an artificial grotto which I have seen ... with a clear spring of water falling from it; the walls were composed of various sorts of sea shells, lying roughly together, some reversed, some with their mouths outwards, their colours being so artfully blended as to form a very beautiful variety.'[3] Such deliberate attempts to create the picturesque could hardly fail to relax the austerity of classical canons.

Other influences were at work to raise the rocaille style on to another level. In constricted town sites, especially in Venice, the grotto became more and more a part of the architectural whole. In the middle of the seventeenth century Count

[1] Pages 56, 59, 68.
[2] Shells had been curiously little used in medieval decoration. Cybo of Hyères decorated a page of manuscript with them about 1390 (British Museum, MS. B 369).
[3] *De re aedificatoria*, trans. Leoni, p. 192.

Giacomo Cavazza's Venetian palace is described as having a double flight of stairs opening off a saloon on the ground floor to form 'an open space converted into a grotto, with incrustations on its walls formed of pebbles and sea-shells of every kind and colour, which are in themselves a delight to the eye, and enchant one by the skill with which they are arranged and for the various figures, even human, which they compose'.[1] Italy, too, was developing her own baroque style into a picturesque freedom; and unconsciously the two influences combined to create a style more picturesque than classical, more *rocaille* than Roman, in which strict symmetry of detail was explicitly rejected. The canons of Chinese ornament had become as familiar to the eye as those of Rome,[2] and an idea of asymmetrical beauty was becoming familiar to the intellect. As early as 1685 Sir William Temple [3] was willing to believe that:

'there may be other forms wholly irregular, that may, for ought I know, have more beauty than any of the others; but they must owe it to some extraordinary dispositions of nature . . ., or some great race of fancy or judgement in the contrivance, which may produce many disagreeing parts into some figure, which shall yet, upon the whole, be very agreeable. Something of this I have seen in some places, but heard more of it from others, who have lived much among the Chinese; a people whose way of thinking seems to be as wide of ours in Europe as their country does. . . . Their greatest reach of imagination is employed in contriving figures, where the beauty shall be great, and strike the eye, but without any order or disposition of parts, that shall be commonly or easily observed. And though we have hardly any notion of this sort of beauty, yet they have a particular word to express it, and where they find it hit their eye at first sight, they say the Sharawadgi is fine or is admirable, or any such expression of esteem. And whoever observes the work upon the best Indian gowns, or the painting upon their best screens or purcellans, will find their beauty is all of this kind, without order.'

The European tradition of symmetry was to some extent influenced by such doctrines and examples. Designs were no longer to be definitely architectural in inspiration, or necessarily symmetrical along any median line. Interior decoration lost its architectonic qualities, its columns and cornices, and became a veil of ornament that flowed over the surface of the room as a dress flows over the body of a woman. Elaborate compositions of C and S curves took the place of the frieze, metope, and pediment shapes with which classical architecture had endowed ornament. The rich mouldings that framed the work of the late seventeenth century disappeared, and anomalous growths of forms neither of rock, nor seaweed, nor water, nor vegetable growth, yet partaking in some degree of all these natures, took the place of olive and acanthus. Nothing that could be gracefully curved was left straight, neither outline, nor surface, nor relief;[4] often nothing that with any

---

[1] Molmenti, *Venice, the Decadence*, ii. 6.

[2] It is indeed difficult to say whether it is Chinese or baroque influence that inspires the asymmetry of some late seventeenth-century Venetian silks.

[3] *The Gardens of Epicurus*. Addison borrows from him in the *Spectator* of 25 June, 1712.

[4] Hogarth, in his *Analysis of Beauty*, describes a curling motion as 'always pleasing . . . I never can forget my frequent strong attention to it, when I was very young, and that its beguiling movement gave me the

appearance of elegance could be balanced into irregularity was left symmetrical. Even mirrors were no longer arranged to increase the symmetry of a room, but rather to lessen its architectural mass and to give an illusion of lightness to the walls. The new style first appeared in Sardi's organ-loft of the Maddalena at Rome, begun soon after 1680; it was soon used on a smaller scale by the Genoese woodcarvers. Gradually it invaded baroque architecture; in the Palazzo Doria and the Palazzo del Grillo, for example, it is as if classicism were being seen askew through *rocaille* spectacles. In the first quarter of the eighteenth century the style became general in Italy; Lecce, the perfect example of a rocaille town, for the most part dates from before Serpotta's death in 1732. In decoration rocaille was freely used in plaster for the decoration of small rooms, in carved wood for furniture, and in bronze for grilles[1] and railings; but, since it was a style essentially of perspective, and indeed of exaggerated perspective, its most successful ensembles were in the work of such artists as Tiepolo, who succeeded in giving it an air of artistic probability that lesser men failed to do.

Such creations as garden grottoes were an Italian invention, and have a strangely artificial air outside Italy, where there is no mass of classic ruins to explain their origin; but the travels of northern artists in Italy[2] and the strong Italian influence on stage-settings helped to make them familiar in other countries.[3] They came to be recognized as a characteristic element in an Italianate garden, and Italian *rocailleurs* travelled to France and Germany to make them. Such a grotto was one of Louis XIV's first creations at Versailles.[4] Already the style was beginning to be naturalized; Italian workmen made it, but Lepautre designed[5] a 'Pilier orné de coquillages et de rocailles avec un bassin de marbre en forme de Coquille.' The façade of the Palace on the side of the grotto was brought into relation with it by having the keystones of the window arches of the lowest story decorated with

same kind of sensation then, which I since have had in seeing a country dance. . . . This single example might be sufficient to explain what I mean by the beauty of a composed *intricacy of form*, and how it may be said, with propriety, to lead the eye a *kind of chace*.'

[1] A fine example is the grille in the Scuola di San Rocco at Venice.

[2] The inventories of Henry VIII include 'a goblett of golde wt. a cover chased rockey' and two golden salts 'rockey fasshion.' Palgrave, *Kalendars and Inventories*, ii. 285, 288, 289. The sides of the triumphal arch set up for the entry of Charles IX into Paris in 1572 (engraved by Olivier Codoré) were all of rockwork. Before 1538 Albrecht Altdorfer designed a covered cup decorated almost entirely with ribbed shells in relief. Victoria and Albert Museum, EO 2, E 627, 1911. Rocks and shells appear in the fantasies of Cornelis Floris about 155 (Victoria and Albert Museum, Dept. of Engraved Ornament, EO 18, 2170, 5a, 7, 8, 27699, 2) and occasionally reappear in such freak designs as the goblet designed by Daniel Boutemie for M. Hesselin in 1636 (Victoria and Albert Museum, EO 8, E 2401, 1913). More restrained work of the same type was published by Johann Schmischek in 1630 (Victoria and Albert Museum, EO 39, E 2397-9, 1913), and but for the details of costume might be dated much later.

[3] As early as 1651 the scenery of Corneille's *Andromaque* shows the influence of Italian grottoes in its design. Lulli entered the royal service in 1653, and in the next year an Italian opera was produced in Paris under the patronage of Mazarin—Carlo Caproli's *Le Nozze di Peleo e Teti*—with a regular grotto background.

[4] Destroyed towards the end of the reign of Louis XIV.

[5] Engraved in 1673. He also published in 1661 'Fontaines ou jets d'eau à l'Italienne' and in 1667 'Grottes et fontaines', besides four undated series.

'testes ornées de coquillages, de corail, et de rocailles'.[1] Thus rocaille forms
gradually crept into pure ornament in France; the acceptance of its elements may
have been assisted by the fashion for collecting shells and other marine rarities.[2]
Certain Louis XIV decoration already shows in the architectural framing to its
cascades and fountain figures

> La beauté des contours observés avec soin,
> Point durement traités, amples, tirés de loin,
> Inégaux, ondoyants, et tenant de la flamme
> Afin de conserver plus d'action et d'âme . . .
> Faisant briller partout de la diversité
> Et ne tombant jamais dans un air répété.[3]

Oppenordt, the greatest of the rocailleurs, the son of a Dutch cabinet maker, came
from Rome to Paris in 1698. As a scholar of the École Française he had measured
the column of Trajan, but by virtue of his youth and his foreign birth, he had been
equally attracted by the broken lines of Italian baroque and the grottoes of Italian
gardens. During the domination of Watteau France had found her need of
variety and intricacy satisfied by the crossing planes of rhythm which he translated from the landscapes of Poussin into the lighter and more fanciful scenes of
decorative art, and rocaille was hardly needed.[4] When Watteau went to England
in 1719, two years before his death, the French vogue for rocaille decoration
began: and the great 'soleil' of Rheims, made by Thomas Germain in 1722, is
definitely rocaille in style. Oppenordt's work was seconded by that of J. A.
Meissonier, born and bred at Turin, of whom Cochin said, 'Il sçavoit assez
d'architecture ancienne pour ne pas contrecarrer directement ceux qui y tenoient
avec trop d'obstination; mais il la déguisoit avec tant d'adresse qu'il avoit le
mérite de l'invention, et qu'on ne la reconnoissoit qu'à peine.'[5]

By 1743 the Duc de Luynes records that the new decorations of the Chambre de
le Reine at Versailles 'sont tout de travers, suivant le goût nouveau'.[6]

French rocaille usually gains direct inspiration from garden grottoes, and though
far removed from solid fact keeps rocks, water, and garden architecture as its
theme (fig. 358). Another *genre* shows children, animals, and flowers among the
tortuous curves—half rock, half tree—of its design.[7] Such designs, however, are

---

[1] Félibien, *Description de Versailles*, p. 298.

[2] La Bruyère includes the 'connoisseur de coquilles' among his collectors. *Caractères*, de la Mode, 1687–96.
The fashion was at its height in the early eighteenth century, and rose and fell with the cognate style of
decoration. Sevins's collection was sold in 1749 for 4,500 livres. Courajod, *Livre journal de Lazare Duvaux*,
xlix. P. Mazell in 1755 published designs with swags of shells and flowers.

[3] Molière, *La Gloire de Val-de-Grâce*.

[4] Watteau, however, uses the batswing of rocaille in the frame to his *Printemps*.

[5] *Mercure*, Dec. 1754. Meissonnier's drawings and the engravings after them, for plate, carriages, rooms,
and even tombs in the rocaille manner (now in the Cabinet des Estampes of the Bibliothèque Nationale) are
dated from 1723 to 1735. For French rocaille see R. Sedlmaier, *Grundlagen der Rokoko-Ornamentik in Frankreich*,
Strassburg, 1917.   [6] *Mémoires*, v. 13.

[7] A typical subject is Mondon's *Les Heures du Jour*, published about 1738. Other designs of the sort are by

LA FONTAINE.

Paris chez Huquier fils rue St Jacques au grand St Remy

J. de la Joüe *in*

Huquier *sculp*

FIG. 358. Design by J. de la Joue, engraved by Huquier fils, c. 1745.

very slight in their structure, and are intended for painting rather than for relief.

In France, indeed, pure rocaille always remained a style for decoration on a small scale. As de Brosses wrote, 'Le goût gothique (by which he designated rocaille) étant petit, délicat, détaillé, peut convenir aux petits objets, jamais au grands.'

Before it could be admitted into the fabric of French architecture rocaille had to be chastened by the discipline of classic regularity. French rocaille decoration on a large scale is *not* asymmetrical; the purist may deny its claim to be called rocaille at all, though every formal element of strict rocaille is employed in its design. Its planning is light, varied, and gay; its shells, its broken curves with their fringed serrations, 'ondoyants, et tenant de la flamme', its batswing scrolls, are all rocaille; but in all its most studied manifestations it respects the rule of median symmetry.[1] Even so it was felt to present difficulties to those who lived with it; the Duchess de Valentinois tried to get a harmonious effect by furnishing her *cabinet de rocaille* only with 'piles de carreaux de drap d'or et de vases de porcelaine remplis de fleurs',[2] and Blondel[3] and Cochin raised their voices in protest against the style.[4] Cochin writes:

'Goldsmiths, chasers, carvers in wood for panelling and others, are humbly entreated by men of good taste to be so kind as henceforward to hold themselves in subjection to certain laws dictated by reason. The goldsmiths are begged, when they make an artichoke or a celery stem of natural size on the lid of a sauceboat,[5] to be so kind as not to set beside it a hare as big as a finger . . . not to change the purpose of things, and to remember that a candlestick had better be straight and perpendicular to carry the candle. . . . At least let us hope to obtain the concession that when things can be square, they will not twist and torture them; that when the pediments can be arched they will not break them up with those S curves that they seem to have learned from the writing masters. If they do this, a man of good taste who comes in for a house of this sort can chip off all this vegetation, batswings, and other horrors with a chisel, and find beneath a bare moulding which will be decoration enough for him. We allow them, however, to serve this twisted stuff to all Provincials and strangers, who may be bad enough judges to prefer our modern taste to that of the last century. The more these inventions are disseminated abroad, the more may one hope to preserve some superiority of taste for France.'

Cochin represented the view of the 'homme du monde', and the procedure which he advocates became the fact of history. Not only was rocaille designed in France chiefly by men of foreign birth like Meissonier, Oppenordt, and Slodtz, and executed by foreigners like Caffieri, but the Frenchmen who practised the style all

Boucher and de la Joue (engraved by Huquier), Hubert and G. de Marteau (1743). The same style is represented in Italy by G. Guercino, who published *c.* 1750 rocaille designs framing pastoral subjects.

[1] Even this modified form is associated with the name of a foreigner, Verberckt, though designs for it were also published by Nicholas Pineau and others.   [2] Mme. de Villedieu, *Journal amoureux*, x. 31.

[3] *Distribution des maisons de plaisance*, ii, 1738, p. 67. 'Les attributs les plus respectables paraissent confondus avec des ornements qui ne doivent leur naissance qu'à une imagination bizarre, et l'on trouve partout un amas ridicule de coquilles, de dragons, de roseaux, de palmiers et de plantes qui font à présent tout le prix de la décoration intérieure.'

[4] *Mercure Galant*, Dec. 1754.   [5] This is a hit against Oppenordt's *Livre de légumes*.

emigrated. It is significant that the best French rocaille *ensembles* are near the eastern frontier, at Nancy, and that they were built for the Polish Stanislas Leczinski.[1]

Even in England, where the *London Magazine* in 1738 tells us that 'the ridiculous imitation of the French has now become the epidemical distemper of the King-dom', the style remained for some time in the hands of foreigners. The earliest pattern-book was that published in 1736 by an Italian, Gaetano Brunetti: sixty plates of designs 'very useful to painters, sculptors, stone carvers, wood carvers and silversmiths' with the usual mixture of shells, flowers and crooked scrolls and cartouches. This was followed two years later by a set of plates for jewellery by the German Flach, and in 1743/4 by the comparatively symmetrical chimney-pieces of Abraham Swan.[2] Rocaille in England was nearly always modified by Chinese influence;[3] Thomas Johnson, in his pattern-book of 1758, definitely mixed *chinoiseries* with his wild and slender rocaille; and Matthew Lock diversified one of the fanciful but not inelegant table-designs he published in 1746 with an English dog hunting a Chinese dragon through a wilderness of French rocaille.

Only where Jesuitism had planted baroque architecture in an alien soil—in Portugal, Germany, and Poland—did the rocaille style have an unfettered vogue. There it succeeded baroque as naturally as the lighter French style succeeded that of Versailles. In these countries actual buildings were erected in the style. In Germany, introduced by Italians and Frenchmen, it took deep root and flourished. One of the most surprising of its earlier manifestations is the Klosterkirche at Ottobeuren, designed by the Italian Amiconi in 1738; another is that of the Church of St. Peter at Mainz, decorated by Appiani of Milan between 1748 and 1756. The wall decoration, in false perspective, is definitely asymmetrical; and even the capitals follow suit. Moreover, there is no attempt at congruity of subject; the piers are decorated with little rocaille *imagini* of the seasons, with autumn personified as an infant Bacchus seated on a wine barrel. Such Italian designers as Amiconi and Appiani[4] were succeeded by Frenchmen like the two François Cuvilliès (1698–1768

[1] Even there rocaille ornament is reserved for the delicate grilles that add the piquancy of contrast to the calm and classic symmetry of the whole. For a study of the rocaille ironwork at Nancy see Ch. Cournault, *Jean Lamour*.

[2] Delacour published rocaille designs in London in 1741; H. Copland in 1746; P. Glazier in 1754; T. Johnson in 1753, 1758, and 1761; and A. Heckell, J. Collins, and J. Linnell undated pattern-books. The fashion for collecting shells reached England later, and is often alluded to in the memoirs of Mrs. Delany and other leisured ladies of the time. To make a grotto was a fairly common occupation; a surviving example in the east pavilion at Mereworth Castle, later than 1736 and earlier than 1752, has realistic flowers and birds, classical egg-and-tongue mouldings, and Chinese touches, all executed in shells. The fashion is reflected in some English china, for instance in Plymouth salt-cellars of 1768–70. A small room in the Royal Castle at Rheinsberg shows a German version of shell decoration, the shells being arranged as very light trails of flowers. It would seem to date from about 1760.

[3] An exception is a kind of *rustic* rocaille like the goat-and-bee milk jugs first made in silver and then copied in china at Chelsea in 1745.

[4] Another Italian worker in the style was Leopoldo Retti, who did the decorations at Schloss Ansbach. See O. Lessing, *Schloss Ansbach*, Leipzig.

FIG. 359. Fantastic design by François de Cuvilliès père, c. 1750.

360. Moulded plaster entablature, taken from the frieze of the Temple of Antoninus and Faustina at Rome, *c.* 1745. Holkham Hall

361. Carved wood over-door, Dining Room of the Petit Trianon, Versailles, 1768

362. Design for a mantelpiece. By Piranesi, 1769

and 1734–1805), who found in Germany a welcome for their rocaille patterns (fig. 359) that they had outworn at home.[1] In 1754, the year of the fall of the style from favour in France, the rocaille palace of Sans Souci was begun, and every German princeling rich enough to indulge such fancies built, if not a palace, at least a pavilion in the style.[2]

Rocaille was to be found, as Thomas Hope wrote in his *Historical Essay on Architecture*, 'in the temple and in the tomb, in the exterior and interior of houses, in vehicles and vessels, in floors, walls and ceilings, in the stationary parts and in loose furniture, in the altar and the sideboard, in the chair, table, chimney-piece, chandelier, sconce, and picture frame'. An enormous number of German rocaille pattern-books were produced,[3] for the most part in the middle years of the century. These show as great a variety of subject as the most provincial pattern-books of the Renaissance; and indeed they draw their themes from the same repertory.[4]

Just as the splendid classicism of Louis XIV could not endure for ever, so the graceful frivolity of his successor's court palled in time. Its very frivolity was a cause of change; as Grimm wrote in 1763,[5] 'Bizarrerie in decoration, in ornament, in design and in form . . . had reached its climax in France; they had to be changed every moment, since a thing which is not reasonable can only please by its novelty.' So Society demanded that its music should fall into fresh cadences, its plays find other endings, and its pictures make a new appeal. Decoration followed in their wake, and the style of Louis XV was modulated into forms of ornament that better fitted the changing tastes of society.

[1] The elder went to Bavaria soon after 1721. It is remarkable how far more graceful and reasonable is his work for the French than for the German market. Indeed the intensity of rocaille is a matter of its distance from France, and that of the Rhineland is for the most part moderate. French influence is evident, for instance, in the Festsaal at Bruchsal, finished between 1743 and 1754: the architectural members are regular, and asymmetry is confined to light garlands of flowers.

[2] See C. Gurlitt, *Geschichte des Barockstiles und des Rococo in Deutschland*, Stuttgart, 1889, and *Das Barock und Rococo Ornament in Deutschlands*, Berlin, 1885.

[3] 1721, J. E. Heiglen, Augsburg; *c.* 1725, Johann Jacob Baumgartner, Augsburg; 1728, Bergmuller; 1730, Craaz, Augsburg; G. S. Rosch; 1736, J. C. Junck, Augsburg; *c.* 1750, J. M. Feichtmayer; J. C. Schmidhammer, Nuremberg; J. J. Preisler, Nuremberg; J. G. Thelot, Augsburg; J. W. Baumgartner, Augsburg; Q. Loh; Christian Freidrich Rudolph, Augsburg; Caspar Gottlieb Eister; Johann Baur, Augsburg; C. Klauber, Augsburg; J. G. Hertel, Augsburg; E. X. Habermann, Augsburg, &c.

[4] J. H. Haid of Augsburg and Vienna (1710–76) published rocaille patterns with the emperors of the four monarchies of the ancient world, Death, Eternity, the four Humours, Aeneas, Androcles, 'Tumultus, Servitium, Amor Patriae, Providentia, Sapientia, Veritas, Clementia, Mathematica, Philosophia, Solon, Perisander, Cleobulus, Thales, Vita Humana'. The subjects are those of Etienne de Laune: the style is rocaille and the dates run from 1740 to 1776. Nor was Haid alone in his work: G. B. Göz of Augsburg (1708–70) published patterns of rocaille scrolls with the figures of Theophrastus, Paracelsus, the Disasters of War, Lucretia, Fortuna, Croesus, Christian Martyrs, Humilitas, Eleemosyna, Avaritia, Amor Proximi and the Virgin and Child. Such subjects eventually palled, and J. J. Nilson of Augsburg (1721–88) tried to give new life to rocaille in its declining years by designing in that style scenes from Gessner's Idylls—*La Cruche cassée*, *La Fable de l'Instrument à cordes et du Chant des Oiseaux*, *Damon and Philis*, and, in fact, a complete iconography of the Return to Nature.

[5] *Correspondence littéraire*, iii. 224.

IX

THE RETURN TO ANTIQUITY

I

THE Renaissance had in it a romantic element, for it was a return to the remote past, and its clarities were veiled at first in the mystery of distance. But with increasing knowledge the Latin countries lost this romantic sense, and had instead a feeling of their nearness to Rome: time was forgotten and they entered into a delayed inheritance and made it their own. The eighteenth century was for England what the sixteenth had been for Italy and the seventeenth for France: as a distant province of the Empire, she too entered upon her inheritance. Moreover in virtue of her remoteness and of the relative slightness of her link with ancient Rome, she brought back to classicism the sense of Romance and revivified it for the rest of Europe.

The exile of the English King and Court for twenty years of the seventeenth century had lessened the wonted insularity of England; Bishop Burnet, in 1685, begins his *Letters from Italy* with the apology: 'It may look like a presumptuous affectation to be reckoned among voyagers, if [one] attempts to say anything upon so short a Ramble, and concerning places so much visited, and by consequence so well known,' and Lassels, publishing his *Voyage of Italy* in the following year, has five journeys to Italy, as bear-leader to young Englishmen, to his credit, and regards the stay-at-home as 'a meer *Onocephalus*, and a homeling *Mammacuth*.'[1] Thomas Coke was sent on his travels at fifteen, and spent six years in acquiring classical tastes abroad; Horace Walpole set out in 1739, at the age of twenty-two. In the next year Lady Pomfret was of opinion that the Grand Tour was 'carried a great deal too far among the English'. The fashion, however, continued to grow: the *Letters concerning the Present State of England* (1772) state; 'Where one Englishman travelled in the reign of the first two Georges, ten now go on the Grand Tour. Indeed, to such a pitch is the spirit of travelling come in the Kingdom that there is scarce a citizen of large fortune but takes a flying view of France, Italy and Germany in a summer's excursion.'[2] Between 1763 and 1765 no less than forty thousand English passed through Calais.[3]

[1] Travelling, he assures us, 'preserves my young nobleman from surfeiting of his Parents, and weans him from the dangerous fondness of his Mother. . . . I would therefore have my young nobleman's *governour* to carry him immediately into *Italy* at fifteen or sixteen, and their [*sic*] season his mind with the gravity, and wise maximes of that Nation, which hath civilized the whole World and taught Man Man-hood. Having spent two or three years in *Italy* in learning the *Language*, viewing the several *Courts*, studying their *Maximes*, imitating *their Gentile Conversation*, and following the sweet Exercises of *Musick*, *Painting*, *Architecture*, and *Mathematicks*, he will at his return, know what true use to make of *France*.'

[2] Quoted Lenygon, *Decoration in England, 1660–1770*, p. 11.

[3] Jourdain, *English Decoration and Furniture, 1750–1820*, p. 2.

Therefore, with the return to England of men who had spent the formative years of youth in Rome, Classicism was born anew. Walpole could write in 1780,[1]

'Before the glorious close of a reign that carried our arms and victories beyond where Roman eagles ever flew, ardour for the arts had led our travellers to explore whatever beauties of Grecian or Latin taste still subsisted in provinces once subject to Rome; the fine editions in consequence of those researches have established the throne of architecture in Britain, while itself languishes at Rome, wantons in tawdry imitations of the French in other parts of Europe, and struggles in vain at Paris to surmount their prepossession in favour of their own errors.'

England's political troubles had deferred the maturity of her Renaissance, and the beginning of the century did not bring to her, as it did to France, an unconscious reaction against the antique. Men of the world sincerely attempted to see classicism in its greatness as well as in its detail; Chesterfield, for all his French tastes, warned his son against viewing Italy 'knick-knackally'. By 1732 Berkeley was aware that classical architecture, 'the noble offspring of judgement and fancy ... peculiarly conversant about order, proportion and symmetry', was most likely to help his generation to 'some rational notion of the je ne sais quoi in beauty'.[2] England seriously attempted to follow in the footsteps of Rome. Kent, who had rediscovered the beauties of classicism at first hand during a nine-year stay in Rome, when he returned to England in 1720 became the arbiter of English taste.[3]

Naturally such classicism was that of the Renaissance rather than of antiquity: his new Houses of Parliament were strongly influenced by the Pitti Palace; while the smoking-room he designed at Rousham in 1724 and the Presence Chamber at Kensington Palace (probably planned in the following year) show ceilings in the classical manner of the sixteenth-century Roman *grottesche*.[4]

The Englishmen who made their way to Italy a little later in the century not only saw with unwearied eyes the remains that had inspired Joachim du Bellay, but were also faced with fresh revelations of Roman greatness. Herculaneum had been accidentally discovered in 1709, and by 1738 a new development in the history of classical influence was inaugurated by the excavation of the site,[5] followed by the beginnings of excavation at Pompeii in 1755.

---

[1] *Anecdotes of Painting in England*, ed. Dallaway, iv. 207.

[2] Walpole declares that 'his oracle was so much consulted by all who affected taste that nothing was thought complete without his assistance. He was not only consulted for furniture, as frames of pictures, glasses, tables, chairs, &c., but for plate, for a barge, for a cradle.'

[3] Alciphron, *Works*, ed. Sampson, ii. 261.

[4] The early diaries of Robert Adam show him susceptible to the same influence; and he uses a definitely Renaissance scheme with patterned columns, shallow arched recesses and dolphin friezes in the little round room off the Long Gallery at Syon House. A similar Raffaelesque inspiration is evident in Biagio Rebecca's plasterwork in the Cupola Room at Heaton Park, done about 1780. Such work may have been encouraged by Winkelmann's dictum that Raphael, alone of the moderns, had approached the Greek ideal. Hautecœur, *Rome et la Renaissance de l'antiquité*, p. 32.

[5] Fresh excavations were undertaken in 1750 and 1756; the publication of the paintings and objects found

In England a Roman classicism gradually became the accepted language of the cultivated aristocracy. English patricians who often, even in their physical type, approached nearly to the antique Roman mould, found in London and India a life such as Pliny had once led in Rome and Syria, and in their country houses the delights and the responsibilities that he had found at Laurentum. Funeral monuments show that even in face of death Englishmen of the eighteenth century could believe themselves to be Roman. The strength of the illusion lay in the absence of artificiality; there was no masquerade and no pretence. The English, lacking the dramatic sense, could live straightforwardly as Englishmen against a classical background. They did not change their manner of life, but adapted classicism to their own needs. So Chambers wrote in 1759,[1] 'The Tuscan Order, as it conveys ideas of strength and rustic simplicity, is very proper for rural purposes, and may be employed in farmhouses, in barns, and sheds for implements of husbandry, in stables, maneges and dog-kennels, in greenhouses, grottos and fountains, in gates of parks and gardens, and generally wherever magnificence is required and expense to be avoided.' So Sir John Soane and the Bishop of Derry, exploring the villa of Lucullus near Terracina in 1778, decided to plan a classic dog-kennel. Classical magnificence was felt to be congruous with English country life. Coke, the student of turnip culture, by 1745 had erected for himself the most splendid classical palace in England, built of bricks specially baked of the Roman shape and colour, with a great Hall shaped as a Roman basilica, its colonnade of African marbles taken from that of the Temple of Fortuna Virilis at Rome, its entablature copied from the portico of the Temple of Antoninus and Faustina at Rome (fig. 360),[2] its garden portico from that of the Pantheon. Nor was such splendour unusual; even Bubb Doddington had pillars in his house encased in lapis lazuli at four shillings the ounce. Nothing that was classical could be extravagant; and indeed, when we remember that the Attic reserve of Athens, the urbanity of Rome, and the good taste of England are all expressions of ideals which have much in common, the apparent incongruity is resolved and we admit the right of the English dilettanti to live under the colonnades of a classic order.

Meanwhile the classical revival had begun in France.[3] Its first manifestation was

in the *Antichità di Ercolano* began in 1757. Even in baroque Italy (and especially in Venice) there was a certain revival of classicism. Carlo Lodoli (1690–1771) preached a return to Vitruvius and Palladio, and the fruits of his teaching are evident in a new Venetian academic school of architects: Scalfurotto, d. 1764, Lucchesi, d. 1776, Maccarucci, d. 1798, and others.

[1] *Decorative Part of Civil Architecture*, ed. Gwilt, p. 183.

[2] These were both taken from the measured drawings in Desgodetz's *Édifices antiques de Rome*. It is interesting that the ceiling is based on designs of Inigo Jones and Webb, so that the great hall is a *summa* of the middle stage of English classicism.

[3] The foundation of the French provincial academies, which had markedly slackened after 1685, proceeded apace: 1700 Lyon; 1705 Caen; 1706 Montpellier; 1712 Bordeaux; 1720 Pau; 1723 Béziers; 1726 Marseille; 1729 Toulouse; 1730 Montauban; 1732 La Rochelle; 1738 Arras; 1740 Dijon; 1744 Rouen; 1747 Clermont-Ferrand; 1749 Auxerre; 1750 Amiens and Nancy; 1752 Besançon; 1755 Bourg; 1757 Metz; 1758 Lille; 1772 Grenoble; 1775 Mulhouse; 1776 Agen, &c.

a strong archaeological interest in antiquity.[1] As early as 1719 eighteen hundred copies of Bertrand de Montfaucon's *L'Antiquité expliquée* were sold in two months, and Stosch's *Recueil des pierres gravées* of 1724 had also a considerable success. The French Académie des Inscriptions became more and more archaeological in its interests; in every department of scholarship curiosity was focussed on material things, and interest was once more turned from criticism to discovery. Nor was this all. Fénélon had had the historian's idea of resuscitating the past, of showing the life of nations and the progress of civilization; and ancient Rome began to be a living reality to eighteenth-century France with Montesquieu's *Grandeur et Décadence des Romains* of 1734. As he tells us in the Preface to his *Esprit des Lois* 'quand j'ai été appelé à l'antiquité j'ai cherché à en prendre l'esprit', and he succeeded in giving his generation a sense of the lasting vitality of Roman civilization. The ground was being prepared for a fresh sowing of the classic style, that reached its flowering point twenty years later. By 1738 Blondel was pleading for 'simplicity of form, economy of ornament',[2] and by 1747 classical canons were recognized as the basis of French artistic criticism.[3]

If the reaction against the antique of the beginning of the century had been partly due to feminine influence, the return to the antique was in turn assisted by a woman. Madame de Pompadour exerted her influence when at its highest point in favour of a classical style, and sent her brother, afterwards Marquis de Marigny, to study 'true beauty' in Italy from 1748 to 1751, before becoming Director-General of the Royal buildings, gardens, and works of art. He was accompanied by the young architect Soufflot, who was later to bring back strictly classical style into French building, and by the artist Cochin, who was later to do his best to bring back classical regularity into French decoration.[4] Yet they were not solitary pioneers, but men early influenced by a strong general current of feeling for antiquity. The study of the antique, in 1750, 'recommended' in the French Academy, was soon 'commanded';[5] and the Académie de Peinture, which up to 1762 had always given biblical subjects for its prize compositions, between 1762 and 1780 gave twenty-five out of thirty-five of its prizes for subjects drawn from Greek and Roman antiquity.[6] The chief agent in this revolution of taste was the Comte de Caylus, who had travelled in Italy, the Levant,[7] England, and Holland. He found in the newly discovered antiquities of Herculaneum and Pompeii fresh material for establishing his philosophical belief 'à l'éternel recommencement des choses', and compiled from his own collection a corpus of antique models—

[1] It is significant that the classical style of the middle of the century is first presaged in the coin cabinet designed for the King by the brothers Slodtz in 1739, now in the Cabinet des Médailles at Paris.

[2] Quoted Blomfield, *History of French Architecture*, ii. 55.

[3] Michel, *Histoire de l'art*, vii. 542.

[4] Hubert Robert and Fragonard undertook a similar journey in 1756.

[5] Rocheblave, *Goût en France*, p. 180.   [6] Dreyfous, *op. cit.*, p. 150.

[7] He visited Constantinople, Ephesus, and the Troad, but was called home before he had reached Greece itself.

medals, vases, gems, statuettes, and fragments—for modern use. He writes to his friend Paciaudi:[1] 'Je triomphe sur l'étrusque, mon romain est singulièrement étoffé, l'égyptien va un peu,[2] mais le grec respire à peine.' His *Recueil* remains a monument of industry rather than of constructive ability; it is a collection of detached objects, without system or classification beyond an attempt at a chronological arrangement.[3] His influence was upon detail only;[4] and the real importance of his collections lay in his avowed intention of collecting the small objects of everyday life. Thus he not only influenced the Fine Arts as one of the chief 'donneurs d'idées' of his time,[5] but also brought the ideal of the imitation of antiquity into a new sphere. It was to serve not only for the noble art of architecture, but also for the lesser crafts of ordinary life.

Yet, however strictly classical his later work, there can be little doubt that at first the return to antiquity meant for him, as for many Frenchmen of his day, the return to the French classical style of Louis XIV. Blondel, in his *Architecture française* of 1752, states that the study of the buildings of the Grand Siècle 'ne contribue pas moins à perfectionner les Architectes de nos jours, que les ouvrages des Grecs ont servi autrefois à instruire les Architectes d'Italie.'[6] Cochin's attitude to the paintings of Herculaneum was definitely critical; and the world of fashion did not take archaeology too seriously, but found with Walpole that classical antiquities were 'a little dear, but ... most entertaining'.[7] They were not ready for a rigorous classicism, but agreed with M. de Vandières: 'Je ne veux point de la chicorée moderne, je ne veux point de l'austère ancien. Mezzo l'uno, mezzo l'altro.'[8] For some years, indeed, the classical was but one of several parallel styles. This parallelism is reflected in Hogarth's *Analysis of Beauty* of 1753; he bases it upon fitness, variety, uniformity, simplicity, intricacy, and quantity; and though his view of variety and intricacy shows the influence of rocaille decoration,

[1] Rocheblave, *Le Comte de Caylus*, p. 119.

[2] On such early Egyptology see Hautecœur, *Rome et la Renaissance de l'antiquité au XVIIIᵉ siècle*, p. 102.

[3] He explained his procedure thus: 'Les antiquailles m'arrivent, je les étudie, je les fais dessiner à des jeunes gens ... je jette ces gravures dans un coin avec leurs explications et quand il y en a de quoi faire un volume je les donne à quelqu'un de notre académie.' Hautecœur, *Rome et la Renaissance de l'antiquité au XVIIIᵉ siècle* p. 24.

[4] Marmontel, his avowed enemy, waxes indignant over his pretensions: 'il avoit tant dit, tant fait dire par ses prôneurs, qu'en architecture il était le restaurateur du *style simple*, des *formes simples*, du *beau simple*, que les ignorants le croyaient; et, par ses relations avec les dilettanti, il se faisait passer en Italie et dans toute l'Europe pour l'inspirateur des beaux arts.' *Œuvres complètes*, Paris, 1818, i. 359.

[5] Caylus published in 1755 *Nouveaux sujets de peinture et de sculpture* and two years later *Tableaux d'Homère et de Virgile*.

[6] Inspiration was drawn even from earlier sources. The columns of the Salle d'Opera at Versailles (1753–70) show a clear recollection of Philibert de l'Orme's 'Ordre français'. It is a significant fact that the standard edition of Jean le Pautre's work is still the three folio volumes published in 1751 (Chez Ch. A. Jombert, libraire dur Roi, rue Dauphine), and that the most useful engravings of the vases of Versailles and Marly are those published by Marie Michelle Blondel about 1780 (*Profils et ornements de vases ... dans les jardins de Versailles, Trianon et Marly*).

[7] Letter to Lady Ossory, 14 December 1771. Ed. Toynbee, viii. 118.

[8] Letter to Soufflot, 1760. Quoted, Michel, *Histoire de l'art*, vii. 450.

his view of fitness is classical: 'Fitness of the parts to the design for which every individual thing is formed, either by art or nature, is first to be considered, as it is of the greatest consequence to the beauty of the whole. This is so evident, that even the sense of seeing, the great inlet of beauty, is itself so strongly biassed by it, that if the mind, on account of this kind of value in a form, esteem it beautiful, though on all other considerations it be not so, the eye grows insensible to its want of beauty, and even begins to be pleased, especially after it has been a considerable time acquainted with it.' Cochin in the next year expressed the same view in France, asking the craftsmen:

'to give credence to the assurances we give them . . . that straight, square, round and oval regular forms are as rich ornaments as all their inventions. . . . We assure them, in conscience and honour, that all obtuse and acute angles, unless one is absolutely forced to use them, are architecturally bad, and that right angles are the only ones that there create a good effect. . . . It is unnecessary to suppress cornices in order to avoid the difficulty of properly disposing the ornaments suitable to them. They will find that they need not substitute grasses and other paltry prettinesses for the modillions, dentils and other virile ornaments used hitherto.'[1]

The admirers of classicism were beginning to show impatience with rival styles; Briseux, in 1752, found that while diversity of feeling was an advantage to the progress of the arts and sciences, yet its excess became dangerous. He called men back to the study of proportion in architecture on the ground of its analogy with music; the scientific study of the laws of sound once more induced men to find beauty in ratio.[2]

By his time the study of the minor objects of antiquity had begun to introduce their subjects into decoration. The first appearance of such ornament in the goods sold by Lazare Duvaux dates from November 1750.[3] In 1754 cameo decoration came into fashion for Sèvres,[4] and five years later Wedgwood started his factory, finding inspiration for his designs in Sir William Hamilton's collections of antique gems and Etruscan vases. Classical interest, indeed, was no longer focussed on the great monuments of architecture, but rather on the lesser relics of antiquity.[5] Other collectors hastened to supplement Caylus's repertory of such things,[6] and consequently design was dominated by antique form—urns,

[1] *Mercure Galant*, December 1754. Cochin was in fact preaching to the converted; Gilles Marie Oppenordt's later work before his death in 1743 is perfectly reasonable classic of a light and graceful kind.

[2] *Traité du Beau Essentiel dans les Arts*, 1752, pp. 1 et seqq. Blondel, in his *Architecture française* of 1752, uses the same analogy.

[3] *Op. cit.* ii. 67: Madame de Pompadour. 'Un feu représentant Apollon et la Sibylle . . . un feu représentant l'amour.'

[4] Cf. *op. cit.* ii. 210 et seq. Hautecœur, *Rome et la Renaissance de l'antiquité*, p. 215. The Meissen price-list of 1766 mentions various things 'à la Grecque' and with Etruscan borders.

[5] Designs *en camaïeu* were introduced for toile de Jouy in 1769.

[6] e.g. for engraved gems in the *Recueils* of Mariette (1750), Winckelmann (1760), Lachau and Leblond (1780) &c.; and for wall-paintings in the works on Pompeii and Herculaneum of Caylus (1750), Cochin and Bellicaud (1757), Richard (1770), and best of all in Caylus and Mariette's publication (1757–83) of Bartoli's *Recueil de peintures antiques* (1789). Ponce, *Les Arabesques des Bains de Livie*, &c.

sarcophagi, vases, lamps—and architecture by antique bas-relief, and by Pompeian painting. Piranesi, in his *Diverse maniere d'adornare i camini* published at Rome in 1769, though he apologized for using antique designs intended for urns and vases for other purposes, and tried to find some classical justification for his practice, was yet willing to reproduce Greek vases and Roman plate in marble (fig. 362), and to borrow Egyptian motives from Caylus's collection. He published designs for sculptured chimney-pieces ornamented with classical rhytons, kyathoi, and sistra, and for clocks shaped as Roman cippi and lamps, and statues of the Ephesian Diana; he even included a mummy mustard-pot. Excavations at Herculaneum not only brought to light such types for the craftsmen to copy as the exquisite bronze vases of the Villa dei Papiri,[1] but also set other models than those of temple-architecture before the classical designer. Walpole writes,[2] 'at least the discoveries at Herculaneum testify that a light and fantastic architecture of a very Indian air made a common decoration of private apartments'. Light classical rinceaux and mouldings were used to produce effects as airy as those of the other styles of the Régence[3] and women could have classical *boudoirs* without fear of being depressed by their austerity.

2

Such qualified classicism suffered a great change between the years 1760 and 1766. Three fresh impulses added new life to it and transformed the whole. First, Piranesi in his *Della Magnificenza ed Architettura de' Romani* of 1761 gave new force to the sense of structural power that lies in the enormous mass of such Roman buildings as those of the Palatine and of the Baths of Caracalla.[4] He endued them with that terrifying greatness that haunts his *Carcere d'Invenzione*; and the peasants that he drew camping in the weeds under their shadow served to point the contrast between their purpose and their destiny, and to make the link between past and present that constitutes romance.

By 1770 his work[5] had spread the heroic scale through Europe; Doric virtues were in fashion, and the Encyclopedists were busy reconciling megalomania with sensibility. Whenever architectural mass is admired for its own sake the decoration of minor objects becomes architectural, in order that they may share in the reflected glory of magnitude. The *Comptes du Roi* of the middle of the century

---

[1] Published by the Accademia Ercolanese in 1757. Rather similar objects are represented on a puce ground on some Aubusson tapestry settee and chair seats of about 1790 in the Victoria and Albert Museum.

[2] *Anecdotes of Painting in England*, ed. Dallaway and Wornum, iii. 58.

[3] The style is represented in England by Matthew Darly's *New Book of Ceilings* of 1760.

[4] His earliest work, *Antichità Romane de' Tempe della Republica e dei primi Imperatori*, dates from 1743. His work was seconded by that of a French imitator, Le Geay, who published *Tombeaux* and *Rovine* at Rome in 1768.

[5] The direct influence of his pattern-books seems to have been less strong than the indirect influence of his more picturesque engravings. On the influence of the temples of Paestum and Sicily see Hautecœur, *Rome et la Renaissance de l'antiquité au XVIIIᵉ siècle*, p. 138.

363. Printed cotton. By R. Jones, Old Ford, 1761

364. Detail of Etruscan Rome at Osterley Park. By Robert Adam. Designed in 1775

quickly show this tendency. Among the snuff-boxes made for the King in 1758 is one by Herbault, 'de forme carrée, à motifs d'architecture en or de couleur', and the same influence may be seen in contemporary engraved designs. Piranesi himself published in 1769 designs for chimney-pieces with motives borrowed from Roman sarcophagi, friezes from the Temple of Antoninus and Faustina, trophies from the base of Trajan's Column, details from the triumphal arches, and reliefs from the *stucchi* of Roman tombs. Chintzes were adorned with classical façades; candlesticks were shaped as columns of a classic order; inkstands were formed of the members of a classic building; even embroidery had its dentils and its vitruvian scrolls.

Moreover, Piranesi succeeded in turning the natural defects of time-worn antiquity into beauty, and by richness of detail and truth of form gave a reality to his ruin pictures that had been lacking from the earlier compositions of Panini (1692–1765) and his school. It was under his influence that Hubert Robert, who had met him in Rome during his stay there between 1754 and 1764, some twenty years later exhibited a painting of the Grande Galerie of the Louvre as it would appear in ruins, and that Robert Adam in 1761 sketched a design for a great Roman ruin to be erected at Kedleston.[1] Diderot, in his criticism of the salon of 1767, explains their charm: 'Les idées que les ruines réveillent en nous sont grandes; tout s'anéantit, tout périt, tout passe. . . . Oh! les belles, les sublimes ruines! . . . L'effet de ces compositions, bonnes ou mauvaises, c'est de vous laisser dans une douce mélancolie.'[2]

The tradition of the decorative use of such scenes, that had begun with the engravings of Ducerceau as early as 1576,[3] was revived and strengthened by Piranesi's work. In 1745 Cuvilliès published his 'Morceaux de Caprices propres à diverses usages', including cartouches framing views of classical ruins; and a few years later Babel, Le Prince, and Le Geay were publishing similar ruin scenes for decorative use. They appeared alike on French and English chintzes (fig. 363),[4] pottery and china,[5] and on a more important scale in wall decoration.[6] The picturesque

---

[1] The sketch is in the C. J. Richard collection in the Victoria and Albert Museum. On the English taste for 'ruins' in Gothic style see p. 162.

[2] In 1768 the Académie offered a prize for a poem on 'Les Ruines.' See also E. M. Mainwaring, *Italian Landscape in eighteenth-century England*, 1925; R. Haferkorn, *Gotik und Ruine in der Englischen Dichtung des Achtzehnten Jahrhunderts*, Leipzig, 1925. Ruins, of course, had early been used as a background to such scenes as the Adoration of the Magi.

[3] A comparatively rare instance of their decorative use in the seventeenth century is afforded by some Nevers pottery in the Musée de Cluny.

[4] On toile de Jouy designed by Huet and on such English imitations as one in the Victoria and Albert Museum, made by R. Jones of Old Ford in 1761.

[5] e.g. on the pottery of Tournai and on transfer printed Worcester china of about 1765 and its numerous derivatives.

[6] e.g. in 1761 the French artist Delacour painted large pictures of Roman ruins for the panels of the saloon of Yester House, Midlothian. Paolo Anesi painted ruins on the walls of the Villa Albani, Vivani and the Priola painted a little room in the Palazzo Rosso at Genoa as a temple of Diana with a ruined stone roof, and

decay of ancient monuments was admired on any scale; and about 1770 engraved title-pages, frontispieces, and trophies for ornament showed the cracks and fractures of ancient bas-reliefs.

The second influence that modified classicism, and to some extent negatived the picturesque influence of Piranesi,[1] was that of Winckelmann. He sent men back to Roman originals and to the Roman copies that were accepted as Greek; he enriched the criticism of classical art by establishing the conception of its growth and attempting to define the phases of its beauty; and thus by setting it once more in its true place in its sphere of history, he gave back to it in the sphere of intellect the Romance that Piranesi had rediscovered in the sphere of sight.

But his influence had another and less happy side. For the first time in the history of aesthetics, a philosopher based his theory of art not on modern work, but on antique creations that had hardly begun to be a part of the art of his own day and that had been almost unknown to the generations just before his own. Consequently the philosopher's theory had not lately found expression in art, but instead exerted a real influence over the work of the generations that immediately succeeded him. Beauty, Winckelmann maintained, is always heightened by simplicity and by an absence of individuality. Beauty should be like the purest water, drawn from a spring: the less definite taste it has, the more healthful it is, because free from foreign admixture.[2] In classic ornament he found that the ruling principle was simplicity, whereas modern decoration was complicated and inharmonious, and far removed from the 'majestic gravity' of the ancients.[3]

His history of art, which was almost contemporary in publication with Lessing's *Laocoon* (1763) and the first volume of the *Monumenti Inediti*, was translated into French in 1766, and its influence is apparent in Diderot's criticism of the Salon of 1767.[4] Its effect upon art was intensified by the third impulse towards the revivification of Classicism: the rediscovery of Greece.[5] This to some extent resulted from the work of the learned antiquaries; the Académie des Inscriptions and the Society of Dilettanti[6] took a keen interest in chance discoveries in Greece and in Ionia, and the traveller who braved fever, brigands, and Turkish administration in those lands was sure at least of an audience on his return. As early as 1751–2 Richard Dalton published a series of drawings of Greece made there two years before. By 1753 the ex-Jesuit Laugier was praising Greek architecture at the

Adam's friend Clerisseau painted for Father Le Sueur a 'hermitage' room designed as a ruined temple. Hautecœur, *Rome et la Renaissance de l'antiquité au XVIIIᵉ siècle*, p. 6.

[1] Piranesi, it must be remembered, stood definitely for richness against austerity and for Rome against Greece.

[2] *Histoire de l'art*, bk. iv, chap. ii, § 20.

[3] *Ibid.*, French trans. An. II de la République, ii. 651.

[4] The Works of Winckelmann and Caylus are the sources of the article on Greek Art in the *Grande Encyclopédie*.

[5] On the relations between England and Greece see Michaelis, *Ancient Marbles*, p. 113.

[6] Founded in London in 1733.

expense of Roman,[1] though six years later Sir William Chambers was unfavourably comparing the Parthenon with St. Martin's-in-the-Fields.[2]

The chief agents in bringing the designers of France and England into closer touch with Hellenic Art were the Englishmen James Stuart and Nicholas Revett, who started for Greece in 1751 and spent two years in Athens measuring and drawing. They returned in 1754, but spent eight years in preparing the *Antiquities of Athens*, so that it was preceded by the *Ruines des plus beaux monuments de la Grèce*, published in 1758[3] by the ex-Jesuit Leroy, who had only reached Athens in 1755. Stuart and Revett's measured architectural drawings made the Parthenon and the Erectheum as accessible to imitation as the monuments of Rome, and their influence was seconded by such publications as Paciaudi's *Monumenta Peloponnesiaca* (1761) and Soufflot's *Ruines de Paestum* (1764).[4]

A new canon was established to strengthen and to purify the classical art of modern times. Greek influence was felt in every branch of art, from literature[5] and official and domestic[6] architecture and decoration[7] down to snuff-boxes. Among these last, indeed, it appeared almost earliest; the *Comptes Royaux* include three snuff-boxes 'garnie à la Grecque' in 1762, another in 1763, and two more in 1764. By this year Greek tastes had become general; Grimm tells us,[8] 'Depuis quelques années on a recherché les ornements et les formes antiques; le goût y a gagné considérablement, et la mode en est devenue si générale que tout se fait aujourd'hui à la Grecque. La décoration intérieure et extérieure des bâtiments, les meubles, les étoffes, les bijoux de toute espèce, tout est, à Paris, à la Grecque. Le goût a passé de l'architecture dans les boutiques des marchandes de modes ...'[9]

[1] *Essai sur l'architecture*, p. 3. 'L'architecture doit ce qu'elle a de plus parfait aux Grecs, nation priviligiée, à qui il était réservé de ne rien ignorer dans les sciences et de tout inventer dans les arts. Les Romains, dignes d'admirer, capables de copier les modèles excellents que la Grèce leur fournissait, voulurent y ajouter du leur et ne firent qu'apprendre à tout l'univers que, quand le degré de perfection est atteint, il n'y a plus qu'à imiter ou a déchoir.' The London *Investigator* of 1755 started an argument whether Rome owed her monuments to Etruscan or Greek models, the *Investigator* avowing that the Romans had been a barbarous people before the conquest of Greece. See A. Samuel, *Piranesi*, p. 8.

[2] *Decorative Part of Civil Architecture*, ed. Gwilt, p. 117.

[3] Second edition, 1770.

[4] The French usually gave the credit of this Hellenic Renaissance to England: e.g. Prince de Ligne, *Belœil*, p. 278. Panini's engravings entitled 'Ruins of Attica' and 'Ruins of the Peloponnese' are entirely conventional, and reproduce the pyramid of Cestius and the temple of Castor at Rome.

[5] Grou translated Plato's *Republic* in 1763, Moutonnet Clairfons the *Pastoral Poets* in 1773, and Le Brun the *Iliad* in 1776.

[6] Tapestries of heroic scenes from the *Iliad* were begun at Beauvais in 1761. Badin, *La Manufacture de Tapisseries à Beauvais*, p. 35.

[7] As early as 1756 Joseph Le Lorrain decorated a 'cabinet à la Grecque' for La Live de Jully. Michel, *Histoire de l'art*, vii. 542.

[8] *Correspondance littéraire* (1 May 1764), iii. 244. Paris, 1829.

[9] Cf. the *Comédie de l'amateur* of the same year (quoted Havard, *Les Styles*, p. 151).

          ... Heureusement pour nous
     La mode est pour le Grec; nos meubles, nos bijoux,
     Étoffe, coiffure, équipage,
     Tout est grec ...

Walpole writes from Paris in April 1764,[1] 'Everything must be à la Grecque, accordingly the lace on their waistcoats is copied from a frieze.' By 1771 the style had reached a point when parody was possible, and in that year Pettitot published a series of half-human vases: La Vivandière, le Grenadier, la Bergère, la Mariée, l'Epoux, and le Jeune Moine, all *à la Grecque*. Greece, indeed, had usurped the place of Rome in men's imaginations. Empire, power and law were no longer their preoccupations, and the 'philosophes' felt nearer to Academe than to the Capitol.

Yet too little of purely Greek decoration was known to make it the single basis of a style of ornament. Men were only beginning to study Greek vase painting, and that in the late Etruscan vases collected by Sir William Hamilton and his friends from the tombs of Magna Graecia.[2] This inspired the colour of Robert Adam's Etruscan manner—chocolate, terra cotta, yellow, black, and blue—first used about 1775;[3] but Adam's sphinxes and tripods owe little to the vase painter.[4] Greek architectural style, however, had a greater influence, though this influence was exerted rather in the sphere of theory than in that of decorative detail. It, and the principles it represented, served to bind together the scattered and accidental elements of classical decoration into a coherent whole; its proportions and its elegance served to chasten even Roman elements into an art as 'pure' and impersonal as the doctrines of Winckelmann.

Robert Adam, who had gained his experience in France in 1754 and in Italy in the following year,[5] and had then studied the palace of Diocletian at Spalato,[6] at first practised a classic style diverse in inspiration and rather rich in ornament. In the hall and anteroom at Syon House, for instance, the influence of Spalato itself is evident; while in the gallery, of which the decoration was begun in 1762, the curved fluting of the lower panels is taken from Roman sarcophagi, and the rich decoration of the upper panels shows definite French influence. He owed something to Caylus in his thesis 'that the domestic Architecture of the Greeks and Romans was entirely distinct from that of their temples'; but in establishing an anti-Palladian style for the expression of this view he became the high priest of 'Grecian' decoration. As early as 1763 its refinements appear in his designs for the Great Room at Bowood. Though his patterns are based on archaising Roman work such as the delicate stuccoes of the *Tombe Latine* the influence that made him

---

[1] *Letters*, ed. Toynbee, vi. 47.

[2] His first collection was acquired for the English nation in 1772. The factory at Naples was producing 'Etruscan' services from 1786 onwards.

[3] In Lord Derby's house in Grosvenor Square and at Osterley Park.

[4] This is equally true of Pergolesi's 'Etruscan' decoration in England, 1776–7.

[5] He was a friend of Piranesi, who set his name upon the plan of the Campus Martius engraved in 1757.

[6] He published his *Ruins of the Palace of the Emperor Diocletian* in 1764. It had a good deal of influence as Spalato was the first *private* building to be published in detail and so, without incongruity, could serve as a model for private buildings on a lesser scale. Clérisseau, his companion, decorated the coffee-room of the Villa Albani with views of the ruins of Spalato.

turn to them rather than to the more robust and more truly Roman style is the influence of Greece itself. In 1761 he was using Roman armour in the decorations of Syon House, but by 1774 he was designing 'Grecian trophies' for Kedleston.

Greek elements enjoyed the factitious importance of association that the Five Orders had enjoyed in the early Renaissance; the anthemion and mouldings of the Erechtheum were enough to stamp anything they ornamented as Greek. In the rest of the work the artist had to avoid sins of commission, even if sins of omission took their place. By 1780 a calculated lightness inspired every branch of ornament:[1] a regular arrangement of medallions, linked by geometrical members lightened with anthemion or *rinceau* decoration or emphasized by plain, tongued, reed, guilloche, or Vitruvian scroll mouldings, was the basis of ornament in every art. Nothing was irregular; nothing was marked; nothing was personal. Really personal work was in fact absent: the development of industry and the gradual rise of mass production meant that frieze and moulding, medallion and ornament, were each year more mechanically produced. Casting and impressing began to take the place of sculpture and chiselling; ornament began to be 'applied' rather than to form a part of the whole. The same medallion, itself copied from an antique gem, would serve in painting for the ceiling, in plaster for the panel, in jasper ware for the mantelpiece, in silver for the tea urn, in porcelain for the tea set, in lacquer for the tray, in inlay for the commodes, in bronze for the candelabra, in brocade for the curtains, in each instance used as the central medallion of a large surface very lightly decorated with classical ornament. Even the carpet reflected the design of the ceiling.[2] Symmetry, from being an expression of luxury, became an economy, not only of craftsmanship but also of thought. Decoration was static and not dynamic; the designers agreed with Burke, 'A bird on the wing is not so beautiful as when it is perched'.

The seventeenth-century instinct, that made the inhabitants in some sense actors in the symmetrical design of the room, was dead; human scale and human proportion were ignored. An Adam room looks best empty, for its inhabitants have always the air of interlopers.

Hardly ever has a style been more consistent or more universal in its application; but for the first time the art that was beginning to be industrialized was claimed as the prerogative of wealth and education. Even Reynolds stated that, 'having . . . frequently revolved this subject in my mind, I am now clearly of opinion that a relish for the higher excellencies of art is an acquired taste, which no man ever possessed without long cultivation and great labour and attention;' and

---

[1] e.g. in Leverton's decorations of the saloon at Woodhall Park, with very slight arabesques, only covering (and that lightly) about a quarter of a plain wall. 'Grecian' influence is the more evident since they rise from red-figured Greek vases.

[2] e.g. in the Music Room at Harewood, designed by Robert Adam in 1765.

Wedgwood, in his Introduction to his Trade Catalogue of 1777,[1] writes: 'Beautiful forms and compositions are not made by chance, and they never were made, nor can be made in any kind at a small expense.'

The 'pure' taste created a liking for simplicity of surface; ornament was an extraneous thing, applied in order to heighten the effect of such simplicity. Mouldings were flattened; fluting was made as shallow as possible; plaster decoration was repeated and uniform; painting was confined to pilasters and medallions; and the relief of the whole was reduced to a cameo-like scale.[2] Rhythm of surface was driven out of ornament to find expression in form. The brothers Adam wrote 'The rising and falling, advancing and receding, with the convexity and concavity, serve to produce an agreeable and diversified contour . . . and create a variety of light and shade which gives great spirit, beauty and effect to the composition.'[3]

Such an impoverishment of the tradition of classical decoration could not be endured without a protest from those who knew it in other forms than that of Robert Adam's work. Horace Walpole calls Adam's later manner 'filagraine and fan painting' in 1775 and 'gingerbread and sippets of embroidery' ten years later; Sir William Chambers went so far as to say that painted ceilings might be said not to be in use in England, 'for one cannot suffer to go by so high a name the trifling, gaudy ceilings now in fashion, which, composed as they are of little rounds, squares, hexagons and ovals, excite no other idea than that of a dessert upon the plates of which are dished out bad copies of indifferent antiques'.[4] English design, indeed, was almost completely dominated by classical work in relief, without the counterbalance of a pictorial tradition. Reynolds is typically English when he states:[5] 'All the inventions and thoughts of the Antients, whether conveyed to us in statues, bas-reliefs, intaglios, cameos or coins, are to be sought after and carefully studied; the genius that hovers over these venerable relicks, may be called the father of modern art.'

Though classical designs that were fuller and rounder in style than Adam's were published in London by Placido Columbani,[6] Matthew Darley,[7] Isaac Taylor,[8]

---

[1] Quoted, Hulme, *Birth and Development of Ornament*, p. 231.

[2] James Adam, visiting the so-called temple of Serapis at Pozzuoli in 1761, had admired the stucco on one of the vaults 'very flat but very elegant in a sort of hexagonal compartments, which has a pretty effect'.

[3] The bow-fronted and serpentine chests which Adam introduced are to be found (greatly exaggerated) in the pattern-book published by Emanuel Eichel of Augsburg, *c.* 1770.

[4] Quoted, Lenygon, *Decoration in England, 1660–70*, p. 16. Chambers was born in Sweden and his work shows strong French influence.

[5] 'Discourse to the Academy, 1774': *Works*, 1819, i. 172.

[6] *Vases and Tripods on Twelve Plates*, 1770; *A New Book of Ornaments containing a Variety of Elegant Designs for Modern Pannels*, 1775; *Capitals Freezes and Corniches*, 1776.

[7] *Sixty Vases by English, French and Italian Masters*, 1776–70; *A New Book of Ornaments in the Present (antique) Taste as now used by all Professions*, 1772.

[8] 1775, *Plaster Work*.

Samuel Alken,[1] Pergolesi,[2] Richardson,[3] Pass,[4] and Dulouchamp,[5] Adam's remains the strongest influence, and it is his style that has the most imitators.[6]

3

France was less archaeological than England; while the Royal Academy was listening to Reynold's Discourses, the Académie des Inscriptions was offering a prize for a dissertation on the attributes of Venus.[7] Moreover, French artists were not content merely to reproduce antiquity with elegance. David, starting as a young man for Rome, declared: 'L'antique ne me séduira pas, l'antique manque d'action, il ne remue pas',[8] and even after his return he had his own methods of making antiquity palatable. First he copied his model carefully: 'Voilà ce que j'appelais alors l'antique tout cru. Quand j'avais copié ainsi . . . avec grand soin et à grand peine, rentré chez moi . . . *je l'assaisonnais à la sauce moderne.*' His process is the converse of that of the seventeenth-century artist, who strove to produce modern work 'assaisonné des grâces antiques'; but it remains typically French.

Strict classicism was practically confined to architecture; Soufflot and Gabriel were as classical as Adam, but they knew how to use straight lines without austerity, and unlike Adam they did not decorate their interiors as academically as their façades.[9] Occasionally the metope-forms filled with swags with falling ends that are characteristic of Louis XVI architecture appear in decoration,[10] but it generally followed a much freer style. At the Petit Trianon, for instance, the decorations planned in 1768 are far less classical than is the exterior; the thought that it was a country house, destined to be little more than a pavilion in an exquisite garden, induced Guibert to seek in the garden, rather than in Rome, the models of his rose garlands, his lilies, his laurels, and his asters. Even Cochin, who

[1] 1779–80, Acanthus and other foliage, and friezes.   [2] 1787, 1791, and 1792.
[3] *Capitals of Columns and Friezes measured from the Antique*, 1793.   [4] Designs for ceilings, 1797.
[5] Dulouchamp succeeded Pergolesi and published classical designs in 1801.
[6] *A New Book of Ornaments designed by T. Laws, Carver*, 1773; patterns by W. Darling, 1775; designs for chimney-pieces by the sculptor R. Westmacott, 1777; *Vases in the manner of the Antique*, by P. Begbie, 1779; patterns by W. and J. Pain, 1786; Fanlights by Joseph Bottomley, 1793; George Richardson's *Collection of Ceilings*, 1793; J. Carter's *Ceilings*, &c. Denmark tended to follow the English style; Liselund, for instance, shows marked Adam influence, probably derived from his *Works in Architecture* of 1773, and the Englishman Cameron introduced the same style into Russia.
[7] In 1776: Bertrand, *La fin du classicisme*, p. 5. There were only four French subscribers to Adam's *Ruins of the Palace of the Emperor Diocletian*, 1764; and Charles Louis Clérisseau, his companion on the journey, is the only artist among them.
[8] Dreyfous, *L'Art au temps révolutionnaire*, p. 152.
[9] Cf. J. F. Blondel, *Architecture française*, 1752, i. 117. 'Nous ajouterons ici que pour réussir dans la décoration intérieure, les meilleurs préceptes, sans la partie du goût, seront insuffisants, de même que dans l'ordonnance des dehors, le goût sans principes ne produit souvent que des parties désunis.' Watelet considers it a pity that architects should be 'les arbitres de la décoration' and would give a larger share of influence to painters and sculptors. *Dictionnaire des arts de peinture*, 1792, i. 561.
[10] Engraved designs in Gabriel's style were published by Caillouët and G. M. Fontanière; and his influence is clear in the work of Delafosse. Adam used panels with swags of this type on his façade of the Register House of Scotland about 1775.

as Secretary to the Academy provided a list of subjects for the pictures to adorn its walls, found Homer 'trop sérieux' and chose instead the flower myths of the Metamorphoses.[1]

In France, moreover, the earlier assimilation of classical style and the tradition of pictorial dominance in decoration prevented an undue plastic influence. Antique wall-paintings were the chief source of ornament, and the French style progressed in the direction, not of Grecian, but of Pompeian elegance. Forms were fuller and richer than in England; and even in their severest work, the French decorators, trained in the school of rocaille, could make the four-square lines imposed by architectural convention graceful and even sinuous in effect. The so-called Pompeian style, too, had been naturalized in France nearly two centuries before Pompeii was discovered. Its ponderation, its sweet curves, its hanging trophies, its female terminals, all appear as early as 1560 in the arabesques of Ducerceau and of Marc Duval.[2] Thus it was natural that when Pompeii and Herculaneum yielded up their treasures of painting, the French decorators should at once accept them as models.[3] Already in 1757 Caylus had published his *Recueil de peintures antiques,*[4] and the style was only waiting for the artists to bring it to life again. Some of the earliest designs of the sort, almost excessively light and elegant in character, date from 1770 and are by the Italians Carloni and Brenna; but before his death in that year Boucher was already producing arabesques of the same kind. Watelet describes the style as the painters of his day understood it:[5] 'Les arabesques[6] . . . peuvent offrir des assemblages qui plaisent, ou faire naître des idées riantes. . . . (Ils) présentent donc le plus souvent des objets agréables et partiellement vrais, mais dont la réunion et l'agencement sont chimériques.' They are to painting what dreams are to life; their perspective and their background are arbitrary, and the only link between their subjects is often the most delicate of flowering branches.

'Does the painter of arabesques wish to depart from Nature in order to enrich and give character to his compositions? He has but to recall to his memory the ingenious metamorphoses hymned by the Poets. He reproduces their Sirens, their Sphinxes, their Dryads, and Fauns, Genii, and those winged children who fly caressing or wounding mortals at will. These accomplished artists further people their compositions with real or chimerical animals. They recall the strange cults which have been held in their honour, as well as those of the divinities so often celebrated in all the arts; by the statues of Diana, Venus, Flora or Hebe, they hang garlands, wreaths, musical instruments and trophies; they raise altars and tripods

[1] De Nolhac, *Le Trianon de Marie Antoinette*, p. 63.

[2] Victoria and Albert Museum, EO 15. 25292.

[3] It is interesting to compare its English version—for instance the decoration of the Etruscan room at Osterley Park—with some of the work of Prieur.

[4] It was issued in thirty copies, each of which cost 1,500 livres. George III's copy is now in the British Museum.

[5] *Dictionnaire des arts de peinture*, 1792, vol. i, pp. 90 et seqq.

[6] After the seventeenth century the term 'arabesque' takes the place of the older 'grotesque'.

365. Ball Room ceiling at 20, Portman Square, London. The paintings by Angelica Kauffmann, the plaster work in the style of Robert Adam, *c.* 1780.

366. Panel of carved wood. Perhaps by Rousseau, *c.* 1775

bearing censers whence the smoke of incense arises. Vases of the most graceful form are crowned with chaplets of flowers; leafy branches frame bas-reliefs, cameos, pictures that recall the votive offerings dedicated in temples; symbolic ornaments adorn and characterize grave deities, or those that preside over human pleasures.'

Exactly such arabesques were designed by Prieur,[1] Leriche, Cauvet,[2] Michel and Tibesar; less graceful movements are characteristic of Dugourc[3] and Queverdo,[4] but the essentials of their style are the same. Two important sets of arabesques from Roman sources were engraved,[5] but the French style remained individual and unmistakable. Its artists were familiar enough with this tradition to take liberties with it; a series of panels in the style of Van Spaendonck[6] are designed in the Pompeian manner, but with flowers arranged not in urns or amphorae, but in graceful vases of French china. They might use medallions of classical subjects, volutes and urns, amphorae and fillets, but they also included natural flowers and a natural ease of style, and the personal touch of the artists marks their work alike in design and execution. The art was not industrialized; plasterwork was not turned out by the yard, and painting was not confined to isolated medallions which alone, of all the decorations, had to be painted by an artist.[7] Watelet even condemned the substitution of cameo-painting for painting in natural colours as 'une sorte de luxe parcimonieux'.[8]

The only elements of weakness lay in the divorce of decoration and construction, which reduced architectural motives to the rank of minor detail, and the lack of a real idea to express which reduced attributes and symbols to the level of mere ornament.[9] Nothing but outward grace was modified if one element of the design was changed for another; and indeed the artist's first sketch often shows several motives that could indifferently be applied to his scheme. Yet artistic elegance alone has undoubted charm, and classical decoration has rarely been produced in which gaiety and force, sobriety and liveliness have been so gracefully expressed as they are in the Grand Salon of Marie Antoinette's Petits Appartements at Versailles[10] (fig. 368).

[1] Prieur was primarily a painter, but some of his designs were engraved: *Recueil de sujets arabesques, Cahiers de sujets arabesques*, and *Suites de frises et ornements* (1783).

[2] His *Recueil d'ornemens*, 1777, definitely shows two manners, both classic, but one sculptural and the other Pompeian in inspiration.

[3] *Arabesques*, 1782. A French writer claims Dugourc as the originator of the Pompeian style in France; see P. Lafond, *L'Art décoratif et le mobilier sous la République et l'Empire*, p. 10.   [4] *Cayer de Panneaux*, 1788.

[5] Lavallée Poussin, *Nouvelle collection d'arabesques propres à la décoration des appartements . . . dessinés à Rome*, and another by C. Lasinio, 1789. Watelet recommends fragments from the Baths of Titus, engraved by M. Ponce, as admirable models.   [6] Now in the Pierpont Morgan Collection.

[7] It is exceptional, and characteristic of the decline of the style, that Reveillon in 1785 published wallpapers with panels designed by Prieur.   [8] *Op. cit.*, i. 292.

[9] A somewhat similar tendency is to be found in the Fine Arts; M. de Marigny used to order pictures and statues of which the price, the size, and the subject were fixed, though their destination was left to chance. Delécluze, *L. David*, p. 117.

[10] A curious contrast is afforded by the use of the same elements in the drawing-room ceiling of Brocket Hall, Herts., by James Paine. He uses candelabra radiating from the centre of the ceiling, with sphinxes and tripods between, but the whole scheme is clumsy and lacking in significance.

The decline of the monarchy prevented the full development of the style, for, as the glories of the French Court diminished, English influence crept in.[1] In 1786 the Treaty of Commerce between France and England permitted the import of English goods at moderate duties, and Heppelwhite, in the preface to his *Cabinet Maker's Guide* of 1788, definitely assumes that the English style has been accepted abroad.[2] The Château de Bagatelle, built in the year of the treaty,[3] already begins to show a certain English frigidity of treatment[4] (fig. 370), as do Vaudoyer's decorations of the Princesse de Salm's music-room. Three years after their erection the emigration of the French nobility began, and only twelve months later the phrase 'Ancien Régime' was in use.[5]

It was natural, therefore, that the English classical style which was just coming into fashion and had not yet been identified with the monarchy should be accepted by the Revolutionaries. All the elements of the Revolutionary and Empire styles—chimaeras, griffins, eagles,[6] sirens, trophies, masks, lamps, fasces, tripods, lozenge-shaped medallions and heavy acroteria—were derived through England from Piranesi; Adam's trophies at Syon House are the direct precursors of the Empire trophies at Versailles.[7] The French democracy, like the English aristocracy before them, learned to use the models of antiquity as their own. The main lines of the design are broken; the ornament no longer fits the panel so well; but the detail is more classical than ever. Half the symbols of the Revolution are Roman: the Phrygian bonnet was that worn at Rome by enfranchised slaves; the fasces of the law,[8] the pike of armed force, the oak of civic virtue, and the poplar

[1] See Madame de Genlis, *Dictionnaire des étiquettes de la cour et de la société au XVIIIᵉ siècle*, Paris, 1818, i. 37. A better understanding of England had been fostered by the Abbé Prévost's more sympathetic interpretation of her peculiarities, and this led to a wave of *Anglomanie*. Such influence was intensified by the dominance of English taste in the academic life of Rome. It is significant that in 1782 the Academy at Paris say of the design for a theatre sent in by a student at Rome 'le style de la décoration et surtout de l'intérieur est infiniment trop sévère'. Hautecœur, *Rome et la renaissance de l'antiquité au XVIIIᵉ siècle*, p. 136.

[2] 'The English taste and workmanship', he writes, 'have of late years been much sought for by surrounding nations, and the mutability of all things, but more especially of fashion, has rendered the labours of our predecessors in this line of little use; nay, at this day they can only tend to mislead those foreigners who seek knowledge of English taste in the various articles of household furniture.'

[3] From the designs of Bélanger. G. Mourey gives its date as 1779; Molinier dates it to 1777.

[4] Molinier calls its style 'une abominable simplicité'. *Le mobilier au XVIIᵉ et au XVIIIᵉ siècle*, p. 192. A more archaeological influence is apparent; in 1790, for instance, Dugourc designed a settee for the Comte de Provence with its back painted with figures of satyrs copied from Greek vase paintings (H. Lefuel, *Georges Jacob*, Plate XXI). The influence of France on England in classical decoration made itself felt at the same time. Walpole describes the ornament of Carlton House, 'delicate and new with more freedom and variety than Greek ornaments; and though probably borrowed from the Hôtel de Condé, and other new palaces . . . rather classic than French'. Letter to Lady Ossory, 17 September 1785 (ed. Toynbee, xiii. 320).

[5] It first appeared in the *Projet d'utilité et d'embellissement pour Paris* of 1789.

[6] After 1794 the French craftsmen made some use of Albertolli's drawings and designs of eagles.

[7] The affiliation is evident between such English decoration as the saloon ceiling at Brocket Hall, finished soon after 1779, and the Directoire style; and between such silver work as a candelabrum and candlesticks of 1791–2, belonging to Lord Yarborough, and the later and heavier Empire style (Jackson, *English Plate*, ii. 875).

[8] These appear as the badge of Cardinal Mazarin on his books and on carved doors of the middle of the seventeenth century, in the Palais de l'Institut.

367. Panel of gesso on wood. French, *c.* 1775

368. Detail of the Grand Salon of the Petits Appartements of Marie Antoinette,
Versailles. Carved by the brothers Rousseau, 1783

of the majesty of the people are all antique.[1] The only modern symbols are masonic: the level and the equilateral triangle that appeared in 1789 to mark the equality of the three orders, the compass, the table of the law, and the eye that, in 1791, appeared as the symbol of the Constitution. The Revolution was effected as gradually yet as swiftly in art as in politics.[2]

With the flight to Varennes in 1791, revolutionary decoration began. Royal portraits disappeared from Sèvres porcelain, and instead there are tricolour decorations 'à la nation'. Cruder symbolism than this was accepted even at Sèvres, and cups and saucers were produced with the levels, balances, bonnets, and eyes of masonic symbolism, while the china painters put their decorations into mourning for Mirabeau. In 1793 Jacquemart printed paper and silks with all the Republican emblems—tricolour ribbons and cockades, civic crowns of oak, fasces, levels, balances, pikes, and the rest (fig. 372). Yet this topical style was an ephemeral thing, reappearing only at moments of crisis, and interesting men for a month on end at the most. It was soon confined to buttons, snuff-boxes, and the like, that could be taken up and thrown away, and never had a serious part to play in real decoration.

Decorative style resembled politics in being dominated by theory; the art of the Revolution, the Directorate, the Consulate, and the Empire is the embodiment of Winckelmann's aesthetic doctrines. Abstract classicism was the canon for every art. 'Prétendre se passer de l'étude des antiques et des classiques,' said Ingres,[3] 'ou c'est folie, ou c'est paresse. Oui, l'art anticlassique, si tant est que ce soit un art, n'est qu'un art de paresseux. C'est la doctrine de ceux qui veulent produire sans avoir travaillé, savoir sans avoir appris.' Moreover, the men of the Revolution and of the Empire could not bear their archaeological knowledge as lightly as had the dilettanti of the Ancien Régime; it had come to be the brevet of the true democrat, and had therefore to be insisted upon and taken as seriously as the aristocrats had taken the art of the return to nature. 'Il fallait se *défranciser* et se *débaptiser* et redevenir grec et romain par l'âme.'[4] The *Voyage du jeune Anarcharsis*, which Barthélemy, the keeper of the King's coin collection, had begun in 1757 and published in 1788, became for many an epitome of classical knowledge. It showed antiquity as a background to human life, and even inspired

[1] This rather arid symbolism may derive from England, where a similar style was prevalent about 1784. Cf. the state chair at Carlton House, described in the *European Magazine* of March (quoted, Jourdain, *Furniture and Decoration in England, 1750–1820*, p. 178) with 'on each corner of the feet, a lion's head, expressive of fortitude and strength; the feet have serpents twining round them to denote wisdom'.

[2] In both the king initiated destruction. In the financial difficulties of September 1789 he announced to the National Assembly that he had sent the 'Argenterie de la Couronne' to the mint. The Assembly passed a resolution begging him to give up the idea of such a sacrifice, since the royal gold and silver formed 'un ensemble impossible à reconstituer jamais, capable de fournir à l'art de l'orfèvrerie et à celui du ciseleur des enseignements qui, eux disparus, leur manqueraient à tout jamais'. The king, however, took no notice of this resolution and his plate was melted (Dreyfous, *op. cit.*, p. 16).

[3] Quoted Guerlin, *L'Art enseigné, le dessin*, p. 74.

[4] Chamfort, quoted Bertrand, *La fin du Classicisme*, p. 28.

Madame Vigée le Brun to give an archaeologically correct Greek supper.[1] If such books educated the public, many more were issued to educate the artist. Between 1790 and 1814 over a hundred and fifty works on archaeology and the history of ancient art were published in France, for the most part by subscription.[2]

The strict imitation of antiquity appeared in every department of art. Caylus had inaugurated the study of classical dress in his *Tableaux tirés de l'Iliade et de l'Odyssée d'Homère et de l'Enéide de Virgile, avec des observations générales sur le costume*, in 1787, and Talma, who had seen classical dress on the English stage, made his first appearance in a toga as Brutus in 1789. Such a figure demanded an appropriate background, and the first accurately classical scenery was designed by Percier and Fontaine for *Lucrèce* in 1791.

The theatre, moreover, had to play the part hitherto filled by the Church and the Court; the dramatic pageants of the Revolution took the place of the solemnities of the churches and the splendours of Versailles. Thus drama, and the pictures of dramatic scenes that made the only important *genre* in painting, were less strictly divided from ordinary life than before. The Roman eagles that were to lead the armies of Napoleon first appeared in the theatrical pageant of the *Translation des cendres de Voltaire* in July 1791, and those who bore them in that procession initiated a movement to imitate classical dress in everyday life.

David not only took the pose of many of his pictures[3] from antique engraved gems and sculptured medallions, but also copied much of his classic detail from the plates of d'Hancarville's *Antiquités étrusques, grecques et romaines* (1787), a publication of Sir William Hamilton's collection. From these drawings he and his pupil, Moreau, in 1789 made models of furniture, bronzes, and textiles for Jacob to execute, for use in David's pictures *La Mort de Socrate, Paris et Hélène* and *Les Horaces*, and thus initiated the Empire style in furniture. As early as 1790 the *Cabinet des Modes* gives designs for a 'lit à la Fédération' (with its columns composed of victors' fasces), 'fauteuil antique et chaise étrusque', and the Convention, for whom David was a prophet, adopted the style for practical use.[4] The Revolution was a moment when Time brought in his revenges, and as Corneille and

[1] The fowls and eels were cooked according to the recipes of the *Jeune Anarcharsis*; the Comte de Paroy lent Greek vases to decorate the table, the walls were draped 'comme on en voit dans les tableaux de Poussin', and hostess and guests wore classic dress. Madame Vigée le Brun, *Souvenirs*, 1869, i. 67.

[2] Some of the most important are: 1780–99, J. A. David, *Antiquités d'Herculaneum*; 1793, translation of Stuart and Revett's *Antiquities of Athens*; 1798, Delettre and Boutrou, *Galerie antique*; 1799, Delagardette, *Ruines de Paestum*; 1800, Piranesi, *Antiquités grecques et romaines*; 1801, Tischbein's plates of Greek vases; 1802–6, Millin, *Monuments inédits*; 1803, Legrand, *Galerie des antiques*; 1804, Beauvallet, *Fragments d'architecture . . . antique*; Normand, *Recueil d'ornements*; Piroli, *Monuments antiques du Musée Napoléon*; 1805, Piranesi, *Antiquités de la Grande Grèce*; 1808, Landon, pirated edition of Stuart and Revett's *Antiquities of Athens*; Clener and Millin's plates of Greek vases; Willemin, *Parallèle des plus anciennes peintures et sculptures antiques*; 1810, Bouillon, *Musée des Antiques*; Lenoir and Willemin, *Peintures, vases et bronzes antiques de la Malmaison*, &c.

[3] Notably *Paris et Hélène* and *Les Sabines*. The influence of English classicism on his work is not always recognized; his bas-relief style is plagiarized from the work of Gavin Hamilton twenty years before.

[4] See H. Lefuel, *Georges Jacob*, p. 142.

369. Painted door, Directoire style, c. 1795

370. Panel of carved wood from the Round Saloon, Château de Bagatelle, 1786

371. Dome of the Music Saloon, Château de Bagatelle, 1786

372. Printed silk. By Jacquemart, 1793

373. Design for Toile de Jouy. By J. B. Huet. *c.* 1800

Racine had once dressed the heroes of antiquity in the trappings of a modern court, Society had now to have ballrooms and boudoirs decorated like a stage set for a classic tragedy. The old decorative traditions came to an end, and even French painting was approximated to classical sculpture. Ingres's advice was: 'Point de couleur trop ardente, c'est anti-historique. Tombez plutôt dans le gris que dans l'ardent.' Colour, indeed, took a second place and was confined to details; the Merveilleuses might dress in 'jaune queue de serin, amarante, abricot, pistache et lilas', but Ingres could state, without fear of ridicule, 'Je mettrai sur ma porte: *École de Dessin*: et je formerai des peintres.'[1] Classical sculpture and the Tuscan Order symbolized the Roman virtues, and Pigalle had to carve Voltaire for the Institut in a state of 'heroic nudity'.

A change of background was needed for a changed society. The Revolution had succeeded in destroying the civilization of eighteenth-century France, and its creations and its possessions had to meet one of two fates: destruction or such alienation as involved destruction of purpose, or a lifeless conservation in Museums.[2] Preservation was usually accidental: destruction was one of the preoccupations of the new government. In 1793 the Convention decreed that the 'signes de la féodalité' should be removed from all objects of ordinary use. The fleurs-de-lis and the royal blazon were proscribed even in the watermarks of paper. Their removal from all the national works of art created some difficult problems; Cellini's stag at Anet was damaged by a crowd which considered that, since the feudal right of chase had been abolished, the emblems of the chase must also be destroyed. An unfortunate resident of Auteuil had to present a petition to the Convention that the decorations of his house might be spared, as the committee of his district maintained that their acanthus, masks, and chimeras appeared at Versailles as 'signes de la féodalité'.[3]

Meanwhile the impulse of construction in classical style was slowly gaining force, even in the unessential art of decoration. The jury that censored the *signes*

[1] Quoted, R. de la Sizeranne, *Les questions esthétiques*, p. 66.

[2] In 1790 the Commission des Monuments was formed to inventory and preserve ecclesiastical goods. This was succeeded on 11 August 1792 by a new Commission, to take over the Mobilier de la Couronne and to inventory and classify the collections of the Musée National. The Provincial Museums of France date from Barrères' proposal of 6 February 1793, to found 'des établissements pareils que vous vous proposez de former dans chaque département de la république. Il ne doit pas plus y avoir une capitale des arts, qu'une capitale politique dans un pays libre' (Dreyfous, *op. cit.*, p. 61).

[3] Dreyfous, *op. cit.*, pp. 19, 30, and 72. It was proposed at a meeting of the Conservatoire 'de faire effacer autant qu'il sera possible, sans les endommager, de tous les tableaux de Rubens, par les plus habiles restaurateurs, les signes de féodalité qu'ils rencontrent', but the proposal was not carried out. Courajod, *op. cit.* i. lxx. A jury was sent in September 1894 to censor the tapestries in course of fabrication at the Gobelins. They condemned the *Siege of Calais*, after Barthélemy, because, 'le pardon accordé aux bourgeois de Calais n'est arraché que par les larmes et les supplications d'une reine et des fils d'un despote'. Raphael's *Heliodorus driven from the Temple* was 'un sujet consacrant les idées de l'erreur et du fanatisme.' De Troy's composition of Medea's poisoned robe had to have the diadems removed from the heads of Creusa and her father, while in the companion piece of Jason overcoming the bulls, 'il demeure entendu qu'on ne tissera point les personnages de Médée et du roi son père, qui blesseraient les yeux d'un républicain'. Out of 321 subjects 120 were condemned as reactionary, and 136 as frivolous. (Havard and Vachon, *Les Manufactures Nationales*, p. 233.)

Fig. 374. Designs by Percier and Fontaine, *c.* 1805.

375. Decoration of the ceiling of Napoleon's bathroom. Rambouillet, *c.* 1800

376. Ceiling of the Salon Rose of the Hôtel de Beauharnais, *c.* 1805

de la féodalité at the manufactory of the Gobelins in 1794 was the first to give official help to the renaissance of decoration by organizing a prize competition for tapestry designs. Their advice to competitors was full of windy phrases: they were to celebrate the heroes of the Revolution and of antiquity; they were to 'stimulate the imagination by pleasing subjects, drawn from fiction . . . to cover a useful truth with the skilful veil of allegory, to charm the eyes, to please the mind, and to teach it to respect the morals and the austerity of Republican principles'; [1] but none of the compositions submitted were ever executed.

Not until a Dictatorship was established in decoration could it progress. Percier established himself as the arbiter of style, and developed a French version of really strict classicism. He was a former student of the French school at Rome. There, he tells us, 'M. Peyre, par ses savantes leçons m'avait initié à la connaissance de l'antique; Drouais me le montrait de l'âme et du doigt, et il me le montrait, non plus en perspective, non plus aligné froidement sur le papier, mais debout sur le terrain, mais vivant de toute la vie de l'Art et animé de tous les souvenirs de l'histoire.' [2] But Drouais died at the age of twenty-five, and Percier's conception of the antique, like Adam's, suffered a chill after he left Rome. The society which he served lived by theory, and was evolving a new and painfully logical aesthetic. Its basis was not a free idea of proportion, but a strict application of geometry. A writer of the fourth year of the Republic [3] expresses the theory in all its rigour:

'It remains to make a new application of mathematics to the arts to prove, directly and without consulting the eye, what forms are the most gracious, what scheme the most agreeable. . . . For it is possible to reduce the unknown laws of beauty to a few fundamental principles, and once these principles are established, their application to particular instances will come into the sphere of geometry.'

Révérony St. Cyr expanded the theme to fill a volume. [4] Geometry lay at the root of all beauty; 'N'en doutons point, les grands littérateurs, les grands artistes eussent été bons géomètres en application.' [5]

With such views in currency, it is hardly surprising that the work which Percier carried out [6] and the designs which he published from 1793 onward in collaboration with the architect Fontaine are frigid, abstract, and in essence monotonous.

---

[1] Havard and Vachon, *op. cit.*, p. 236. The subjects accepted were *L'Etude voulant ramener le Temps ; Borée et Orythie ; L'Education d'Achille ; La Paix ramenant l'Abondance ; L'Innocence se réfugiant dans les bras de la Justice*, and revivals of Guido Reni, Correggio, and Le Sueur. Guiffrey, *Histoire de la tapisserie*, p. 133.

[2] Dreyfous, *op. cit.*, p. 278.

[3] *Décade*, An. iv, t. viii, p. 270: the article is signed H. S.

[4] *Essai sur le perfectionnement des Beaux Arts par les sciences exactes*, 1803.   [5] *Ibid.*, i. 3.

[6] In collaboration with Fontaine (who had visited England and studied its architecture some time before 1798) he repaired the Revolutionary damages to the Tuileries, restored St. Cloud, transformed La Malmaison, and decorated Fontainebleau and Compiègne. The first house he decorated was for M. de Chauvelin, a former Ambassador to England.

Stiff *appliqués* of cast metal appear on a ground of mahogany in furniture, on gilt metal on clocks, on porcelain on vases, on bronze on lamps, and the same design appears brocaded on silk for hangings and applied in plaster for decoration. The designs are usually based on diagonal intersections or lozenge-shaped panels; maeanders and frets, diapers and medallions are all geometrical. From the use of human forms, except of an unreal kind in minor work, Percier was at first debarred by the feeling of his day. The instructions of the jury of October 1794 to would-be designers for the Savonnerie ordered them 'not to employ any human figures, since it would be revolting to tread them underfoot under a government that had recalled Man to his dignity; exception made, however, to any kind of chimera, such as centaurs, tritons and other monsters'.[1] Percier and Fontaine followed this precept in all their early work, and diversified their designs with a variety of composite figures that recall archaistic Roman reliefs. The men of the Revolution loved the winged sense of liberty; and David, at all the National Fêtes which he planned, had thousands of caged birds released to carry the joy of freedom even into the upper airs. Similarly Percier and Fontaine used many winged figures on their decoration—Victories, Psyches, Pegasi, sphinxes, and seahorses—but their wings are fixed and still. Theirs is a static and motionless art; there is a certain military precision about it, a formal accuracy, a want of freedom.[2] They themselves wrote:[3] 'Le genre ne nous appartient point; il est tout aux Anciens', and they treated their classic foliage, their wreaths and paterae, their urns, torches, lamps, and lyres with the respect due to antiquity. They agreed with Quatremère de Quincy,[4] 'Mieux vaut imiter et copier que créer des productions qui préparent la chute des arts.' So Attic red figured vases were even copied in their natural colours on Lyons silks.[5]

But if the elements of their design were stereotyped, at least they brought back to decoration a classic sense of appropriateness. Architecture, decoration, and furnishings were once more united: 'Furniture is too closely connected with interior decoration, for the architect to remain indifferent to it. . . . Construction and decoration are in close relation, and if they cease to appear so, there is a flaw in the whole.'[6] Moreover, they made their designs for a particular purpose and often for a particular person: a bedroom for a painter with the symbols of the arts and medallions of the artists of antiquity; a bedroom for a girl, designed as a temple of Diana; a bed for 'un guerrier grand chasseur'; a bedroom adorned with the poppies of sleep.[7]

[1] Havard and Vachon, *op. cit.*, p. 324.

[2] It must be remembered that Napoleon himself hated any elaboration of ornament; a design of Percier's bears the significant inscription: 'Simplifier les ornements, c'est pour l'Empereur' (H. Lefuel, *Jacob Desmalter*, 1926, p. 78).   [3] *Recueil de décorations intérieures*, 1812, p. 7.

[4] *Archives littéraires*, 1804, iii. 7.   [5] By Grand frères. Musée des Tissus historiques, Lyons.

[6] Percier and Fontaine, *op. cit.* N. Dellbruck evolved a simpler bourgeois style, but in essentials its principles are the same.

[7] Cf. Percier and Fontaine's own preface to their *Recueil* of 1812 (p. 11) which protests against 'l'abus

FIG. 377. Design for the decoration of a boudoir by Percier and Fontaine, *c.* 1810.

With this conception of appropriateness they linked the whole development of the style; and the commonplace classicism of the Consulate gained in force with the triumphs of Napoleon. The arrows, spears, helmets, cuirasses, trumpets, and short swords of Rome were paralleled by the cannon, bayonets, shakos, tunics, and drums of the Napoleonic legions[1] (fig. 378). Each new conquest brought fresh trophies into art; during the campaign in Italy Josephine ordered a bed with its tester 'simulant une tente des tons tricolores', and a set of stools to go with it, all shaped like drums;[2] the campaign in Egypt brought in oblique lines, sphinxes, obelisks, hieroglyphics, winged globes, and pyramids in 1808;[3] the Eastern campaign the crescents and mail of Turkey in 1809; even the Russian campaign introduced the knout into the trophies of war. Tablets and cartouches gave place to shields; draperies and curtains took the lines of tent hangings.[4] Such allusions explained themselves; but for special occasions a more elaborate and more literary symbolism was freely employed. Prud'hon, for instance, thus describes the cradle he designed for the Roi de Rome:

'This cradle is supported on four horns of plenty, near which are set the genii of Strength and Justice; it is . . . powdered with bees. A shield, bearing the cipher of the Emperor and rimmed with a triple border of palms, ivy, and laurel, forms the head. Glory, soaring over

désordonné que l'on fait des plus belles formes, des plus belles inventions, dans les sujets qui les comportent les moins. Si, par exemple, des sphinx, des termes à l'égyptienne, peuvent convenir par la sévérité de leurs formes et par leurs sens allégorique à tel ou tel emploi dans certains objets de l'architecture ou de l'ameublement, avant peu l'on verra toutes les enseignes, tous les dessins de portes à l'égyptienne. Si les légèretés de l'arabesque . . . conviennent à de petits compartimens, et s'accordent avec les pièces dont l'étendue comme le caractère ne demandent que de la gaîté; bientôt, si la mode s'empare de ce goût, l'arabesque deviendra l'ornement universel.'

[1] Cf. Dubois and Marchais, *Recueil de dessins des armures, casques, cuirasses, etc., tirés du Musée Impérial de l'artillerie de France et des cabinets particuliers*, 1808.

[2] Napoleon complained of their expense on his return (H. Lefuel, *Jacob Desmalter*, 1926, p. 44). The tented room of Josephine at La Malmaison dates from 1812.

[3] Piranesi in 1769 had used Egyptian motives—Isis, Osiris, Apis, cats, hawks, sphinxes, &c.—in his designs, and in the decoration of the English café in the Piazza di Spagna. Asprucci built an Egyptian temple in the gardens of the Villa Borghese, and decorated a room in the villa in the Egyptian style of Piranesi, oddly completed with flying cupids bearing wreaths. Egyptian terminal figures appear in France—perhaps thanks to Caylus—on some work of Gouthière's for the Duc d'Aumont in 1782 (Molinier, *Le Mobilier au XVIIe et au XVIIIe siècle*, p. 162.) After the Egyptian expedition Denon ordered from Jacob a complete set of bedroom furniture designed after his own drawings of ancient objects at Thebes; and provided Sèvres with designs in Egyptian style. A Sèvres breakfast set designed by him given to Charles Schulmeister in 1809 has the coffee pot shaped as a canopic jar, a crocodile on the sugar basin, and cartouches everywhere. (It is now in the Musée des Arts décoratifs at Strasbourg.) The famous Egyptian service of 140 pieces, painted with hieroglyphics on a blue ground, was made in 1811. The style owed much to illustrated books of travel: 1787, Volney, *Voyage en Égypte*; 1795, French translation of Norden, *Voyage d'Égypte et de Nubie*; 1799, Grohmann, *Restes d'architecture égyptienne*; 1802, Denon, *Voyage dans la basse et haute Égypte*; 1803, Quatremère de Quincy, *Architecture égyptienne*, &c. One of the finest surviving Egyptian rooms is the *salon* of the Villa San Martino in Elba, which Napoleon used as a country house during his exile there in 1814–15. It has a lotus cornice and hieroglyphic frieze and door frames, while the walls are decorated with panels of Eastern scenes divided by Egyptian columns.

[4] This fashion was derived from pre-revolutionary times. At Bagatelle 'les chambres à coucher étaient en forme de tente . . . avec des pilastres faits de faisceaux d'armes; les jambages de cheminées, de canons posés sur la culasse; les chenets, figurés en bombes, en boulets, en grenades; les bias de cheminée, en cors de chasse'. *Mémoires secrets*, xv. 188.

379. Panel of Beauvais tapestry, *c.* 1816

378. Trophy of arms from the Salle du Sacre, Versailles, *c.* 1805

380. The Eagle of Napoleon. Tapestry, *c.* 1805. Probably designed by Debret and Dubois. Malmaison

the world, holds up the crowns of Triumph and Immortality, in the midst of which shines the star of Napoleon.[1] A young eaglet, set at the foot of the cradle, already gazes upon the heroic star; it flutters its wings and seems to try to raise itself thereto. The genius of Justice leans upon the foot of the cradle; the expression on his face, his grave and serene pose, make him easily recognizable, even without the balances of Themis and the sacred band that wraps his brow. At the head of the cradle stands the genius of Strength, leaning on the club of Hercules; with the other hand he holds a crown of oak leaves. Above him glitter the Imperial arms. In the first of the two bas-reliefs the Seine, lying upon her urn, receives the precious child that the gods confide to her; the arms of the City of Paris, placed beside the nymph, recall both the birthplace of the Prince and the city that offers him his first cradle. The second relief represents the Tiber, and beside him a fragment on which the Wolf of Romulus can be discerned; the river god raises his reed-crowned head and sees rising on the horizon the new star that shall bring back to his banks their ancient splendour.'[2]

The Empire style might have progressed into real vitality but for circumstances. For one thing the French school at Rome had had to be closed in 1793 because of the Papal hostility to the revolutionaries, and for a time the younger generation of French artists lost close touch with the monuments of antiquity. For another, the French *maîtrises*, which had survived the attacks of Turgot in 1776, had been finally suppressed by the Constituent Assembly in 1791, so that the system of apprenticeship broke down, the ancient craft traditions were weakened, the general standard of technique was lowered, and the actual number of artists reduced. Finally, the Empire style was that of a political system that might be imperial in its government, but was democratic in its society. Art had been able to live only by ceasing to be suspect as a prerogative of aristocracy.[3] Consequently the level of democracy passed over decoration. Its triumphs date from the Paris Exhibitions, the first of their kind, of 1798 and 1801. Mass production began. Percier and Fontaine wrote their own indictment of the process:[4]

'It is neither a truer feeling nor a more generally enlightened taste that is thus bringing such forms and such work into general use. . . . They are not desired because they are beautiful, but are considered beautiful because they are desired; and so at once they suffer the fate of every product of fashion. Industrial manufacture takes possession of them, reproduces them in a thousand cheap ways, brings them within the smallest means. Every kind of falsification distorts their value. Plaster takes the place of marble, paper plays the part of painting,

[1] The star of Napoleon is derived from the stars that figure on the original Bonaparte coat of arms.
[2] H. Lefuel, *Jacob Desmalter*, p. 33. The cradle was presented to Marie Louise a fortnight before the child's birth. It was fortunate that the baby proved to be a boy.
[3] Cf. the description of the revolutionary peasant before an art he does not understand in the *Notice de l'An XI* (1803): 'Ces maisons, ces palais, qu'il regarde encore avec les yeux de l'indignation, ne sont plus à ses ennemis; ils sont à lui. Ces décorations contre lesquelles les mains égarées se soulèvent, ce sont des simples feuilles d'acanthe ou de lierre; ce sont des masques, des chimères antiques. Ce sont des lions égyptiens, ce sont des groupes d'enfants, que l'on menace et que l'on détruit. Tu crois rencontrer l'effigie d'un roi; ici c'est la statue de Linnaeus, de cet immortel ami de la nature; là c'est le dieu des bergers; plus loin, c'est une tête de Minerve que tu mutiles. Le trident de Neptune, le caducée de Mercure, le thyrse de Bacchus te semblent être autant de sceptres, et tu les brises! Dans ce bosquet, ce ne sont point des tyrans que tu vois; ce sont des dieux champêtres et bienfaisants dont tu réduis les statues en poussière.' Dreyfous, *op. cit.*, p. 29.
[4] *Op. cit.*, pp. 11-12.

pasteboard imitates sculpture, glass is used instead of precious stones, sheet iron replaces wrought metal, japanning imitates porphyry.[1] From all this a first abuse arises, that comes from the very essence of fashion, which is to make vile all that becomes common. . . . But a yet graver abuse . . . is to take from them by economy of work, by imitation of material, and by systematic or mechanical processes, that perfection of execution, that delicate finish, that touch of original feeling, that theory alone separates from conception and creation, and that in truth is inseparable from them.'

There was nothing in the 'geometric beauty' of even the best-designed work to prevent its being mechanically produced; a trade catalogue of 1813[2] shows how Percier and Fontaine's classicism was reproduced and sold by the square metre.

Democracy dimmed the richness of royal colour. The hues of the Empire were dull and muddy; the dark green of ancient bronzes, the terra cotta and buff-yellow of ancient pottery, violet, maroon, and blue. These might all be combined in a single decorative scheme; the *Journal de la Mode* of February 1791[3] describes a room with a ceiling adorned with a parasol-rosette in maroon, a sky-blue frieze with horns of abundance in white; the mirror framed in pilasters with white vine leaves on a sky-blue ground bordered with violet, and the panelling of light brown with a violet border decorated with rosettes and cameos with white figures touched with maroon on a blue ground. Here too, the progress of industrialism made itself felt: the invention of Prussian blue in 1810 marks the beginning of chemical dyeing. Richness was felt to consist not in plenitude of form or splendour of colour, but in mere material quantity. So hangings, instead of being flat upon the wall, were arranged in folds and loops to display as great a quantity of stuff as possible;[4] and these hangings were even imitated on brocade[5] and wall-paper[6] to be used flat.

The coronation of Napoleon brought new elements into decoration; it linked him not only with Rome but also with France, not only with Caesar, but also with Charlemagne. When he came to see David's great picture of the ceremony, he is reported to have said: 'C'est très bien, très bien, David. Vous avez deviné ma pensée. Vous m'avez fait chevalier français.'[7] The imperial factories soon expressed the new standpoint. The bees of Merovingian goldwork that had been found in the tomb of Childeric became the imperial emblem, and at Sèvres

[1] A rather later book, A. Teyssèdre, *L'Art de décorer les appartements*, 1824, is mostly taken up with practical directions for the manufacture of substitutes for marble and other costly materials.

[2] The *Recueil des dessins d'ornements d'architecture* of J. Beunat's factory at Sarrebourg.

[3] Quoted, E. de Goncourt, *Histoire de la société française pendant la révolution*, p. 73.

[4] Cf. Madame de Genlis, *Mémoires*, v. 105. 'On plissoit sur les murs les étoffes, au lieu de les étendre; on calculoit sans doute que de cette manière l'aunage étoit infiniment plus considérable, et que cela étoit beaucoup plus magnifique.'

[5] Examples are in the Musée historique des tissus at Lyon; one made for the Salle des Maréchaux at the Tuileries imitates lace with a gathered flounce at the foot; others have imitation tasselled fringes.

[6] By Joseph Dufour and Jacquemart, Ackermann, *Wallpaper*, p. 48, c. 1808.

[7] Bertrand, *op. cit.*, p. 307. Napoleon did not respond easily to the stimulus of antiquity. He told Madame de Rémusat: 'En Égypte, on a voulu me faire lire l'Iliade. Elle m'a ennuyé.' Mme de Rémusat, *Mémoires*, i. 279.

medallions of Napoleon and Charlemagne, Rome and Paris were allowed to balance each other.[1] The toga was no longer the heroic garb; fashion turned to the velvets, the ruffles, the gold lace and the *panaches* of the royal court.[2]

Even classical models were preferred with a Gallic flavour.[3] It is significant that the Madeleine, of which the colonnade dates from 1814, is based not on any building in Rome, but on the Maison Carrée of Nîmes.[4] Its difference lies in size, for the greatness of Napoleons's schemes necessarily resulted in megalomania in art. Quatremère de Quincy in 1816 wrote in his *Éloge* of Chalgrin, the architect of the Arc de Triomphe, 'We shall not fear to assert that material greatness is one of the chief causes of worth and effect in architecture. The reason is that the greatest number of impressions produced by this art depend upon a feeling of admiration. Now it is a human instinct to admire greatness, of which the idea is always associated in the human mind with that of power and force.'[5] The weakness and the strength of Napoleonic France is seen in the mixture of admiration of greatness in architecture and of the appreciation of mechanical repetition of small units of decoration in ornament.

The admiration of grandeur and the reacceptance of the French past did more than modify classicism; it set up an undercurrent that the progress of the nineteenth century made of primary importance. France returned once more to the inspiration of the *style Louis XIV*; the late Empire style shows a marked return to the fuller forms, the scrolling volutes, the natural flowers and the fuller colours of the art of Versailles (fig. 380). The symbolic idea was lost; the old congruity was gone; but the forms were as nearly the same as a nineteenth-century pencil could make them.

To this influence the strangely slight change of a style at the Restoration is due.[6] The decoration of the late Empire was in its inspiration monarchical; only a few emblems had to be altered to make it fit for Bourbon use. The king inherited the art of the Emperor, and Bellanger and Dugourc, survivors of the Ancien Régime,

[1] Cf. the Emperor's New Year present to the Duchesse de Bellune in 1814. Bouchot, *La Toilette à la cour de Napoléon*, p. 130.

[2] In 1806 the exportation of marabout from the East began; Leroy, the court dressmaker, used as much as 28,000 francs worth of feathers in six months. Such tastes were reflected in the designs of embroidery, which were inspired by the *panaches* of plumes.

[3] Hubert Robert and Clérisseau, the companion of Robert Adam on his Spalato journey, had been the first to paint the Roman remains of Provence and Languedoc, and that late in the eighteenth century. Robert sent several pictures of Nîmes, Orange, and the Pont du Gard to the Salon of 1787.

[4] Four years later H. Lebas designed a printed linen, 'Les Monuments de Paris', and another 'Les Monuments du Midi'.

[5] Quatremère de Quincy, *Notices historiques*, i. 18. On the parallel cult of the colossal in England, see C. Hussey, *The Picturesque*, 1927, p. 198.

[6] There was a slight recrudescence of the 'topical' style in decoration: e.g. a wall-paper of 1815, having a pale blue ground with white stripes of running vine intertwined with scrolls with all the names of the allied generals, with medallions of the ciphers of the allied monarchs, finished at the top with a frieze of military medals. Ackermann, *Wallpaper*, p. 55. On Restoration decoration see J. Robiquet, *L'Art et le Goût sous la Restauration, 1814–30*.

helped to bring it back into monarchical channels. The crown had a different form, the Bourbon fleur-de-lis replaced the Napoleonic bees, natural lilies[1] took a more important place in the design: but these were almost the only changes for the first decade of the new régime.[2] Sèvres continued to manufacture 'dans l'antique' and 'dans l'Egyptien' and up to 1823 followed the Etruscan models with classic decoration that Napoleon had approved. Indeed, the more archaeological of the Empire types were perpetuated into the third decade of the new century; as late as 1832 Dauptain was printing wall-paper designed by Poterlet with medallions of groups of Greek vases and panels of decoration copied from such vases.

France, enriched by Napoleon with the spoils of Italy,[3] had still her instinct for antiquity. The classic style of Napoleon was still part of the artistic patrimony of the countries which had formed his Empire. France, Holland, Italy, Spain, Sweden, Germany, and Russia followed its dictates with little modification. As late as 1832 Quatremère de Quincy could write: [4]

'Today a common civilization unites in the same tastes and in the practice of the same arts, nearly on the same level, all the nations of Europe, who in this respect seem to be but provinces of a single empire. Moreover, Greek architecture, which is that of all the nations, has through their influence on a great part of the rest of the globe, spread far beyond the confines of Europe. . . . This architecture has thus become in some sort universal.'

4

England, though not subject to Napoleon, remained under the yoke of classicism; her dilettanti, if cut off from Italy, could have 'beautiful carpets made of very large dimensions from the Roman pavements . . . lately discovered in Gloucestershire';[5] the humblest of her squires could have chairs imitated from those of Greek funerary reliefs, and even a cottage might have a foot or two of Greek fret or Vitruvian scroll frieze to make it classical.[6]

[1] The *Liliacées* of Redouté provided models. Jacob Desmalter, for instance, used it. H. Lefuel, *Jacob Desmalter*, p. 13. It is curious to note that natural lilies are used in conjunction with the bees on a *garniture de lit* of Point d'Alençon given by Napoleon to Marie Louise in 1809, which must have taken some years to make. It was offered for sale at Messrs. Marshall & Snelgrove's in 1925–6.

[2] Some other modifications were curiously inappropriate; winged monsters à la Percier were invested with 'le cordon de l'ordre de St. Michel'. Lefuel, *op. cit.*, p. 101. In 1815 it was reported of a set of furniture covers that were in course of being woven at Beauvais for Napoleon's palace on Monte Cavallo: 'les dessins ne représentant aucun emblème ou ornement relatifs au dernier gouvernement rien ne s'opposera à ce que les meubles puissent servir partout où l'on voudra les placer.' Badin, *La manufacture de tapisseries à Beauvais*, p. 45.

[3] These collections even had a direct influence on decoration. In 1808 Brongniart planned a Sèvres service for Fontainebleau 'd'après l'antique . . . Le bord de l'assiette est en fond d'or avec un laurier peint en gris sur le fond; au milieu se trouve une tête imitant un camée, faite d'après les figures du musée Napoléon et les médailles et pierres gravées de la Bibliothèque Nationale.' This service was repeated in 1812–13. As late as 1826 Dufour was printing wall-paper with scenes of the Italian campaign of 1796–7.

[4] *Dictionnaire de l'architecture*, p. 690.

[5] Walpole, Letter to Lady Ossory, 13 November 1796, *Letters*, ed. Toynbee, xv. 428. The 'progress' of industrial art is shown by the fact that floor-cloths imitated from these same pavements were shown as a novelty at the Exhibition of 1862.

[6] Taste, however, was increasingly conditioned by national prejudices. In February 1790 Wedgwood

381. Sèvres vases, c. 1825

382. The Front Parlour, Pitzhanger Manor. By Sir John Soane, 1802

Robert Adam died in 1792, in the year when British insularity became a political fact; but he had founded a school, and England, for the first years of the new century, remained rigidly Greek. The hall of Ickworth, built about 1800, is characteristically decorated with friezes in bas-relief copied from Flaxman's illustrations of the *Iliad* and the *Odyssey*. Faint ripples of the French currents reached our shores; some of James Wyatt's designs for ceilings show the Adam tradition modified by a certain broken angularity of form that recalls the Directoire style; even the lictor's fasces appear in a few of Busby's designs.[1] Thomas Hope, a wealthy dilettante who knew Percier and admired his work, endeavoured to introduce his style in England, but found it necessary to employ foreign modellers and craftsmen.[2]

England had her share in the Egyptian campaign, and after 1804,[3] the year of Denon's publication, a mild interest was felt in the Egyptian antique; but even Hope, though he decorated a little room in Egyptian style to receive his collection of Egyptian antiquities, warns the young artist never to adopt it 'except from motives more weighty than a mere aim at novelty', as hieroglyphics are unintelligible, their outline is never agreeable, and the whole style needs immense solidity of construction to give it meaning.[4] He was aware, too, that England could do little with 'those straight lines which seem so little attractive to the

writes to Flaxman, then in Rome, 'The history of Orestes is an excellent classic subject . . . but there is one objection which I am afraid is insurmountable and that is the nakedness of the figures . . . the same objection applies to the *Judgment of Paris* and the other pieces; and indeed the nude is so general in the works of the ancients that it will be very difficult to avoid the introduction of naked figures. On the other hand, it is absolutely necessary to do so, or to keep the pieces for our own use, for none, either male or female, of the present generation, will take or apply them as furniture, if the figures are naked.' W. G. Constable, *John Flaxman*, p. 12.

[1] In *A Collection of Designs for Modern Embellishments*.

[2] His collection was dispersed in 1917; some examples of his furniture are now in the picture galleries of the Ashmolean Museum, Oxford. Some of his schemes are remarkable for their completeness and their richness of allusion. He thus describes the decoration of a room of which the central object was a marble group by Flaxman, of Aurora visiting Cephalus on Mount Ida. 'The whole surrounding decoration has been rendered, in some degree, analogous to these personages, and to the face of Nature at the moment when the first of the two, the goddess of the morn, is supposed to announce approaching day. Round the bottom of the room still reign the emblems of night. In the rail of a black marble table are introduced medallions of the god of sleep and of the goddess of night. The bird consecrated to the latter deity perches on the pillars of a black marble chimney-piece, whose broad frieze is studded with golden stars. The sides of the room display in satin curtains, draped in ample folds over pannels of looking-glass, and edged with black velvet, the fiery hue which fringes the clouds just before sunrise: and in a ceiling of cooler sky blue are sown, amidst a few still unextinguished luminaries of the night, the roses which the harbinger of day, in her course, spreads on every side around her.' (The Plate shows these as a stiff border of stars and a formal wreath in the most severe Empire style.) 'The broad band which girds the top of the room, contains medallions of the ruddy goddess and of the Phrygian youth, intermixed with the instruments and emblems of the chace, his favourite amusement. Figures of the youthful hours, adorned with wreaths of foliage, adorn part of the furniture, which is chiefly gilt, in order to give more relief to the azure, the black, and the orange compartments of the hangings.' (*Household Furniture and Interior Decoration executed from Designs by Thomas Hope*, 1807, p. 25.)

[3] The designs of J. Taylor, published in London in that year, include one for a sideboard in Egyptian style, and some more appear in R. Brown's pattern-book of 1807, in which year a wall-paper with sphinx borders was also produced.

[4] *Household Furniture and Interior Decoration executed from Designs by Thomas Hope*, p. 26.

greatest number'. England lacked the stimulus of conquest that enriched the Empire style, and the general trend of her decoration was towards a negative purity of ornament, only mitigated by an exact imitation of antiquity.[1] Sir John Soane, who began to practise in 1780, soon did his best to limit the influence of classical architecture upon decoration.

'The ancients,' he told his pupils, 'with great propriety decorated the temples and altars with the skulls of victims, ram's heads, and other ornaments peculiar to their religious ceremonies, but when the same ornaments are introduced in the decoration of English houses, they become puerile, and disgusting. . . . It is impossible for me to impress too much upon your minds that modillions, mutules, dentils and triglyphs cannot be admitted in the interior of any edifice with even a shadow of propriety.'[2]

But if he thus swept away the commonplaces of classical decoration, Soane produced little or nothing to take its place. A meagre fret, a rigid rosette, or more rarely a stumpy winged figure, assort indifferently with pure and reasonable architectural form, and appear but rarely in his work (fig. 382). Even his structural forms are flattened and simplified into a well-proportioned bareness. Repton characterizes 'the new style' as being of no character. It

'consists of a plain building, with rows of square windows set at equal distances, and if to these be added a Grecian Cornice, it is called a *Grecian Building*; if instead of the cornice certain notches are cut in the top of the wall, it is called a *Gothic Building*. Thus has the rage for simplicity, the dread of mixing dates, and the difficulty of adding ornament to utility alike corrupted and exploded both the Grecian and the Gothic style in our modern buildings.'[3]

Burke's identification of smoothness with beauty continued to dominate both theory and practice; Uvedale Price writes in 1810,[4] 'Almost all ornaments are rough, and most of them sharp, which is a mode of roughness; and, considered analogically, the most contrary to beauty of any mode. But as ornaments are rough, so the ground is generally smooth; which shows that, though smoothness be the most essential quality of beauty, without which it can scarcely exist, yet that roughness, in its different modes and degrees, is the ornament, the fringe of beauty, that which gives it life and spirit and preserves it from baldness and insipidity.' So not only in architecture, but also in minor forms of decoration, ornament, except as a 'fringe of beauty', almost disappeared. Furniture followed the pure outline and smooth surface of Attic models,[5] until by 1828 Walter Scott could find that an ordinary chair had 'something of Grecian massiveness'.[6] Walls were

---

[1] Inwood, author of a *Monograph on the Erechtheum*, when he built St. Pancras Church between 1819 and 1822, used the Erechtheum order and doorways for the façade, and composed his tower by setting the choragic monument of Lysicrates on top of the Tower of the Winds.

[2] *Plans, Elevations, &c. of Buildings erected in the Counties of Norfolk, &c.* 1788, p. 9.

[3] *Designs for the Pavillon at Brighton*, 1808, p. 21.   [4] *On the Picturesque*, p. 107.

[5] The development of this Anglo-Greek style owes much to the work of Charles Heathcote Tatham. See Jourdain, *Furniture and Decoration in England, 1750–1820*, p. 50.

[6] *Quarterly Review*, 1828, vol. xxxviii, p. 318.

bare of arabesque and medallion, but showed instead a surface as smooth and shining, if not as beautiful, as marble. Textiles were no longer scrolled like a classic frieze, but had the 'geometric beauty' of stripes and squares. Even the sculptor Flaxman's most popular work was his engravings in pure line. In everything there was a deliberate bareness: the riches of classicism had been expended and its coffers were empty. 'Our English way of liking nothing and professing to like triglyphs'[1] found its full expression.

The fall of Napoleon brought England into fresh touch with France,[2] and by 1816 Richardson's designs[3] showed the influence of the French revival of seventeenth-century classicism in their rich and rounded curves. It was thence that the florid and complacent classicism of the Regency derived: classicism reduced from chiselled bronze and marble to cast iron and stucco.[4] Even Soane's classicism lost its restraint after 1815, and a contemporary critic complains that in the Bank of England 'we meet with remnants of Mausoleums, Caryatides, Pillars from Temples, Ornaments from the Pantheon—and all heaped together with a perversion of taste that is truly admirable. He steals a bit here and a bit there—and in piling up these collected thefts, he imagines he has done the duty and earned the honours of an Artist.'[5]

In France the classic tradition found more wherewith to renew its force; the *École française d'Athènes*, founded in 1847, added to the treasures of Hellenic antiquity, and the acquisition of the Campana Collection in 1850 renewed the classic tradition in the goldsmith's art. In the years about 1852, when Gautier's *Émaux et Camées* and de Vigny's *Poèmes Antiques* appeared, there was a flickering revival of classic ornament.[6] Chenevard published designs almost academic in the severity of their classicism, though their application was in fact[7] less severe. Indeed, the 'néo-grec' has been described as the only *style* of the second Empire.[8] In 1860 Prince Napoleon built his Pompeian villa in the Avenue Montaigne, complete with atrium, impluvium, triclinium, and tablinum. Rossigneux designed antique furniture for it, and Christofle copied its plate from Greek models.[9] In

[1] Ruskin, *Stones of Venice*, vol. i, chap. ii, p. 13.
[2] In 1825, for instance, George IV sent for F. H. G. Jacob Desmalter to decorate his rooms at Windsor.
[3] *A Collection of Ornaments in the Antique Style.* Similar influences are evident in H. Moses' designs published in 1817, in R. Hebblethwaite's gates at Hyde Park Corner, c. 1825, in M. A. Nicholson's furniture designs of 1826, and in the patterns for plate published by Maguire about 1830.
[4] It is unnecessary to follow the history of the style in nineteenth-century architecture. Its chief exponents in England were W. Wilkins (d. 1839), Smirke, Decimus Burton (d. 1881), W. H. Playfair (d. 1857), Thomas Hamilton (d. 1858), H. L. Elmes and Cockerell. In Germany Schinkel made it even more academic than in England: a tendency that culminates in Leo von Klenze's Munich Propylaea.
[5] *Champion*, newspaper, 1815.
[6] *Recueil des compositions exécutées ou projectées sur les dessins de A. M. Chenevard . . .* Lyon, 1860.
[7] e.g. in the *salon* of the theatre of Lyons.   [8] H. Clouzot, *Des Tuileries à Saint Cloud*, p. 94.
[9] About this time Alfred Stevens, who knew Italy well, was designing in classic style. In 1850 he made classical designs for Sheffield stoves and fenders; in 1856 he painted a music-room ceiling in the Pompeian manner; and in 1858 designed a classic sideboard for Dorchester House. See *Alfred Stevens and his Work*, Autotype Company, 1891.
3620.2   S

the 1862 Exhibition curtains,[1] carpets,[2] and glass [3] were exhibited decorated with Greek vase palmettes; and 'a cabinet in Pompeian style' [4] with decoration based on wall paintings but translated into marquetry in New Zealand woods. Industrialism and classicism are not easily wedded; and instead of the riches of the *grand siècle*, the graces of Trianon, and the refinements of the Empire, French commerce was content to produce objects like the table which Rudolph of Paris exhibited at the 1851 Exhibition,

'a round table of cast silver, composed of a hollowed flat plate, in the centre of which is the front face of the head of a Naiad, surrounded by Titans and Naiads, with Hylas and a Nymph; the hollowed portion and the border are ornamented with heads, birds and foliage, after models by the late Wagner: the leg of the table is formed of the stem of a reed and foliage, ornamented with a kingfisher: upon the three claws are the bird's nest attacked by a rat, and intoxicated infant Bacchantes . . .' [5]

Even the archaeological discoveries of the middle of the century served only to inspire the production of black marble clocks with a pediment engraved with the outlines of the Aeginetan statues. In industrial art, indeed, the survivals of classic tradition came to be sternly reproved by its professional critics. 'The funeral urns of the Greeks revived as drinking vessels for the table, the columns of temples turned into candlesticks, and Sarcophagi into wine coolers; while the decorations of ceilings are applied to carpets, and the carved frieze of an Ionic temple to a muslin curtain: all these errors arising from an indiscriminating use of those materials with which antiquity has supplied us' [6] appeared out of date beneath the vaults of the Crystal Palace.

'It is to this, then, that our Doric and Palladian pride is at last reduced! We have vaunted the divinity of the Greek ideal—we have plumed ourselves on the purity of our Italian taste —we have cast our whole souls into the proportions of pillars, and the relations of orders— and behold the end! Our taste, thus exalted and disciplined, is dazzled by the lustre of a few rows of panes of glass; and the first principles of architectural sublimity, so far sought, are found all the while to have consisted merely in sparkling and space.'[7]

[1] By Messrs. Templeton of Glasgow.   [2] By Messrs. Henderson of Durham.
[3] By Messrs. Lloyd and Summerfield of Birmingham.   [4] By Mr. Levien of London.
[5] 1851 Exhibition, *Reports of Juries*, ii. 1125.   [6] *Reports of Juries*, ii. 1591.
[7] J. Ruskin, *The Opening of the Crystal Palace*, 1854, p. 5.

383. Boudoir in the Villa von Arnim, Sans Souci, Berlin, c. 1860

384. 'The Music Lesson', adapted from François Boucher's painting 'L'Agréable Leçon'. Engraved by J. E. Nilson. Chelsea china, c. 1765

X

THE RETURN TO NATURE

I

THE illusion of Watteau's style, the elegant unreality of French rocaille and the romance of *chinoiseries* heralded an age in which feeling was to reign over reason. There was a reaction against deliberate bizarrerie and calculated hedonism: a new kind of pleasure was needed and found in the delights of sensibility. The seventeenth century, an age of psychology, had sought forms of purely human invention; the eighteenth, a century of sensibility to external impressions, sought forms that brought with them the connotations of nature.

The impulse originated in the honest and sincere English pleasure in 'feasting our eyes with hawthorns and our ears with nightingales' [1] which is a part of our medieval heritage. The parterres of classicism could never altogether fulfil the need for such delights, and even in 1712 Addison was dreaming of the charms of a wild garden.[2] 'A little wandering rill' was to run through it, 'in the same manner as it would do in an open field, so that it generally passes through banks of violets and primroses, plats of willow, or other plants that seem to be of its own producing.' Twenty years later Pope was pleading the cause of 'artful wildness' [3] and Kent was putting his precepts into practice and planting dead trees to add to the 'natural' beauties of Kensington Gardens.[4] The world was soon able to rest from its horticultural labours and to indulge in the emotions which Nature could not fail to rouse in men of sensibility.

Thomson was the first prophet of the new religion: a voice crying in the wilderness of the town: 'I know no subject more elevating, more amusing, more ready to awake the poetical enthusiasm, the philosophical reflection, and the moral sentiment, than the works of Nature.' [5] His point of view differed from that of the pastoral poets of the seventeenth century in establishing a direct relation between the beauties of nature and the sensitive mind of the poet; it is his own personal impressions which are cherished and recorded that they may stir a sympathetic chord in the mind of the reader. The treatment is paralleled in the

[1] Mrs. Boscawen, *Letters, c.* 1750. [2] *Spectator*, No. 447, Sept. 1712.
[3] *Epistle to the Earl of Burlington.*
[4] For an account of English landscape gardening see C. Hussey, *The Picturesque*, 1927. The most recent account of parallel feeling in literature is C. de Haas, *Nature and the Country in English Poetry of the First Half of the Eighteenth Century*, Amsterdam, 1928. An example of the influence of such tastes on decoration at this date is afforded by the Worsley Cup, given by Charles Worsley to the Honourable Society of the Middle Temple, and made in London by Fred. Kandler in 1739. The bowl is enclosed by an avenue of naturalistic trees, with the upper part wreathed in vines. Jackson, *English Plate*, i. 229.
[5] Preface to the second edition of *The Seasons*. (First thought of in 1725: *Winter*, published in 1726, and the series finished with *Autumn* in 1730.)

Idylls of Gessner,[1] which were written some years before their publication in 1758 and 1762.[2] It is true that Gessner's pastorals are closely modelled upon Theocritus and Ovid; it is true that (unlike his Scottish contemporaries) he takes no account of his environment in his descriptions of Nature;[3] but none the less he breaks new ground in such work as the 'Contemplations amid the grass'— a sympathetic survey of the microcosm at our feet that childish eyes know best.

In early eighteenth-century France it was a mark of elegance to despise the country and everything that had to do with it, but gradually Frenchmen became accustomed to another way of thinking. For the most part they knew as little of real country life as they did of England or Switzerland, and could invest all three with the artificial charm of romance. Addison's *Spectator* essays were translated into French in 1720,[4] and Thomson's *Seasons* influenced France even before it was translated in 1759.[5] Saint Lambert, a Lorrainer who shared to some extent in Germanic sensibility, worked at his *Saisons* for nearly twenty years before he published them in 1766; and by then they were only a single manifestation of an interest that had become general.[6]

Lacking any true feeling for country pleasures, the Frenchmen of the early eighteenth century were quick to exaggerate the purely emotional side of the return to nature. Sensibility of every kind and degree was cultivated, and even philosophy found a new standpoint. Condillac[7] derived all man's highest facul-

---

[1] His preface tells us: 'It sometimes happens that I can tear myself away from the town and seek a refuge in the unpeopled countryside. There the sight of the beauties of Nature clears away from my soul all the weariness and all the painful impressions which I have brought with me. Filled with a thousand delightful feelings, I am as happy as a shepherd of the golden age.' He would seek in his Swiss retreat the simple pleasures of the country: 'Hazels trained to form an arbour would shelter my lonely house with their shade. . . . Before the door, in a little enclosure bounded by a quickset hedge, a limpid spring would murmur under a trellis of rushes. . . . A close hedge of nut-trees would wall this garden, with an arch of wild creepers at each corner' (vol. i, Preface, p. 31). The few who explored the reality were disappointed. Madame de Genlis went to see Gessner at Zurich, and tells us (*Souvenirs de Félicie*, p. 91) 'Je m'imaginais que l'habitation de Gessner devait être une élégante chaumière entourée de bocages et de fleurs, que l'on n'y buvait que du lait, et que, suivant l'expression allemande, *on y marchait sur des roses*. J'arrive chez lui. Je traverse un petit jardin uniquement rempli de carottes et de choux, ce qui commence à déranger un peu mes idées d'eglogues et d'idylles, qui furent tout à fait bouleversées en entrant dans le salon par une fumée de tabac qui formait une véritable nuage, au travers duquel j'aperçois Gessner fumant sa pipe et buvant de la bière, à côté d'une bonne femme en casaquin, avec un grand bonnet à carcasse et tricotant; c'était Madame Gessner.' A. Cassagne, *Le dessin enseigné par les maîtres*, p. 478, quotes a letter from Gessner instancing the influence of Thomson on landscape painting.

[2] The first French translation dates from 1761; the first edition in English was not published until 1802.

[3] The only one of his pastorals with such a setting is 'The Wooden Leg, a Swiss Idyll' as against some forty classical ones.

[4] By Charles Dufresny. It is significant that it was he who later designed an irregular English garden for Versailles.

[5] Bret, *Les Quatre Saisons*; Gentil Bernard, *Les Trois Saisons*; Peyrot, *Les Quatre Saisons*; Coninck, *Les Saisons*, &c. See D. Mornet, *Le Sentiment de la Nature en France au XVIIIᵉ siècle*, p. 398.

[6] Ever since the traditions of the seventeenth century had been rejected between 1735 and 1740, *Anglomanie* had increasingly dominated thought, and from 1763 the salon of Mademoiselle de l'Espinasse served as a focus to its influence.

[7] *Traité des Sensations*, 1754; Diderot's *Interprétation de la Nature* was published in the same year.

ties from sensation; and Helvetius found that 'dans l'homme tout se réduit a sentir'.[1] The only expression of this glorification of sentiment in the visual arts was in such work as that of Greuze. Its only important result was to give a false basis to any art that was in close relation with nature by making its chief function moral and didactic.[2] It was inevitable that such a view should permanently impoverish decorative art; the casual associations of its elements became of more importance than their intrinsic beauty and their artistic fitness. Moreover, every form of art that did not tell a story became of inferior interest, and a definite break-up of the traditional schemes of formal decoration was a result of the attempt to apply the new canons to ornament.[3]

The return to Nature is characteristic of England and Switzerland, the countries whose civilization was most firmly rooted in the soil. Neither country, however, found a natural expression for their feeling in decorative form,[4] though the generation that felt with Gray that 'not a precipice, not a torrent, not a cliff, but is pregnant with religion or poetry', made some extraordinary experiments in the attempt to express their sensibility in decoration. At Drakelowe there is still a panorama-room, decorated about 1790 and attributed to Paul Sandby. A contemporary tells us:

'Sir Nigel hath adorned one of his rooms with singular happiness. It is large, one side painted forest scenery, whose majestic trees arch over the curved ceiling; through them we see glades, tufted banks, and ascending walls in perspective. The opposite side of the room exhibits a Peak Valley, the front shows a prospect of more different country; real pales, painted green, and placed a few inches from the walls, increase the power of that deception.'[5]

In France Marie Antoinette set a clear pane of glass above a chimney piece at St. Cloud to frame an exquisite natural view as a landscape; but we hear of no panorama-rooms. In that country, indeed, sensibility was centred in human rather than natural interest.[6] Men felt with the Prince de Ligne that 'un tableau sans figures ressemble à la fin du monde.'[7] But men were tired of the pastoral

---

[1] *De l'Esprit*, 1758.

[2] The idea started in England with Shaftesbury's *Essay on Merit and Virtue* which was translated into French in 1745. A few years later Diderot could express without fear of contradiction the view that two qualities only were necessary for an artist, 'la morale et la perspective.' His views had considerable influence through his annual criticisms of the *salons*, beginning in 1759.

[3] Even Montgolfier's ascent in a balloon was made the subject of at least two patterns for Toile de Jouy about 1785, and at least two designs were made to represent the *Fête de la Fédération* in 1791. An English chintz was printed showing George III with his horse, and Queen Charlotte with her six children, as well as a group of the whole family with Windsor Castle in the background. (Example in the Victoria and Albert Museum.) Similarly such popular novels as the *Nouvelle Héloïse* and *Paul et Virginie* furnished pictorial designs for chintzes. Such influence, however, depended to some extent upon the development of the illustration of novels by engravings. Most of such chintz patterns are derived from engraved plates, while their lesser motives come from vignettes and culs de lampe. On these see H. Clouzot, *Histoire de la manufacture de Jouy et de la Toile imprimé en France*, 1928.

[4] Even Chelsea only produced one good peasant figure, the Reaper.

[5] *Letters*, ed. Gosse, ii. 45 (1739).

[6] A curious attempt is made to introduce it in Saint Aubin's *Premier essai de papilloneries humaines* where half human butterflies disport themselves.   [7] *Belœil*, p. 207.

written from a personal point of view, and agreed with Beaumarchais: 'Rien n'est plus insipide que ces fades camaïeux, où tout est bleu, où tout est rose, où tout est l'auteur, quel qu'il soit.'[1] The direct observation possible when the author was describing his own sensations would have produced a *genre* of no appeal to the eighteenth century if it had been faithfully applied to the contemporary life of the French peasantry. A family of painters—the brothers le Nain—and a single author—La Bruyère—had had the courage to face the facts a hundred years before, but their efforts had only served to bring the seventeenth-century pastoral movement to an end by driving men to seek romance further afield.[2] La Bruyère described the peasantry of France as he saw them: 'L'on voit certains animaux farouches, des mâles et des femelles; répandus par la campagne, noirs, livides, et tout brûlés du soleil. . . . Ils ont comme une voix articulée, et quand ils le lèvent sur leurs pieds, ils montrent une face humaine, et en effet ils sont des hommes.' Here was no theme for a pastoral, and the passage of a century saw little change.[3] Fêtes champêtres were fashionable, complete with peasants in holiday dress, village fairs and country dances; but only rarely—as in the fête given to the King of Poland at Bagatelle in 1757—did real villagers take part;[4] far more often—as in the famous fête given by the duchesse de Mazarin—it was the dancers of the opera who played the part of peasants, and led their beribboned lambs into the *salons* of the nobility. All the atmosphere of charming unreality is caught in Boucher's designs for the set of tapestries known as the *Nobles pastorales*, made in 1755: *La fontaine d'Amour, Le joueur de flûte, Le pêcheur, La pipée aux oiseaux, Le déjeuner, La bergère*;[5] and François Casanova's set of *Les amusements de la campagne*, designed in 1772,[6] are just as far removed from reality. In such pictorial fashion alone could such fêtes influence decoration; only Frederick the Great went so far as to have a straw-yellow wicker pattern service copied from peasant platters made at the Berlin china factory for his use at Sans Souci.[7]

[1] Quoted Martha, *La délicatesse dans l'Art*, p. 215.

[2] It is possibly due to their influence combined with that of the Dutch painters that Beauvais wove a tapestry of a 'Noce de Picardie' in 1670 (Badin, *La manufacture de tapisseries à Beauvais*, p. 7). An inventory of the Royal plate made after 1686 includes 'un vigneron d'or émaillé, portant une bêche de la main gauche et un fagot sur son épaule, cœffé d'un bonnet.' J. Guiffrey, *Inventaire général du Mobilier de la Couronne sous Louis XIV*, Paris, 1885, i. 50.

[3] Even Diderot found that 'Certaines formes sont-elles en usage parmi les paysans, ou des gens dont la profession, les emplois, le caractère nous sont odieux ou méprisables; ces idées accessoires reviendront malgré nous, avec celles de la couleur et de la forme; et nous prononcerons contre cette couleur et ces formes, quoiqu'elles n'ont rien en elles-mêmes de désagréable.' *Grande Encyclopédie*, Art. Beau.

[4] Such naturalistic pastorals are represented in decoration by Audran's *Fêtes de Village*, woven at the Gobelins about 1750, and in the *Couronnement de la Rosière*, printed at Jouy some thirty years later.

[5] They continued to be woven up to 1778. Badin, *La manufacture de tapisseries à Beauvais*, p. 35. See also H. Lemonnier, *L'Art moderne*, p. 215.

[6] *Ibid*. They included *Le rendez-vous de chasse, La pêche aux filets, La chasse aux canards, L'abreuvoir, Le repas, Le fauconnier assis, La blanchisseuse*, and *La charette de poissons*. Another set of pastorals—that 'à draperies bleues et à arabesques' designed by Huet was woven at Beauvais in 1780.

[7] Between 1770 and 1790 the china factories of Copenhagen and Petersburg were producing little statuettes of peasants in the traditional dress of their provinces.

385. Snuff-box enamelled with a Dutch subject. French, *c.* 1760

386. Design for printed linen in the Dutch style. French, *c.* 1760

387. Details of the frieze of the Pavillon du Jeu, Grand Trianon, Versailles. By Verberckt, *c.* 1750

The modern pastoral needed to be re-introduced to literature in a new dress; and in consequence of the *rapprochement* which contemporary theory had produced between literature and all other arts, its introduction was quickly and directly reflected in decoration.

The new pastoral was first sought in the remote country of China, then enjoying a literary vogue; and Huet painted Chinese pastorals in *camaieu bleu* for the Château de Champs (fig. 337). But China, by reason of its exotic artificiality, could not provide the thrill of contrast that scenes of rustic life seen in a courtly setting had to provide. New inspiration was sought in Italy, distant enough for romance, and classical enough to provide a sufficiently dignified background. In 1736 Boucher designed for Beauvais a set of 'Fêtes de Village à l'Italienne' in fourteen panels, some of which were reproduced as many as seventeen times,[1] with peasants and ruins and fêtes in the manner of 'Le delizie del fiume Brenta'. Holland next enjoyed a fleeting vogue. De Beaumarchais' *Le Hollandais* (1738) was followed in the next year by *Les Amusements de la Hollande* and in 1747 by Aubert de la Chesnaye des Bois' *Lettres Hollandaises*. France had its school of 'peintres hollandisants'; the engravers found new subjects for their plates and a 'hameau à la flamande' or two appeared in French gardens. The fashion was reflected in decoration. Figures of Dutch peasants were produced in porcelain, silver, and gold;[2] Horace Walpole hung his dining-room with paper imitating Dutch tiles, and about 1745 the looms of Brussels and Aubusson produced their 'fêtes flamandes' and 'fins Teniers'. The *Comptes Royaux* for 1758 mention snuffboxes 'émaillées à figures, d'après Teniers'; those for 1760 three 'a figures flamandes' (fig. 385),[3] and similar subjects were used by J. B. Huet and his school in their designs for Toile de Jouy (fig. 386). But Holland lacked both elegance and remoteness, and its associations were rather commercial than poetical. Diderot might exclaim:[4] 'J'aime mieux la rusticité que la mignardise; je donnerois dix Watteau pour un Teniers'; but the Dutch vogue soon languished and a fresh effort had to be made in a new direction.

Here again England and Switzerland gave the lead. The idealization of country life initiated by Gray's *Elegy* (begun in 1742 and finished in 1750) was continued alike in the *Devin du Village* of Rousseau (1755) and in the paintings of Greuze. France, however, soon got away from the facts of peasant life to the old visionary

[1] Badin, *La manufacture de tapisseries à Beauvais*, p. 31.
[2] *Livre Journal*, ed. Courajod, ii. 31. In 1749 Mme de Rochechouart bought of Lazare Duvaux 'Un Hollandais de porcelaine des Saxe'; *ibid.*, ii. 254. In 1755 Madame de Pompadour acquired 'Deux figures en or sur des terrasses, composées à l'usage de salière et poivrière, l'une représentant un Hollandois qui présente une huitre, l'autre un paysan qui tient un gros sac', *ibid.*, ii. 305, and in the following year Mme de Mirepoix bought 'une maison flamande, formant une cassolette, ornée d'attributs, figures et animaux, 480 livres'.
[3] Mazé Sencier, *Livre des Collectionneurs*, pp. 169–70. Cf. the Teniers' tapestry at Langborough in 1754 (R. Pococke, *Travels through England*, Camden Society, ii. 57). Teniers' scenes are stock subjects in Berlin and Frankenthal porcelain from about 1765 to 1770, and Dutch peasants are included in the Meissen price list of 1765 (Hannover, *op. cit.*, Rackham, iii. 94).   [4] *Pensées détachées*: du goût.

ideal, and Saint Lambert, describing the villagers returning homewards worn out, hot and hungry from haymaking, is content to refresh them with nothing more solid than strawberries and raspberries.

Such pastorals were possible only if their treatment was extremely tactful and their background extremely vague. They had to be set in some decently remote pastoral country—Switzerland[1] or the Pyrenees—or in some ideal village unknown to the geographer. No French writer dared to draw inspiration from anything as near to Paris as Stoke Poges is to London.[2] French pastorals, indeed, are as artificial as was the Hameau at Chantilly, where cottage walls in a state of picturesque and carefully achieved dilapidation masked a saloon of the Corinthian order hung with rose-coloured taffetas.[3]

Madame de Pompadour, however, brought rusticity into fashion, and kept cows and fowls at the Grand Trianon.[4] Her country tastes soon influenced decoration; the Pavillon de jeu of the Petit Trianon, built in 1749, has the interior decorated by Verberckt with a gilded frieze of the Marquise's poultry yard: pigeons, cocks, hens, ducks, and swans (fig. 387). Her purchases from Lazare Duvaux in the following year reflect the same interests; a fire-back with a fowl and pigeons, and another with a shepherd and shepherdess with their dogs and sheep.[5] But all these manifestations of new sensibilities lacked conviction. Some fresher and more human form of the 'return to nature' had to be found, and was discovered in the noble savage.

2

The beginnings of the study of anthropology had provided the philosophers with a new foundation for their theories. They had early found the romance of distance in admiration of the 'noble savage'; by 1672 Denys was already chanting his praises, and the Utopia of Vairasse's *Histoire des Sévérambes* of 1667 was succeeded by Fénelon's more famous *Bétique* in 1699. The increase of ethnological knowledge was enough to add reality to the dream, but not enough to destroy it. Buffon had published his *Observations on Human Varieties* in 1749, and in the next year Rousseau took advantage of the new point of view in his essay for a prize offered by the academy of Dijon on the moral effects of science and the arts. His thesis was that 'man's age of innocence was his happiest and best, and civilization had been his ruin'. Eleven years later it reached a larger public in the opening

---

[1] Cf. the group of the *Bergère des Alpes* designed for Sèvres by Falconet in 1766.

[2] French linguistic taste, too, was fastidious; Huber, the translator of Gessner's pastorals, wrote in his preface: 'La langue allemande a des hardiesses, que non seulement je ne pouvais pas, mais que je ne devais pas même rendre en français. Il m'a donc fallu en quelques endroits affaiblir les images, en choisissant à dessein des expressions moins énergiques.'

[3] de Nolhac, *Le Trianon de Marie Antoinette*, p. 267. The Hameau was built in 1774. Cf. the china painted by Lagrenée le jeune for the Trianon in 1788, in Pompeian style, with rustic cows and calves. In 1803 a room in the Casa del Labrador at Aranjuez was made to reproduce the ruined labourer's cottage that the Palace replaced.

[4] de Nolhac, *op. cit.*, p. 42.   [5] *Livre Journal de Lazare Duvaux*, ed. Courajod, ii. 75.

LA CHASSE

FIG. 388. Design for a panel by Boucher père, c. 1745.

words of *Émile*: 'Tout est bien sortant de la main de l'Auteur des choses, tout dégénère entre les mains de l'homme.'

The noble savage dispossessed the peasant in pastoral,[1] but however convenient an abstraction for literary purposes, he had hardly any decorative value. Only the interest in America felt[2] in the two decades between 1770 and 1780 could endow him with a little life. A panel of Cauvet's (fig. 389) shows the bow and arrows, the feathered head-dress and the tomahawk of the Iroquois, and the charming trophies of the *Cabinet du Roi* at Versailles, decorated in 1788, are all crowned by an American-Indian coronet of feathers.[3] Thus even monarchy could be glorified by the romance of savagery. Such symbols, however, remained artificial. The savage was most truly admirable when he did not even carry an attribute to be added to the vocabulary of decoration; 'l'habit de la Nature c'est la peau; plus on s'éloigne de ce vêtement, plus on pêche contre le goût.'[4]

There was, however, another age of innocence than that of the savage which art could glorify: childhood. Universal in its appeal, it none the less shared in the romance of unfamiliarity for a generation that sent away its babies to be reared in their nurses' homes; and the charming decorations of Boucher père show how well the subjects it afforded could be accommodated to the prevailing taste (fig. 388). The interest was bound up with the philosophical interest in education which had been felt even before Rousseau's *Émile* appeared in 1762.[5] So Boucher painted Madame de Pompadour's boudoir at Crécy with children engaged in drawing, sculpture, building, chemistry, music, gardening, dancing, fishing, and shooting; Arrivet designed fan-patterns with figures of children saying their lessons to their mother; the Meissen factory included no less than fourteen sets of figures of children in its price list of 1765,[6] and Casanova designed for Beauvais a set of tapestries, *L'Éducation ou les Quatre Ages*, woven between 1778

[1] Cf. *Émile*: 'Généralement il n'y a rien de plus lourd qu'un paysan, ni rien de plus fin qu'un sauvage.' The Prince de Ligne advises, 'Pas trop de Chinois; cela est trop colifichet et devient trop commun. Si l'on veut dans un canton désert faire construire quelques habitations de sauvages, et dépayser par des usages éloignés, cela ne peut être que très agréable.' *Belœil*, p. 213.

[2] Walpole, letter to Sir Richard Bentley, 3 Nov. 1754: 'The West Indian war has thrown me into a new study; I read nothing but American voyages, and histories of plantations and settlements.' *Letters*, ed. Toynbee, iii. 260.

[3] A more topical political reason inspired the well-known Toile de Jouy, *Hommage de l'Amérique à la France*, printed about 1795.

[4] Diderot, *Pensées détachées sur la peinture*, 1798. Political events arrested the progress of the glorification of the savage in decorative art. There is a letter from M. de Montucla, dated 8 April 1789, forbidding the Sèvres factory to make medallions with the head of a negro and the legend 'Ne suis-je pas homme?' (Havard and Vachon, *Les Manufactures Nationales*, p. 438). Cf. the use of wall-papers with scenes from Uncle Tom's Cabin in England and America, *c.* 1855; see *The Times Literary Supplement*, 15 July and 9 December 1926.

[5] Marmontel's *Contes Moraux* appeared in the *Mercure*, 1755-9, before they were published in book form in 1761 (two editions) and 1765. His second series appeared in the *Mercure*, 1790-3, and were published as a book in 1801. Others are La Dixmerie's *Contes philosophiques*, 1765, and Mme le Prince de Beaumont, *Contes Moraux*, 1773 and 1776.

[6] Hannover, *Pottery and Porcelain*, ed. Rackham, iii. 94.

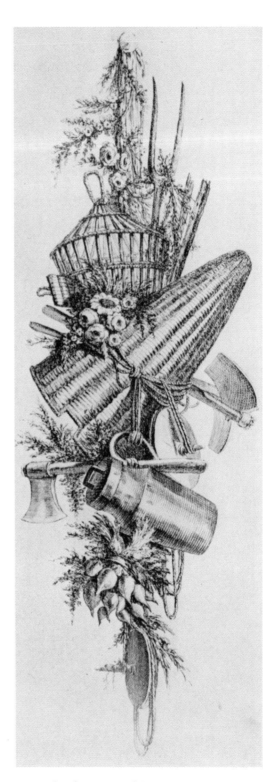

389. Design for a panel by Cauvet
with Red Indian attributes, c. 1775

390. *Attributs pastorals* by Delafosse, c. 1780

391. Design for printed linen. French, c. 1780

and 1780.[1] But this style in its turn could rule only for a short time, since it held few potentialities of development.

Philosophic influence on the decorative arts was more fruitful in the next phase, when a new interest and a new beauty were discovered in human avocations. The beginnings of industrialism, and the growth of the study of political economy[2] were accompanied by a real interest in the technique of manufacture. The *Grande Encyclopédie*, of which the first volume appeared in 1751, was a glorification of tools and technical processes.[3] The work even found a direct reflection in decoration. The china painters of Vincennes produced a dinner service decorated with figures representing all the *métiers*, from the gardener to the macaroon seller;[4] and Meissen and Lunéville followed suit about 1765 with their little figures of the 'Cris de Paris'. Madame de Pompadour bought in 1757 'Une petite tabatière, forme ronde, en or gravé et émaillé, à figures représentant des chimistes';[5] Huet made in 1783 a design for Toile de Jouy showing all the processes of calico-printing and the allied trades; and another design exists which shows *amorini* playing with retorts, electrical machines, telescopes, and other scientific instruments, and even a little satyr-encyclopedist belabouring a baby in clerical bands. The recognition of the importance of trade was similarly reflected in tapestries,[6] chintz-patterns and china painting[7] with scenes of mercantile shipping. Manufactured products were reproduced in decoration; ribbons—which had crept in from classical ornament— were used independently or with an admixture of flowers in goldwork,[8] woven silks, printed stuffs, and inlaid wood in such designs as those of Pillement's *Cahier de six nœuds de rubans* of 1770. Even woven and printed imitations of lace were admitted into ornament.[9]

Before long the process of the return to nature brought these technical processes into even closer relation with the lives of the leisured classes. Rousseau in 1762 preached in *Émile*:[10] 'He who eats in idleness what he has not earned, steals it.

[1] Badin, *La manufacture de tapisseries à Beauvais*, p. 35.

[2] The *Société des Économistes* was founded in 1767.

[3] D'Alembert says in his Preface that Diderot 'est l'auteur de la partie de cette encyclopédie la plus étendue, la plus importante, la plus désirée du public, et, j'ose le dire, la plus difficile à remplir; c'est la description des arts. M. Diderot l'a faite sur des métiers qui lui ont été fournis par des ouvriers ou des amateurs . . . ou sur les connaissances qu'il a été puiser lui-même chez les ouvriers, ou enfin sur les métiers qu'il s'est donné la peine de voir et dont quelquefois il a fait construire des modèles, pour les étudier plus à son aise.'

[4] Lent to the exhibition of the *Société des arts décoratifs* in 1865. The fashion reached England later; in 1796 J. C. Ibbetson painted oval medallions at Kenwood with scenes of industrial life. M. Jourdain, *English Furniture and Decoration, 1750–1820*, p. 75.

[5] *Livre Journal de Lazare Duvaux*, ii. 336.

[6] About 1750 Daniel Leyniers the younger was weaving tapestries with trading scenes at Brussels, and others were woven about the same time at Aubusson.

[7] e.g. on the porcelain of Meissen, Zweibrücken, and Doccia.

[8] Ribbons begin to appear in the decoration of goods in Lazare Duvaux's stock in the summer of 1754. See his *Livre Journal*, ii. 203, 207, and 306.

[9] Furs had appeared earlier in silk design out of compliment to Marie Leczinska, and the fashion for immense plumes which Marie Antoinette and the Princesse de Lamballe brought in in 1774, introduced them also into silk design.   [10] Book iii; *Œuvres*, viii. 102 and 109–10.

Every idle citizen is a rogue. . . . Of all the occupations by which a man may earn
a living that which brings him nearest to the state of nature is manual labour. . . .
Learn a trade.' The trade must be a serious one; the pupil must be 'neither gilder
nor embroiderer, nor lacquerer like Locke's gentleman . . . nor musician, nor
actor, nor writer of books. . . . I had rather that he were a shoe-maker than a poet'.
His advice was taken seriously; the king had his locksmith's forge in the attics of
Versailles, and Madame de Genlis, governess to the children of the Duc d'Orléans,
taught them all kinds of crafts as part of their Royal education: leatherwork,
basket making, ribbon weaving, cardboard modelling, artificial flower-making,
wire netting, paper marbling, hair work of all kinds, with carpentry and cabinet
making for the boys.[1] But such occupations were not the most admirable of all;
Rousseau found[2] that 'Le premier et le plus respectable des arts est l'agriculture,
je mettois la forge au second, la charpente au troisième.'

Agriculture, like the pastoral, entered court life in a decorated dress. The noble
did not, unless driven by the extreme of poverty, cultivate his own land, but took
to gardening[3] instead. Even the system of rotation was reduced to the scale of
a garden plot.[4] The new taste brought country landscapes into decoration, and
made gardening and other country pursuits a part of court life. The acting of
pastorals passed from the private theatre into everyday life, and the young queen
playing dairy-maid in her Hameau could find a satisfaction, however artificial, for
a sincere desire for peace in simple surroundings. Buildings very much like the
Hameau of Versailles appear on Toile de Jouy as a background to a charming
group of a lady playing with her children; and the same tastes are reflected in a
whole series of printed linens, *Les plaisirs de la ferme, Les vendanges, Les délices des
quatre saisons, L'éducation maternelle.*

The taste for gardening had behind it the authority of the sentimental novel.
Rousseau always chooses the garden as the centre of family life, the refuge of
disappointment, and the scene of calm. He makes the friends of Monsieur and
Madame de Wolmar pass their mornings there, 'à l'angloise, réunis et dans le
silence, goûtant à la fois le plaisir d'être ensemble et la douceur du recueillement.'
But the gardens of the novelist were always romantic and irregular, and in consequence every effort was made to give the splendid vistas and parterres of royal
parks the 'natural wildness' of some parsonage or farm.[5] 'They distorted our

---

[1] *Mémoires*, ed. Barrière, p. 195.   [2] *Émile*, Book iii; *Œuvres*, viii. 79.

[3] The interest in landscape gardening began in England, but since the strictly formal style was less general
there than in France it effected a milder revolution in taste. Delille's *Jardins* notes that Kent there introduced
an irregular style into gardening. The Prince de Ligne began his English garden at Belœil in 1775.

[4] Walpole, Letter to Chute, 5 Aug. 1771, ed. Toynbee, iii. 64. . . . 'English gardening gains ground
(in France) prodigiously—not much at a time indeed. . . . There is a Monsieur Boutin, who has tacked a piece
of what he calls an English garden to a set of stone terraces. . . . In a corner enclosed by a chalk wall are . . .
a strip of grass, another of corn, and a third *en friche*.'

[5] See Le Rouge, *Détail de nouveaux jardins à la mode ou jardins anglo-chinois*, 1776–85. (Whateley) *L'Art de
former les jardins modernes ou l'art des jardins Anglois*, 1771. Translation of Walpole, *On Modern Gardening*, 1785.

majestic avenues as far as the eye could reach; they destroyed our pools and fountains; they dug muddy little brooks, glorified by the name of streams; they overburdened our parks with bridges, hermitages, and tombs.'[1] The true end of the *ancien régime* is the moment immortalized by Hubert Robert when the formal trees of the Park of Versailles were cut down in 1775 by the orders of Louis XV.

It was in consequence of this taste for gardening that the impulse of the 'return to Nature' found its real expression in decoration. The trophies which the seventeenth century had consecrated to the arts of war were transformed into trophies of the pursuits of peace, since rakes and spades, like the instruments of music, art and science, symbolized the interests of those for whom they were made.[2] Cochin *fils* was one of the first to meet the need with his *Attributs et trophées de Jardinages,* which was followed by J. B. Huet's *Premier Livre de différents trophés* in 1772 and by Peyrotte's book of the same name with trophies of 'L'Astronomie, la Pêche, la Sculpture, la Marine, la Musique, l'Agriculture, le Jardinage et la Guerre.'[3] Such trophies appear in every kind of wall decoration; in painting, carving, stucco, tapestry, embroidery, and even on the bronze lantern in the hall of the Petit Trianon.

Trophies of the same occupations as those of Peyrotte's pattern-book decorate the *Cabinet du Roi* of Versailles (1788)—the room which had to be guarded with iron bars to protect the king from the possible attacks of his people. But since they were confined to the houses of the over-sophisticated who alone found pleasure in the artificial pastoral, they passed away with other *signes de la féodalité* before the tide of Revolution.

3

The strongest and most natural of all the decorative manifestations of the return to nature was a revival of floral ornament. England had maintained the tradition of such decoration alike in gardening, literature, and the minor arts. As early as 1709 John Harris had produced a theory of criticism that reduced poetry, music, and painting to the imitation of nature,[4] and national taste was ready to make the

The Prince de Ligne (*Belœil*, p. 232) in 1786 preaches, 'Amateurs des jardins, soyez amateurs de l'humanité. C'est dans les champs que vous trouverez moyen de l'exercer. . . . Éloignez de chez vous la triste image de la pauvreté.'

[1] Madame de Genlis, *Dictionnaire des Étiquettes de la Cour*, 1818, i. 37. The allusion is probably to Chantilly, which had its 'hameau' and gothic chapel *à l'anglaise*.

[2] At Marly, which Louis XIV planned as an escape from the grandeurs of Versailles, Le Brun had designed trophies of rakes and spades, scythes and flails, nets and baskets.

[3] Others were published at Paris by Demarteau l'aîné; Cherpitel; Juillet; J. Dumont and R. Charpentier, both engraved by Huquier; de Lalonde; and in London by Dodd, 1769. (One design for a room decorated with them appears in I. Johnson's book of 1758.)

[4] Cordier de Launay later based a whole theory of aesthetic on this point of view (*Théorie circosphérique des deux genres du beau*, 1806). His thesis was that man could create no form, but could only borrow from nature. The objects of human artistic creation are either exact imitations of nature, or mixtures of scattered natural forms in a composite chimerical whole.

most of such philosophic justification.[1] Thomson could describe the glories of English gardens—perhaps the most flowery gardens in Europe:

> Fair-handed Spring unbosoms every grace;
> Throws out the snowdrop and the crocus first,
> The daisy, primrose, violet darkly blue,
> And polyanthus of unnumbered dyes,
> The yellow wallflower, stained with iron brown
> And lavish stock that scents the garden round;
> From the soft wing of vernal breezes shed,
> Anemones: auriculas, enriched
> With shining meal o'er their velvet leaves;
> The full ranunculus of glowing red . . .
> No gradual bloom is wanting, from the bud
> First-born of Spring to Summer's musky tribes;
> Nor hyacinths, of purest virgin white,
> Low bent, and blushing inward; nor jonquils
> Of potent fragrance; nor gay-spotted pinks;
> Nor, showered from every bush, the damask rose.[2]

The embroidresses rejoiced in flower patterns, and rivalled the poet in their profusion. Mrs. Delany records 'a black satin court petticoat with sprays . . . of bugloss, auriculas, honeysuckle, wild roses, lilies of the valley, and white and yellow jessamine.'[3] Even natural landscape had its influence on embroidery. At one court, she tells us,

'The Duchess of Queensberry's clothes pleased me best. They were white satin embroidered, the bottom of the petticoat *brown hills* covered with all sorts of weeds, and every breadth had *an old stump of a tree* that ran up almost to the top of the petticoat, broken and ragged, and worked with brown chenille, round. which were twined nasturtiums, ivy, honeysuckles, periwinkle, convolvuli and all sorts of twining flowers, which spread and covered the petticoat. Vines with the leaves variegated as you have seen them by the sun, all rather smaller than nature, which makes them look very light; the robings and facings were little green banks filled with all sorts of weeds, and the sleeves and the rest of the gown loose twining branches of the same sort as those on the petticoats; many of the leaves were finished with gold, and parts of the stumps of the trees looked like the gilding of the sun.'

Such tastes spread even into architecture and furniture; Decker in 1759 published under the misleading title of *Gothic Architecture*, 'a large Collection of Temples, Banqueting, Summer and Green Houses, Gazebos, Alcoves . . . Hermitages for Summer and Winter, Obelisks, Pyramids, etc., many of which may be executed with Pollards, Rude Branches and Roots of trees, Being a taste entirely new,' while Robert Mainwaring in 1765 published 'The Cabinet and Chairmakers' Real Friend and Companion . . . containing . . . some very beautiful designs supposed

---

[1] Cf. Prince de Ligne, *Belœil* (1786), p. 48: 'La simplicité, la nature et le désordre appartiennent aux Anglais de même que les lignes droites, les percés, les grands morceaux sont aux Français.'

[2] The importance of Thomson's *Seasons* in the history of taste was first pointed out by Warton. (See Alison, *Essays on taste*, 1825 ed., ii. 102 note).   [3] Jourdain, *English Secular Embroidery*, p. 107.

392. Embroidered linen hanging. English, *c.* 1750

393. Detail of a commode. French, c. 1775

to be executed with the Limbs of Yew, Apple, or Pear Trees, ornamented with Leaves and Blossoms, which, if properly painted, will appear like nature.' [1]

In France the hold of style was stronger; but the tradition of flower patterns was still a living one, however much it had become subordinated to a succession of architectural styles; weaver, embroiderer, sculptor, jeweller, painter, and engraver had all a special technique ready for its use and development. As early as 1745 the lilies of France appeared in natural form, wreathed in roses, in the headpiece to the account of the festivities given by the city of Paris to celebrate the Dauphin's marriage,[2] and thirty years later they were perpetuated in bronze on furniture for royal use (fig. 393).

Once more the poetry of nature and of flowers was re-created against a background of scientific study. Such study, too, was admitted and encouraged even in court circles. Men like Linnaeus, who published the first edition of his *Genera Plantarum* in 1737, and Bernard de Jussieu, had ladies of fashion as their pupils and patrons;[3] the botanical painter Ehret in 1749 began to give lessons to the Duchesses of Norfolk and of Leeds, and to the daughters of the Dukes of Bridgwater and Kent and of many other noble houses.[4]

Such scientific studies were at first directly imitated in decoration. Buffon had his 'édition de Sèvres' with all the birds he describes painted on a dinner service,[5] and about 1790 the Copenhagen porcelain factory began the famous *Flora Danica* service, derived from the botanical engravings of Holmskjold, the first director of the factory.[6]

As a taste for flowers and birds became more widespread their representation became less severe. The engravers began to produce flower-plates intended to be of use alike to the botanist and to the designer,[7] and these were soon followed by definitely decorative flower patterns that could be adapted to any of the arts.[8]

[1] Some of Chippendale's mirror designs show frames of naturalistic branches.

[2] *Fêtes publiques données par la Ville de Paris à l'occasion du mariage de Monsiegneur le Dauphin*, 1745.

[3] Jussieu reminded the Academy of the collection of 6,000 miniatures of plants begun by Robert, painter-embroiderer to Gaston d'Orléans, for the use of embroiderers. In 1759 he laid out a botanic garden at the Trianon to replace Madame de Pompadour's farmyard.

[4] *Proceedings of the Linnaean Society*, 1894–5, p. 57.

[5] Shown on loan at the Musée des Arts décoratifs in 1865. Up to 1770 the birds on Meissen porcelain were taken from the coloured plates of Buffon. In 1787 a set of plates of Tournay porcelain were painted for Philippe d'Orleans by Joseph Mayer with birds from Buffon's plates; the set is now in the Victoria and Albert Museum. Chapuis decorated other Sèvres services with birds in 1753, 1759, and 1763, and he and the Evans family of Sèvres influenced the china paintings of Chelsea about 1760, and of Worcester, Bristol, and Plymouth porcelain, which used bird decoration between 1770 and 1780. Birds were also used on Sceaux pottery about 1765.

[6] The service is now the Rosenborg Slott at Copenhagen. Hannover, *Pottery and Porcelain*, ed. Rackham, iii. 433. Rather later the Spanish royal china factory at Buen Retiro produced a set decorated with medicinal herbs taken from the *Icones et descriptiones plantarum*, published in 1791.

[7] The earliest of these are by Dutchmen and published in London; e.g. P. Casteels, London, 1730, and *A Select Collection of the most beautiful flowers* by A. Heckell, c. 1760.

[8] Among the most important are those by Vivares (London, 1756), Bertren (Paris, 1765), Berthault (Paris, c. 1770), Roch (Paris, 1770), T. Major (London, 1775), G. F. Reudel (Augsburg, c. 1775), &c.

Similarly about 1765 Philippe de la Salle designed splendid bird patterns for Lyons silks, in which the various species are recognizable enough but the whole intention is decorative.

Just as flowers had once obeyed the conventions of classicism, so now they followed the canons of the rocaille style. They are never shown growing, as in the Middle Ages; they are never stylized into symmetry, as in the Renaissance, but instead are balanced into a graceful irregularity. Always they appear freshly cut, as if just given to some charming visitor to a garden; and always thrown with artful carelessness upon the background, as if she had let them slip from her fingers. They are sophisticated by a court discipline of gaiety; they dance, they curtsey, they glide across a panel or a plate, with all the graces and some of the mannerisms of a fine lady.

The poet Gray said that he took to botany to save himself the trouble of thinking, and half the world followed his example. All over Europe flowers became the dominant motive in china painting. The Meissen factory adopted 'teutsche Blumen' as a standard type of decoration in 1740, using the prints of Schmidhammer and J. D. Preisler as models before they had evolved their own types. The French factory adopted them very shortly after its foundation in 1748, and they appear on the wares of Stockholm, Venice, Le Nove, Capo di monte, Dresden, Nymphenburg, Höchst, Frankenthal, Vienna, Zurich, Chantilly, Mennecy, Lille, Volkstedt, Etterbeek, and indeed in every china factory of any importance in Europe. It was perhaps in the English factories—and notably at Chelsea—that they were most naturalistically treated and most consistently used. Pottery was not slow to imitate the more delicate wares, and flowers appear on the pottery of Rennes, Marseilles (fig. 396), Sceaux (fig. 395), Aprey, Lunéville, Meillonnas, Niederwiller, Strasbourg, Rouen, Saint Clément, Moustier, Marieberg, and many other provincial centres.

Flowers were not only painted, but were even plastically imitated in porcelain (fig. 397). The royal manufactory of Vincennes (later Sèvres) began to make them in 1748. Soulavie tells us [1] how Madame de Pompadour introduced them to her royal lover.

'She awaited him one day in that fairy palace of the Bellevue, that had cost him so dear, and as he entered, she received him in a room at the back of which was an immense greenhouse and a bank of flowers in the middle of a severe winter. As fresh roses, lilies and pinks predominated, the enraptured king could not admire enough the beauty and sweet scent of this bank of flowers. Nature was there counterfeited. These vases, these flowers, these roses, these pinks, these lilies and these sprays were all in porcelain, and the sweet scent of the flowers was caused by their essences artificially distilled.'

It is hard to conceive a more artificial tribute to natural beauty, but it greatly pleased the king. D'Argenson records [2] that 'the king ordered from the factory at

---

[1] *Mémoires du duc de Richelieu*, quoted in Havard and Vachon, *op. cit.*, p. 340.   [2] *Mémoires*, vii. 122.

394. Panel of embroidered silk, presented by the City of Lyons to Louis XVI, *c.* 1770

396. Dish of Marseilles pottery, c. 1765

395. Dish of Sceaux pottery, c. 1775

Vincennes porcelain flowers painted like nature with their vases, to the value of more than eight hundred thousand livres, for all his country houses'.[1] In 1749, the first year when these china bouquets were offered for public sale, the demand was such that more than thirty-six thousand livres worth was sold, representing five-sixths of the factory's total output of porcelain.[2] Vegetables—cabbages, lettuces, artichokes, cauliflowers, melons, and asparagus—were imitated as tureens and teapots[3] between about 1750 and 1760. Sèvres with flower decoration was even applied with unhappy effect to furniture, which also received floral ornament in the more suitable inlaying and painting.[4] The goldsmiths were quick to avail themselves of the theme. The *corbeille* of Marie Josèphe de Saxe, who was married in 1747, included a gold box decorated with a hawthorn spray with enamelled leaves and diamond flowers, and others with ears of corn, pansies, and cherries. Two years later Hébert was producing innumerable snuff-boxes with roses, pinks, anemones, hyacinths, and tulips.[5] In 1754 Heimmerich published at London a pattern-book of 'Bouquets de Fleurs pour orfèvre'. The Austrian watch-makers a little later revived the designs and style of Légaré and his school, while in France charming work was produced with floral frets of gold over a ground of agate or other precious material (fig. 399). The interaction of craftsmanship and poetry may indeed be traced in the pastorals of the time:

> L'émail des gazons frais, des ruisseaux argentés,
> Et le jeu des rayons dans ces perles liquides . . .
> Les rubis des pavots qu'emportent les zéphyrs
> Et le bleuet flottant, qui sème ses saphirs. . . .[6]

The pictorial art of tapestry was soon affected by the work of men like Tessier,

[1] The Dauphine, Marie Josèphe de Saxe, bought of Duvaux two pair of candlesticks of which the description shows the elaboration; his day-book records (ii. 6) 'Posé à la cheminée de son cabinet à Versailles une paire de bras à trois branches, composés de branchages vernis imitant la nature, avec les fleurs de Vincennes assorties à chaque plante; le haut de ces bras d'une branche de lys, tulipes, jonquilles, narcisses et jacinthes bleues, les branches du milieu en roses, celles en dehors d'anémones et semi-doubles, celles en dedans de giroflées rouges et violettes, la jonction des branches garnies de différentes fleurs, le bas, de boutons d'or et oreilles d'ours; les bassins de la même porcelaine avec les binets dorées d'or moulu, 1,200 livres. Une autre paire de même grosseur, posée en trumeau vis-à-vis, dont le haut de trois œillets doubles, barbeaux, branches de fleurs d'oranger, tulipes, campanules; les branches du milieu d'anémones et semi-doubles, celles en dehors de jacinthes d'Hollande a quatre cœurs; celles en dedans de jonquilles doubles. La jonction des bras ornée de différentes fleurs, le bas de boutons d'or et grosses jacinthes à cœur de rose, avec les bassins de porcelaine et binets dorés, 1,200 liv.' A bouquet of such flowers that she sent to her father, the Elector of Saxony, is still preserved in the Porcelain Collection at Dresden (fig. 397).

[2] See Duvaux, *op. cit.*, ii. 3, 6, 59, 67, &c.

[3] As tureens at Delft, Brussels, Proskau, Holitsch, Strasbourg, Sleswig, Eckernförde, Kastrup, Höchst, and Lille; while cauliflower teapots and basins were produced in Staffordshire; Hannover, *Pottery and Porcelain*, ed. Rackham, i. 490.

[4] e.g. Duvaux, *op. cit.*, i. 1, Sept. 1748, 'M. de Boulogne, Deux armures d'encoignure en bois satiné à fleurs'; ii. 54, June 1750, 'S.A. Mme la Princesse de Rohan, douairière; Deux commodes à pieds de biche en vernis blanc poli et peintes avec des guirlandes de fleurs sur la face et les côtés.'

[5] *Ibid.*, p. 153. In 1754 Jean Moynat made a snuff-box with roses, narcissus, pinks, anemones, tulips, and jonquils enamelled in natural colours on a ground of blue and brown. Mazé-Sencier, *Livre des Collectionneurs*, p. 152. (2) *ibid.*, p. 150. [6] Saint Lambert, *Les Saisons*, chant i.

'peintre du Roi pour les fleurs', and a profusion of flowers bloomed on the hangings, screens, and chair-coverings produced at the Gobelins and at Beauvais. The
most eminent of the designers in this style was Ranson, who besides designing for
the Royal tapestry works published many pattern-books in 1778 and the subse-
quent years. It is noticeable that his repertory includes only simple garden
flowers and fruits—roses, larkspurs, cornflowers, poppies, pinks, iris, lilies, tulips,
anemones; grapes, apples, plums, oranges, pears, and gooseberries. They are never
closely massed, but always scattered in light and airy fashion over the ground that
is to be filled.[1] Lyons silk, with its long tradition of flower decoration, paid
homage to the new taste in another way. The flowers that under Louis XIV
had been of heroic largeness were under Louis XV represented in their natural
size. At the same time the weavers and embroiderers reproduced many wild
flowers, such as buttercups and sorrel.[2]

Not only the minor arts but also the mistress art of architecture accepted flowers
as one of the chief elements of decoration. By 1750 Frederick II had even the
library at Sans Souci[3] decorated with naturalistic leafy sprays; Chambers introduced flowers into his architectural decorations after his return to England in
1753,[4] and by 1768 country flowers—daisies, stocks, violets, and anemones—were
enough appreciated at Court to furnish the decoration for Marie Antoinette's
bedroom at the Petit Trianon.[5] Even the strict classical style could be influenced
without loss of correctness, since Augustan art had treated flowers naturalistically
in its ornamental sculpture.[6] In 1780 de Lalonde was publishing designs for
classical orders with a frieze of rose-rinceaux, and mouldings of closely-packed
naturalistic roses, besides several of oak and acorns and one of fruit,[7] and the use
of flowers marks the last stage of the architectural style of Robert Adam. Georges
Jacob decorated furniture in the classic style of Louis XVI with lilac, violets,
roses, poppies, sunflowers, water-lilies, parsley, lilies of the valley, apple blossom,
medlars, pea-pods, and ears of corn.[8] Diderot even tried to express the beauties

---

[1] Other pattern-books of the sort were produced by such different artists as Saint Aubin, who soon after
1750 published *Bouquets champêtres dédiés à Madame la Maréchale de Biron*, and another series dedicated to
Madame de Pompadour, Pillement the designer of *Chinoiseries*, who about 1760 published at London two
'Recueils de différens bouquets de fleurs', and Thomas Bertien.

[2] e.g. on waistcoats of about 1783 in the Musée des Tissus historiques of Lyons.

[3] By the German sculptor Merk. Cf. Hoppenhaupt's designs for wall decoration published in 1753, and
the Kaiserzimmer in the grand-ducal castle at Carlsruhe.

[4] Gwilt, prefatory memoir to Chambers's *Decorative Part of Civil Architecture*, p. xlix. Cf. the very naturalistic swags of flowers hanging from bucrania on the frieze of the north-east room at Mereworth Castle, and
the boudoir ceiling at Kyre Park, Worcestershire, c. 1755.

[5] Cf. the many flowers used in the decoration of Madame du Barry's garden pavilion at Fontainebleau
three years later.

[6] M. Reymond has pointed out that S. Maria dell'Orto, the gardener's church in Rome, built in 1690, is
full of painted garlands of flowers and fruit applied to a classic baroque scheme, and indicates its possible
influence on eighteenth-century decoration (Michel, *Histoire de l'Art*, vi. 35).

[7] Victoria and Albert Museum, EO26, E5174 and 5177, 1910; cf. Albertolli's similar mouldings of 1787.

[8] H. Lefuel, *Georges Jacob*, p. 119.

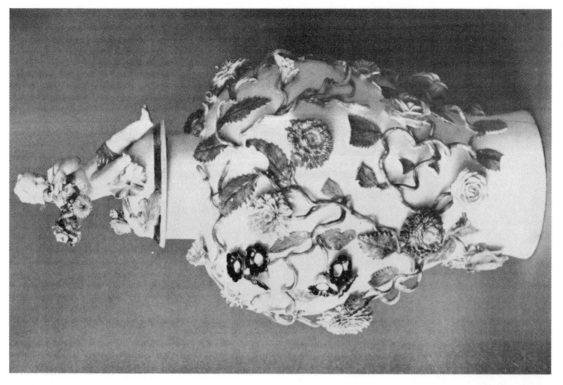

398. Vase of Berlin China, *c.* 1755

397. Bouquet of Vincennes china flowers given by the Dauphine to the Elector of Saxony in 1749

399. Etui with gold decoration on an agate
ground. French, *c.* 1775

400. Etui of agate with applied decoration in gold and precious
stones. French, *c.* 1760

of classical architecture in terms of nature. 'Ce qui est riche en architecture . . . c'est cette belle touffe d'acanthe qui entoure le vase de Callimaque; c'est une frise où rampe une vigne abondante, ou qu'embrasse un faisceau de chêne ou de laurier.'[1] In the trophy of the arts in the Cabinet du Roi at Versailles (1788) a palm tree appears as the symbol of the column and its capital. Every one agreed with Voltaire: 'Comme le mauvais goût au physique consiste à n'être flatté que par les assaisonnemens trop piquans et trop recherchés, aussi le mauvais goût dans les Arts est de ne se plaire qu'aux ornemens étudiés, et de ne pas sentir la belle nature.'

Paradoxically the return to nature in decoration owed much to the gradual industrialization of the arts. In consequence of the weakening of their craft-traditions, a more universal style of ornament was possible, and was fostered by the general taste. Its adoption may well have been hastened by the 'École gratuite de Dessin' of Paris, founded by the flower painter Jean Jacques Bachelier in 1766 under the patronage of Madame de Pompadour.[2] It was 'une école élémentaire de dessin en faveur des métiers relatifs aux arts', and taught the elements of geometry and architecture, and the drawing of figures, animals, ornament, and flowers. Its pupils numbered over fifteen hundred in the first few years, and it is easy to believe that its influence must have tended to level the styles of the different crafts. At the same time the development after 1750 of cotton spinning and weaving led to the production of vast quantities of calicoes, prints, and muslins of which the designs were printed and not woven, while the introduction in 1770 of cylinders instead of blocks in printing cotton made a short repeat of not more than ten or twelve inches necessary, and encouraged the use of small detached sprigs of flowers.[3] At Lyons, Jean Revel's discovery of 'points rentrés', which made it possible to give greater play of light and shade to the fabric, helped to approximate silk-weaving to painting, and led to the free adoption of realistic flower-patterns.[4] Similarly the invention of transfer printing on china, an English process discovered in 1756, helped to prolong the life of the style.

The influence of the taste for flowers likewise appeared in more subtle forms than these. Sainte Beuve says that Rousseau's phrase 'l'or de genêts et la pourpre de la bruyère'[5] marks an epoch in French prose; at the same time flower hues enter decoration to make an epoch in French art.[6] The pearl-grey and gold and

[1] *Grande Encyclopédie*, art. Goût.

[2] After 1792 École Nationale du Dessin, now École Nationale des Arts décoratifs. See Dreyfous, *L'Art français aux temps révolutionnaires*, p. 86.

[3] At the Revolution the Société Populaire et Républicaine des Arts at its session of the 26th Germinal, an II, demanded 'Que peut une fleur, un paysage sur les mœurs? . . .' A member replied: 'Je prétends que les peintres de fleurs sont utiles au commerce et que les manufactures en tirent un grand parti.' The assembly agreed, 'Qu'on les renvoie donc aux manufactures' (*Journal de la Société*, p. 310; quoted, Courajod, *A. Lenoir*, i. lxvii).

[4] A curious style which had few imitators is shown in Pillement's *Fleurs Idealle* [sic] of 1770, giving designs of fantastic flowers made with feathers.

[5] Used in a letter to M. de Malesherbes of 26 January 1762.   [6] The change reached England in 1766.

lacquer colours of the first half of the century were succeeded by the colours of porcelain: *bleu du Roy* discovered at Sèvres in 1749, *bleu céleste, bleu turquoise* (1752), *rose Pompadour* (1757) and by other china tints—*violet pensée, vert pomme, jonquille, œil de perdrix*, taken directly from nature. They satisfied a growing wish for clarity of colour: as early as 1741 Père Andre had proposed to grade colours according to their luminosity: first yellow, then red, green, blue, and last violet. 'Qu'y a-t-il de plus naturel et de plus raisonnable, que de mesurer leur beauté par leur éclat?'[1] It is such colours as these which made Burke say:

'Those which seem most appropriate to beauty, are the milder of every sort: light greens, soft blues; weak whites, pink reds; and violets. . . . If the colours be strong and vivid, they are always diversified, and the object is never of one strong colour; there are almost always such a number of them (as in variegated flowers) that the strength and glare of each is considerably abated.'

In the autumn of 1753 Gray was observing the autumn colouring in new detail: 'the hazel and whitethorn were turning yellow in the hedges, the sycamore, lime and ash (where it was young, or much exposed) were growing rusty', and the general appreciation of such colouring was reflected in the vogue of *feuille morte* and such subdued tints.[2]

Purely naturalistic tastes, however, could not last indefinitely. Flowers lack certain qualities without which art cannot live. Lessing discovered that 'the inorganic and vegetable world are incapable of an ideal'[3] and Uvedale Price failed to find them picturesque.[4] The fashion, indeed, had begun to decline by 1780, and Delille's belated production of *Les Jardins* in 1782 failed before the ridicule of Rivarol's *Lettres critiques sur le poème des jardins, suivies de la plainte du chou et du navet.*

The flowers of the sentimental return to Nature lived just long enough to symbolize the political return to anarchy which the philosophy of sentiment had helped to bring about. In the terrible days of the Convention every woman wore or carried a bunch of flowers, and the tricolour found decorative expression in the cornflower, the poppy, and the daisy of the fields (fig. 403). The theorists of the

---

[1] *Essai sur le Beau*, p. 10.

[2] The effect of colour on a sensitive mind began to be of interest: Goethe used to wear coloured glasses in order to experience the change of feeling produced by a world that was green, blue, or yellow, and quotes a Frenchman who maintained that the tone of his conversation with Madame X had changed after she had altered the colour of her boudoir from blue to red. Diderot was interested in the question of the associations of colours, and found them half rational and half capricious. Such analogies, however, were strong enough to make startling or vivid hues 'une marque de vanité ou de quelqu'autre mauvaise disposition de cœur ou d'esprit'. The Abbé Castel went farther and invented a 'Clavecin à couleurs' for the interpretation of music in terms of colour.

[3] Notes for Part II of *Laocoon*, quoted Bosanquet, *History of Aesthetics*, p. 229.

[4] *On the Picturesque*, 1810, p. 93. 'If we turn from animal to vegetable nature, many of the most beautiful flowers have a high degree of symmetry; so much so, that their colours appear to be laid on after a regular and finished design: but beauty is so much the prevailing character of flowers, that no one seeks for anything picturesque among them.'

401. Screen of Gobelins tapestry. By Neilson, 1764

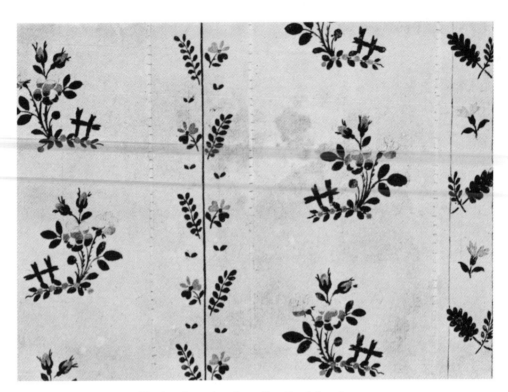

402. Design for printed textile. By Advenier, *c.* 1770

403. Design for textile with Revolutionary poppies and
cornflowers, *c.* 1791.

404. Silk brocade. French, *c.* 1800

405. Design for Toile de Jouy. By Horace Vernet, 1815

Empire, however, soon reduced flowers to geometrical abstractions. Révérony St. Cyr found that 'the enormous variety of these favourites of Nature leaves no hope of determining their form in a satisfactory and geometric manner'.[1] Percier did not banish them from decoration, but so stiffened and formalized them that there seems no lack of harmony between his geometric forms and his marguerites, palms, myrtle, olive, acanthus, and fern. A typical Empire velvet brocade is decorated with single laurel leaves laid flat in rows.[2] The pastoral was dead; and the agriculturist and artizan celebrated the fleeting triumphs of democracy, not with the insignia of their own crafts, but with the trophies of patrician Rome.

4

Not until a measure of aristocratic life was restored did the pastoral reappear. Then Delille could hymn the occupations of the country in his *Homme des champs* of 1802;[3] de la Borde could write of the delights of 'un beau jardin et une vie tranquille';[4] and Marie Louise—another Austrian—could order from the imperial manufactory of Sèvres a service of milk pans and pitchers for use in her own dairy.

But the aristocratic sport of hunting had a greater charm for the bourgeois. By 1810 'new invented Borders for Rooms, etc., of Field Sports' were being published in London,[5] and five years later Horace Vernet's design for Toile de Jouy—*La Chasse à courre*—was in great vogue in France (fig. 405). 'Natural Wildness' was added to other designs of the same sort by a background of gothic ruins, pine trees, snow mountains, and Swiss chalets. Swiss scenery, indeed, enjoyed a vogue of its own[6] as a subject of decoration; scenes that could serve as illustrations to *Contes Moraux* were produced in wall-paper by Mongin about 1803[7] and in Toile de Jouy by Demarne in 1814. Then with the return of the monarchy pastoral was once more domiciled in France; and about 1820, Normandy was producing printed cottons with *Les plaisirs de la campagne*.

If industry destroyed the romance of the arts,[8] a more urban life once more gave a fresh charm to flowers.[9] Moreover, the new link between Napoleon and the Imperial House of Austria revived the royal style of simplicity; in 1810 Girodet

---

[1] *Essai sur le perfectionnement des Beaux Arts par les sciences exactes*, 1803, i. 27.

[2] A piece is in the Musée des Tissus historiques at Lyons.

[3] In the same year appeared Morel's *Théorie des jardins ou l'art des jardins de la Nature*.

[4] *Description des nouveaux jardins de la France et de ses anciens châteaux*, Paris, 1808.

[5] 'Engraved by Merke after R. B. Davis and published by C. Random at the Sporting Gallery, 65 Pall Mall'; see Ackerman, *Wallpaper*, p. 58.

[6] Swiss travel came into fashion after the publication of the *Nouvelle Héloïse* about 1777, and about 1780 engravings of Swiss scenery began to be produced in considerable quantities. See D. Mornet, *Du sentiment de la Nature en France au XVIIIᵉ siècle*, p. 54.

[7] Ackerman, *op. cit.*, p. 50. A similar paper was produced by the Alsatian Zuber in the following year.

[8] The *Service des Arts Industriels* made at Sèvres in 1823 is a curious survival from the preceding century.

[9] At the same time a flower—the crown imperial—was added to the Napoleonic emblems. It appears on a carpet woven for Napoleon at the Savonneries and given by him to the King of Saxony in 1809, which is now at La Malmaison.

painted the panels of the salon des fleurs at Compiègne for Marie Louise with the different sorts of lilies, and for the boudoir at Versailles, Bony designed silks that have their circular and octagonal medallions filled with birds and butterflies instead of thunderbolts and eagles, and their grounds adorned with light and irregular sprigs of flowers.[1] For Saint Cloud he mingled the traditions of Monarchy and Empire, and the Napoleonic thunderbolts and panoplies alternate oddly with the golden pheasants of the tradition of Philippe de la Salle. For Fontainebleau Richard produced painted velvets, on which panels of naturalistic oleander boughs are framed first by a strictly classical anthemion and then by a garland of natural roses. The Restoration had therefore only to bring back the lilies of Versailles to replace the Imperial bees, and to add to its *pastiches* of the classicism of Louis XIV the pine boughs of the Swiss pastoral,[2] and the many-hued convolvulus which Bernardin de Saint Pierre had introduced into French art. But the flowers of the Ancien Régime returned sobered by their years of exile; they had lost their former grace and had become a trifle plebeian; they suggest a conservatory[3] rather than a court, mature well-being rather than youthful elegance.

Decorative treatment became more and more naturalistic and pictorial as the century progressed.[4] Classicism was confined to a border that framed a naturalistic bouquet, and when the traditional rinceaux of the classic style were retained for furnishings of state they were naturalized by the addition of such flowers as the newly discovered dahlia.[5] Flowers had come back into French decoration with the revival of aristocracy and monarchy; as aristocracy declined before the influence of a wealthy bourgeoisie such comparatively simple decoration was modified in sympathy. It had to be enriched and vulgarized by the addition of tropical birds and of glowing jewelled ornaments, which hang in complacent incongruity from the frame[6] (fig. 407). But while in France the parvenus were demanding styles with historic pedigrees, in Victorian England the national taste for flowers and flower-patterns was reaching its zenith, unhindered by any sophisticated canons of style.[7] Craftsman and amateur alike embarked upon a career of pitiless naturalism, and even its critics preached a servile imitation of Nature.

The remorseless detail of the pre-Raphaelites—which included a minute study of

---

[1] These hangings, still in a marvellous state of preservation, form part of the Mobilier National.

[2] e.g. in the *Service forestier* with pine and fir sprigs framing views of famous trees made at Sèvres in 1835.

[3] The influence that brought in this naturalism was definitely horticultural. By 1830 Sèvres was producing its 'Service de la culture des fleurs'.

[4] Naturalism was encouraged in colour printing on cotton by Oberkampf's discovery of solid green in 1809.

[5] e.g. in the Savonnerie carpet woven for the throne-room of the Tuileries in 1840. Havard and Vachon, *op. cit.*, p. 326. A similar mixture is to be found in the designs published in London rather earlier by H. Boullemier, and in Aglio's pattern-book of 1821.

[6] About 1840 Mancherat de Longpré resuscitated Pillement's feather flowers.

[7] Even Pugin was affected. In 1840 he wrote (*Floriated Ornament*, p. 2) that a cast of natural flowers he had seen in Antwerp had given him 'an entirely new view of mediaeval carving', but he was himself too architecturally minded to produce more than stiff quatrefoils and powderings.

407. Screen panel of Beauvais tapestry, c. 1830

406. Beauvais tapestry, c. 1825

408. Porcelain vase and cover, painted by Edwin Steele, Swinton, *c.* 1830

a

b

FIG. 409. Carpets exhibited by Messrs. Turberville Smith of London at the 1851 Exhibition. Designed by E. T. Parris; the first was executed in shades of bright green, the second in many colours.

plant-form—began to appear in Art about 1845[1] and the writings of Ruskin helped to make the way clear for naturalistic decoration. By 1849 he was destroying all that remained of architectural power over ornament:

'The laws of Art', he declared, 'are best learnt from the observance of Nature; and though architectural ornament is not to be a congeries of imitated objects, it is to be treated as Nature would treat it. Now the colour of Nature does not emphasize the form; it ornaments the animal, or the flower, or the mountain, by partial confusion and concealment of structure. And in good architecture the colouring should not bring out the forms, but cross them and dapple them. As in Nature, the colour should play about the surface, inter-changing and complicating the forms.'[2]

In style, too, nature was to have the upper hand; 'the presence of conventionalism is no bar to great Art; but the absence of naturalism is. All vital art represents what its public really likes, and the best uses the best as its subject, that is, the forms of nature, and not the spirals and zigzags of children and savages.'[3] In subject and treatment Ruskin's teaching is thus summarized by his interpreter, Mr. Collingwood:

'The notion that the best decoration is the product of incomplete, and therefore inadequate, art, has led to the fallacy that its artistic inadequacy is its virtue; that, whereas in picture-making and architecture grand proportion and intricate composition are virtues, in decoration mere symmetry is the right principle; that colour, which must always be gradated and variegated to be good in painting, may better be flat in decoration; that form, which must have meaning when pictorial, should have none when ornamental. And on these three errors . . . our modern system of pattern making is based. It has been strengthened in its erroneous position by the necessities of mechanism, which can reproduce flat colour, and symmetrical pattern, and nonsense form, with more ease and cheapness than beautiful colour and infinitely varied form. . . . But thanks to Mr. Ruskin's teaching, primarily, we are in a way to a better civilization in this respect. The fallacies of conventionalization are likely to be forsworn by all who pretend to a love of Art; and a truer view of the nature of ornament is gradually introducing itself. And this is a sign not only of better things for Art, but also of better things for society; for the lower forms of conventional decoration, based on nothing better than order, symmetry and definition, are the marks and tokens of a low form of culture and public morality . . . while the decoration that is based on natural form, and does its best with that, in its own material, is always a sign of health and vitality in the nation.'[4]

The taste of mid-Victorian England, with its gardens and its greenhouses, its pressed flowers, and its smattering of botany, was fully represented at the Great Exhibition of 1851. In every branch of industrial art the most popular designs were naturalistic; in chintzes, we are told, 'the taste is to cover the surface almost entirely with large and coarse flowers—dahlias, hollyhocks, roses, hydrangeas, or others which gave scope for strong and vivid colouring, and which are often

[1] A similar tendency is shown in France in such work as Grobon's *Groupes de fleurs et de fruits*, but they hardly rise above a drawing-master's level.   [2] *Seven Lamps of Architecture*, chap. iv.
[3] *Stones of Venice*, i, ch. ii.   [4] Collingwood, *Art Teaching of John Ruskin*, p. 248.

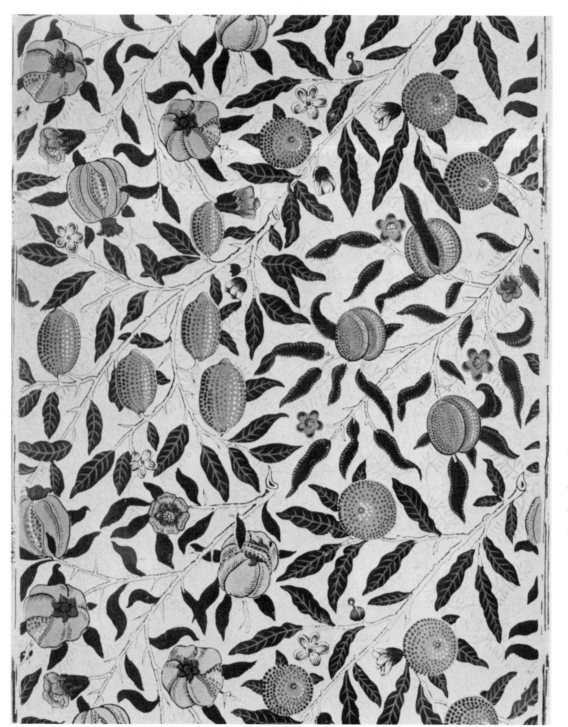

410. Design for wallpaper: *Fruit* pattern. By William Morris, *c.* 1870

411. Printed linen : *Honeysuckle* pattern. By William Morris, *c.* 1880

FIG. 413. Jug in chased silver, designed and made by MM. Faunière frères, and exhibited at the Paris Exhibition of 1878.

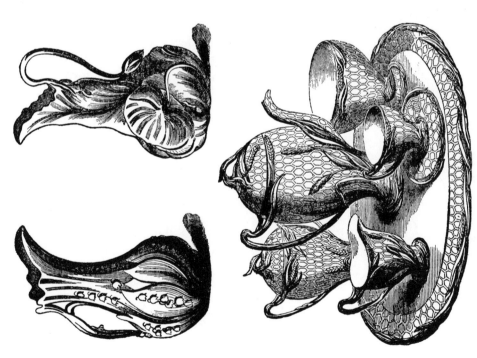

FIG. 412. Tea set and jugs exhibited by Messrs. Grainger of Worcester at the 1851 Exhibition.

magnified by the designer much beyond the scale of nature'.¹ Carpets rivalled chintzes in their horticultural interest; of two carpets exhibited by Messrs. Turberville Smith of London we are told:

'in the first (fig. 409 *a*) we have only the fern plant, one of the most graceful productions of the woods and hedgerows, and, as seen, worked out in this carpet in shades of the liveliest green, nothing can be more ornamental. For the second pattern (409 *b*), the flower garden seems to have been rifled of its gayest and choicest flowers, to furnish the designer with materials for his work, so much that it almost requires one well instructed in Botany to make out a list of its contents; and yet there is nothing overdone, nor any absence of the most elegant harmony.'²

Indeed trade descriptions became more and more botanical, and we read of one carpet that 'the design is a cordon of leaves of the *Clitoria arborescens,* enclosed by a trellis work of flowers, among which the *Lilium tigrinum* is conspicuous'.³

In pottery and porcelain the imitation of nature invaded form as well as design, and the Worcester factory exhibited jugs and cups covered with leaves and flowers or formed of interlacing leaves (fig. 412).⁴ The Court jewellers of St. Petersburg exhibited 'a diadem wreath in imitation of the leaves and fruit of the bryony, in emeralds and diamonds; a berthe of bouquets of currant branches in diamonds and rubies; a bouquet of eglantine and lily of the valley in diamonds, and a branch of ipomea in diamonds and turquoises'.⁵

The first criticism of the naturalistic style came from the Exhibition's official critic of design, Mr. Redgrave.⁶

' . . . . There has arisen a new species of ornament of the most objectionable kind which it is desirable at once to deprecate on account of its complete departure from just taste and true principles. This may be called the *natural* or merely imitative style, and it is seen in its worst development in some of the articles of form. Thus we have metal *imitations* of plant forms with an attempt to make them a strict resemblance, forgetting that natural objects are rendered into ornament by subordinating the details to the general idea, and that the endeavour ought to be to seize the simplest expression of a thing rather than to imitate it . . . Ormolu stems and leaves bear porcelain flowers painted to imitate nature, and candles are made to rise out of tulips and china asters, while gas jets gush forth from opal arums. . . . In the same way, and doubtless supported by great authority, past and present, enormous wreaths of flowers, fish, game, fruits, &c., imitated *à merveille*, dangle round sideboards, beds, and picture-frames . . . In Fabrics where flatness would seem most essential, this imitative treatment is often carried to the greatest excess; and carpets are ornamented with water-lilies floating on their natural bed, with fruits and flowers poured forth in overwhelming abundance in all the glory of their shades and hues; or we are startled by a lion at our hearth, or a leopard on our rug, his spotted coat imitated even to its relief as well as to its colour, while palm-trees and landscapes are used as the ornaments of muslin curtains.'

---

¹ *Reports of Juries,* ii. 1638.   ² *Art Journal Illustrated Catalogue,* p. 135.
³ *Ibid.,* p. 118.
⁴ *Ibid.,* p. 76. Similar forms are included in *A Collection of Ornamental Cups and Vases* by G. E. S., *c.* 1855.
⁵ *Reports of Juries,* ii. 1128.   ⁶ *Ibid.* ii. 1592.

414. Lyons silk brocade, 1889

415. Lyons silk brocade, *c.* 1900

But naturalism had a fatal attraction for the British mind,[1] and the designer, trained for his work by the drawing of sculptured detail in the round,[2] was not going to modify the relief of his designs even for woven fabrics. As late as 1879 the critic could still object:[3]

'. . . One may knock for admittance with the head of a goat, wipe one's feet upon a New-foundland dog, approach the hostess over a carpet strewn with bouquets, converse with one foot upon a Bengal tiger, and contemplate birds of Paradise upon the walls; . . . one may be called upon to interpose the Bay of Naples between an elderly lady and the fire-place, to slice a pine-apple upon a humming-bird, and place one's finger-glass upon the countenance of a Tyrolese peasant. . . . Do we not everywhere find flowers upon floor carpets, fruit upon dessert plates, insects and birds upon the walls? Are not the ladies of the family still called upon to embellish the door panels with "subjects from life"? . . . Do not the Misses Garrett advocate flowers and leaves, "as suggestive of the sweet smell that household things ought to have"? And has not Mr. Cross told the art students of the Metropolitan schools that it is a proper thing to depict "a rose or a butterfly upon a chest of drawers"? One of the cele-brated Gillow's newest designs is a bordering of flowers, peacocks, and butterflies drawn and coloured after life. . . . Hindley has shown bouquets of flowers twenty-four inches across, and Hampton similar things three feet across. Sporting scenes are depicted upon wall-papering; episodes in the Prince's Indian tour have been commemorated, and in the most noted emporiums . . . as many animals as might have tenanted Noah's Ark are imitated in crockery, and displayed in the window to captivate the public eye.'

In France, it is true, the hold of style was far stronger than in England and Germany, but even there much naturalistic work was produced, particularly in metal. In 1857 Michelet was advocating insects as a source of inspiration for the designer, and was writing with true artistic sympathy of their beauty, both hidden and revealed. 'L'orfèvre, le lapidaire feront bien de leur demander des modèles et des leçons.'[4] By 1863 all the fashionable jewels were in the form of lizards, snakes, beetles, dragon-flies and other insects.[5] A little later Viollet-le-Duc was preaching the doctrine that in flowers the modern artist might find inspiration as rich and as varied as the medieval craftsman had done;[6] Loeuillard was producing wild roses, maidenhair-fern, banana-leaves, daisies, and fuchsias in diamonds. By 1880 even mimosa was so imitated.[7] The Exhibition of 1878 showed much naturalistic silver work, with sprays of wild flowers creeping over forms imitated from wood and wicker (fig. 413.)

5

In the second half of the century such naturalism came under the influence of two other prevailing currents in decoration and was consequently regenerated.

[1] In 1857 G. G. Scott was proclaiming that 'an implicit and unconditional falling back on [nature] must be the great, all pervading characteristic of the future style . . . the rejection of all *merely* conventional forms of ornament in ancient styles'. *Remarks on Secular and Domestic Architecture*, p. 264.
[2] See A. Proust, *L'Art sous la République*, 1892, p. 187.
[3] G. L., *The Science of Taste*, 1879, p. 90.   [4] Quoted, *Art et décoration*, xv, 1904, p. 1.
[5] Vever, *La bijouterie française au XIXᵉ siècle*, ii. 224.
[6] *Dictionnaire raisonné de l'architecture*, 1861, v. 515, s.v. Flore.   [7] Vever, *op. cit.*, ii. 415.

Stylization brought it back into the sphere of true decoration and gave it form, rhythm, and beauty.

In England the taste for medievalism led Morris[1] to seek, not only in his garden, but also in Gerard's *Herbal* for his models, and to interpret flowers in a style that, however individual in effect, is eclectic in origin. The first wall-paper he put upon the market—the 'Daisy' of 1862—is definitely inspired by early herbal woodcuts, as is one of the best of all his designs, the 'Fruit' paper (fig. 410). Even his later work, if less pleasantly archaic than this, is that of a man who felt more at home in the fifteenth century than in any other period. Moreover, instead of pandering to the bad taste of the gardeners of his day he returned to the flora of the late Middle Ages: the Oxford fritillary and wild tulip, the Cotswold rose, columbine, peony, poppy, honeysuckle, carnation, iris, larkspur, anemone, daisy, and marigold. He warns the designer against the exotic[2] and against the merely horticultural:

'Be very shy of double flowers; choose the old columbine where the clustering doves are unmistakable and distinct, not the double one, where they run into mere tatters. Choose... the old china aster with the yellow centre, that goes so well with the purple-brown stems and curiously coloured florets, instead of the lumps that look like cut paper, of which we are now so proud. Don't be swindled out of that wonder of beauty, a single snowdrop; there is no gain and plenty of loss in the double one.'[3]

He had the poet's love of trees; his house in Kent was built with such care that hardly a cherry or an apple-tree had to be cut down, and the trees were so near the house that the apples fell in at the windows as they stood open on hot August nights. So Morris draws fruit and tree-forms as a lover, and brings them back to their true place in decoration. He rarely introduces live creatures into his patterns, but when he does they are English doves, thrushes, woodpeckers, partridges, and rabbits. He shuns the strange and the outlandish; his patterns are the translation into decorative art of Ruskin's feeling[4] that 'No scene is continually and untiringly loved, but one rich by joyful human labour; smooth in field; fair in garden; full in orchard; trim, sweet and frequent in homestead; ringing with voices of vivid existence'.

Morris's designs are formal and frankly repeating patterns; he draws his forms from nature, but adapts them to his own use. It is his decorative doctrine that Ruskin reflected when about 1870 he recanted, and said that his pupils were wrong if 'they think if they carve quantities of flowers and leaves, and copy them from the life, they have done all that is needed. . . . The difficulty is not to carve quantities of leaves. Anybody can do that. The difficulty is, never anywhere to have an *unnecessary* leaf'.[5]

[1] His first purely decorative work, for his own Red House at Upton, dates from 1860.
[2] The passage is quoted in Aymer Valence, *William Morris*, p. 134.
[3] *Ibid.*, p. 133.
[4] *Unto this Last.*
[5] *Lectures on Art*, § 166.

While in England naturalism was thus married to tradition,[1] in France the influence of Japanese art[2] created a new interest in natural form which eventually resulted in 'L'Art nouveau'. As early as 1867 M. Bracquemond designed for a wealthy French manufacturer a porcelain dinner set 'dans le genre rustique . . . style japonais'.[3] The style was no pastiche, but a personal interpretation of oriental art; the artist took the herbs and flowers of the French kitchen-garden and the birds and beasts of the French farm-yard, and borrowed from Japanese art not the letter, but the spirit: a calculated freedom of his spacing, a skilful summariness in his modelling, a deliberate accentuation of the essential character of his forms. Like the artists of the rocaille style, he put balance in place of symmetry; but unlike them he confined such asymmetry to decoration and did not let it encroach on form. His work inspired others; Lalique had the idea of designing a service of table silver 'où les herbes potagères auraient été les seuls éléments de décoration. J'avais commencé par le chou et par le céleri, dont le côté cannelé donne une moulduration pittoresque et solide; j'aurais continué en empruntant au persil, à la carotte, à toute la jolie flore si dédaignée qui s'épanouit au potager, ses feuilles, ses tiges, ses racines, ses fleurs et ses fruits'.

In the characterization of such forms Lalique brings out a quasi-human element; his practice agrees with the theory of his contemporary, Sully Prudhomme: 'On peut dire qu'en général les formes des minéraux, des végétaux et des animaux qui peuplent la terre, au lieu de nous représenter les essences latentes qui les revêtent, ne font à nos yeux, avant toute réflexion, qu'imiter et symboliser l'essence humaine.'[4] There is in his work something of the quality that Verlaine demands for poetry:

De la musique avant toute chose;
Et pour cela préfère l'Impair
Plus vague et plus soluble dans l'air
Sans rien en lui qui pèse ou qui pose . . .
Rien de plus cher que la chanson grise
Où l'Indécis au Précis se joint . . .

However airy Lalique's work might be, it did not fail to influence design of a more solid sort. In 1892 Gallé, himself an accomplished flower-grower of Lorraine, made a set of dining-room furniture inspired by the plants of the

[1] A few exceptional Englishmen—notably Whistler and William de Morgan—were early sensitive to Japanese influences. Such plates of de Morgan's as 'Stranded fish', 'Sea bird's island' and 'The Snake Eater' show him interpreting his own love of nature and the sea in terms of Japanese art. He began potting in 1870. See May Morris, 'William de Morgan', in *Burlington Magazine*, xxxi, 1917, p. 77.

[2] Before 1878 Tiffany had his own Japanese workmen in New York.

[3] *L'Art moderne à l'Exposition de 1878*, p. 464. See also 'L'influence de l'art japonais sur l'art décoratif moderne' in *Bulletin de la Société franco-japonaise de Paris*, 1911, p. 109.

[4] *Théorie générale de l'expression*, 1883, p. 106. For human forms with curiously 'Art nouveau' style the reader is referred to a Pre-Raphaelite design for window tracery dating from 1854. Holman Hunt, *Pre-Raphaelitism*, i. 363.

vegetable garden. Thence he developed a new theory of appropriateness of subject and form; it was natural, he thought, that wooden furniture should follow the lines of vegetable growth, and that each piece—or preferably each room—should have the whole of its decoration derived from certain definite natural forms: so he designed the whole furnishing of a room from the dahlia, makes a sideboard called 'la blanche vigne', and a chiffonnier 'd'après la clématite sauvage'[1] (fig. 416). It was not only in his general conception of such decoration that he was original; like Lalique he renounced naturalism, but he did not, like Lalique, see his plants in human guise. For him they remained plants, with lives, aspirations, passions and gestures of their own that the artist could apprehend and reflect in his compositions.[2]

Gallé and his 'École de Nancy' used few elements outside the rich flora of Lorraine; Lalique himself draws his designs from all the vegetable world of France.

'The yellow daffodil, the wood-anemone, jasmine, violets are not neglected. He loves mistletoe for the strength and sharpness of its slender stems, the ear of corn for the multiple richness of its elements, the thistle for its spiky strength and the sharp edges and prickly points of its leaves, and the clinging silk of its flowers. He has found in the pine-cone and the acorn a decorative value unperceived before. He uses waterweed, seaweed, algae. He has patiently explored the infinity of the plant world.'[3]

His work has one great weakness which it transmits to all its derivatives; it stylizes natural forms according to the same formula for every craft: wood-carving, marquetry, pottery, tapestry, embroidery, all show the same curves, the same irregularities, the same quaintnesses. If there is any craft to which such designs are really accommodated it is the typical craft of the century: just as rocaille is a style for chiselled gilt bronze, so 'l'Art nouveau' is a style for moulded glass and metal.

Naturally, as the style spread, it came to include fresh decorative elements. In 1900 Tiffany exhibited a tea-set with decoration from the characteristic flora of America. Grasset's *La plante et ses applications ornementales* (1898–9) was a useful pattern-book for the unoriginal. Corn and grass became classical for the decoration of brocade. The orchids[4] of the wealthy that had inspired the naturalistic silk-weavers of Lyons (fig. 414) provided the theme also of the frieze of the 'Pavillon de l'Art nouveau' of the Paris Exhibition of 1900; misletoe, pine, cow-parsley, and sycamore became decorative commonplaces, water-lilies as frequent in French decoration as in French verse. Such verse, indeed, might itself help to inspire the designer: Gallé made vases, 'où l'inquiétude des inflorescences, verticilles et pendeloques, s'échevèle au rude éveil de février;' a tea-table 'd'après les nénuphars et les iris de rivière; marqueteries sur un thème de Maurice Bouchor;

[1] V. Champier, *Les industries d'art à l'Exposition de 1900*, i. 83.
[2] See E. de Vogüé, *Remarques sur l'Exposition du Centenaire*, 1889, p. 129.
[3] A. Beaumer, quoted G. Geffroy, *René Lalique*, 1922, p. 33.
[4] See E. de Puyat, *Les Orchidées, histoire iconographique*, 1880, &c.

416. Dining-room Chiffonier, design of traveller's joy.
By Gallé, 1900

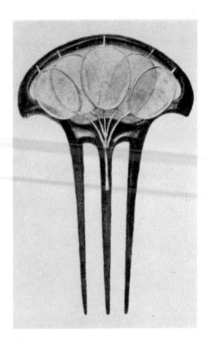

418. Comb. By Lucien Galliard,
c. 1900

417. Corsage ornament. By René Lalique, 1900

419. Bracelet. By René Lalique, *c.* 1900

"la musique de l'eau, des feuilles et du ciel" ',[1] as well as pottery inspired by Shake-speare, Baudelaire and Villon.

Préaubert designed tapestry in a pattern of carrot-blossom, Lambert friezes with the leaves, flowers and fruit of cucumbers, and Vilder attempted a new sphere with a pattern of lobsters and gurnards. The Belgian architect Horta founded a school that took not leaf or flower or fruit for its theme, but roots; and thence arose the most extreme and most fantastic manifestations of 'l'Art nouveau'. Like the worst extravagancies of rocaille, they could only flourish outside France; but they provided models for the manufacturers of Brussels, Geneva, Munich, Berlin, and Pforzheim, and ended by bringing even 'l'Art nouveau' within the sphere of industrialism.

[1] Champier, *op. cit.*, i. 91.

XI

THE ROMANCE OF THE PAST

I

'WHATEVER is familiar', wrote Reynolds,[1] 'or in any way reminds us of what we see and hear every day, perhaps does not belong to the higher provinces of art. . . . The mind is to be transported, as Shakespeare expresses it, *beyond the ignorant present* to ages past.' England, in the course of the eighteenth century, had made classical art so much a natural form of expression that it became part of what was seen every day; chinoiseries and pastorals had not the glamour of antiquity; therefore, in the search for the mysterious greatness of past ages, she turned her eyes back to her own creations of the Middle Ages. They had a double charm; their appreciation was unfamiliar, and yet came easily to a nation that had never fully renounced her medieval past. The age of reason, too, pressed a little hard on a nation capable of poetic sensibility, and Gothic architecture seemed an emotional antithesis to the classic orders. 'It is difficult', wrote Walpole in 1762, 'for the noblest Grecian temple to convey half so many impressions to the mind as a Cathedral does of the best Gothic taste. . . . One must have taste to be sensible of the beauties of Grecian architecture; one only wants passions to feel Gothic.'[2] Moreover, even on the Continent, a fuller grasp of architectural and literary principles was introducing new canons of judgement. Seventeenth-century France had disliked the Gothic style[3] since it represented the gulf for ever fixed between antiquity and modern times. Racine found Chartres Cathedral 'grande, mais un peu barbare'; La Bruyère stated 'on a entièrement abandonné l'ordre gothique, que la Barbarie avait introduit pour les palais et pour les temples'. Furetière gives the reason for this condemnation; Gothic architecture is 'éloignée des proportions antiques, sans correction de profils ni de bon goût dans ses ornements chimériques'.[4] But others were finding standards for architecture that differed from the dogmas of Vitruvius. The anonymous author of *Mémoires critiques sur l'Architecture*, published in Paris in 1702, wrote:[5]

'L'architecture est un art de bâtir selon l'objet, selon le sujet, et selon le lieu. Par cette définition, je désigne que l'architecture n'est rien moins que la simple connaissance des cinq ordres. . . . Entre tous les ouvrages qu'il y a dans Paris, je choisirai . . . l'église Notre-Dame, la Sainte-Chapelle . . . deux édifices faits selon l'objet, selon le sujet, et selon le lieu.'

Such opinions found expression in action, and in 1708 Robert de Cotte designed

---

[1] *Discourse*, xiii, 1786, 1819 ed., ii. 125.   [2] *Anecdotes of Painting*, ed. Dallaway, i. 194.
[3] Fénelon, for example, condemns it out of hand.   [4] *Glossaire*, s.v. *Gothique*.   [5] p. 22.

420. The Gallery, Strawberry Hill, *c.* 1760

a church façade in 'gothique troubadour', though it was not executed.[1] Some arabesques in the style of Bérain have ladies in fifteenth-century dress and high hennins set within their classical frames;[2] and about 1675 tapestries with scenes from medieval romances were woven at Beauvais, with figures in fairly accurate medieval dress.[3] Such students as Gaignières were at work upon the historical background of a Gothic revival, and it was probably only the creation of other minor styles such as chinoiseries and the development of picturesque decoration that prevented the formation of a French Gothic style in the early years of the eighteenth century. As it was, however, France gave this Gothic revival a cold welcome; when Gaignières died in 1715, leaving his collections to the king, out of them all only one picture—a portrait of Jean le Bon—was thought worthy to enter the royal collection;[4] and Montfaucon's *Monuments de la Monarchie française*, published between 1729 and 1733, had small success and little influence.

English taste[5] was more inclined to the medieval, since it was less prejudiced by classical canons and less influenced by feminine taste. In 1739 the Président des Brosses found St. Mark's at Venice 'un vilain monument s'il en fut jamais, massif, sombre et gothique, du plus méchant goût';[6] while in the same year the Englishman, Gray, characteristically found Rheims Cathedral 'a vast Gothic building of surprising beauty and lightness'.[7] In England, too, interest in the literature and art of the Middle Ages was growing.[8] Chaucer's poems were reprinted in 1687 and again in 1721; Dryden himself 'translated' them and Addison wrote approvingly of the ballad of *Chevy Chase*.

In 1715 Hawksmoor's quadrangle at All Souls was begun, that (however ignorantly) carried on the tradition of Oxford Gothic where Wren had left it. Even Kent dabbled in Gothic in the Court of King's Bench at Westminster and in the choir-screen at Gloucester.[9] By 1724, William Stukeley was advocating the revival of the Gothic style in domestic architecture, and justifying his advocacy by an appeal to nature. 'I judge for a gallery, library or the like, 'tis the best manner of building, because the idea of it is taken from a walk of trees, whose branching heads are curiously imitated by the roof,'[10] and ten years later Ivory Talbot was

[1] Courajod, *Leçons professées à l'École du Louvre*, iii. 131. Before 1676 Chauveau had designed *culs-de-lampe* for *St. Louis ou la sainte couronne conquise*, in which the saint is represented in a more or less Gothic niche.
[2] e. g. on some embroidery on yellow silk in the Musée historique des Tissus at Lyons.
[3] One is now in the State Collection, Wurtenburg. See H. Goebel, *Wandteppiche*, II. Teil, *Die Romanischen Länder*, Band II, fig. 203.
[4] R. Lanson, *Le goût du Moyen Age en France au XVIIIᵉ siècle*, p. 9.
[5] I regret that Mr. Kenneth Clark's *The Gothic Revival, an Essay in the History of Taste*, 1928, appeared too late for me to make use of it. I can only refer the reader to it for a full and interesting discussion of the revival in England. [6] *Lettres*, i. 174. [7] *Letters*, ed. Gosse, ii. 28.
[8] Saintsbury (*History of Criticism*, iii. 27) considers that this literary revival began twenty years earlier in Germany than in England, but the earliest date he adduces is 1748. In Scotland Watson (1706–11) and Allan Ramsay (1724–40) had earlier reprinted a good many old ballads. Collections of these also appeared in England in 1723 and in 1737. [9] Now destroyed.
[10] *Itinerarium Curiosum*. Raphael seems to have been one of the first to compare Gothic architecture and the growth of interlacing trees; see T. G. Jackson, *Gothic Architecture*, i. 2.

3620.2　　　　　　　Y

having plaster tracery attached to the walls of his stable in order to give the impression of blocked up Gothic windows.[1] Another decade passed, and Sanderson Miller built a Gothic cottage as a 'hermitage'; but for the most part Gothic buildings were like Lord Hardwicke's, 'merely the walls and semblance of an old castle to make an object from his house'. They served 'to terminate a prospect' or to mask some useful building; so Mason suggested that an ice house should be disguised as a 'time-struck abbey',[2] and Ivory Talbot disguised his kitchen chimney as a pinnacle.[3] Sir George Lyttelton felt that 'even Lord Leicester's (Holkham) wants the view of a Gothick castle to make it compleat'.[4] It is this view of Gothic architecture as a kind of scenic decoration which caused the eighteenth-century versions of it to be built of such flimsy materials that Walpole could 'outlive three sets of his own battlements'.[5]

Indeed, in the eyes of the men of the eighteenth century, Gothic architecture partook of the incoherence and wildness of the stonework grotto or the stage scene rather than of the regularity of consistent architecture. Berkeley in 1732 considered it 'fantastical, and for the most part founded neither in Nature nor in reason, in necessity nor use'.[6] Even Walpole contrasts its 'unreserved licentiousness' with the 'rational beauties of regular architecture',[7] though he found there was 'a magic hardiness' in Gothic architecture that could not have been sustained had it been dictated by pure caprice. Its constructive principles were ignored, and its ornaments alone were seen, just as the conceptions of medieval literature were ignored and its epithets and phrases alone appreciated. Montesquieu clearly expresses this point of view:[8]

'Gothic architecture appears to be most varied, but the confusion of its ornaments wearies by their pettiness, so that there is none that we can distinguish from another, and by reason of their multitude there is none on which the eye may rest; so that it displeases by the very parts that have been chosen to make it pleasing. A building in Gothic style is a kind of enigma to the eye that sees it, and the spirit is troubled, as if it were faced with an obscure poem.'[9]

None the less this failure of comprehension did not prevent the Gothic style from influencing design, for the eighteenth century, to a great extent, divorced function and ornament, and elevated pure decoration to the rank of a separate art. Reynolds, the apostle of the Fine Arts, wrote:[10]

'Though we by no means ought to rank these (the ornaments of the arts) with positive and

---

[1] *An eighteenth-century correspondence . . . letters . . . to Sanderson Miller Esq. of Radway*, ed. by L. Dickens and M. Stanton, London, 1910, p. 301.   [2] *The English Garden*, 1772.
[3] In 1753. Dickens and Stanton, *op. cit.*, p. 303. He justifies himself by remarking that 'the Beauty of Gothic Architecture (in my opinion) consists, like that of a Pindarick Ode, in the Boldness and Irregularity of its Members'. On other Gothic structures of this type see C. Hussey, *The Picturesque*, 1927, p. 144 et seqq.
[4] July 1755, *ibid.*, p. 235.   [5] *Gentleman's Magazine*, 1834, 2nd series, i. 24.
[6] Alciphron, *Works*, ed. Sampson, 1898, ii. 260.   [7] *Anecdotes of Painting*, ed. Dallaway, i. 201.
[8] *Grande Encyclopédie*, art. Goût.
[9] Rousseau considered that Gothic cathedrals existed only 'pour la honte de ceux qui eurent la patience de les faire'.   [10] *Discourse VII*, 1776, 1819 ed., i. 227.

substantial beauties, yet it must be allowed that a knowledge of both is essentially requisite towards forming a complete, whole, and perfect taste. It is in reality from the ornaments that arts receive their peculiar character and complexion; we may add that in them we find the characteristical mark of a national taste, as by throwing up a feather in the air we know which way the wind blows better than by a more heavy matter.'

Reynolds, moreover, admitted a certain condescending admiration for the Gothic style. Four years before he painted the New College windows—some of the most emphatic denials of medieval tradition that exist—he wrote: [1]

'. . . Very finished artists in the inferior branches of the art will contribute to furnish the mind and give hints, of which a skilful painter, who is sensible of what he wants, and is in no danger of being infected by the contact of vicious models, will know how to avail himself. He will pick up from dung hills what, by a nice chemistry, passing through his own mind, shall be converted into pure gold, and under the rudeness of Gothic essays, he will find original, rational, and even sublime inventions.'

It was in this spirit that men transformed their houses into the Gothic style; 'the old mansion immediately shot up into Gothic spires, and was plastered over with stucco; the walls were notched into battlements; uncouth animals were set grinning at one another over the gate-posts, and the hall was fortified with rusty swords and pistols.' [2]

In England, indeed, as classicism became more strict, its unfamiliar discipline began to cause a reaction.[3] In 1742 Batty Langley published his 'Ancient Architecture, restored and improved by a great variety of grand and useful designs in the Gothick mode', with five new orders of columns to be applied to the various features of a building 'in the Gothic manner'. The second edition of his book reverses the proportions between classic and medieval; it is entitled 'Gothic Architecture, improved by Rules and Proportions'.[4] Walpole began to feel that 'The Grecian is only proper for magnificent and public buildings. Columns and all their beautiful ornaments look ridiculous when crowded into a closet or cheese-cake house. The variety is little, and admits no charming irregularities'.[5] In 1750 he began to turn Strawberry Hill into a monument of romantic Gothic, and already the style was prevalent enough for him to find ready-made wall-paper for his hall painted in perspective to represent fretwork,[6] of a sort that Gray calls 'rather pretty, and nearly Gothic'.[7] But, however domestic such work might be, its

---

[1] *Discourse VI*, 1774, 1819 ed., i. 176.

[2] *The World*, 12 April 1753.

[3] By 1746 Sanderson Miller was busy designing in the Gothic style for his friends Lord Guernsey, Sir Edward Turner, and Lord North.

[4] Such a stage is represented by the hall of Lacock Abbey, rebuilt by Ivory Talbot between 1753 and 1755. The ceiling has a network of quatrefoils filled in with shields, above an ordinary classical frieze, while the walls are decorated with ogival canopied niches with statues in cedar wood.

[5] Letter to Mann, 25 February 1750; ed. Toynbee, ii. 433. He did not publish the *Castle of Otranto* until 1764.

[6] In 1753, made by Jackson of Battersea.   [7] *Letters*, ed. Gosse, iii. 120.

elements were derived from ecclesiastical sources.[1] Alison, summing up the style in 1790, writes:[2] 'Everything was now made in imitation, not indeed of Gothic furniture, but in imitation of the forms and ornaments of Gothic Halls and Cathedrals. This slight association, however, was sufficient to give beauty to such forms, because it led to Gothic manners and adventure, which had become fashionable in the world from many beautiful compositions both in Prose and Verse.'

Walpole found no incongruity in applying ecclesiastical decoration to his toy-house;[3] he had a bedroom chimney-piece modelled on Bishop Dudley's tomb in Westminster Abbey, borrowed the ceiling of his picture-gallery from the vault of Henry VII's Chapel (fig. 420), took its principal entrance from the north door of St. Albans, with recesses (finished with gold network over looking-glass) imitated from Archbishop Bourchier's tomb at Canterbury, and designed the piers of his garden gate 'after' the choir of Ely Cathedral. Gray describes his bedroom: 'The ceiling is coved and fretted in star and quatre-foil compartments, with roses at the intersections, all in papier maché. The chimney on your left is the high altar in the Cathedral at Rouen. . . . whose pinnacles almost reach the ceiling, all of niche-work.' But comparatively few people were prepared to be as thorough or as archaeological as this;[4] even Gray concludes: 'It is mere pedantry in Gothicism to stick to nothing but Altars and Tombs, and there is no end of it, if we are to sit upon nothing but Coronation chairs, nor drink out of nothing but chalices or flagons.'[5]

For most people Gothic remained but one of several styles. In America, in 1757, a surveyor advertised that he designed 'all sorts of Rooms after the manner of the Arabian, Chinese, Persian, Gothic, Muscovite, Palladian, Vitruvian, and Egyptian';[6] and this enumeration, however artificial, puts the beginning of the style into proper perspective. Its vogue ranked in England equally with the Chinese taste; Chippendale even transfers some decorative motives from the one to the other. William and John Halfpenny's *Pocket Companion* of 1752 contains plates of 'Chinese and Gothic architecture properly ornamented'; Chippendale's *Director* of 1754, besides chinoiseries, has designs for chairs, 'Gothic, and fit for

[1] Occasionally family tradition provided another source of inspiration; the Astleys, for instance, had their Chippendale chairs covered with petit-point pictures of the combat between Sir Philip Buyl and John Astley at Smithfield in 1441, taken from a seventeenth-century picture based on fifteenth-century drawings. Sold at Christie's on 5 July 1917. Lady Evans, *Lustre Pottery*, p. 66.

[2] *Essays on Taste*, 6th edition, 1825, ii. 195.

[3] Repton, writing in 1806, seems to have been the first to recognize any incongruity. 'In adapting the Gothic style to buildings of small extent there may be some reasonable objection; the fastidiousness even of good taste will perhaps observe that we always see vast piles of buildings in ancient Gothic remains, and that it is a modern, or false Gothic only, which can be adapted to so small a building as a keeper's lodge, a reposoir or a pavilion.' He further remarks that any modern imitation of a castle must produce the effect of a prison, while an abbey provides models only for a chapel, hall, and library (*Designs for the Pavillon at Brighton*, p. 17; *An Enquiry into the Changes of Taste in Landscape Gardening*, p. 75).

[4] Even Walpole had the chimney-piece in his round drawing-room 'taken from the tomb of Edward the Confessor, but improved by Robert Adam'.

[5] *Letters*, ed. Gosse, iii. 120. (1761.)

[6] Lenygon, *Decoration in England*, 1660–1770, p. 21.

eating parlours,' and the decorations of many houses were divided between the two styles. Walpole says of Latimer's:[1] 'The house has undergone Batty Langley's discipline: half the ornaments are his bastard Gothic, half of Hallett's mongrel Chinese. I want to write over the door of most modern edifices, "Repaired and beautified; Langley and Hallett, Churchwardens".'

Often the structure was classical, the detail Gothic:[2] about 1780 Landi could still publish patterns in which a mild Attic style is married to Gothic of this sort, with acanthus string-courses to complete its arcadings. The English-Attic armchair and the usual urn are Gothicized with surprising results. But when the antiquaries began to study the architectural remains of their own country, then gradually the neo-Gothic style rose to a different level. Such works as Grose's *Antiquities of England and Wales* (1773–87)[3] helped to give a truer view of the history of Gothic art.

Buildings more permanent than Strawberry Hill began to be erected in the style; Sir William Chambers built the Earl of Dorchester a Gothic house at Milton Abbas in 1771;[4] and a generation of architects arose as willing to practise the Gothic style as the Greek.

Men gradually realized that constructive form lay behind Gothic ornament; Blake had vision enough to see that 'Grecian art is mathematical form . . . only eternal in the reasoning memory,' while Gothic is 'living form, that is to say, eternal existence,'[5] and architects began really to construct, and not merely to ornament, in the style. By the beginning of the new century, Wyatt, Nash, and Smirke were building great houses,[6] such as Ashridge and Eaton Hall, in Gothic, 'castellated' and Tudor styles; and Dallaway was finding perfection in the architecture of the fourteenth century. Their constructions, however, were in the nature of *pastiches*, and the purpose of the building was often forgotten in the attempt to ape an Abbey or Castle. They are among the worst-planned houses in England for modern life, and for the same reason provide the most awkward of backgrounds for furniture and decoration.

[1] *Letters*, 5 July 1755. John Crunden, in 1770, published 'The Joyner and Cabinet Maker's Darling . . . containing 60 different designs . . . 40 of which are Gothic, Chinese, Mosaic and ornamental frets, proper for friezes, Imposts, architraves, Tabernacle frames, Book-cases, Tea-tables, tea stands, trays, stoves and Fenders'. Cf. the thin and spindling designs for Gothic book-case frets published by Lowes and Elbon in 1788, and the similar patterns for 'Gothic windows for chapels and summer houses', produced by Joseph Bottomley five years later.

[2] e. g. Decker, *Gothic Architecture*, 1759, and Wallis, *The Carpenter's Treasure*, a collection of designs for temples, with their plans, gates, doors, rails, &c. in the Gothic taste. 1774.

[3] Others are Carter, *Ancient Architecture of England*, and Halfpenny, *Gothic ornaments in the Cathedral Church of York*, both of 1795.

[4] He set Gothic above Greek in his *Decorative Part of Civil Architecture*, written in 1759, ed. Gwilt, p. 129. Other typical houses are Llanerchydol, Montgomery, 1776; Beeston Hall, Norfolk, 1786. Robert Adam employed a Gothic style at Culzean and Lander, but only for exterior work; their interiors are strictly classical.

[5] *Sibylline leaves*. His *Songs of Innocence* were printed from his own handwriting with ornamental borders of his composition in emulation of the illuminated manuscripts of the Middle Ages.

[6] Wyatt 'restored' Salisbury Cathedral in 1782: built Fonthill in 1796 and Ashridge in 1806.

None the less, the style became international, at least in the northern countries. The men of the eighteenth century had been bred and nurtured on history, and when they wearied of ancient history and ancient architecture, which had become almost platitudinous in their familiarity, they turned quite naturally to the history and architecture of medieval times. An appreciation of Gothic construction is found in Germany by 1773.[1] Goethe pictures an Italian, a Frenchman, and himself, looking at Strasbourg Cathedral. 'It is in petty taste,' says the Italian, and passes by. 'Quite childish,' lisps the Frenchman, and triumphantly taps his snuff-box *à la Grecque*. 'What have you both done, that you should despise it? The Column is in no sense an element of our dwellings; it contradicts the essence of all our buildings. Our houses do not arise out of four columns at four corners; they arise out of four walls on four sides, which serve instead of columns; exclude columns, and where you add them, make them a burdensome superfluity.'[2]

2

The revival of Gothic style in France followed a rather different course. The early stage of interest in picturesque ruins had been felt as strongly there as in England, but had been satisfied by expression in a classic guise.[3] Through literature, however, medieval influence gradually crept in. The *Roman de la Rose* was reprinted in 1735; in 1738 the Benedictines of St. Maur abandoned the ecclesiastical field for the study of early French history and literature, and in 1753 La Curne de Sainte Palaye's *Mémoires sur l'ancienne chevalerie* did much to resuscitate for eighteenth-century France the images of knight and lady, tournament and battle. Legrand d'Aussy completed the romantic background by his publication in 1779 of *Fabliaux ou Contes des XIIe et XIIIe siècles,* and by 1760 timid versions of medieval dress were appearing on the French stage.[4] The Jesuits, whose great educational force was directed against national feeling, and consequently against the study of national history, were expelled from France in 1764. In the next year a ballet[5] was performed at Fontainebleau with a chorus in the dress of the time of Dagobert. Gradually the Middle Ages ceased to be barbarous, and the poetry and picturesqueness of ruins that were medieval began to rank with the charms of those that were antique. Blondel found in 1752[6] that certain Gothic churches were 'construites avec tant de légèreté et de hardiesse qu'on ne peut

---

[1] For special purposes more or less Gothic detail had been used earlier. The Baroque Lodge of the Teutonic Order at Mainz, built between 1730 and 1735, has romantic medieval helmets, plumed and vizored, carved over the windows, in odd contrast to the classical quivers on the consoles.

[2] *Deutsche Baukunst*, quoted Bosanquet, *History of Aesthetics*, p. 308.

[3] See p. 105.

[4] R. Lanson, *Le goût du Moyen Age en France au XVIIIe siècle*, p. 29. On Gothic taste in France see also P. Schommer, *L'Art décoratif au temps du Romantisme.*

[5] *La Fée Urgèle.*   [6] *Architecture française*, i. 14.

leur refuser de l'admiration.' Medieval themes began to appear in French literature,[1] though in art such influences were little felt.

Walpole's French friends had found it difficult to be polite about Strawberry Hill,[2] and in 1764 Le Roy, the Historiographer of the Royal Academy of Architecture, was able to publish a memoir on Christian Temples, which started from the ancient basilicas and ended at Soufflot's Pantheon without once mentioning a Gothic church or cathedral. French works on the Middle Ages, such as Montfaucon's, were historical in their point of view; the artistic standpoint had not yet been reached. Gothic architecture, however, little by little began to take its place in the arts; first in paintings and engravings of medieval scenes, then as ruins: first in such engravings as one of the plates of owls in Buffon's *Histoire naturelle des oiseaux* of 1770, then as a background to hunting scenes on a few Lyons brocades.[3] Slowly the Middle Ages came into fashion in Court circles. In 1780 Monsieur gave a fête to the Queen with fifty knights in medieval array, and a romantic tournament, and in the same year a few Anglomaniacs erected little Gothic pavilions in their gardens.[4]

Gothicism on the English scale, however, was felt to offend the *convenances*. The Prince de Ligne in 1786 found that 'l'image de la destruction est toujours affreuse et tous ces airs de tremblements de terre sont de fort mauvais air... Une église catholique n'est pas plus gaie dans un jardin qu'ailleurs.' The lapse of nine years found him unchanged in his opinion, though the style was spreading:

'Les maisons gothiques deviennent aussi trop communes ... J'aime assez qu'à l'aide de créneaux et murs, ou tours découpées, on répare, et traite ainsi un vieux Château ... mais pourquoi se donner de la peine de faire croire que son Château est une Église qu'on trouve partout? ... D'ailleurs, on ne peut plus faire le découpé, le svelte, le hardi et le précieux de ce genre.'[5]

It was, indeed, not through archaeological or artistic influence that Gothicism

---

[1] Dorat's *Abailard et Héloïse* of 1758 was followed in 1760 by Voltaire's *Tancrède*, and the *Castle of Otranto* appeared in a French version in 1781. The first French version of Ossian dates from 1762, the second from 1763 and the third, by Le Tourneur, from 1776. Yet another influence, which to the classically trained French mind was medieval in its strangeness, was that of Shakespeare, which also made itself felt in the middle years of the century. (Ducis's version of *Hamlet* dates from 1769; Le Tourneur's translation of the plays from 1776.)

[2] See Letter to Mann, 29 Dec. 1764 (Toynbee, vi. 162). Madame de Boufflers owned she did not approve of it, and that it was not 'digne de la solidité anglaise', and 8 June 1771 (viii. 37), 'When I once asked Mme du Deffand what her countrymen said of it, she owned that they were not struck with it, but looked upon it as natural enough in a country which had not yet arrived at true taste.' In 1786 the Prince de Ligne found that Walpole's 'Château de la Tamise' was as mad as his Castle of Otranto and not more amusing.

[3] Examples in the Musée des tissus historiques at Lyons.

[4] e.g. in the garden of the Duc de Penthièvre, at Armainvilliers, where a 'salle de bains gothique' and a Gothic tomb were erected, together with a Turkish bridge and pavilion and a Chinese Kiosk. In 1780 Blaikie built a 'Tour des paladins' in the gardens of Bagatelle, and Bernard a Gothic chapel and observatory in the Abbey of Ourscamp; while in 1787 Kléber covered the grounds of the Prince de Montbéliard with little Gothic buildings—an Anabaptist chapel, a concert hall, a shooting gallery, and servants' quarters (R. Lanson, *Le Goût du Moyen Age en France au XVIIIe siècle*, p. 40). A little Gothic house was even built by Prince Potemkin near Tsarskoe-Selo before 1786 (de Ligne, *Belœil*, p. 184).

[5] *Belœil*, p. 273.

was reintroduced, but through sentiment. The romantic simplicity of the Dark Ages came to be emotionally linked with the complexity of Gothic ornament. As early as 1764 Diderot was objurgating Soufflot for his classic Panthéon, and declaring that 'Les modernes. . . . n'ont réussi qu'à faire regretter la beauté agreste, mais raisonnée, des églises gothiques.'[1]

The classicism of the Revolution was severe enough to provoke a reaction, and Gothicism began to be felt as an undercurrent to the prevailing style.[2] At first, however, the revolutionary attitude to Gothic art—the art of the medieval monarchy and the medieval church—was wholly destructive. Much of this destruction was unorganized and complete, but the official confiscation of ecclesiastical and noble property brought together an immense accumulation of medieval works of art. In September 1793 the former convent of the Petits Augustins was turned into a clearing-house for dealing with this; bronzes were to be melted, wood to be used for fuel, and marble to be converted into lime. Mercifully, however, the collectors and dilettanti of the Ancien Régime had fostered an archaeological attitude of mind, and the idea of a Museum in the Palace of the Louvre had become familiar, though nothing had been done to make it a reality.[3] Lenoir, who was put in charge of the storehouse of the Petits Augustins, was an ardent, if not a learned archaeologist, anxious to preserve what was antique, even if it were not classical. He lived in the convent and spent all his salary and all his means in the rescue of medieval works of art. He made friends with a stonemason, who let him use his cart to bring his treasures to the Petits Augustins, wrapped in curtains and counterpanes from Lenoir's room. He had the courage to hide silver figures at a time when precious metals were concealed under pain of death, and when the Comité du Salut Public demanded bronzes, he whitewashed them and so disguised them as stone. The house, however, was so cold, and his remaining means so small, that he had to use most of the wooden statues as fuel for his stove.[4] Meanwhile men interested in other periods of art were reviving the idea of a Museum in the Louvre to contain the statues and pictures from Fontainebleau, the Luxembourg, and other once-royal possessions, and the Museum of the Louvre was formally opened on 10 August 1793, the first anniversary of the fall of the monarchy. At first, however, Gothic remains were not thought worthy of inclu-

[1] Quoted, Harvard, *Les Styles*, p. 173.

[2] The Revolution, like all times of political crisis, witnessed many translations from foreign works, since these alone had no marked political bias. Consequently Mrs. Radcliffe's Gothic romances were all translated in the last years of the century (*The Italian* in 1796, *Mysteries of Udolpho* 1797, *Julia* 1798, *Children of the Forest* 1800), and in 1795 Madame de Genlis was writing *Les Chevaliers de la Cygne ou la Cour de Charlemagne*.

[3] In 1750 the first vague idea appeared, and in that year the picture gallery of the Luxembourg was opened free to the public twice a week. In 1773 another vague project for centralizing the Royal Treasures at the Louvre was brought forward, but though a committee was formed in 1778, nothing was done until the question of its lighting came up ten years later. Dreyfous, *op. cit.*, p. 49.

[4] For the whole story see Courajod, *A. Lenoir*. The Petits Augustins was on the site of the present École des Beaux Arts, and the sculptures still in its courtyard are some that Lenoir brought there.

sion: the idea of a museum was necessarily classical.[1] Two years later, however, from being a clearing-house, the Petits Augustins was constituted as a secondary museum of the sculpture that Lenoir had succeeded in saving, and became the fountain head of the Gothic revival in France.

'How many minds', says Michelet,[2] 'have caught in this museum the spark of history, the interest of great memories, the vague wish to go back through the centuries! I can still recall the emotion, always the same and always strong, that made my heart beat, when as a child I use to come beneath these sombre vaults and to contemplate these pallid faces, when I used to go seeking, ardent, curious, fearful, through room after room and age after age.'

It was chiefly for reasons of sentiment or of literary interest that people came to Lenoir's museum. He early put together tombs from fragments which he represented to be those of Abelard and Héloïse; he soon added to their number and arranged a fitting *décor* for them. A writer of 1814[3] tells us that,

'Le jardin, planté avec autant d'art que de goût, peut être considéré comme un Elysée, puisqu'il renferme non seulement les statues de plusieurs rois et guerriers célèbres, mais encore les cendres des hommes de lettres les plus illustres dont la France s'honore ... Des fleurs éparses çà et là, opposées à des cyprès, à des ifs, à des saules pleureurs et à des peupliers, groupent les monuments funèbres qui provoquent le regret et l'admiration.'

As early as 1791, the year in which all monastic property passed to the State, the Théatre du Marais had been rebuilt, in the 'genre . . . gothique . . . absolument l'architecture de nos anciennes chapelles,'[4] and by 1793, when the parish churches and the property of the émigrés was sequestrated, a taste for Gothic ornament was beginning to make itself felt: 'Nous avons tant épluché les modes, tant raffiné sur les goûts, tant retourné les meubles et les ajustements, que rassasiés, épuisés de jolies choses, nous redemandons le Gothique comme quelque chose de neuf, nous l'adopterons; et nous voilà revenus tout naturellement au XIVe siècle.'[5] Millin published his *Antiquités nationales* in 1798, and the first volume of Lenoir's *Musée des monuments français* appeared in 1800,[6] but the progress of Gothic taste was still slow.[7] Schlegel, in his Letters on Paintings in Paris of 1802-4,[8] wrote:

'A great number of old French memorials, fragments torn from ruined churches and

---

[1] Varon's report of the second year of the republic states, 'A quelque degré de gloire qu'il soit intéressant de porter l'industrie de la France, on ne saurait nier que la plus belle vaisselle et la plus belle porcelaine ne soient déplacées auprès des formes simples at pures d'un vase étrusque...' Equally out of place would be 'l'art gothique, si l'on peut qualifier du mot d'art ou l'enfance ou la décrépitude des siècles passés.'

[2] *Histoire de la Révolution*, vi. 117.

[3] Quoted, Benoît, *L'Art français sous la Révolution et l'Empire*, p. 121.

[4] de Goncourt, *Histoire de la Société française pendant la révolution*, p. 131.

[5] Almanac, *Petites Affiches* of August, 1793; quoted *ibid.*, p. 74.

[6] Twelve editions of the catalogue of his museum were issued between 1792 and 1816.

[7] At the Salon of 1800, Petit Radel brought forward a plan for the scientific destruction of Gothic churches by means of fire, by hewing a hole in every column, filling it with dry wood and then lighting the tinder. 'Toute l'édifice croule sur lui-meme en moins de dix minutes.' Michel, *Histoire de l'Art*, ii. 11. A somewhat similar plan, with explosives in place of wood, was used by the Germans for the destruction of Gothic churches in the Great War.   [8] Bohn's trans., p. 99.

monasteries, mutilated and in many instances more than half destroyed, have been carefully collected, and are now exhibited, in chronological order, in the ancient monastery of the Petits Augustins. . . . This collection . . . possesses at least one useful property, shewing, in the clearest and most remarkable manner, what the imitative arts, especially sculpture, ought *not* to be.'

Nine years after the Revolution Deseine could still write against the 'monuments celtiques, et vous, statues momies du XIIIe siècle, qui jouissez dans votre obscure retraite d'un respect idiot.' [1]

Chateaubriand, who during his eight-year sojourn in England had acquired a romantic taste for the Gothic style, naturalized Gothic in France by his *Génie du Christianisme* of 1802. He made Christianity, and the Christian art of the Middle Ages, picturesque and obscurely romantic. Just as the *Génie* owed much of its remarkable success to its apposite appearance at the time of the Concordat, so the neo-Gothic style owed its further development to the foundation of the Empire.[2] The events of 1804 changed men's attitude towards the past. Pre-Capetian France came to be regarded as the direct ancestor of the Napoleonic Empire; the reliquary of Charlemagne[3] became the palladium of his dynasty. For Napoleon's coronation Percier and Fontaine masked the façade of Notre Dame with pseudo-gothic arcades, in which the eagles and N's of the new dynasty appeared framed in the architectural motives of old France.[4] At the same time the Frankish and Teutonic elements in early French history were emphasized at the expense of the truly French element, which was too closely associated with the Ancien Régime. By a strange perversion of fact medieval remains came to be looked upon as monuments of a Teutonic civilization, and therefore became admirable. Schlegel in 1805 expressed this change of view in his *Gothic Architecture*,[5] 'The Gothic may possibly be styled in the next work on architecture the German style, from its having been common among all the nations of ancient Germany, and the grandest, heretofore called Gothic, edifices in Italy, France, and even in Spain, being also the work of German architecture.' Therefore he changed his view of the style, and instead of condemning it, as he had done before, stated: [6]

'I have a decided predilection for the Gothic style. . . . It unites an extreme delicacy and inconceivable skill in mechanical execution, with the grand, the boundless and infinite, concentrated in the idea of an entire Gothic fabric; a rare and truly beautiful combination of contrasting elements, conceived by the power of the human intellect, and aiming at fault-

[1] Floreal IX, *Opinion sur les Muses*.

[2] As early as 1802 Napoleon, an enthusiast for the translations of *Ossian*, published in 1795 and 1801, endeavoured to bring Ossianic subjects into decoration. He commissioned Girodet and Gerard to paint scenes from *Ossian* in 'epic-classic' manner for La Malmaison; but David's criticism—'je ne me connais pas à cette peinture-là'—was enough to doom the scheme. Ossian, however, with Voltaire and Dante, represents the moderns among the medallions of classic authors in the library at La Malmaison.

[3] Presented to Napoleon in 1804.

[4] See the engraving by Dupréel after Isabey and Fontaine (Chalcographie du Louvre).

[5] p. 156.   [6] *Ibid.*, p. 155.

421. Design for Toile de Jouy, c. 1817

422. Panel of Beauvais tapestry, *c.* 1830

less perfection in the minutest details as well as in the lofty grandeur and comprehensiveness of the general design.'

But French interest remained for the most part sentimental or literary; the *Salons* from 1806 to 1810 might exhibit pictures of medieval subjects,[1] the archaeology of the Middle Ages might be treated seriously,[2] Noverre might even suggest in 1807[3] that the Gothic style was, by its lightness and variety, well suited to the construction of a theatre; but decorative art remained classical.[4]

With the Restoration the political basis of the taste for medievalism was completely changed. Gothic art could once more take its true place as the creation of monarchical France, since the fall of Napoleon made the Capetian Monarchy and the Medieval Church once more living parts of French historical consciousness. Thierry's *Les Normands* of 1815, Michaud's *Histoire des Croisades* (finished in 1822) and Sismondi's works brought the Middle Ages to life for France. The Troubadours came into fashion[5] and the Salon of 1814 was full of pictures of noble paladins, sentimental châtelaines, and gay minstrels.

In 1810 Beaumer and Rathier had begun to publish a great '*Recueil des costumes ou la Collection des plus belles figures françaises, des armures, des instruments, des meubles dessinés d'après les monuments, manuscrits, peintures, vitraux .... depuis Clovis jusqu'à Napoléon I*[er]*;* and it is a significant fact that the publication only proceeded as far as the reign of Louis XII. Men like Chateaubriand, who had acquired the habit of Gothic decoration during their exile in England, found in it the natural monarchical antidote to the imperial classicism of Percier and Fontaine.[6]

Gothicism and Romance were identified, and the glamour of distance was added to the charm of a national style by giving ogival architecture a Saracenic pedigree.[7] Lenoir wished to call Gothic architecture Saracen, Syrian, or Arab.[8] The theory

[1] 1802, Richard, *Valentine de Milan*; 1806, Vafflard, *Honneurs rendus à Duguesclin*; Regnault, *Héloïse et Abailard*; 1808, Gois, *Jeanne d'Arc à l'assaut*; 1810, Révoil, *L'Anneau de Charles Quint*.
[2] 1805, Willemin, *Monuments français inédits du VIe au XVIIe siècle*; 1811, Lenoir, *Histoire des Arts en France*; Leroux d'Agincourt begins *Histoire de l'art par les monuments depuis sa décadence au IVe siècle jusqu'à son renouvellement au XVIe*. Another influence was the rediscovery of the Italian Primitives. See T. Borenius in *Quarterly Review*, April 1923.   [3] *Observations sur la construction d'une salle d'opéra*, p. 242.
[4] De Jouy, however, notices 'la création des meubles gothiques' in 1813. *L'Ermite de la Chaussée d'Antin*, iv. 250.
[5] 1813, Marchangy, *La Gaule poétique*; 1814, Roquefort Flamericourt, *État de la poésie française dans les XIIe et XIIIe siècles*.
[6] It is interesting that Percier had himself taken a personal interest in Gothic and Renaissance work; it is to him that we owe the illustrations of Lenoir's *Musée des Monuments français*.
[7] Some English architectural designs of about 1780 (V. and A. M. 93 B. 21) include a few Gothic plans called 'Moorish' or 'moresque' and Watelet (*Dict. des arts de peinture*, 1792, ii. 430) ascribes Gothic architecture to the Saracens. The doctrine is hinted at in Chaussard, *Ode Philosophique sur les Arts Industriels* (an VI) p. ii, and expressed in a subject put forward for discussion by the Société libre d'émulation de Rouen in 1806. (Benoît, *op. cit.*, p. 128). Lenoir tried to combat the earlier view that Gothic architecture was an English invention (*Musée des monuments français*, vii. 1, 125); the doctrine did not really die until Hallam's *Europe in the Middle Ages*, translated into French 1820-2, proved that Canterbury was designed by a French architect.
[8] *Musée des monuments français*, i. 35 and vii. 41, and 129. J. F. Blondel gives it an Arab derivation in his *Architecture française* of 1752, i. 15.

gained the weight of popular approval with the vogue of Walter Scott's *Ivanhoe*, which began soon after its publication, and was at its height about 1820. Even decoration was influenced; a design for toile de Jouy shows citadels and minarets, knights and Bedouins, shrines and trophies,[1] against a background where Gothic tracery ingeniously takes the place of the lozenged reticulations of the Empire style (fig. 421). Paradoxically Gothic began also to be considered as the typically Christian style. In 1822 the King ordered a book-case for his own library of religious books, ornamented with Sèvres plaques painted with Gothic figures of Christian heroes.

The architects of the Restoration—Bellanger, Le Fevre, L'Abbé, Choffard, Courtépée and Renard—designed in the 'style troubadour'; but their knowledge of the history and traditions of Gothic art was superficial. The restitution of sequestrated church property decimated the Museum of the Petits Augustins, and in 1816 the remains of its portable collections were merged in those of the Louvre. The style in France was conditioned by certain limitations. The men of the Restoration were very poor, and Louis XVIII himself had so little taste for pomp and ceremony that the wits said that it was only at his splendid funeral that he 'réellement fit bonne contenance'. In the absence of visible productions, the immaterial art of literature had become the arbiter of decoration, and this condition further fettered the craftsmen; all French nineteenth-century Gothic is historically or romantically literary. Its most familiar expressions are the title-pages and bindings of books,[2] or clocks and *garnitures de cheminée* that represent their heroes and heroines.[3] The style fell between the two stools of literary falsification and pure archaeology. Either it was treated as an historic document or it was admired as Chateaubriand admired it, *sub specie naturae*: 'Les voûtes ciselées en feuillages, les jambages qui appuient les murs et finissent brusquement comme des troncs brisés, la fraîcheur des voûtes, les ténèbres du sanctuaire, les ailes obscures, les passages secrets, les portes abaissées, tout dans l'église Gothique retrace les labyrinthes des bois.' The books that had, perhaps, the greatest influence in the propagation of the style—Taylor, Nodier, and de Cailleux' *Voyages pittoresques et romantiques dans l'ancienne France* of 1820—attempted to reconcile archaeology and romance; but the two currents of interest were contemporary rather than identical.[4] Influences so derived are more powerful in detail than in mass, and French neo-Gothic, except for the restoration of medieval buildings damaged in the Revolution, had no wider scope than rocaille or the Chinese style.[5]

[1] P. J. de Loutherbourg published trophies of crusading and tilting armour in London in 1794, 1795, 1799, and 1804.

[2] e. g. the 1838 edition of Chateaubriand's *Génie du Christianisme*.

[3] See the Quentin Bauchart Bequest, Musée des Arts Decoratifs, Paris.

[4] The École des Chartes dates from 1821 and the Commission des Monuments Historiques from 1837; the culmination of neo-Gothic romanticism, Victor Hugo's *Notre-Dame de Paris*, comes between the two in 1831.

[5] Even Viollet-le-Duc's early work (about 1834) was in designing small objects like clocks, candlesticks, and vases. (P. Gout, *Viollet-le-Duc*, p. 102.)

A Gothic house was an 'antithèse adorable au siècle des boutiques': and Madame Salomon de Rothschild had a Gothic dining-room like the nave of a cathedral.[1] A young French girl writes to her friend: 'Cette Geneviève est-elle heureuse d'avoir un amour de mari comme le sien! Il va lui faire bâtir un pavillon gothique, un tout petit pavillon, avec tourelles, poivrières, créneaux, enfin toutes les choses qu'on voit en un château féodal. Nous irons l'inaugurer à la prochaine saison. On jouera à la châtelaine, on aura de belles robes traînantes, des aumonières, des pages, des lévriers.'[2] Such a style was naturally subject to eddies of fashion; in 1830 Jérôme Paturot finds everywhere 'le gothique à lancettes, le gothique rayonnant ou rutilant, enfin le gothique flamboyant,' and even dresses are trimmed with Gothic arcadings; and then by 1836 Chateaubriand declares that the style has become so wearisome 'qu'on en meurt d'ennui'.

But as mere fashion turned away from the Gothic style, true and serious knowledge of its principles and its history was at length attained. Viollet-le-Duc's profound and acute studies of Gothic architecture[3] recreated the sense of its structural principles, and by making the art of the Middle Ages seem once more logical, skilful and consistent, made Frenchmen once more conscious of the continuity of their national tradition. Thus the Gothic style appealed to critics of the middle years of the nineteenth century for exactly opposite reasons to those that had constituted its charm in the years before the Revolution. Its dynamic qualities were recognized; its evident constructive origin and the structural forces that control its form in themselves compelled admiration.

Viollet le Duc made an impassioned plea for the adoption of Gothic architecture as the basis of artistic education.[4]

'We do not wish to bring the progress of architecture in France to a standstill, it would be madness to dream of it. . . . We ask that our architecture of the thirteenth century should first be studied as a man should study his own language, that is so that he may know not only the words, but also the grammar and the spirit; we ask that official teaching should take this course; that the study of antiquity should become what it ought always to have been, archaeology, and the study of French thirteenth-century architecture, art. Once this principle is taught without restriction, let every one do as he pleases; in our country, in the midst of modern activity and industry, such national art will not be slow in making progress. You will begin by having copies, that is inevitable, that is even necessary to understand all the resources of Gothic architecture; we will say more, you will probably have bad copies. . . . But since the principle is good, and the art a type educationally inexhaustible, the artists will soon get hold of the sense of it; their copies will become intelligent and well thought out, and finally our national architecture, while keeping its unity and its entirely French basis, will be enabled to reach such perfection as our language has already attained.'

[1] Duchess de Dino, *Chronique*, ii. 26 (1836).
[2] Germaine de N... à Madeleine de B..., 6 April, 1833. Maigron, *Romantisme et la Mode*, p. 127.
[3] He began to study Gothic about 1834; his great work, the *Dictionnaire raisonné de l'architecture française du XIe au XVIe siècle*, was published in 1854.
[4] *Annales Archéologiques*, iv. 351–2. June 1846.

The first steps of his programme were carried out; Didron tells us, for instance:[1] 'M. Leduc has already in his portfolios the measured drawings of a hundred houses of the twelfth and thirteenth centuries. He will show that one can, that one *ought*, to copy these medieval houses, as one must copy the churches.' Viollet-le-Duc, moreover, realized that the first condition of satisfactory design was to take account of the characteristic properties of the material employed and of the way of using it, and that it was through neglect of this condition that ugly monotonous work was produced that offended reason and taste alike.[2] Yet in spite of this study of historic fact and this appreciation of artistic truth, the time had gone by for a Gothic renaissance in France; restoration and reconstruction were everywhere undertaken, but hardly any creation was attempted. Even in decoration it was literary and not artistic influence that was at work; in 1841 Victor Hugo was addressing verses to M. Froment Meurice to tell him:

> Le poète est ciseleur
> Le ciseleur est poète

and by the next year the grateful jeweller was producing bracelets in pure Gothic style with scenes from the life of St. Louis, followed two years later by others called *Esmeralda* and *Jeanne d'Arc*. But public support was lacking; in 1846 the Academy was protesting against the building of churches in Gothic style, and a year later Froment Meurice was designing only in the Renaissance manner.[3] Gothic had become ecclesiastical and archaeological, 'le style diocésain'; Viollet-le-Duc might design metal work of real beauty for the relics of Notre Dame (fig. 424), he might restore Pierrefonds from top to bottom (fig. 426), he might even design the decorations of the railway carriages of the imperial train in modified fifteenth-century style with some earlier details; but still the world in general wanted something fresh.

By 1853 Guilmard classifies contemporary work under three schools: the conservative academic, the eclectic, and the third school,

'who gallantly display the banner of the Middle Ages. They dare not maintain any longer that the art of this period is the pre-eminently Christian art, for facts too categorically deny this proud and useful statement; but driven off grounds of religion, they establish themselves on national soil; and claim that the Gothic style is the only French style that, born and created in our midst, belongs to us. The strange thing is that these bold innovators, starting a few years ago from the disdain which they felt for the servile imitation or copying of antiquity, have come, intoxicated, as one may say, by their own enthusiasm, to the same sad end in which the Empire style fell, to servile imitation and to copying. . . . Whereas at the end of the last century artists went for their models to the Capitol or the Acropolis, so now

---

[1] *Annales Archéologiques*, v. 383. December 1846.
[2] *Histoire d'un dessinateur*, p. 280. The same plea is made in Gilbert Scott's *Remarks on Secular and Domestic Architecture* of 1857; he says that the 'despicableness' of stucco, veneer, and falsified design was first exposed by Pugin.
[3] Vever, *La Bijouterie française au XIXᵉ siècle*, i. 154.

423. Painting of a Boudoir in the Gothic style. French, *c.* 1835

424. Reliquary of the Holy Crown. By Viollet le
Duc, 1862. Paris, Notre Dame

FIG. 425. Two brooches and a casket exhibited by Froment Meurice at the 1851 Exhibition.

they take a shorter road and find them close at hand at Amiens, Rheims and Beauvais. So according to this school . . . art can find salvation only in retrogression.'[1]

Viollet-le-Duc was appointed Professor at the École des Beaux Arts in 1863; but his doctrines were so unpopular that he soon saw fit to resign his chair.

3

Only in England did the Gothic style really take root.[2] The somewhat arid taste of the early nineteenth century found Gothic ornament of any sort 'neat and simple, yet *venerable* in character'; and in England the religious standpoint towards art and learning, which Lamennais[3] failed to make the general view in France, ennobled the Gothic style as being national, serious, and Christian.

Gradually its history became better known; Rickman published the first intelligent analysis of the variations of Gothic style in 1817, and by 1822 L. N. Cottingham was publishing full-size working drawings of Gothic ornament,[4] and the craftsmen were making full use of them. Pugin's *Gothic Furniture*, published in 1826, has 'Gothic' designs for all the needs of modern houses in the abbatial or baronial style: sideboards, cheval-glasses, card-tables, jardinières, book-cases, bureaux, dressing-tables and sofas, all strangely tricked out with tracery, crockets, cusps and pinnacles (fig. 428). The aridity of Neo-Atticism had impoverished men's vision, and industrialism had hardly yet filled their purses: Eastlake is justified in his criticism of the carved Gothic detail of the time: 'Beautiful no one expected it to be. But it also was not clever; it was not interesting; it was not life-like; it was not humorous; it was not even ugly after a good honest fashion—it was deplorably and hopelessly *mean*'.[5] Church and State alike, however, came to recognize Gothic as the true national style. The Parliamentary committee who, in 1834, invited designs for the new Houses of Parliament, decided that Gothic or Elizabethan were the only permissible styles;[6] and the Tractarians, who started to rebuild the ritual fabric of the Church at about the same date, set the ecclesiastical archaeology of the Middle Ages but little lower than their dogmas.[7] By 1840 there

[1] Guilmard, *Connaissance des Styles*, 132–3.

[2] See H. Repton, *Observations on the Theory and Practice of Landscape Gardening*, 1803, p. 151. 'So prevalent is the taste for what is called Gothic, in the neighbourhood of great cities, that we see buildings of every description, from the villa to the pigsty, with little pointed arches; or battlements to look like Gothic; and a Gothic dairy is now become as common an appendage to a place, as were formerly the hermitage, the grotto, or the Chinese pavilion.'

[3] For his interpretation of Gothic art see *Esquisse d'une philosophie*, 1840, iii, bk. 8, p. 147.

[4] As early as 1803 Edwards was making careful sketches (bought by Beckford of Fonthill) of court cupboards and early pottery, disinterred from attics and gardeners' outhouses.

[5] *History of the Gothic Revival*, 1872, p. 134. It is characteristic that Soane made three designs, all equally dull, for Marylebone Church, in the classic, Romanesque, and Gothic styles, and that the classic was finally accepted as the cheapest.

[6] Soane in 1820 proposed to make part of the new Law Courts Elizabethan to match the old part; but the old part was pulled down by mistake during the dreary muddle of controversy and in the end the whole was built in the classical style.

[7] Newman, curiously enough, confessed himself a classicist at heart, while among the Gothicists, Pugin was a Catholic and Rickman a Quaker.

426. Château de Pierrefonds. Door of the Salle des Preuses. Designed by Viollet le Duc, *c.* 1865

428. Design for a Gothic bookcase. By A. W. N. Pugin, 1835

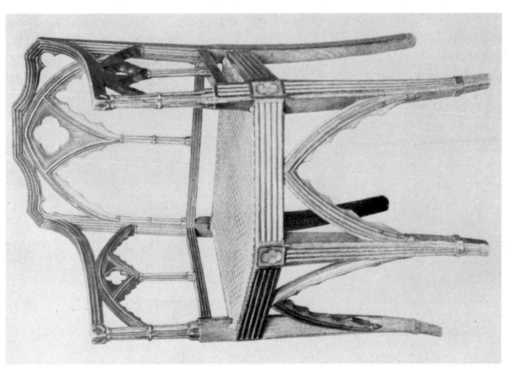

427. Oak chair in Gothic style, c. 1825

were critics learned enough to 'damn a moulding that was half an hour too late,' and architects and designers familiar enough with medieval styles[1] to attempt constructive imitation on a new scale. The leading spirit of the new movement was Pugin. The English-born son of a French *émigré*, he was educated by a father devoted to the study of Gothic,[2] and brought to its appreciation an inherited sense of style. When only fifteen years of age he was employed on the designing of furniture in medieval style for Windsor Castle, and by 1836 he was sufficiently sure of himself to publish *Contrasts, or a Parallel between the Architecture of the Fifteenth and Nineteenth Centuries*, in which his own drawings of the finest examples of the perpendicular style are amusingly confronted with the aridities of contemporary neo-Gothic and neo-Attic architecture. Pugin's real gifts never found their full scope. He had a French sense of craftsmanship, and set up a quasi-medieval workshop, but all his work was cramped by the modern stinting of labour and expense; his most important civil decoration—the detail of the New Houses of Parliament, that occupied him from 1837 to 1843—gives, like his ecclesiastical work, an unsatisfactory impression of dryness and poverty.

> I doubt if they're half baked, those chalk rosettes,
> Ciphers and stucco-twiddlings everywhere;
> It's just like breathing in a lime kiln. . . .[3]

He had a true sense of the beauty of soaring vertical line; but being limited, as he was, in expense, he spent too much on height and spoiled his effects by the poorness of his materials. Indeed, he had far less sense of architecture than of decoration; his best work is ornament pure and simple.[4] Here again the gold work, the glass, the embroideries, the carpets, and the mural decoration done from his designs are far less living than the designs themselves: these may be derivative, but his nervous pencil gives them a life which his craftsmen could not perpetuate.[5] Whatever a modern critic may miss in Pugin's resuscitations, they satisfied a generation more occupied with pedantry than spirit. At Oxford by 1850 'the University taste for modern Gothic was established beyond recall, and every don, and indeed every undergraduate, descanted of the features of their Gothic buildings like a glossary, and each took care to discriminate nicely between the different dates of construction, and to speak with pity of all that was not of the "correct style"'. They elevated the Gothic style into a religion, and chanted with

[1] Intelligent drawings of old examples were made by Henry Shaw (published in 1834 as *Specimens of the Details of Elizabethan Architecture* and *Specimens of Ancient Furniture*); C. J. Richardson, after 1839 (likewise Elizabethan); C. Sprosse, 1840 (Romanesque from the churches of Halberstadt); Pugin and Le Keux, 1841 (published as *Architectural Antiquities of Normandy*); W. Burges, in the sixties; and many more.

[2] The elder Pugin published *Specimens of Gothic Architecture* and *Examples of Gothic Architecture* (1831).

[3] Browning, *Bishop Blougram's Apology*.

[4] Some interesting pen and ink designs of his for furniture are in the Victoria and Albert Museum, E 2588–2600, 1910.

[5] The most important of his published pattern-books are the *Glossary of Ecclesiastical Ornament*, 1844, and *Floriated Ornament*, 1849.

FIG. 429. Oak Bookcase, designed by R. Norman Shaw and exhibited by
James Forsyth at the 1862 Exhibition.

FIG. 430. Sideboard in Gothic style, exhibited by Messrs. Hindley & Sons at the 1862 Exhibition.

Ruskin, 'Whatever has any connexion with the five orders, or with any one of the orders; whatever is Doric or Ionic or Corinthian or composite, or in any way Grecized or Romanized; whatever betrays the smallest respect for Vitruvian laws or conformity with Palladian work—that we are to endure no longer.'[1] The style that had diverted Horace Walpole had become more 'learned' than archaeology had ever succeeded in making classicism; the ritualists endowed it with a hieratic sanctity, the naturalists with a divine spontaneity, the travellers with the glamour of Italy. Even science lent a hand, and in 1857 provided models of the flora of the carboniferous forests for the Gothic capitals of the Oxford University Museum.

This very 'learning', this identification with religion and science, limited the influence of neo-Gothic on the essentially industrial ornament of the time. The manufacturers of 1851 did their best, but the critics took a lofty tone. If the designer had hoped to find safety in a close adherence to architectural models, they upbraided him for 'a false adaptation of Gothic stone forms to wood-carving', and told him his wardrobe 'would be more characteristic as an oratory';[2] if he had sought sanctuary in religion, they took a high moral tone: 'In one case the most sacred symbols of religion serve as decoration for the borders of plates, while the centres of them, and of the dishes of the same set, consist of angels, copied from an illustrated prayer-book, flying in the midst of a blue heaven diapered with stars. Such incongruities, improper in any case, are sadly and strangely inapplicable to a dinner service.'[3] Only Romance offered a safe shelter: 'One of the most costly and admirable works . . . is the buffet, designed by Messrs. Cookes & Sons, of Warwick. Any attempt to describe this elaborately carved piece of workmanship would . . . be out of the question. All we can do is to explain that the designs are chiefly suggested by Scott's *Kenilworth*.'[4] The only constructive criticism that was offered was the suggestion that the medieval practice of ornamenting furniture with mottoes or texts should be revived, 'as having far more significance than the commonplace conceits of much of the ornament of the present day.'[5] The manufacturers continued to do their best. They called in architects to design for them, and produced such monstrosities as the bookcase designed by R. Norman Shaw and exhibited in 1862 (fig. 429), and the oak billiard-table, shown at the same exhibition, 'in the style of the fifteenth century, the panels of the sides and ends carved in low relief, illustrating the history of the Wars of the Roses,' which appears to have been supported on thirteenth-century fonts.[6] Mr. Poynter exhibited a buffet, painted with the combat of Sir Bacchus and Sir John Barleycorn. 'Some of the emblematic heads on this piece', we are told, 'Pale Ale, Sherry, Port, etc., were marked by much individuality, and the entire effect was very rich and harmonious.

1 *Stones of Venice*, vol. iii, chap. iv, § 35.   2 1851 Exhibition, *Reports of Juries*, ii. 1625.
3 *Reports of Juries*, ii. 1647.   4 *Art Journal Catalogue*, p. 123.
5 *Reports of Juries*, ii. 1622.
6 1862 Exhibition, *Illustrated Catalogue of Industrial Department*, British Division, vol. ii, No. 1542.

It has been purchased for the South Kensington Museum.'[1] For humbler use coffin-Gothic was produced, 'adapted from the New Museum of the University of Oxford'.[2]

But Oxford, among all her Tractarians and critics of architecture, reared one son who was pre-eminently a craftsman, with a craftsman's scorn of pedantry and a craftsman's sense of style. Scott's novels had taught William Morris to love Gothic as a boy; in his Oxford days Chaucer converted him altogether to the Middle Ages.[3] Never was he in any degree classical; Iceland came to be for him what Greece is for most men.[4] He translated Latin and Greek, it is true, but transmuted them into medieval guise; he went to Celtic romance and Scandinavian epic for poetic inspiration; to Germany, Burgundy, Holland, and England for decorative inspiration. His outlook was steadily and instinctively northern; the Italianism of the Pre-Raphaelites did not influence him. So he was able to elide the centuries of the Renaissance,[5] and to breathe life into medieval craftsmanship. At first he trod cautiously along almost forgotten paths; his Red House of 1859 is definitely based on North-French Gothic; his firm in the early sixties deliberately copied details from Norfolk and Suffolk churches. At first, indeed, they described themselves as 'a company of historical artists', and the details of their exhibits in 1862 are praised as 'satisfactory to the archaeologist from the exactness of the imitation'.[6]

But Morris was more than a maker of *pastiches*; he not only introduced detail of a fresh kind, but also a fresh method of visual generalization. Since classicism did not influence him he was free from the tyranny of its sculptural and pictorial traditions; his textiles are textiles and not pictures, his furniture is woodwork and not statuary, his colours are vegetable dyes and not borrowed from the palette of a naturalistic painter. He found that 'the age is ugly—to find anything beautiful we must "look before and after"'. But it was less a question of imitating the models of any particular century than of merging himself in the spiritual life of that century; 'if a man nowadays wants to do anything beautiful, he must just choose the epoch which suits him and identify himself with that—he must be a thirteenth-century man, for instance'.[7] So all the six hundred and more patterns he designed are definitely and indubitably his own; he may have become a fifteenth-century man, but he exactly copied no fifteenth-century models. By reason of this individuality his influence was limited; he had imitators in England, his work indirectly helped

[1] J. B. Waring, *Masterpieces of Industrial Art and Sculpture*, iii, Letterpress to Plate 155.

[2] *Ibid.*, ii, No. 5825. A pattern-book of Gothic furniture of the same type as that exhibited was published by J. Gibbs in 1854 (*Designs for Gothic Ornaments and Furniture*).

[3] He first read the *Canterbury Tales* in 1853.

[4] He travelled in Iceland before he went to Italy, and wrote: 'Do you suppose that I should see anything in Rome that I cannot see in Whitechapel?'

[5] 'For us to set to work to imitate the minor vices of the Borgias, or the degraded and nightmare whims of the blasé and bankrupt aristocracy of Louis XV's time seems to me merely ridiculous.' Quoted, A. Valence, *William Morris*, p. 264.   [6] Quoted, *ibid.*, p. 59.   [7] Quoted, *ibid.*, p. 243.

in some degree in the revival of Folk art in the Scandinavian, Teutonic,[1] and Slavonic countries, but the Latins found him 'impitoyablement anglais'.[2]

4

In France the nineteenth century was an age of eclecticism in both philosophy and art. The philosopher, Cousin, had taught that all truth had already been formulated in some form or other; the critics that all beauty had already found decorative expression. For the Romantics, too, life was a dramatic spectacle, and every writer became painfully conscious of his background. Precision in historic truth, exactitude in local colour, were artistic pre-occupations for the decades after 1830. So men strove to fill in the background of their own lives with a suitable *décor*, and art remained imitative and allusive.

But the romance of the past now shed its glamour over other centuries than those of the Middle Ages. A decadent society lives upon the past; its illusion of vitality depends upon its memories of what it has survived. As early as 1825 the *Souvenirs de la Marquise de Créqui*[3] prophesy 'comme le penchant de la mode est toujours glissant, comme le changement sera la maladie des temps futurs, vous passerez par la Renaissance avant d'en revenir au temps du Grand Roi'.[4] The current of historical research had begun to set in that direction.[5] In 1828 the Duchesse de Berri had initiated the restoration of Chambord,[6] while in the next year Boieldieu's *La Dame Blanche* inspired her to organize a 'quadrille de Marie Stuart' at the Tuileries, that helped to turn the mode into Renaissance channels. The architect, Chenevard, the decorators, Liénard, Vechte, and Georges Grohé, and the jeweller, Marchant, exploited the scrolls, the cartouches and the chimeras of the Renaissance; and then the monarchical revival of the art of Versailles became general when the palace was constituted a national museum in 1837. So the designer[7] could mingle Gothic arcades, Renaissance arabesques, Louis XIV cartouches and rocaille decoration in a stock-pot of style, and trust to a vague sense of historic continuity to give coherence to his work.

[1] His wallpapers were directly imitated in Germany by Otto Eckmann and Walter Leistikow, and in Belgium by Henri van der Velde. Ackerman, *Wall-paper*, p. 63. He seems to have exercised a certain influence over Eugène Grasset before he turned to *L'Art nouveau*; but on the whole his influence on continental work has been slight.

[2] H. du Cleuziou, *Chronique de l'Art industriel*, p. 42. In 1867 the French were amazed at 'la roideur, la sécheresse et la perpendicularité (qui) donnent aux imitations gothiques un caractère si particulier, si original'.

[3] The Marquise died in 1803; the *Souvenirs*, published in 1825, are probably a fake by Cousen de Courchamp.

[4] Quoted, Havard, *Les Styles*, p. 176.

[5] The eighteen volumes of Petitot and Montmerqué, *Collection des Mémoires relatifs à l'histoire de France depuis l'avènement de Henri IV jusqu'à 1763* were published between 1820–29, and Sainte Beuve's sixteenth-century criticism was published in 1828.

[6] Viollet-le-Duc notes that the very idea of restoration dates only from the second quarter of the nineteenth century.

[7] e.g. Julienne in 1840 in his *L'Ornemaniste des arts industriels*. In 1834 Weale republished Johnson's designs as Chippendale's, and in 1858–9 reproduced Chippendale, Inigo Jones, Johnson, Lock, and Pether under the title *Old English and French Ornaments*. More serious and archaeological in intention is Reynard's *Ornements des Anciens Maîtres des XVᵉ–XVIIIᵉ Siècles*, published in 1845.

The Revolution, moreover, had set back the eighteenth century into the perspective of history, and though the decorative impulses of the nineteenth century—naturalism, classicism, orientalism, and romanticism—were no more than the decadence of the impulses of the Ancien Régime, they could none the less find romance even in their own origins. The nineteenth century, too, was a century of the study of heredity, and therefore the work of generations that had but lately passed away acquired a new interest and a new importance. After 1855 the view that Augustin Thierry had applied to history was taken to include all human production: 'Les sociétés humaines ne vivent pas seulement dans le présent, et il leur importe de savoir d'où elles viennent pour savoir où elles vont.'

Eugénie could take as her model Marie Antoinette;[1] and the craftsmen who exhibited at the Paris Exhibition of 1857 could practise not only Etruscan, Egyptian, Byzantine, Chinese, Renaissance and even Celtic[2] styles, but could also imitate the *style Louis XVI*. The *surtout de table* exhibited by Froment Meurice at the Exhibition of 1867 was in this style, and by 1878 practically every piece of modern furniture exhibited was either copied or adapted from eighteenth-century models. Even chinoiseries were copied, and silks were woven in the faded colours that Louis XVI brocades had acquired with time. By this date, however, Renaissance decoration was beginning to take the lead:[3] designs were once more *à la Marie Stuart*. Alphonse Fouquet's jewels were in Renaissance style; Avisseau was copying the wares of Palissy; Tissot was damascening in the manner of De Laune and Mignot; and others were less happily translating the patterns of sixteenth-century Venetian reticella into gold and diamonds.

But though one past style might dominate for a few months, it was in fact the whole repertory of history which inspired the ornament of the mid-nineteenth century. The Comte de Laborde in 1856 saw the only hope of raising the level of the arts in the study of the models of past times in museums,[4] and already the engravers were busy providing the craftsmen with models. A typical pattern-book of 1853—Guilmard's *La Connaissance des styles*—gives well-documented and accurate information and plates of French styles from Gallo-Roman times to the Restoration.[5] Guilmard describes the point of view that the artist of his day had

[1] See E. Rouyer, *Les Appartements privés de S. M. l'Impératrice au Palais des Tuileries*, Paris, 1867.

[2] Alexander Gueyton exhibited a buckle and a penannular brooch in Celtic style. See Vever, *La Bijouterie française au XIXᵉ siècle*, ii. 23. West and Son of Dublin had exhibited 'brooches and trinkets in gold, copied with much taste, yet not servilely, from the antique fibulae in Ireland' at the Great Exhibition of 1851. *Reports of Juries*, ii. 1130.

[3] As early as 1850 Alfred Stevens was designing hunting-knives in the manner of 1560, and in 1861 plates imitating Gubbio ware with the four Domestic Virtues—Sincerity, Gaiety, Amity, and Generosity.

[4] *Quelques idées sur la direction des Arts et sur le maintien du goût public*, Paris, 1856. About 1832 the de Sommerard and Debruge-Duménil Collections had become important centres of interest at Paris, and in 1844 the former became the nucleus of the Musée de Cluny. In 1852 the London Museum of Ornamental Art was formed at Marlborough House, and five years later transferred to South Kensington.

[5] Others are Destailleur, *Recueil d'estampes relatives à l'ornementation des appartements aux XVIᵉ, XVIIᵉ et XVIIIᵉ siècles*, Paris 1863, and R. Pfnor, *Portefeuille des Arts industriels*, 1866–7.

to take; he had to consider the whole sphere of archaeological science, with intelligence and industry, but with judgement rather than enthusiasm. He had to draw inspiration from models of many periods, and use his creative power to harmonize the diverse elements thus gathered together; he had to imitate with judgement and understanding, but not to copy. His doctrine, in fact, was to be eclectic: moderate, accurate, skilful, and a little cold.[1]

The craftsman, like the poet, had first to acquire a varied and archaistic vocabulary,[2] and then to turn it to the best use he could. Each no longer inherited a living tradition, but instead had right of entrance to a museum of arts that were dead. The official report on the furniture exhibited at the Exposition Universelle of 1878 complacently remarks: 'A perfect comprehension of any style and a complete assimilation of ancient technique have made this exhibition resemble a museum in which an extremely wealthy collector has gathered together the most perfect types of furniture of all ages.' Creation ceased; adaptation became the watchword of the craftsmen. Theoretically such adaptation was free: 'Faire du Louis XIV, cela ne signifie pas ou plutôt ne devrait pas signifier "imiter textuellement une commode de Boule ou un panneau de Berain"; c'est . . . s'approprier les lois qui présidaient pendant le XVIIᵉ siècle aux effets décoratifs de la masse et du profil, de la couleur et du détail, et, avec ces éléments, créer des objets qui n'aient avec leurs ancêtres qu'un air de famille.'[3] In fact style changed so rapidly that, for all but a few artists, decoration became a veneering of heterogeneous detail on to a featureless frame.

'Mais à peine un artiste s'est-il bien pénétré de ce style et croit-il faire acte d'originalité relative, que le vent a changé, et qu'il souffle au Louis XVI. Tout est à refaire . . . tout a été refait . . . lorsque la Renaissance, ou le gothique, ou l'antique vient à son tour régner despotiquement . . . une preuve assez curieuse de ce que nous avançons, c'est que tous les ouvrages que l'on publie pour servir de matériaux dans les ateliers sont de recueils de modèles de tous les styles; et plus ils sont variés, plus ils obtiennent de succès.'[4]

In 1864 the *Union centrale des Beaux-Arts appliqués à l'Industrie* founded its museum at Paris to serve as a visible corpus of style for the French craftsman; in 1852 the first nucleus of the South Kensington Museum was collected in England. Little wonder that the designer, in an effort to please everybody, should mix his styles; Ruskin preached[5] 'That art is greatest which conveys to the mind of the

---

[1] Guilmard, p. 132. Cf. Viollet-le-Duc, *Dictionnaire raisonné de l'architecture*, 1863, vi. 34, s.v. Goût. 'Personne ne naît homme de goût. Le goût, au contraire, n'est que l'empreinte laissée par une éducation bien dirigée, le couronnement d'un labeur patient.'

[2] Théodore de Banville advised the poet: 'Je vous ordonne de lire le plus qu'il vous sera possible des dictionnaires, des encyclopédies, des ouvrages techniques traitant de tous les métiers et de toutes les sciences spéciales, des catalogues de librairie et des catalogues de ventes, des livrets de musées, enfin tous les livres qui pourront augmenter le répertoire des mots que vous savez et vous renseigner sur leur acceptation exacte. . . . Une fois votre tête ainsi meublée, vous serez bien armé pour trouver la rime.' Quoted Guyau, *Problèmes d'esthétique contemporaine*, p. 200.

[3] *Le Beau dans l'utile* (Exposition de l'Union centrale des Beaux-Arts appliquées à l'industrie, 1865), p. 115.

[4] *Ibid.*, p. 115.   [5] *Modern Painters*, lii, 98 *et passim*.

431. Tapestry designed by William Morris and H. Dearle, with subjects from Morris's poem, 'The Orchard', designed *c.* 1875, woven 1890

432. Design for a panel for the Salle d'Apollon of the Elysée.
By P. V. Galland, 1868

spectator by any means whatsoever the greatest number of the greatest ideas'.[1]
Such decoration as that of the Foyer of the Paris Opera House, planned in 1861,
combines every ornate element of decoration from 1520 to 1750 into a whole as
fatiguing as it is sumptuous. The commission on the Sèvres factory of 1875
recommended the young artist to study

'la pureté et la grâce de l'art grec; la sévérité et la vigueur de l'art étrusque; le brillant
et l'originalité de l'art persan; la variété infinie, la coloration merveilleuse de l'art chinois;
les effets frappants du décor de l'art japonais, la grâce et les combinaisons ingénieuses de
l'art arabe; l'abondance et la richesse de l'art italien; la légèreté grâcieuse des arabesques
de Rouen, de Nevers et de Delft; la noble élégance et la distinction du vieux Sèvres de
Louis XVI.'[2]

Some startling hybrids were produced; an escritoire was exhibited at the 1862
Exhibition[3] 'in the Early English style', painted with the story of Cadmus in the
manner of archaic Greek vase paintings. Below were medallions of Pericles saying
to Anaxagoras: 'O Anaxagoras, I am sorry to see thee starving,' Dante composing
the *Divine Comedy*, an Assyrian sculptor and a printer, with a border below of
'porcupines regardant'. In 1869 Grasset designed a wall-paper of which the lines
are Louis XVI and every element Egyptian,[4] and nine years later another French
designer was producing cabinets 'dans un style néo-grec que nous appellerons
flamboyant, avec décoration empruntée à la flore de l'art indou'.[5] It is no wonder
that the French delegate to the international jury of the Exhibition of 1867
declared, 'according to the creations of our age future generations will take us for
a fantastic race, living sometimes like Greeks, sometimes like the men of the
Italian Renaissance or the women of the eighteenth century, but never having had
any life of our own'. Yet the very variety of the sources of design brought a certain bastard originality into decoration; the mere fact of regarding ornament as a
stereotyped thing to be applied to any surface, however incongruous, created new
forms and effects. But a *style* is not made thus; it is significant that the decorative
art of the middle of the nineteenth century has no name. A critic said of the
Exhibition in 1878: 'Je dirai du palais du Trocadéro qu'il est à la fois grec, roman,
byzantin, arabe, florentin si l'on veut, et qu'en même temps il n'est rien de tout
cela. Il appartient à la famille des monuments essentiellement modernes.'[6] Yet an
art so derivative could hardly be called 'essentially modern' in perpetuity. Moreover, it had no wish to be modern; every design had an antique label, however
inappropriate.[7]

---

[1] This view even found expression in France; see Martha, *La Délicatesse dans l'Art*, 1884, p. 128.

[2] Havard and Vachon, *op. cit.*, p. 535.

[3] By Messrs. Harland & Fisher of London; it was dated 1858. J. B. Waring, *Masterpieces of Industrial Arts and Sculpture*, vol. ii, Plate 155.   [4] *Revue de l'Art décoratif*, xvii, 1897, p. 184.

[5] *L'Art moderne à l'Exposition de 1878*, p. 396.   [6] *L'Art moderne à l'Exposition de 1878*, ed. L. Gonse, p. 262.

[7] W. S. Gilbert, *Patience*:

Saph. . . . You are not Empyrean. You are not Della Cruscan. You are not even early English. Oh! be
early English ere it is too late! . . .

Jane. Still, there *is* a cobwebby gray velvet, with a tender bloom like cold gravy, which, made Florentine

In England the names of the dead were bandied about until a plea was made: 'If people would but let poor Anne rest in her grave! The confusion her ghost has created is ludicrous. Only the other day I was shown a French mirror (Louis XIV) by some really cultivated folks as "Queen Anne—Empire, you know. Genuine Chippendale!"'[1] But eventually the very habit of labelling made people realize the incongruity of fashionable furnishing in the antique manner. A doctrine of colourlessness was preached:

'In what we may call the typical English house of the present day there is really no architecture, and if such a building is to be decorated, it is almost legitimate to employ any style of decoration. In such a case I should choose a style which has no very marked features— which is not strongly Greek, or strongly Gothic,[2] or strongly Italian, and if there is the necessary ability, I should say try and produce ornaments having novelty of character and yet showing your knowledge of the good qualities of all styles that are past.'[3]

This doctrine failed to satisfy. Timidly and uncertainly the doctrine of 'period furnishing' began to be preached. 'Without tiresome adherence to a given date, we must study unity of plan, and banish all really discordant elements. For instance, a room furnished notably in the Georgian style should not contain obtrusive Victorian manufactures. A very Japanese room should not be marred by an early English work, such as would be unlikely to reach Japan. On the other hand, a Georgian room may contain Jacobean furniture. A Jacobean room may take hints from old Japan or Egypt, for objects of contemporary or earlier date may be assumed to have a possible right in the room, which those of a *later* date cannot have by any stretch of the imagination.'[4] Lenoir in 1887 published a typical collection of decorations for French rooms: some 'style Louis XV', with the legs of chairs and sofas in tasselled draperies; some 'Salons Renaissance', complete with ottomans and étagères, and one room with 'décoration Louis XIII, meubles genre japonais'.

Gradually the doctrine of congruity strengthened and developed;[5] as a rest from the stress of the present, men 'made believe' in their own homes, trying to capture the peace and beauty of the bygone past in rooms set as scenes in that past. The parvenu acquired a 'Louis room' in proof of the antiquity of his family; the Jew a Gothic one in proof of his knightly descent. Museums were built with the same piety that had inspired the foundations of churches, monasteries, and colleges in

fourteenth century, trimmed with Venetian leather and Spanish altar lace, and surmounted with something Japanese—it matters not what—would at least be early English!

In 1862 Howell and James exhibited jewels variously labelled, without too serious a regard for style, Etruscan, Benvenuto Cellini, Celtic, Anglo-Saxon, Greek, Gothic, Holbein, and Alhambresque.

[1] Mrs. Haweis, *Art in Decoration*, 1881, p. 42.

[2] Cf. C. Dresser, *Studies in Design for House Decorators, Designers and Manufacturers*, Plate XVI: 'Design for a dado and dado rail, of Gothic spirit, but not with the marked features of any style.'

[3] Dresser, *Principles of Artistic Design*, p. 74. (1873.)

[4] Haweis, *op. cit.*, p. 28.

[5] The first *Exposition Centennale* was held in 1889.

433. Detail of the Salle des Fêtes, Hôtel de Ville, Paris, c. 1885

434. Part of the decoration of a bathroom exhibited at thè Paris Exhibition of 1900

the Middle Ages; [1] and at the same time much antique building that served a useful and ordinary purpose was destroyed.[2] Beautiful decoration detached from its purpose was preserved in halls of terra cotta and cast iron, and the suburbs of every city in Europe burst into hideous being. Objects of everyday use, of form and design more ugly and meaningless than any seen heretofore, were mechanically produced by the thousand, while the skilled craftsman found a new and profitable calling in manufacturing sham antiques. Even work frankly original was given a meretricious appearance of antiquity (fig. 434). At the Paris Exhibition of 1900 Vernon Lee criticized

'that sickly imitation, in a brand new piece of work, of the effects of time, weather, and of every manner of accident or deterioration: the pottery and enamels reproducing the mere patina of age or the trickles of bad firing; the relief work in marble or metal which looks as if it had been rolled for centuries in the sea, or corroded by acids underground. And the total effect, increased by all these methods of wilful blunting and blurring, is an art without stamina, tired, impotent, short-lived, while produced by an excessive expense of talent and effort of invention.' [3]

The age of advance and progress in mechanical industry was the age of decadent and archaistic romanticism in design.

---

[1] *c.* 1900: Paris, Musée des Arts Décoratifs, Musée Guimet, Musée Galliéra, Musée Cernuschi, &c., London: Tate Gallery, Victoria and Albert Museum rebuilt.

[2] Cf. Turner's drawing of the Cornmarket at Oxford with its present state.

[3] *Laurus Nobilis*, p. 254.

XII

THE AGE OF THEORY

I

THE great aesthetic philosophers have based their theories upon other arts than that of decoration; the literary aesthetics of the Renaissance and the aesthetics of Fine Art of such thinkers as Kant and Hegel lie outside the sphere of this book. But in the latter half of the eighteenth century there arose a school of lesser men who turned decoration itself into a basis for theory, and by their theory influenced decoration in their turn. As early as 1761 Henry Home of Kames enunciated the view that a circle is more beautiful than a square, because 'the attention is divided among the sides and angles of a square; whereas the circumference of a circle, being a single object, makes one entire impression'; and similarly a square is more beautiful than a hexagon or an octagon; and since it is more regular, than any parallelogram.[1] His compatriot Donaldson based the idea of empathy on an architectural appreciation a few years later: 'Circular and changing shapes are semblative of motion . . . thus beauty of figure becomes a kind of substitute for elegance of motion. . . . The rising foliage of the Corinthian capital makes the column seem to bear its weight of superstructure, not only with ease, but with cheerfulness.'[2] Alison, in his *Essays on the Nature and Principles of Taste*, published in 1790, elaborated Home's theories of the relative beauty of geometric forms,[3] and proceeded to analyse the qualities of more complex forms. 'The beautiful Form of the Vase, for instance, is employed with many different kinds of ornament, and may either be magnificent, elegant, simple, gay or melancholy. In all these cases, however, the composition is different. A greater proportion of uniformity distinguishes it when destined to the expression of simplicity, magnificence or melancholy, and a greater proportion of variety, when destined to the expression of elegance or gaiety.'[4]

Every nineteenth-century thinker concerned himself with the idea of the beautiful; not as a creator, a connoisseur, a collector, a patron or a student, but simply as a theorist.[5] In the preceding century scholarly 'donneurs d'idées' had dictated

[1] *Elements of Criticism*, ed. Boyd, N.Y. 1865, p. 113.
[2] *The Elements of Beauty*, Edinburgh, 1780, p. 22.
[3] Sixth Edition, 1825, i. 67.
[4] *Ibid.*, ii. 32.
[5] Proudhon, for instance (see *Du Principe de l'art et de sa destination sociale*, pub. 1865, but written earlier), emphasized the social aims of art, decreed that it must be a collective product, and found that only thought matters while form is negligible; but he cheerfully confessed to an almost complete ignorance of the reality of which he talked: 'Je ne sais rien, par étude ou apprentissage, de la peinture; pas plus que de la sculpture et de la musique . . . (*ibid.*, pp. 10–11). Je n'ai pas l'intuition esthétique; je manque de ce sentiment prime-

his subject to the artist; now theorists, with no craft-sense and no traditions, were to dictate his style. If the philosophers decreed that form were subservient to idea, the designer had to take some abstract conception and express it pictographically in his pattern.

'I have given in this chapter', says one conscientious man, 'an original sketch (fig. 435) in which I have sought to embody chiefly the one idea of power, energy, force, or vigour; and in order to do this I have employed such lines as we see in the bursting buds of spring . . . especially . . . in the spring growth of a luxuriant tropical vegetation; I have also availed myself of those forms to be seen in certain bones of birds which are associated with the organs of flight . . . as well as those observable in the powerful propelling fins of certain fish.'[1]

The philosopher studied the abstract properties of form; Fechner demonstrated the beauties of the 'Golden Section', the receptivity of the concave and the exclusiveness of the convex;[2] and the artist, ever susceptible to suggestion, tried to analyse his forms into squares and triangles.[3] The geologist considered that geological inspiration was needed: 'the truths of form in common ground are quite as valuable . . . quite as beautiful, as any others which nature presents';[4] and the obedient artist took to petrology. Even the zoologist had some influence on the theory of design: 'If symmetrical animals are superior to radiating animals; if symmetry corresponds to what is most elevated, grand and noble—thought—we must acknowledge that radiation, by the very fact that it characterizes the rudimentary works of creation anterior to the appearance of man upon our planet, belongs to epochs when the world presented nothing but spectacles of sublimity.'[5]

Decoration had passed out of the hands of craftsmen into those of a too literate class of designers, who did their best to follow the theorists. Eastlake writes:[6] 'In the present age, when theory is everything, when volume after volume issues from the press replete with the most subtle analysis of principles which are to guide us in our estimate of the beautiful, it is hopeless to expect that men will work by the light of nature alone, and forgo the influence of precedent.'

Decoration came more than ever before to be considered as a poor relation of the 'Fine' Arts. For three quarters of the nineteenth century the 'richest and noblest' decoration which could be conceived was the imitation of some plastic or pictorial creation. After 1814 Sèvres confined itself almost entirely to imitation of this sort, to be imitated in its turn by the wares of commerce. Similarly the

sautier de goût qui fait juger d'emblée si une chose est belle ou non' (*ibid.*, p. 13). In academic circles the theoretical consideration of beauty and art became a regular part of the philosophic course; in the half century between 1810 and 1864 thirty theses on aesthetics were presented for the doctorate at Paris alone (Lévêque, *La Science du Beau*, preface, p. ix).

[1] Dresser, *Principles of Decorative Design*, p. 17, note. (1873.)   [2] *Vorschule d. Aesthetik*, 1876.

[3] See Guerlin, *L'Art enseigné par les maîtres, Dessin*, p. 7. The doctrine was first enunciated by Eugène Guillaume in 1876; in 1878 the theory was applied to the teaching of drawing in the primary and secondary schools of France.

[4] Ruskin, *Elements of Drawing*, p. 263.   [5] Anon, *Art in Ornament and Dress*, n.d. (before 1879), p. 38.

[6] *History of the Gothic Revival*, 1872, p. 3.

tapestries of the Gobelins gave the lead to the Berlin woolwork of the *bourgeoise*. Decoration inherited not only pictorial subjects, but also pictorial treatment; naturalism, 'le pied-platisme du dix-neuvième siècle' invaded its style. Faithful pictorial imitation, whether of pictures or flowers, of humming birds or jewels, was achieved even in the most unsuitable techniques. Further, each craft imitated another. 'Les peintres introduisent des gammes musicales dans la peinture, les sculpteurs, de la couleur dans la sculpture, les littérateurs, des moyens plastiques dans la littérature, et d'autres artistes . . . une sorte de philosophie encyclopédique dans l'art plastique lui-même.'[1] Potters imitated metal or basket-work; the gold-smith clay; the embroidress textiles and the weaver embroidery; the machine, the processes of hand-work; and the craftsman, the mechanical regularity of the machine. One of the successes of the 1851 exhibition was Odiot's silver plate representing a damask table-napkin,[2] and a few years later Charles Blanc especially lauded a wall-paper representing padded silk, with the folds in relief, held in place by buttons of coloured glass.

Beauty, under whatever form it was envisaged, was no longer sought for unde-filed. The consciousness of the overwhelming contradiction between Christian and economic law which haunted the minds of all the thinkers of the nineteenth century brought the ugly and the incongruous into a new relation with men's theory of life. 'Le laid est un détail d'un grand ensemble qui nous échappe et qui s'harmonise non pas avec l'homme mais avec la création toute entière.'[3] Ugliness became justified as enhancing the beautiful by its contrast; the hideous became the shadow of the sublime. Since a style results from the consistent following, con-scious or unconscious, of a peculiar canon of beauty, this inclusion of the ugly in the artist's cosmos struck at the very roots of decorative style. A strange blind-ness to their surroundings settled upon a generation that cultivated the sensi-bilities of the mind, that loved sunsets and flowers and romance, wept over Byron, collected keepsakes, and regarded their own walls and carpets with uncritical complacency.

For a time, indeed, beauty became of secondary importance. An age of industrialism set its stamp on all that it made. Not only were the objects of ordinary life produced by different methods, but they were modified to satisfy a different public. The commercial wealth of France was nearly trebled between 1830 and 1847,[4] and though England passed through the crisis of the 'hungry forties' her economic basis was changed. 'Nous sommes une démocratie de riches', said Balzac.[5] In 1821 the fête given by M. de Rothschild was more memorable than any of those at Court. Riches, moreover, were unstable and increasing; there was no

---

[1] Beaudelaire, *L'Art philosophique*, iii. 128.   [2] *Reports of Juries*, ii. 1135.
[3] Hugo, *Préface de Cromwell*.
[4] The 'escomptes de la Banque de France' in 1830 were 617 millions; in 1847, 1,800 millions; while the figures for general commerce are 818 millions for 1827 and 2,437 millions for 1847.
[5] *Traité de la Vie élégante*, 1830, 1922 ed., p. 53.

question of creating a permanent and unchanging setting for life, but rather of creating one that could vary with changing tastes and fortunes. France found a model for such decoration in the country that had suffered an industrial but not a political revolution:

'This reckoning of an advanced civilization has undergone its full development in England. In this fatherland of comfort the setting of life is regarded as a great garment, essentially changeable and subject to all the whims of fashion. The rich year by year change their horses, their carriages, their furniture; even their diamonds are reset; everything takes a new form. Similarly lesser furnishings are manufactured in the same spirit; raw materials are wisely used as economically as possible. If we have not yet arrived at this degree of science, we have however gone some way towards it.'[1]

The veneers that in the preceding century had been a revetment of elegance became no more than a mask of tawdriness; ormolu no longer received its chiselled finish at the hands of a master, but was produced with the mechanical grossness of casting and stamping. Ornament was studied and designed apart from the thing that it was to decorate; and, so designed, owed its only originality to the incongruity of the sources from which it was derived.[2] The crafts came under a new classification: from being at the worst 'minor arts' they came to be considered collectively as an *art industriel*.[3] The history of decoration in the nineteenth century is the history of its industrial exhibitions.[4]

The very tools of industrialism became worthy to be included in the repertory of the industrial arts; by 1860 English influence was strong enough in Paris to inspire the goldsmiths to make no jewels but in the forms of cubes, disks, spheres, and cylinders; they were decorated with screws, rivets, nails, locks, and padlocks, and were appropriately called 'bijoux chemin de fer' and 'bateau à vapeur'.[5] Even the rewards of industry are recorded to have inspired ornament: 'More original, and decidedly American in suggestion and design, is a toilet called the "Bullion", in a fine satiny-glazed semi-china. The wide-mouthed ewer, with neck and handle powdered in gold, seems to issue from a bag, shirred and tied up with a carelessly knotted string; the leather-colour of the bag and the scattered gold favour the conceit of the pitcher isuing from a bag of the precious metal.'[6]

Industrialism deprived the minor arts of their traditional individualities: material as such had to be subjugated, not respected. Patterns were transferable from one material to another, and, since they were purposeless, no change of function was

---

[1] *Ibid.*, p. 88.

[2] See, for example, the *Album de l'ornemaniste* of Aimé Chenevard (1836).

[3] 'La Société de l'art industriel' was founded at Paris in 1845, 'La Société du Progrès de l'art industriel' in 1858.

[4] Paris, 1798, 1801, 1802, 1806, 1819, 1823, 1827, 1834, 1839, 1844, 1849, 1855, 1867, 1878, 1889, 1900; London, 1851, 1862; Bordeaux, 1895; Brussels, 1897; Vienna, 1873; Amsterdam, 1883; Philadelphia, 1876; Moscow, 1891 (Exposition française); Chicago, 1893. The first exhibition of industrial art was held at Paris in 1798 on the initiative of François de Neufchâteau.

[5] Vever, *La Bijouterie française au XIXe siècle*, ii. 269.

[6] Quoted, Lucy Crane, *Art or the Formation of Taste*, 1885, p. 81.

involved. Ornament became a kind of merchandise sold by weight. In 1856 the industrial doctrine was clearly expressed:

'Ornament is now as material an interest in a commercial community as even cotton itself, or, indeed, any raw material of manufacture whatever. Such being the case, it is highly important that we should endeavour to comprehend its principles, in order to its most effectual application. We should, therefore, in the first place, study ornament for its own sake, theoretically and scientifically, and not in that limited, narrow sense which would restrict it, in one place as applied to cotton, in another as to iron, and in a third as to clay, and so on.'[1]

The function of ornament is to make raw material valuable; it is a kind of magic varnish which turns everything it touches to gold.

'Take, for example, clay as a natural material; in the hands of one man this material becomes flower-pots, worth eighteen pence a "cast" (a number varying from sixty to twelve according to size); in the hands of another it becomes a tazza, or a vase, worth five pounds or perhaps fifty. A wise policy induces a country to draw to itself all the wealth that it can, without parting with more of its natural material than is absolutely necessary. If for every pound of clay that a nation parts with it can draw to itself that amount of gold which we value at five pounds sterling, it is obviously better thus to part with but little material and yet secure wealth than it is to part with the material at a low rate either in its native condition, or worked into coarse vessels.'[2]

Beauty had passed into the realm of philosophy; ornament into the province of economics. 'Richness' became the true test of pattern: it combined a profusion of ornament with apparent lavishness of effort.[3] Men found with Saint-Saëns that 'la difficulté vaincue est elle-même une beauté,' and discovered even in gross imitations of such *tours de force* the charm of luxury and elegance. One way of achieving richness was the imitation of the work of the goldsmith in other crafts; in Julienne's pattern-book of 1840[4] the designs for porcelain, tapestry, wall-paper, and woodwork are all purely metallic in origin, and about 1862 the best Kidderminster carpets were all 'in the jewelled style'. 'Nor is it necessary to descant upon the superiority of chased, pierced, damaskened, repoussé or even granulated metalwork over Dresden china and such bric-à-brac.'[5]

The doctrine of 'l'art pour l'art', which Gautier had enunciated as early as 1834,[6] came unconsciously to be applied to decoration. 'Ornaments' that served no purpose whatsoever were sufficient to establish the elegance of a room; 'a thousand elegant superfluities' is the consecrated phrase of the novelist. The *ensemble* mattered little so long as the details were sufficiently profuse and varied.

---

[1] Wornum, *The Characteristics of Style*, 1856, p. 6.
[2] Dresser, *Principles of Decorative Design*, p. 2. (1873.)
[3] It had been used by Alison as early as 1790 as a criterion for classifying ornament as simple, elegant, rich or magnificent. *Essays on Taste*, 6th ed. 1825, ii. 34. See also H. Repton, *Observations on the Theory and Practice of Landscape Gardening*, 1803, p. 160: 'Every species of enrichment or decoration ought to be costly, either in its material or in its workmanship.'
[4] *L'Ornemaniste des arts industriels.*
[5] Anon., *Science of Taste*, 1879, p. 122.
[6] Preface to *Mademoiselle de Maupin*.

'There is no more style . . . all rooms are alike . . . square boxes; the financier's taste
dominates everything, and luxury takes the place of style. . . . Every drawing-room is a shop-
ful of bric-à-brac, and usually of new bric-à-brac. Everywhere are the same materials, the
same Brussels carpets . . . the same bronzes turned out by the thousand, the same clocks,
the same bare ceilings painted a dead white that glares among all the gaudy hangings with
which it is surrounded. Here arm-chairs with carved Gothic backs strut beside Louis XV
settees; there tables with twisted legs stand opposite a Boule cabinet, and everywhere, above,
below, on shelves, on tables, on brackets, are Dresden and Sèvres porcelains and Chinese
vases.' [1]

2

By one of the paradoxes of the history of decoration, in this very variety and profusion lay a germ of simplicity. To display such varied bric-à-brac, special furniture of an unobtrusive sort was needed and produced.[2] As early as 1851 a critic
of the Exhibition found that overmuch ornament at the expense of construction
'is apt to sicken us of decoration, and leads us to admire those objects of intricate
utility (the machines and utensils of various kinds) where use is so paramount that
ornament is repudiated, and, fitness of purpose being the end sought, a noble
simplicity is the result.'[3] Another critic[4] made the discovery that 'repose and
harmony are art qualities; glitter and attractiveness if largely indulged in are
vulgarities'. Men began to seek for general principles, and even when like Owen
Jones[5] they discovered as many as thirty-seven, the tendency was towards simplifi-
cation. Owen Jones's main points were that the decorative arts arise from and
should be attendant upon Architecture; that their result should be repose; that all
ornament should be based on a geometrical construction and arranged on certain
definite proportions, so that the whole and each particular member should be a
multiple of some simple unit. All lines should flow out of a parent stem, and all
natural forms should be conventionalized.

The scientific study of colour encouraged the mixture of 'cheerful primaries';
Owen Jones[6] found that no composition could ever be perfect in which any one of
the three primary colours was wanting, either in its natural state or in combination.
'We should place blue, which retires, on the concave surfaces; yellow, which
advances, on the convex; and red, the intermediate colour, on the undersides,
separating the colours by white on the vertical planes.' In other compositions
primary colours should be used on the upper portions of objects, secondary and
tertiary on the lower; and elaborate tables of chromatic equivalents were provided

---

[1] *Le Beau dans l'Utile*, 1866, p. 105.

[2] French criticism of the English exhibit at the Exhibition of 1878 found that all the furniture was influenced
by 'le goût du bibelot', and that in consequence 'cela ressemble trop souvent à du mobilier de théâtre. . . .
Tous ces meubles grêles sans ornementation, sans le travail de l'artiste qui centuple par son talent la valeur
de la matière ressemblent à des bâtis d'accessoires.' *L'Art moderne à l'Exposition de 1878*, p. 392.

[3] 1851 Exhibition, *Reports of Juries*, ii. 1588, et seq. (Supplementary Report on Design, by Redgrave.)

[4] C. Dresser, *Studies in Design*, p. 10.

[5] *Grammar of Ornament*, 1856, p. 5.   [6] *Op. cit.*, p. 7.

to show the proportion. Some decorators elaborated the primary idea into more complicated schemes. Dresser, in his *Principles of Decorative Design* [1] declares:

'This principle I cannot pass without notice—namely, that the finest colour effects are those of a rich, mingled, bloomy character. Imagine a luxuriant garden, the beds in which are filled with a thousand flowers, having all the colours of the rainbow, and imagine these arranged as closely as will permit of growth. When viewed from a distance the effect is soft and rich, and full and varied, and is all that is pleasant. This is nature's colouring. It is our work humbly to strive at producing like beauty with her. Imagine three rooms, all connected by open archways, and all decorated with a thousand flower-like ornaments, and these so coloured, in this mingled manner, that in one room blue predominates, in another red, and in another yellow: we should then have a beautiful tertiary bloom in each—a subtle mingling of colour, an exquisite delicacy and refinement of treatment, a fulness such as always results from a rich mingling of hues, and an amount of detail which would interest when closely inspected; besides which, we should have the harmony of the general effect of the three rooms, the one appearing as olive, the other as citron, and the other as russet.' [2]

Here again profusion of colour, particularly in rooms overlighted by many plate glass windows, eventually encouraged a taste for sober hues.[3] Mrs. Haweis wrote: 'A room is like a picture. . . . The main point of interest to which the decorators should work up is the inhabitants; but as they can never be reckoned upon, the picture must be composed as it were without a subject, like a poem without a point or a story without an end. This must be done by keeping the tone of colour down.'[4] Gilbert Scott asked: 'Could not our principles of decorative painting be reformed and rectified by reference to Nature? How sparing is Nature of her brightest tints, and how lavish of her intermediate hues!'[5] An anonymous *Plea for Art in the Home*, written before 1879, suggests a scheme of startling sobriety; it recommends grey paper for the drawing-room, with inscriptions from the book of Job such as 'Man is born unto travail as the sparks fly upward' painted on it in black letters in diagonal lines.[6] Taste was turning towards simplicity of form and colour in mere weariness of the complications of industrialism. In decoration as in the other arts men agreed with Victor de Laprade: 'le goût dans son sens le plus légitime, le plus élevé, c'est la faculté, toute négative, qui retranche, qui modère.'

[1] p. 46.
[2] Even colour schemes suggested as late as 1881 have a certain vividness and variety; crimson velvet is to be enhanced by pale blue and salmon colour, sage green by amber, orange and crimson, and brown by blue and pink, to suggest the effect of seaweed. (Haweis, *Art in Decoration*, p. 364.)
[3] The peacock blues, rust reds and olive greens traditionally associated with Morris belong to his early years, before he had studied the technique of dyeing. They became fashionable, but Morris himself soon tired of them.
[4] Haweis, *Art of Decoration*, p. 10.
[5] *Remarks on Secular and Domestic Architecture*, 1857, p. 84. He goes on to take the tinting of leaves, sea, rocks, earth, and trees as examples. 'The blue used in our ceilings should not exceed in depth that usually seen in the sky . . .; our greens might be imitated from the varied colours of leaves, and in picking out in different shades of green, we might use together those which we find on the fronts and backs of the same leaf; as, for example, the rich deep green of the olive leaf relieved by a cold whitish green, like that seen on the back of the same leaf'. . . . The tendency towards the 'greenery-yallery' was not felt in Paris until about 1895.
[6] p. 39.

FIG. 435. Design by C. Dresser, 1873

In England two prophets, Ruskin and Morris, arose to preach the new doctrine which in France 'all called for without being able to formulate it'.[1] Both realized that more than a change of style was needed; it was the industrial system itself which had first to be overthrown. The percentage of profit had to be recognized as of less importance than the measure of beauty; in Morris's words: 'The rich must learn to love art more than riches; the poor to hate joyless labour more than poverty.'[2] The aim of both was to annul the existing divorce between design and execution; Ruskin felt that to follow an art which was merely interpretive of the design of another 'has an influence of the most fatal kind on brain and heart, and it issues, if long so pursued, in the *destruction both of intellectual power and moral principle*; whereas art, devoted humbly and self-forgetfully to the clear statement and record of the facts of the universe, is always helpful and beneficent to mankind, full of comfort, strength, and salvation'.[3] Both shared in the eclectic views of their day: both were ready to exchange the realities of the present for an illusion of the Middle Ages. Both brought to their judgement of art a serious concern with the ethical and economic conditions of the artist's or craftsman's life.[4] For Ruskin a work of art was a human action, in which moral, intellectual, and aesthetic activities were all involved; for Morris it was 'expression by man of his pleasure in labour';[5] not only should it be possible to make the matters needful to daily life works of art, but there must be something wrong with the civilization that did not do this.[6]

But a fundamental difference of temperament is reflected in their theories of decoration. Ruskin, the theorist, found reason to analyse Beauty as consisting in Infinity, Unity, Membership, Repose, Symmetry, Purity, and Moderation, and to justify himself by analysis of the beauty of a wild rose. It 'is pretty because it has concentric petals (Unity of origin); because each petal is bounded by varying curves (Infinity); because these curves are dual and symmetrically opposed (Symmetry); because the five petals are bent into the form of a cup, which gives them gradated depth of shade (Infinity); because the shade as well as the light is coloured with crimson and gold (Purity); and because both the gold and the

[1] *Le Beau dans l'Utile*, 1865, quoting M. Auguste Luchet in *Le Siècle* of 15 November.

[2] As early as 1807 Thomas Hope had stated that through his designs for better and more artistic types of furniture 'I hoped to afford to that portion of the community which, through the entire substitution of machinery to manual labour, in the fabrication of many of the most extensive articles of common use, had for ever lost the inferior kinds of employment, a means of replacing the less dignified mode of subsistence of which it had been deprived, by a nobler species of labour; one which absolutely demands the co-operation of those higher intellectual qualities which the former often allows to remain dormant, or even tends to extinguish; and one in which, consequently, the powers of mere machinery never can emulate, or supplant the mental faculties of man.' (*Household Furniture and Interior Decoration from Designs by Thomas Hope*, p. 5.) An appreciation of the baneful effect of industrialism will be found in the *Reports of Juries on the 1851 Exhibition*, ii. 1594.

[3] *The Two Paths*, 1858, s. 15.

[4] Their point of view is linked with Taine's theory of art as the expression of social surroundings.

[5] *Lectures on Art*, p. 58.   [6] *The Lesser Arts of Life*, p. 43.

crimson are used in their most suitable degrees and tints'.[1] Morris, the craftsman, was content to give the world a golden rule: 'Have nothing in your houses which you do not know to be useful or believe to be beautiful.'[2] Ruskin sadly stated, '*We* cannot design, because we have too much to think of, and we think of it too anxiously';[3] Morris was content to set aside the dicta of the theorists on the design of recurring patterns, on merely aesthetic grounds.[4] Ruskin, when he turned to practical things, did 'not despair of seeing at [Oxford] . . . a perfect school of metal work, at the head of which will be, not the ironmasters, but the goldsmiths; and therein, I believe that artists, being taught how to deal wisely with the most precious of metals, will take into due government the uses of all others';[5] while Morris was finding that the making of ugly pottery and stupid glass was 'one of the most remarkable inventions of civilization';[6] and was telling the manufacturer how he might best make use of the peculiar intrinsic qualities of his material.

Ruskin ordained a hierarchy of subject, 'from the abstract lines . . . through the simplest combinations of these lines seen in nature in crystals, waves, and eddies, and the like; the lower shapes of organic life, shells and fish, snakes and other reptiles, the varied suggestions of the vegetable world, branches of trees, foliage, flower and fruit; and through birds and beasts, to the human figure.'[7] Morris was content to find that 'it is necessary to the purity of the art [of pattern designing] that its form and colour when these bear any relation to the facts of Nature (as for the more part they do), should be suggestive of such facts, and not descriptive of them'.[8] Ruskin found art greatest 'on the imminent deadly verge of decadence'; Morris sought inspiration in the vigorous promise of primitive art rather than the accomplishment of maturity: 'You may be sure that the softest and loveliest of patterns will weary the steadiest admirers of their school as soon as they see that there is no hope of growth in them.'[9] Ruskin takes his place as one of many theorists; Morris as the one great decorator of an age when the minor arts have otherwise nothing noble to show to posterity. His real originality lay in his strong technical sense, which revived the craftsman's intuition of the possibilities of his material in an age which generally endeavoured merely to subdue material to industrial use. 'One rule we have for a guide, and whatever we do if we abide by it, we are quite sure to go wrong if we neglect it, and it is common to all the lesser arts. Think of your material. Don't paint anything on pottery save what can only be painted on pottery; if you do it is clear that however good a draughtsman you may be, you do not care about that special art.'[10] It is thanks to

---

[1] *Modern Painters*, v. 97. Note to 1883 edition. Words in brackets added by Collingwood.
[2] *Hopes and Fears for Art*, 1878–81, p. 110.   [3] Oxford Inaugural Lecture.
[4] *Making the Best of it*, quoted Valence, *op. cit.*, p. 85.   [5] Oxford Inaugural Lecture.
[6] *The Lesser Arts of Life*, p. 46, et seq.   [7] *Stones of Venice*, i, chap. xx.
[8] 'History of Pattern Designing,' *Collected Papers*, p. 5.
[9] Aymer Valence, *William Morris*, p. 86. The same note was struck by L. de Laborde in 1856: *De l'Union des arts et de l'industrie*, ii. 9.   [10] *Ibid.*, p. 79.

Morris that a French critic of the end of the century[1] could give our country praise for a simplicity that was not poor.

3

In 1893 Walter Crane said that the revival of handicrafts 'must mean either the sunset or the dawn';[2] and the issue is not yet certain. The tides of creation flow strong in the arts of literature and painting, and stir the waters of music and sculpture; and in decoration itself the influence of modern artists is increasingly felt. Yet artists and craftsmen cannot destroy the industrial system, nor widely influence the taste of a democracy that must depend upon the industrial system for the satisfaction of its wants. Industrial processes cannot with sincerity imitate the craftsman's style or technique, nor with economy attempt a multiplicity of styles.[3] The charm of a lost innocence may attract us to the arts of primitive antiquity or to the peasant crafts of backward countries; but our appreciation of their simplicity is the mark of our sophistication.

Admiration of such simplicity is, however, the true tendency of our age, and may find a real expression even in the arts of industry. We are sincerely interested in significance and structure. Croce has substituted coherence for verisimilitude as a basis of criticism; 'the strength of art lies in being thus simple, naked, and poor. . . . To be the root, not the flower or the fruit, is the function of art.' Instinctively we deprecate what our fathers called 'fancy', and try to draw even dreams and imaginings within the realm of knowledge. What we seek now is a 'belle nudité'; in construction rather than in decoration must the beauty of our day be found: a strength and bareness beautiful, not with the massiveness of Roman travertine, not with the balanced stress of Gothic stone, not with the roughness of Florentine rustication, but with the undifferentiated and negative strength of concrete.[4] We have reached an age when the highest tribute we can pay is silence, when the Lamp of Remembrance is lit not for the supreme commander, but for the Unknown Soldier. We find nobility and even grace only in forms austere to bareness; and may perhaps most honestly seek decorative beauty by surrounding ourselves with pure form and simple colour, and for pattern content ourselves with their shadows on the wall.

One principle alone is evident from the dispassionate study of ornament that here draws to a close: pattern to have life and meaning must derive its inspiration and its significance from the life and the interests of the generation it is to serve.

[1] *Art décoratif*, Nov. 1899, p. 53.

[2] *Arts and Crafts Essays, by members of the Arts and Crafts Exhibition Society.* Preface by W. Morris, p. 15.

[3] Cf. E. de Vogüé, *Remarques sur l'Exposition du Centenaire, 1889*, p. 125: 'Le style attendu, s'il doit apparaître, viendra d'en bas, des milieux où l'industrie est forcée à plus d'initiative, par un plus grand bouleversement de ses habitudes.'

[4] See Le Corbusier, 'Architecture de l'époque machiniste,' in *Journal de Psychologie*, 1928, special number, Nos. 1–3, p. 331. 'L'architecture est totale avant le décor. . . . Les "styles" n'ont donc rien à voir avec l'architecture.'

When Pattern so created is beautiful, it is beautiful for all time, but it does not follow that its use is for all time. Each generation must experience anew a world of which parts at least have but lately been brought within the apprehension of the seeing eye; each generation must thence build up its own schemes for beautifying the essential. What is traditional must necessarily form a part of the visible world; and it is tradition that determines, to a great extent, what we consciously see. In so far as that which created tradition remains a part of our world, tradition is alive; but the blind imitation of the past as such will lead us astray into labyrinths of dead beauty to which we have lost the clue. Conversely, blind negation of the past, by blotting out a part at least of the world that is truly ours, will go far to falsify the significance of what is created. Above everything we must be sincere to our perception alike of fact and vision: for so may we hope to create ornament that shall make our surroundings beautiful for us in our time, and shall truly mirror our age for posterity. 'We shall maintain the fabric of the world; and in the handiwork of our craft shall be our prayer.'

INDEX

Small figures above the line refer to the footnotes

F f